KU-351-561

The Administration of Justice
Second Edition

ROBIN C. A. WHITE

Oxford UK & Cambridge USA

CAT.2
344.707
1045917WHO

Copyright © Robin C. A. White 1991

Robin C. A. White is hereby identified as author of this work in accordance with Section 77 of the Copyright, Designs and Patents Act 1988.

First published 1985

Second edition, revised and updated, first published 1991

Basil Blackwell Ltd
108 Cowley Road, Oxford, OX4 1JF, UK

Basil Blackwell, Inc.
3 Cambridge Center
Cambridge, Massachusetts 02142, USA

All rights reserved. Except for the quotation of short passages for the purposes of criticism and review, no part of this publication may be reproduced, stored in a retrieval system, or transmitted, in any form or by any means, electronic, mechanical, photocopying, recording or otherwise, without the prior permission of the publisher.

Except in the United States of America, this book is sold subject to the condition that it shall not, by way of trade or otherwise, be lent, re-sold, hired out, or otherwise circulated without the publisher's prior consent in any form of binding or cover other than that in which it is published and without a similar condition including this condition being imposed on the subsequent purchaser.

Library of Congress Cataloging in Publication Data
White, Robin C. A.
The administration of justice/Robin C. A. White.—2nd ed.
Includes bibliographical references and indexes.
ISBN 0-631-16751-X:
1. Law—Great Britain. 2. Justice, Administration of—Great Britain. I. Title.
KD660.W45 1991
347.41—dc20
[344.107]
90-28175 CIP

British Library Cataloguing in Publication Data
A CIP cataloguing record for this book is available from the British Library.

Typeset in 10 on 12pt Sabon
by MCS Ltd, Salisbury
Printed in Great Britain by
Hartnolls Ltd, Bodmin

This book is printed on acid-free paper.

THE POLYTECHNIC OF WALES LIBRARY TREFOREST

3/10/9

Contents

Preface

The objectives of this book remain as stated in the preface to the first edition: to meet the needs of students of the English legal system for a text of manageable length and affordable cost, which views the administration of justice in England and Wales from the perspective of the ordinary citizen and seeks to locate the increasing volume of research studies within that perspective. Reaction from students to the first edition has encouraged me to retain these objectives.

Once again, I have tried to keep three objectives in mind. First, assuming no prior knowledge of the legal system, I have tried to deliver in a readable and lively manner basic information about the roles and functions of criminal and civil courts, of tribunals and of lawyers. Second, I have adopted a consumer-oriented perspective on the system to show what difficulties users of the legal system may face, selecting for consideration those areas of business where the ordinary citizen is most likely to experience the workings of the legal system. Third, I have sought to offer some critique of the system where the result of the first two endeavours has been a conclusion that there is a gap between the law in the books and the law in action.

Apart from the task of updating the text, I have made a number of significant changes in structure from the first edition. The volume of material on the role of the police and the Crown Prosecution Service in the pre-trial criminal process warranted the division of the material formerly in a single chapter into two chapters. The division is between the role of the police on the street and in the police station. The work of the Crown Prosecution Service has formed the bridge between the accused in the police station and the accused in court. Part III on the civil process has also been substantially reorganized. A chapter on dealing with debt cases has been added. The social security appeal tribunals and industrial tribunals are both now sufficiently clearly located as key institutions in determining civil claims that each has a chapter devoted to it. There is much less argument about the place of tribunals in the system of adjudication than appeared in the first edition and the thumbnail sketches of other tribunals have been omitted. Developments in the delivery of legal services necessitated the complete re-writing of Part IV of the book in order to attempt to accommodate the new framework established by the Legal Aid Act 1988 and the Courts and Legal Services Act 1990. Readers will, however, need to look elsewhere for a detailed analysis of specific provisions of the 1990 Act.

The manuscript for the new edition was submitted to the publishers in the autumn of 1990 and copy-editing (the last opportunity for significant changes) was completed in January 1991. Page proofs were finalized at the beginning of April. Consequently, the text could not consider the events which have led to the establishment in March 1991 of a new Royal Commission on the criminal process following the overturning of the convictions of the 'Guildford Four' and the 'Birmingham Six'. This Royal Commission should provide the impetus for the much-needed reform of the system of criminal appeals. Oddly, a number of issues relating to the pre-trial criminal process have been included in the terms of reference despite the significant changes which followed the 1981 Report of the Royal Commission on Criminal Procedure. That Commission, of course, post-dated the events which led to the terrible miscarriages of justice which occurred in the Guildford and Birmingham cases.

I have tried to state the law accurately as of 1 April 1991, though a number of changes known to be taking effect later in 1991 have been included in the text.

Robin C. A. White
University of Leicester

Abbreviations

ABWOR	Assistance by way of representation	HCP	House of Commons Session Papers
AC	Law Reports: Appeal Cases	HL	House of Lords
ACAS	Advisory Conciliation and Arbitration Service	J of Crim L & Crimin- ology	Journal of Criminal Law and Criminology
ALAS	Accident Legal Advice Service		
All ER	All England Law Reports	J of Law & Soc	Journal of Law and Society
All ER Rep	All England Law Reports Reprint	JP	Justice of the Peace
Am Soc Rev	American Sociological Review	J Soc Pol	Journal of Social Policy
Brit J of Crim	British Journal of Criminology	JSWL	Journal of Social Welfare Law
		KB	Law Reports: King's Bench Division
Brit J of Law & Soc	British Journal of Law and Society	LAG Bulletin	Legal Action Group Bulletin
		Law & Soc Rev	Law and Society Review
CA	Court of Appeal		
CAB	Citizens Advice Bureau	LCD	Lord Chancellor's Department
CCA	Court of Criminal Appeal	LCF	Law Centres Federation
CCR	County Court Rules	LJKB	Law Journal Reports: King's Bench
Civil J Q	Civil Justice Quarterly		
CID	Criminal Investigation Department	LQR	Law Quarterly Review
		LT	Law Times
CLJ	Cambridge Law Journal	MIND	National Association for Mental Health
CLP	Current Legal Problems		
COIT	Central Office of the Industrial Tribunals	MLR	Modern Law Review
		NACAB	National Association of Citizens Advice Bureaux
Cox CC	Cox's Criminal Cases		
CPS	Crown Prosecution Service	NCCL	National Council for Civil Liberties
Cr App R	Criminal Appeal Reports		
Crim LR	Criminal Law Review	NILT	National Insurance Local Tribunal
DC	Divisional Court		
DHSS	Department of Health and Social Security	OEO	Office of Economic Opportunity (US)
DoE	Department of Employment	OFT	Office of Fair Trading
DPP	Director of Public Prosecutions	OPSSAT	Office of President of Social Security Appeals Tribunals
DSS	Department of Social Security		
EAT	Employment Appeal Tribunal	PAC	Public Assistance Committee
ECJ	European Court of Justice	PL	Public Law
EEC	European Economic Community	Pol Q	Political Quarterly
		QB	Law Reports: Queen's Bench Division
EJO	Enforcement of Judgments Office (Northern Ireland)		
		QC	Queen's Counsel

Abbreviations

RCCP	Royal Commission on Criminal Procedure	SPTL	Society of Public Teachers of Law
RSC	Rules of the Supreme Court	SSAT	Social Security Appeal Tribunal
RTR	Road Traffic Reports	TLR	Times Law Reports
SBAT	Supplementary Benefits Appeal Tribunal	US	United States Supreme Court Reports
SBC	Supplementary Benefits Commission	Western Australia L Rev	Western Australia Law Review
SCB	Solicitors Complaints Bureau		
SI	Statutory Instruments	WLR	Weekly Law Reports
Sol J	Solicitors Journal		

Table of Statutes

Table of Statutory Instruments

Table of Other Documents

Table of Cases

Part I

Institutions and Processes

1

Institutions and Processes

Introduction

It is a truism to say that we live in an ordered society and that social interaction requires a degree of predictability. Law and the legal process contribute to the stable functioning of society by providing a framework of rules governing a multitude of activities. The reach of the law into everyday lives continues to increase, so that there are today few activities wholly unregulated by the law. This does not necessarily mean that there has been an increasing flood of legal disputes. Dispute resolution is just one of the functions of legal processes. It would certainly be a mistake to assume that it was always the intervention of lawyers or adjudication by courts or tribunals which resolved people's problems – and it is primarily about the legal problems of individuals rather than business enterprises that this book is concerned. Very frequently disputes are resolved outside the courtroom by the operation of self-help, legal advice and sometimes even by default. The bulk of lawyers' work is not concerned with court work, but with advice to clients to enable disputes to be settled amicably without litigation, and with the implementation of clients' wishes concerning their property. Examples are the buying and selling of property (conveyancing) and the drafting of wills and the administration of the estates of people who have died (probate).

Disputes arise where parties involved in some interaction disagree as to some fact or point of law involved in the interaction. Such disputes are likely to be resolved in one of the following ways:

abandonment or concession
enquiry
negotiation
conciliation
arbitration
adjudication

All these options may be followed as self-help processes where no legal advice is sought from persons with specialized knowledge, or on advice from an adviser with specialized knowledge. The adviser may or may not be a professionally qualified lawyer, such as a solicitor. Where arbitration or adjudication is involved, the parties are often represented by lawyers.

Let us attempt a working definition of each of the above methods of settlement.

1 *Abandonment or concession:* one or other party regards the matter as insignificant and chooses not to pursue it. Alternatively, one or other party may feel powerless to act or act in ignorance in not pursuing the matter.

2 *Enquiry:* there may be some uncertainty about the facts or the relevant law. Once the uncertainty is resolved the matter may move to one of the other methods of settlement, including the abandoning of the claim by one party.

3 *Negotiation:* this is a process of bargaining on the basis of asserted positions which are not subjected to independent adjudication. Negotiation usually involves compromise; each side makes concessions to the other in order to resolve the dispute by agreement. Such settlements are often made without any admission of liability.

4 *Conciliation:* this is rather like negotiation but a third party is brought in to help the parties come to an agreed settlement. Conciliation is seen as important where a continuing relationship exists between the parties, as in family or employment disputes. Conciliation is invariably a private process.

5 *Arbitration:* each side puts its case to an independent third party chosen by agreement of the parties to the dispute, who then makes a decision between them. It is of particular importance in commercial matters where complex technical and financial detail is involved. Arbitration is usually the result of agreement made in advance of the dispute arising. For example, a commercial contract may provide that any disputes that arise under the contract which cannot be resolved by agreement between the parties shall be referred to arbitration. Such clauses are binding. Arbitration normally takes place in private. Small claims in the county court are often said to be settled by arbitration, but the process is more in the nature of a special form of adjudication (see chapter 9).

6 *Adjudication:* each side puts its case to a court or tribunal, which makes a decision between the parties. The placing of the matter in the hands of the court or tribunal can usually be achieved by unilateral act of one of the parties. The type of business with which particular courts and tribunals can deal is limited by their jurisdiction, which is usually determined by reference to geographical limitations, or the monetary value or seriousness of the dispute, or the nature of the dispute. Adjudication normally takes place in public and a decision is given in open court.

It should be clear from the above that lawyers have an important role to play in all forms of dispute settlement, and indeed perhaps have an even more important role as preventers of disputes, provided, of course, that advice is sought at a sufficiently early stage. Though the above processes seem more naturally to apply to disputes between individuals or business entities, they can have an application in criminal proceedings as we shall see in Part II of this book.

It will also be clear from this conspectus of approaches to dispute resolution that adjudication is just one of many options. It is also the most formal remedy, where concession and compromise have little role to play. But it is important to realize that the various means of dispute resolution do not exist in isolation. Negotiation between parties who have embarked on the process of adjudication often continues right up to the door of the courtroom. Some procedures of adjudication have conciliation built into them in the hope of avoiding the confrontation inherent in adjudication. It is probably true to say that adjudication has a greater importance than other forms of dispute resolution because the outcome of adjudication is normally public and the reasons for a judge's or tribunal's decisions, when treated cumulatively, have an influence on the way in which similar disputes are resolved, whatever the means of resolution. For this reason lawyers tend to have a court-centred view of the legal system.

Distinguishing between Civil and Criminal Proceedings

Understanding the distinction between civil and criminal proceedings is fundamental to an understanding of the English legal system. Different courts and procedures are used for civil and criminal proceedings, though some judges sit in both civil and criminal courts. The distinction between civil and criminal proceedings resides, somewhat unhelpfully, in the legal consequences that follow a particular act. Appreciation of the nature of the distinction and of the terminology associated with it will avoid some serious confusions about the role of various courts in the system.

Civil Law and Civil Proceedings

Civil law and civil proceedings aim to determine the rights and obligations of individuals as between each other. Examples are the determination of rights arising under a contract, of obligations to pay damages for torts, such as negligence, nuisance or defamation, of rights in property and of succession, and of questions of status, such as divorce, adoption and the custody of children. Most of these rights are of a private nature, and are said to belong to the area of *private law*. There is also a body of civil law of a public nature, such as questions of taxation or questions concerning planning or compulsory purchase; these are said to belong to the area of *public law*.

In most civil proceedings the person beginning the proceedings is the *plaintiff* who *sues* or *brings an action* against a *defendant*. The plaintiff will be seeking a *remedy*, usually in the form of *damages* (money compensation), but possibly also in the form of an *injunction* (an order prohibiting the defendant from committing or continuing to commit some wrongful act). There are other remedies that may be appropriate in particular cases, such as a declaration of parties' legal rights and responsibilities. Most civil proceedings are heard by a judge sitting alone; only very rarely (usually in defamation cases) will there be a jury in civil proceedings. The judge *hears* the *action* and delivers a *judgment*.

In some proceedings the terminology is different but it is not appropriate to list all the variations here. For example, in divorce proceedings the party asking for the marriage to be dissolved is the *petitioner*, who petitions for a *decree* against the *respondent*. If the divorce is sought on the ground that the marriage has broken down irretrievably because of the respondent's adultery, it is usual to join in the proceedings the person with whom the respondent is alleged to have committed adultery and this party is called the *co-respondent*.

In civil proceedings, the plaintiff usually has the *burden of proof*; this means that the plaintiff must prove the facts on which the claim is based. The burden of proof in civil cases is said to be *on the balance of probabilities*; in other words the plaintiff must adduce admissible evidence to satisfy the judge that it is more probable than not that what the plaintiff alleges is true.

Criminal Law and Criminal Proceedings

Criminal law and criminal proceedings are concerned with wrongs regarded as committed by the individual against society for which guilty individuals must be punished. In some circumstances even companies can commit criminal offences. Whereas the objective of civil proceedings is to provide a remedy for the person wronged, usually in the form of damages, the objective of criminal proceedings is to determine the guilt or innocence of the accused person and, if that person is found to be guilty, to punish the wrongdoer and to protect society. Part of the purpose of the penalty is also seen as seeking to rehabilitate the wrongdoer. In criminal proceedings a *prosecutor*, usually the police, institutes a *prosecution* against a *defendant* or *accused person* (sometimes referred to simply as *the accused*). The outcome is a determination of *guilt* or *innocence* (by *verdict* if the trial is by jury). A finding that the accused person is not guilty is termed an *acquittal*. If the offence is proved, the court imposes a *sentence* (usually either a *fine* or a *term of imprisonment*) or makes some other *order* (such as a *probation order* or *community service order*).

In criminal proceedings the prosecutor almost invariably has the burden of proof, which is said to be *beyond all reasonable doubt*. The prosecutor must adduce admissible evidence to prove that there is no reasonable doubt that the defendant committed the offence charged and this involves satisfying the tribunal of fact (magistrates or jury) that every essential element of the offence is proved and that the acts of the defendant were done with the requisite intent. When certain defences are raised, such as insanity, the defendant has the burden of proof on the balance of probabilities. In other words, if insanity is raised as a defence, the prosecutor does not have to prove beyond all reasonable doubt that the defendant was sane, but rather the defendant must prove that on the balance of probabilities he or she is insane within the legal definition of that term.

The same set of facts may give rise to both civil and criminal proceedings. The most common example is the motor accident where someone is injured because of a driver's bad driving. A civil action by the injured person often follows as well as a prosecution for a driving offence. Another example of overlap might occur in the case of persons who sell dishonestly goods which are in their possession for repair. Such action amounts to (1) breach of contract (a civil wrong), (2) the tort of conversion (a civil wrong), and (3) theft (a crime).

Appeals

When both civil and criminal cases go on appeal, the terminology again changes. The party appealing is called the *appellant* and the other party who responds to the appeal is called the *respondent*. Appeals to the House of Lords are by *petition* and the Law Lords give *opinions* rather than deliver judgments. In all courts there are fairly strict time limits for entering appeals.

Appeals serve a variety of purposes. Sometimes appeals are available as of right. This means that an unsuccessful litigant does not need any permission to raise the matter before an appeal court. In other cases, a court's permission, known as *leave to appeal* is needed. Leave is often required, where it is felt that there must be present some wider general interest than the dissatisfaction of one of the parties, before the matter should be brought before an appellate court, or where a filter is needed to decide which appeals are meritorious.

In broad general terms, appeals can be divided into those concerned with the merits of the decision under appeal and those concerned with the legality of the process by which that decision was reached. A litigant is entitled not only to a fair and proper decision on the merits, but also to a decision arrived at by due process of law.

Institutions

Some Classifications of Courts

A clear pecking order of courts exists which is of great importance in studying the doctrine of precedent, since decisions of courts higher in the hierarchy are generally binding on those lower in the hierarchy. Lower courts must follow the decisions of higher courts in similar cases unless there is some ground for distinguishing the earlier case. In the tribunal system the doctrine of precedent is not as fully developed but decisions of courts exercising appellate or supervisory jurisdiction (see overleaf) are binding on tribunals. Where there is a tribunal which itself hears appeals from tribunals lower in the hierarchy, decisions of the appellate tribunal normally bind the lower tribunal.

Courts are sometimes classified as *superior* or *inferior* courts. The nature of superior courts is that their jurisdiction is limited neither geographically nor in money terms, whereas it is a characteristic of inferior courts that their jurisdiction is both local and limited. The proceedings of inferior courts are not recorded verbatim but those of superior courts usually are. Inferior courts are also subject to what is known as the supervisory jurisdiction of the High Court. Magistrates' courts and county courts are inferior courts, while other courts are superior courts. The Crown Court is a hybrid, because when it is hearing appeals from magistrates' courts it is deemed to be an inferior court, though for all other purposes it is a superior court. The Supreme Court of Judicature is the collective title given to the Court of Appeal, the High Court and the Crown Court.

Types of Jurisdiction

Reference has been made above to appellate and supervisory jurisdiction. Jurisdiction can be divided into three types as follows:

Original: this indicates that the court or tribunal has jurisdiction to try a case; this is sometimes described as the court or tribunal of first instance.

Appellate: this indicates the court with jurisdiction to review either the decision of the court of first instance or the decision of an appellate court lower in the hierarchy. An example of the latter is the House of Lords reviewing a decision of the Court of Appeal. The exercise of appellate jurisdiction is concerned with the merits of the decision, though appeal to the House of Lords will only be allowed if the case raises a point of law of general public importance beyond the dispute between the litigants in the case.

Supervisory: this indicates the exercise of the jurisdiction of the High Court to ensure that inferior courts and tribunals do not act wrongly in law, in excess of their jurisdiction or otherwise unfairly. Supervisory jurisdiction is exercised either on application for judicial review or by way of case stated. The exercise of supervisory jurisdiction is primarily concerned with the legality of the process by which the decision was reached.

Some Important Institutions

A thumbnail sketch of the courts having jurisdiction in the main areas of civil and criminal law covered in this book will give a slightly more detailed picture of the legal system.

The main courts having jurisdiction in civil cases in contract and tort are the county courts and the Queen's Bench Division of the High Court, with appeal lying to the Court of Appeal, Civil Division, and then to the House of Lords. This is represented in diagrammatic form in figure 1. The Final Report of the Civil Justice Review (Civil Justice Review, 1988) abandoned a suggestion that the county courts and the High Court should become a unified court, but has proposed that all but the most important and complex cases in contract and tort should be heard by county courts.

In criminal cases, there are two entirely separate forms of trial: summary trial before magistrates and trial on indictment in the Crown Court. Trial on indictment in the Crown Court is reserved for the more serious criminal offences; there is an elaborate system of classification of offences for the purposes of determining where trial will take place.

The system of appeals following trial in the magistrates' courts is a complex

Figure 1   Courts having Jurisdiction in Contract and Tort

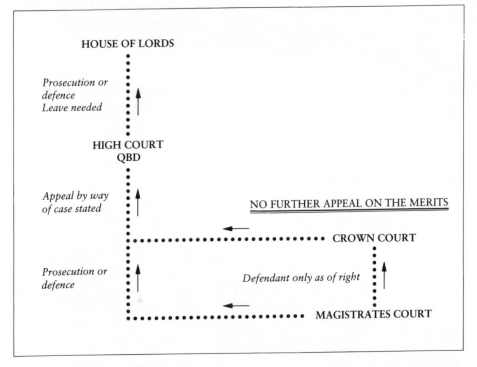

Figure 2   Summary Trial

combination of appeal on the merits and supervisory jurisdiction. Appeal on the merits, that is, against conviction or sentence, lies to the Crown Court as of right, but there is no further appeal on the merits. Appeals in exercise of the supervisory jurisdiction lie by way of case stated from the magistrates' court or the Crown Court to the High Court and then direct to the House of Lords if a sufficiently important point of law is raised. This system is represented in the diagram at figure 2.

Trial on indictment follows the committal of a person for trial by magistrates sitting as examining justices in committal proceedings. Appeal lies, generally with leave, to the Court of Appeal, Criminal Division, and thereafter to the House of Lords if a sufficiently important point of law is raised. This system is represented diagrammatically in figure 3.

The other forum before which the ordinary citizen is likely to appear is a tribunal. This is a generic label for modern forms of court established to meet specific needs and to provide a system of adjudication which is less formal and more accessible than the system of courts with their rituals and complex rules of evidence. Two examples, which are considered in detail later in this book are the

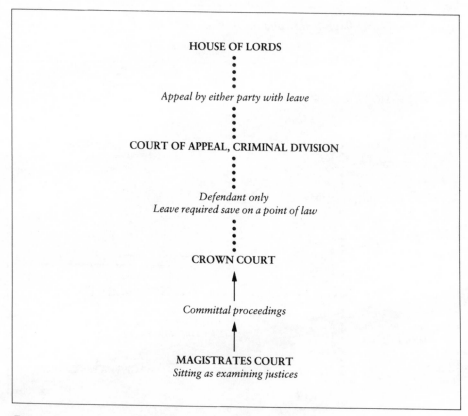

Figure 3   Trial on Indictment

social security appeal tribunals, which hear appeals concerning entitlement to social security benefits from decisions of adjudication officers in the Department of Social Security and Department of Employment, and Industrial Tribunals, which have a wide jurisdiction concerning the relationship of employer and employee.

HOUSE OF LORDS

Type: Superior court
Judges: Law Lords
Jurisdiction: Appellate only; unlimited
Audience: Barristers only

COURT OF APPEAL

Type: Superior court; part of Supreme Court of Judicature
divided into:

Civil Division

Judges: Master of the Rolls
  and Lords Justices
  of Appeal
Jurisdiction: Appellate only,
  civil, unlimited
Audience: Barristers only

Criminal Division

Judges: Lord Chief Justice
  and Lords Justices
  of Appeal
Jurisdiction: Appellate only,
  criminal, unlimited
Audience: Barristers only

HIGH COURT

Type: Superior court
  Part of Supreme Court
  of Judicature
divided into:
  Chancery Division
  Queen's Bench Division
  Family Division
Judges: Puisne judges
Jurisdiction: Appellate,
  supervisory and original,
  civil and criminal,
  unlimited
Audience: Barristers only

CROWN COURT

Type: Superior court
  except when exercising
  appellate jurisdiction
  Part of Supreme Court of
  Judicature
Judges: Puisne judges, Circuit
  judges, recorders
Jurisdiction: original and
  appellate,
  almost always criminal,
  unlimited
Audience: Barristers and in
  some circumstances
  solicitors

COUNTY COURTS

Type: Inferior courts
Judges: Circuit judges,
  District judges
Jurisdiction: Original, civil only,
  limited both geographically
  and by amount of claims
Audience: Barristers and
  solicitors

MAGISTRATES COURT

Type: Inferior courts
Judges: Justice of the Peace
  Stipendiaries
Jurisdiction: Original, civil
  and criminal, limited by
  function and seriousness
  of offence (see chapter 4)
Audience: Barristers and
  solicitors

Figure 4   The Courts

Other major institutions involved in the administration of justice are the legislature, the police, the judiciary and the legal profession. For our purposes more need be said at this stage only about the legal profession. This is divided into two main branches: solicitors and barristers. Each has different functions, though the tasks each performs are not exclusive to it. Barristers often draft documents and give advice, while solicitors often appear as advocates in court. Two points should be noted about the impact of the current division of the profession. First, clients have direct access only to solicitors who alone can instruct barristers to act for clients. Secondly, barristers alone enjoy the right to appear as advocates (known as having a *right of audience*) in the higher courts. Only barristers are currently eligible for appointment as judges in the High Court and above.

The structure and organization of the legal profession has been significantly reformed by the provisions of the Courts and Legal Services Act 1990, which implements proposals contained in the Lord Chancellor's White Paper of July 1989, *Legal Services: A Framework for the Future*, (Cm 740). Part II of the 1990 Act sets up a system of advocacy licensing under which suitably qualified solicitors will be able to acquire rights of audience in the higher courts. Such solicitors will become eligible for any judicial office alongside barristers.

Other changes will affect the work of the profession as well as sharpening up disciplinary procedures against both solicitors and barristers whose work is a source of complaint to their clients.

The institutional picture developed so far can be summarized in figure 4. The hierarchy of courts is also portrayed by putting the highest court in the hierarchy at the top of the chart and ranking other courts beneath it. The principal judges to be found in each court are also noted.

Before moving on there are three courts which warrant mention because otherwise confusion might arise when reference to them is met. None of them is part of the English legal system, though all have an impact on it.

The Judicial Committee of the Privy Council

The Judicial Committee of the Privy Council, often referred to simply as the Privy Council, is the body on whose advice and through which the sovereign exercises her statutory and a number of prerogative powers. The Judicial Committee of the Privy Council is an appellate court which derives its appellate jurisdiction from the right of all the Queen's subjects to appeal to the Crown for redress. The primary function of the Judicial Committee is to act as a final appeal court from the Channel Islands, the Isle of Man, the colonies, protectorates and associated states, and from those independent countries within the Commonwealth, which have not abolished such appeals. Since the legal systems of many of these countries are closely modelled on the English system, many of the decisions of the Judicial Committee are of relevance to the English lawyer and English courts treat decisions of the Judicial Committee with great respect. Another reason is that there is some overlap of personnel, since the Law Lords are members of the Judicial Committee.

Court of Justice of the European Communities

The Court of Justice of the European Communities, which is located in Luxembourg, and is one of the main institutions of the European Communities. Though it is not a part of the English legal system, its decisions have an important impact in English courts. It is rather like a federal court. Since accession to the European Economic Community (EEC) Treaty, it is possible, and in some cases obligatory, for questions on the interpretation of the treaties establishing the European Communities, or as to the validity of acts of Community institutions, to be referred to the European Court from an English court. This occurs most often under Article 177 of the EEC Treaty. The reference is not an appeal. It is a request from an English court or tribunal for an authoritative ruling on the meaning of some aspect of Community law relevant to the issue which the English court or tribunal is deciding. The case is adjourned (put into a state of legal suspended animation) pending the handing down of the opinion of the European Court, on the basis of which the English court will then decide the case. The Court has other important jurisdictions, but this is the only one which need concern us here. The Court of Justice has recently had attached to it a new Court of First Instance, which will take some of the burden of its case load from it, though with an appeal on a point of law lying to the Court of Justice itself.

The European Court of Human Rights

The European Court of Human Rights, which is located in Strasbourg, is one of the main institutions established by the Council of Europe under the European Convention on Human Rights. It is an international court, dealing with human rights complaints against states. It is not open to individuals; only Member States and the Commission established under the Convention may bring cases before the Court. Individual complaints about human rights are made to the Commission which conducts an investigation into those found to be admissible under the Convention's rules and makes a report on them to the Council of Ministers. Following delivery of such reports, the case may be referred to the Court by either the Commission or the Member State against whom the complaint was made. If the case is referred to the Court, the individual whose complaint started the process is able to appear and take part in the proceedings, but not as a party to the case.

Processes

Readers who are beginning to yawn at this stage can be forgiven. The institutional approach to the administration of justice tends to be arid, technical and dull, though a minimum of factual knowledge about the institutions of the system is needed for any consideration of the administration of justice. The problem with focusing on institutions is that it tells us very little about how the system operates.

Much more interesting and exciting is the study of these institutions in action. The study of processes tells us so much more about the system. Is it usable? Is it accessible? Is it fair to litigants? Does it provide an appropriate means of dispute resolution? Without an appreciation of legal processes, it is all too easy to get a distorted picture of the operation of law in society. It will be little use knowing the substantive rules of negligence or of the criminal law, if there is no context in which to place that knowledge. In understanding the law of negligence, it is necessary to know how victims of accidents learn about their rights, of how a typical personal injuries action will proceed, and what factors influence participants in the process. In understanding the prosecution of a criminal offence, it is necessary to know how the offence came to the attention of the police, how the offence has been investigated, what pressures are placed on defendants, whether legal advice defendants receive is effective, and whether the trial process operates fairly and effectively. It is after all processes which ultimately determine the effectiveness of the substantive law.

In recent years there has been increasing emphasis on this perspective on the administration of justice and much research has been carried out that is beginning to enable us to understand how the system operates in practice rather than in theory, or put another way, in the real world rather than in the books. In adopting this perspective greater emphasis is placed on the consumer with attempts made to view the processes through the eyes of the individuals who are caught up in the system. The role of the lawyer is not quite as central, because from this perspective much happens both before and after the lawyer appears on the scene. Indeed in some cases, the lawyer never appears on the scene.

The approach adopted in this book in looking at the civil and criminal justice systems is broadly to follow the fate of a man or woman caught up in a civil or criminal case from the event which begins the process through to the disposition of a final appeal. As we go along necessary institutional and procedural background is given so that by the end of each part of the book the reader should be able to construct an accurate basic account of the institutions and procedures involved, as well as having seen how the system actually operates in the real world.

Part II
The Criminal Process

2

Magistrates' Courts and the Crown Court

Introduction

An appreciation of the distinction between magistrates' courts and the Crown Court is fundamental to an understanding of the criminal process. In essence the distinction is simple: magistrates' courts deal in bulk with less serious or routine crime, including most motoring offences, while the Crown Court deals with a comparatively small number of more serious criminal offences. But beneath this simple distinction is a far more complex difference: the processes by which each court fulfils its functions are dramatically different. It would be quite misleading to think of the process in magistrates' courts as simply a quicker and less formal process than that to be found in the Crown Court.

Magistrates and Magistrates' Courts

There are two types of magistrates: lay magistrates, or justices of the peace (JPs), and stipendiary magistrates. Lay magistrates are amateurs. They are unpaid, though there are allowances for travel, subsistence and loss of earnings. They receive only minimal legal training for the exercise of their functions and rely upon a justices' clerk to advise them as to law and procedure and to undertake the administration of the courts. Stipendiaries are professional lawyers who exercise the functions both of lay magistrates and of their clerks. Stipendiary magistrates have a much shorter history than lay magistrates. They first came to be appointed in the eighteenth century as an alternative to corrupt lay magistrates in some urban areas. (Moir, 1969). There are 63 stipendiaries; most are to be found in London and the rest in large cities elsewhere. By contrast there are about 28,000 lay magistrates (16,000 men and 12,000 women) sitting in about 650 magistrates' courts, each having jurisdiction only in its own area. About 450 of these are located in rural areas. The bulk of criminal business is conducted in the magistrates' courts in the large towns and cities. Dating back to the twelfth century the lay magistracy has survived many major reforms of the legal system.

It is now seen as a central feature of the English legal system and as a great strength of the criminal process. There is undoubtedly a benefit in involving laymen in the administration of criminal justice. The main benefit is summed up neatly, if somewhat idealistically, by Sir Thomas Skyrme in his book on the magistracy:

> The collective views of a cross-section of the population, representing different shades of opinion, can be more effective in dispensing justice acceptable to the public than the decision of a single individual necessarily drawn from a fairly narrow social class and whose experience of local problems may be limited. . . . The system enables the citizen to see that the law is his law, administered by men and women like himself, and that it is not the esoteric preserve of lawyers. (Skyrme, 1983, p. 8)

Magistrates sitting in benches of three (sometimes two) exercise a wide variety of jurisdictions. They try less serious criminal cases; they consider the evidence against those charged with serious offences and determine whether it is sufficient to send them for trial in the Crown Court (see chapter 4); they deal with applications for gaming and liquor licences; they exercise an important civil jurisdiction, principally concerning family matters when sitting as the domestic panel; and, finally, as juvenile courts, they deal with a wide range of cases involving the welfare of those under 17. Part II of this book is concerned with the role of magistrates in the criminal process when dealing with persons aged 17 or over.

Choosing Magistrates

A network of 95 local advisory committees advises the Lord Chancellor of the names of persons thought suitable for appointment. In Greater Manchester, Merseyside and Lancashire appointments are made by the Chancellor of the Duchy of Lancaster. There is still considerable secrecy surrounding the selection and appointment of magistrates. The membership of the advisory committees is currently a closely guarded secret, ostensibly to prevent lobbying for appointment. The Lord Chancellor has announced the start of a process of introducing disclosure of membership of the local advisory committees. By the end of 1992, advisory committee membership must be made public. This is a laudable attempt to respond to criticisms that the present methods of selection lack fairness and openness and serve to perpetuate the middle-class character of the magistracy. The long lead time is to permit the graceful withdrawal of those who regard this openness as a retrograde step; there is nothing to prevent local advisory committees announcing their membership earlier than the 1992 deadline.

Appointment to the advisory committees themselves is also made by the Lord Chancellor who regards the local knowledge they have as important in securing a magistracy that is a microcosm of society. Yet it seems that only nine per cent of members of these committees in 1982 were neither serving nor retired magistrates (King and May, 1985, p. 26). The system has its roots in the recommendations of the Royal Commissions on Justices of the Peace in 1910 (Cd 5250) and in 1948 (Cmd 7463). It was designed primarily to avoid political influence in the appointment of magistrates.

To be eligible for appointment to the magistracy, a person must live locally and not be over 60 years of age, or be in an occupation which might conflict with the role of magistrate. Compulsory retirement arrives at the age of 70. A booklet prepared by the Lord Chancellor's Department (Lord Chancellor's Department, 1988) says:

> When new magistrates are needed, the committees seek nominations. They ask local organisations or business; they may put notices in the press or use another means to find candidates. It is part of the local advisory committee's job to make sure that magistrates are drawn from many walks of life and that the composition of the bench in this sense is broadly balanced.

Some wage earners may be put off by the commitment required; a magistrate is expected to sit at least 26 days each year. This commitment is quite considerable, and even though employers are required to allow persons time off to sit on the bench, they are not required to pay them. The loss of earnings allowance is not overly generous and for some this may present a disincentive to allowing their names to go forward for consideration for appointment. Job and promotion prospects may also be affected by the absences from work.

Training

It is remarkable that it was not until 1 January 1966 that there was a system of compulsory training for new magistrates; native wit, a willingness to learn and the received wisdom of the bench the new magistrates were joining were previously thought sufficient (Skyrme, 1983). Following the recommendations contained in the 1975 White Paper *The Training of Justices of the Peace in England and Wales* (Cmnd 2856), a compulsory two-stage system of training was introduced. The first stage consists of basic training in law and procedure, criminology and penology. It also includes sitting in court as an observer. This stage should be completed before the new magistrate sits on the bench for the first time. The second stage covers the first 12 months of a magistrate's career and consists of further courses of instruction and visits to various types of penal establishment. Those appointed on or after 1 January 1980 are also required to attend approved continuing training totalling not less than 12 hours every three years.

This must be regarded as the barest acceptable minimum of training, and bears no comparison with the years of training required of all other members of the judiciary. There have also been suggestions that the compulsory training is not always fully implemented (Baldwin, 1974). In fairness, it should be added that many courts offer voluntary courses of training both as refresher courses and as guides to new developments relevant to the magistrates' functions to all magistrates, whenever appointed. Attendance at such courses will be expected of all magistrates. How well organized such courses are often depends on the initiatives of senior members of the bench and of justices' clerks.

The training given is basic, designed to equip magistrates to perform their functions rather than to convert lay people into legal experts. The legal expertise is provided by the clerks to the justices. One clerk to the justices has described the tenor of the training given in the following terms:

> Training has to be very practical. You have exercises on sentencing and videos about procedure. You can't come on like a university professor giving a lecture on criminal law. It has to be practical. The whole point of the magistrates is that they are lay people coming in possibly once a fort-night and bringing with them their outside experience as citizens and the fresh approach which legal professionals can lack. A lot of training is to give them confidence, to say to them don't be overawed by lawyers; hold on to common sense; remember what the witness has said, and if you're worried about a legal point, ask the Clerk.

A Cross-Section of the Community?

The booklet prepared by the Lord Chancellor's Department states that the role of local advisory committees is to ensure that magistrates are drawn from all walks of life. It seems that this is not achieved; the difficulties faced by wage earners has already been mentioned.

From time to time attempts are made to produce a profile of the magistracy to determine whether it is representative of the community at large. From these attempts it is clear that among magistrates proportionately more members of political parties are likely to be found than among the public at large. There also seems to be an over-representation of the middle classes (Baldwin, 1976). By contrast women and members of ethnic minorities are under-represented, the latter seriously so (Skyrme, 1983; King and May, 1985). It also seems that women and ethnic minorities are poorly represented on the advisory committees (Burney, 1979).

Such evidence as is available points to a disproportionate social balance among the magistracy with comfortably-off, middle-aged, middle-class magistrates sitting in judgment on the less well-off working-class members of society.

Of particular concern is the very low number of magistrates from the ethnic minority communities; the latest official figures show that only two per cent of magistrates, that is, just over 500, are black. An important study in 1985 (King and May, 1985) showed that recruitment rates of black magistrates varied widely. In eight of the 25 representative courts surveyed, the representation of black magistrates would at least need to double before the composition of the bench reflected the number of black people living in the area.

King and May's conclusion is that there is evidence of racial bias among members of the advisory committees. This takes the form of negative stereo-typing of black people and the imposing of requirements on black candidates, which are not applied to white candidates. One example is the requirement of one committee that Asian candidates be 'acceptable to the whole Asian community' in the area. In general a serious criticism is expressed of the general fairness of the selection process for all candidates. In some areas secret enquiries are made and selection decisions are based on 'soft' information, that is second or third hand information which has not been verified or put to the candidate. No reasons are given to rejected candidates; indeed, in some cases unsuccessful candidates are not even informed that they have been unsuccessful. They simply hear nothing further about the matter.

The study does, however, recognize the difficulty of recruiting ethnic minority magistrates. It found a remarkably small number of black people prepared to be candidates for appointment. This reluctance to serve was, however, itself linked to perceptions of a discriminatory selection procedure and a view of the magistrates' courts as part of the white establishment. The researchers also acknowledge the inherent tension between the concept of popular justice: justice administered, as Sir Thomas Skyrme put it, by men and women like the defendant; and professionalism, which emphasizes the *gravitas* of the judicial function, the need for the magistrate to be a person whose judgment is valued in the community, and the need for efficiency in the despatch of heavy case loads without undue delay.

The Clerk to the Justices

The role of the clerk to the justices is vital to the work of the magistracy. The Clerk to the Justices and his or her staff administer the courts and act as legal advisers to each bench of magistrates when they are sitting. The Clerk to the Justices is often also the bench's training officer.

During hearings the clerk must take care not to overstep the purely advisory role. So a clerk can advise on the admissibility of a piece of evidence (an issue of law) but must not give any hint as to a view on the credibility of a witness (an issue of fact). The dividing line is not always easy to define. A *Practice Direction* ([1981] 1 WLR 1163) issued in 1981 sought to summarize the clerk's responsibilities. The Clerk to the Justices also enjoys some limited quasi-judicial authority, such as the issuing of summonses and the granting of legal aid.

The Work of Magistrates

This small army of minimally trained laymen deal with about two and a half million cases each year, just over half of which will be motoring offences. Many of the other cases will be fairly minor matters; some, of course, will be trivial. But some of the cases dealt with by magistrates are sufficiently serious that each year magistrates send around 20,000 offenders to prison. They will also consider the evidence against about 120,000 persons accused of serious crime to determine whether there is sufficient evidence for them to be sent for trial in the Crown Court. This workload represents a staggering 97 per cent of all criminal

business. The magistrates could not cope if about eight out of every ten defendants did not plead guilty. In cases tried before them, magistrates determine both
guilt and the sentence to be imposed, advised as to law and procedure by their
clerk. The picture which begins to emerge is of an institution which processes
large numbers of individuals, most of whom do not contest the evidence against
them. It is sometimes asserted that magistrates' courts are guilty plea courts and
that there is little point in contesting a case before them because they will
invariably believe the prosecution evidence. In so far as it is possible to extract
information from the criminal judicial statistics, it seems that magistrates find
about half those who contest cases before them not guilty. This is roughly the
same as the proportion acquitted in the Crown Court. Magistrates' courts are
also said to be very cheap and economical; this is only true because of the high
rate of guilty pleas before magistrates' courts. When the hourly cost of contested
cases before magistrates' courts and in the Crown Court is compared, the
resulting figures are remarkably similar. (James Committee, 1975).

The Crown Court

Following the recommendations of the Report of the Royal Commission on
Assizes and Quarter Sessions (Beeching Report) in 1969 (Cmnd 4153), the old
Courts of Assize and Quarter Sessions were replaced in 1972 by a single Crown
Court as the forum for the trial of more serious criminal cases. Though a single
court, the Crown Court may sit anywhere and a national network of trial centres
has been established. When the Crown Court sits in the City of London it is
known as the Central Criminal Court, or colloquially as the Old Bailey. Most
large towns have a Crown Court. Contested trials in the Crown Court, where,
of course, only three per cent of criminal business is conducted, are the epitome
of the ordinary citizen's view of the criminal justice system. Lawyers represent
both prosecution and defence, and, employing formidable forensic skills, seek to
persuade a jury of 12 individuals chosen at random of the guilt or innocence
of the accused. The judge is there to decide points of law and to sum up the
evidence to assist the jury in its task of determining guilt or innocence.
   The jury is perhaps the most sacred institution of the criminal justice system
and has evoked over the years emotive labels from major public figures. In 1830
Blackstone commented that the 'liberties of England cannot but subsist so long
as this palladium remains sacred and inviolate', and in 1956 Lord Devlin
described the jury as 'the lamp that shows that freedom lives'. Equally florid
comments vilifying the jury can be found, but the weight of comment is favourable, and public opinion is massively in favour of the jury (Baldwin and
McConville, 1979a). Whether its popularity is deserved will be considered in
chapter 6.
   Though the process of jury trial appears to be a model of fairness, it is wrong
to isolate it from the processes which have gone before. There is evidence to
suggest that the outcome of cases in the Crown Court is as much dependent upon
what happens to an accused person in the police station, and in the magistrates'

court, as upon the process of jury trial (McBarnet, 1981; McConville and Baldwin, 1981). There have also been persistent complaints that too great a pressure is placed upon some defendants to plead guilty rather than to continue to fight the case (Baldwin and McConville, 1977). Even in the Crown Court seven out of every ten defendants plead guilty.

As a generalization the Crown Court deals with more serious crime, though it is still possible for a defendant to choose to be tried by a judge and jury for comparatively minor matters. For example, a person accused of shoplifting goods costing only a few pence has a right to elect jury trial. When the government of the day sought to introduce in the Criminal Law Bill in 1977 a minimum monetary value of the property stolen as a qualification for the right to elect trial by jury, public opinion was mobilized so strongly against the proposal that it had to be dropped from the Bill. There is also a principle that the more serious the crime the more senior and experienced the judge to try it. The Crown Court is staffed by High Court judges, Circuit judges of whom there are about 400 and part-time judges, called Recorders, of whom there are about 600. This body of over 1000 judges will try about 120,000 cases each year.

In addition to its trial work, the Crown Court deals with persons sent to the Crown Court for sentence where the magistrates do not consider their limited sentencing powers sufficient to deal with a person convicted before them. Generally speaking magistrates cannot sentence a defendant to a period of imprisonment exceeding six months for any one offence or exceeding twelve months for any two or more offences. Nor may they normally fine a defendant more than £2000. Finally, the Crown Court acts as an appeal court against conviction or sentence, or both, in the magistrates' court.

Choosing Judges

Appointment as a Circuit judge is the highest judicial office available through a process of application; higher appointments are by invitation only (Lord Chancellor's Department, 1990). Any solicitor or barrister who has been qualified for at least ten years may apply for appointment as a Recorder. In practice appointments are not offered to those under 40 years of age. Any barrister of at least ten years call or any solicitor who has served as a Recorder for three years may apply for appointment as a Circuit judge. Applicants for these posts are selected and interviewed by members of the Judicial Appointments Group of the Lord Chancellor's Department in much the same manner as they would be for any civil service post.

Appointment as a High Court judge is by invitation only and is open only to barristers who have been qualified for at least ten years. Invitation is based upon recommendations from judges, senior barristers and officials of the Lord Chancellor's Department, which will, in turn, be based upon the reputation acquired by barristers in court. Little dossiers, known in the trade as 'yellow sheets' (but in reality pink cards), build up on potential candidates over a number of years. The final decision to issue an invitation comes after the Lord Chancellor has met with his senior colleagues to draw up an informal short list. The final choice is that of the Lord Chancellor alone; technically appointments are made by the Queen, but by convention she always acts on the advice of the Lord Chancellor. Appointment to the High Court bench by the age of 50 is the mark of a high flier. Comparatively few High Court judges are recruited from among Circuit judges.

Some invitations are turned down. The salary of nearly £70,000 per year is modest compared with the earnings of leading practitioners, though the pension provision is generous. Once appointed, a judge is expected to continue in office until compulsory retirement age: 72 for a Recorder or Circuit judge; 75 for higher judicial appointments. Indeed when Sir Henry Fisher left the High Court bench in 1970 for better paid work, his fellow judges made little secret of their disapproval of his conduct.

A Cloistered Collegiate Group

The overwhelming number of judges recruited from the small world of the Bar invariably gives the judiciary a collegiate atmosphere. The social profile of the judiciary, even today, shows a predominance of middle and upper-class origins and of education at public school and Oxbridge. This will have been followed by two decades or more of life at the Bar. It is impossible to argue that the world of the Inns of Court is not cloistered and full of ritual and tradition. The social-izing influence of the life is powerful. While judges today live more ordinary lives than in the past, it is absurd to suggest that they are a microcosm of society. They are not. Pannick comments:

> It is not surprising that a Bench composed almost entirely of former barris-
> ters should lack expertise and knowledge of many of the matters which are
> central to the lives of those people who come into court as litigants and
> witnesses. (Pannick, 1988, p. 53)

Senior members of the judiciary tend to over-emphasize the 'ordinariness' of judges; the dignity and traditions of judicial office alone prevent that.

Provisions in the Courts and Legal Services Act 1990 pave the way for judicial appointments to be made from among those who have enjoyed certain advocacy rights for a number of years regardless of the branch of the profession to which they belong. This widening of the group eligible for higher judicial office is a welcome reform and will certainly, over time, break down some of the traditions which make it difficult to rebut the charge that judges inhabit a judicial ivory tower remote from the problems of the ordinary citizen. But it is unlikely to make a dramatic difference to the public perception of the majesty of the law embodied in our senior judges. Psychological profiling of those who choose law as a career tends to show a dominance of those with conservative instincts who have a natural liking for working within a clearly defined framework of rules.

Despite all these criticisms, one commentator on judges, who is by no means a sycophantic supporter of every aspect of the judiciary, says:

What has changed markedly is the general standard of judicial performance. Today it is high, most probably higher than ever before in terms of
ability, conduct and understanding of the needs of society. (Pannick, 1988,
p. 15)

Training of Judges

Training of judges has since 1978 been in the hands of the Judicial Studies Board
which has a salaried director and holds regular training seminars in the criminal
jurisdiction both for the newly appointed judge and refresher courses for experienced judges, particularly in matters of sentencing. Only in October 1985 was
the task of the Judicial Studies Board extended to cover the civil and family jurisdictions. The pattern which has emerged is of seminars lasting three or four days.

No real attempt is made to convert from advocacy to judicial skills; it is
assumed that those selected for judicial office will have the 'judicial attitude'
necessary to enable them to perform well in their new role. Snobbery and arro-
gance precludes the acceptance of the need for skills training in these important
areas. The skills will be learned on the job at the expense of advocates, litigants
and witnesses. Pannick argues:

The amateur approach which the English legal system adopts in this
context hinders the effective performance of the judicial function. (Pannick,
1988, p. 73)

The Relationship between Magistrates' Courts and the Crown Court

The nature and seriousness of the offence are the major factors in determining
whether a case will be dealt with by a magistrates' court or the Crown Court.
It is the system of classification of offences for the purpose of determining the
mode of trial that assigns each crime to a particular category. There are now
only three classes of offences:

offences triable only on indictment, that is, in the Crown Court;
offences triable only summarily, that is, in the magistrates' courts;
offences triable either way, that is, either in the Crown Court or in a magis-
    trates' court.

Obviously no problem arises concerning the mode of trial of offences triable
only on indictment or only summarily; there is no choice. Offences triable only
in the Crown Court include the most serious offences, such as murder, manslaughter, rape, robbery or arson, while offences triable only in the magistrates'
court are much less serious; good examples are minor motoring offences. But
there is a whole range of offences which are triable either way, of which the most
significant are burglary and theft. Details of how the choice in such cases
between magistrates' court and the Crown Court is made are to be found in

chapter 5. It is enough to note here that in all such cases the defendant has a right to choose to be tried by a jury in the Crown Court, if the magistrates, after considering the seriousness of the case and all other relevant circumstances, nevertheless conclude that trial in the magistrates' court is more appropriate.

Over the years there has been a tendency to restrict the types of cases for which trial by jury is available. The last major exercise in reclassification was embodied in the Criminal Law Act 1977, and is now largely consolidated in the Magistrates' Courts Act 1980. This followed the recommendations contained in the Report of the James Committee (James Committee, 1975) in downgrading a number of offences. Some offences which could previously be tried only on indictment became triable either way. But more significantly a number of offences became triable only summarily, thus depriving defendants of the right of election for trial by jury. This relieved some pressure on jury trials, but increased pressures in magistrates' courts. There is also some evidence to suggest that the police prefer cases to be tried in magistrates' courts whenever possible and there have been a number of reports in the press in recent years of the practice of deliberately choosing to charge offences triable only summarily to avoid the possibility of jury trial (see, for example, the *Guardian*, 9 August 1983 and 23 January 1984). While attempts can be made to justify such decisions in some cases on grounds of cost, it does tend to lend support to the assertion that magistrates' courts always believe the prosecution evidence and leaves the police open to the charge of manipulating the system to increase the chances of securing convictions.

3

Policing: On the Street

The Work of the Police

Constables and Chief Constables

The police play a central role in the criminal process. The investigation of an offence and the interactions between the police and persons identified as suspects are the core of the criminal process. For many accused of crime, the whole process will be determined by what happens in these pre-trial interactions.

In England and Wales, every police officer, with the exception of the Commissioner of Police for the Metropolis, holds the 'ancient and honourable office of constable' under the Crown. The constable is not an employee, but an independent office holder. Though the police service is run on rigid, quasi-military, hierarchical lines, there are areas where each constable is, at least theoretically, answerable only to the law and not to his or her superiors. In these areas no police officer of higher rank can interfere with the judgment exercised by the constable. But constitutional fiction has been replaced by modern reality. One commentator notes:

> The police officer can no longer be seen as a self-directed decision maker answerable only to the law. Rather he is a person subject to organisational and occupational/professional rules and norms, like other employees. (Lustgarten, 1986 p. 30)

The Police Act 1964, responding to the Royal Commission on the Police of 1962 (Willink Commission, 1962), and as subsequently amended, has established 43 police forces (including the Metropolitan Police District and the City of London Police) each under the direction of a chief officer of police, known in almost every case as a chief constable. Chief officers of police are responsible (except in the case of the Metropolitan Police District and City of London Police) to police authorities and to the Home Secretary for the general efficiency of their forces, but are alone responsible for the way in which they decide to investigate and prosecute offences. Police authorities are local committees consisting of local authority elected members and magistrates charged with the duty to maintain an adequate police force for the area. They have been described as 'extremely tame and timid creatures, unwilling to bark let alone bite' (Benyon, 1986, p. 18).

There is often said to be a distinction between operational matters which are within the sole province of the chief constable and policy matters where the police authority has a role to play. Some doubt the ability to divide police activities into two such distinct areas (Marshall, 1978; Lustgarten, 1986 pp. 20–2).

The Home Secretary's ministerial responsibility for the police extends to his approving the appointment by police authorities of chief constables and assistants. The Home Office also produces regulations governing the appointment, discipline and promotion of officers of the rank of chief superintendent and below. In practice no one becomes a senior police officer without the approval of Home Office civil servants. The Commissioner of Police of the Metropolis is, exceptionally, not a constable and holds office at the pleasure of the Home Secretary. There is no police authority for the Metropolitan Police District. These functions are carried out by the Home Secretary.

Keeping the Peace

Preventing and detecting crime, and making the initial decision to put a case forward for prosecution are just three of eight functions of the police identified by the Willink Commission in 1962. The first and paramount function was stated to be 'the duty to maintain law and order and to protect persons and property'. Many commentators stress this general peace-keeping and community-serving function of the police: 'The core mandate of policing, historically and in terms of concrete demands placed upon the police, is the more diffuse one of order maintenance' (Reiner, 1985, p. 172).

So just as it is a misconception to assume that most lawyers spend a significant amount of their time in court or engaged in court work, so too it is a misconception to assume that crime fighting is the prime activity of the police. One study of police encounters with the public describes police patrol as a 'quite mundane and undramatic activity' which is due largely to the 'mundane nature of the calls which the public make on the police' (Southgate, 1986, p. 53). How then do the police use their time?

How do the Police Use their Time?

A major report by the Policy Studies Institute into policing by the Metropolitan Police, commissioned by Sir David McNee when he was Commissioner of Police for the Metropolis, gives a rough but fascinating breakdown of the time spent by officers in the Metropolitan Police on various tasks (Smith, D., 1983, vol. III). The typical pattern which emerges for a uniformed police constable is that 55 per cent of time is spent outside the police station and 45 per cent of time inside the station. Much of the time in the police station is spent on administrative tasks and around five per cent on training. Outside the police station ten per cent of time is spent on foot patrol and 18 per cent on vehicle patrols. Other time outside the police station is spent attending court, or contacting and interviewing witnesses and informants. Overall it seems that only one per cent of uniformed police time is spent interviewing suspects and witnesses at the police station. This proportion of time is very low; both activities are seen by the police as the most important sources of information leading to the apprehension of offenders.

The figures for detective police officers, the Criminal Investigation Department (CID), show that they spend 55 per cent of their time on police premises and 45 per cent off them. Outside the police station the largest single activity, accounting for 17 per cent of time, is contacting or interviewing informants or witnesses. In the police station 35 per cent of time is spent on administration. Only eight per cent of time is occupied interviewing suspects or witnesses at the police station. For all police only two per cent of police time is spent on this task.

The other significant aspect of the use of police time that emerges from the survey is that police sergeants and inspectors had little time for direct supervision of police constables.

How Good are the Police at Detecting Crime?

One of the early studies of the investigation of crime in this country was conducted by Michael Zander (Zander, 1979b). The results of an investigation into 150 cases tried at the Old Bailey in 1974 were analysed to see how the offender had been caught. In most cases establishing the identity of the offender required no skilled detective work. In nearly half the cases, the person reporting the crime had known the identity of the offender. In a further four in ten cases the offender had been caught at or near the scene of the crime almost immediately, and in one in six cases the police had a good description of the offender or knew the registration number of his car.

In a research study carried out for the Royal Commission on Criminal Procedure, David Steer broadly confirmed Zander's conclusions (Steer, 1980). Three out of four offenders were caught because they were known to the victim of the crime, were caught red-handed at or near the scene of the crime or were one of a small group of people who alone could have committed the offence. One in four cases required traditional skills of detection: fingerprinting, police questioning, tip-offs and local knowledge.

Interrogation of suspects was seen as important in obtaining information about other criminal activity (the suspect's own or that of others) rather than in securing a confession to the crime under investigation. It also seems that an initial assessment is made of the information available about a crime by investigating officers. Those cases which appear to promise some success in detecting the offender are investigated further, while those which do not are quietly shelved. Steer also reports unpublished research by a senior detective police officer which supports this: it found that the average time spent on the investigation of undetected crime was 2 hours 48 minutes and on the investigation of crimes that were cleared up was 4 hours 30 minutes.

In terms of overall success rate the Steer survey showed that the investigation of 959 crimes selected at random produced 373 suspects of whom 34 were cautioned and 289 prosecuted. The 289 prosecutions resulted in 261 convictions. Measuring success in terms of the ratio of convictions to reported crimes suggests that the police secure convictions in only three out of every ten crimes reported.

Fascinating though these figures are, they represent only 'crimes known to the police' and not the totality of criminal activity. In the Steer survey some 80 per cent of offences investigated by the police were reported to them by members of the public rather than discovered by the police. This figure is roughly in line with that produced by other studies. There is a considerable body of research which suggests that crime reported to the police is only the tip of the iceberg. In a 1977 study it was suggested that only one in eleven criminal offences is reported to the police (Sparks et al., 1977). Many of the unreported offences would be trivial and the reasons for non-reporting perfectly valid: for example, a conclusion that the police would be unable to solve the crime. The success rate of the police in the apprehension of offenders noted above is measured against the level of offending the community regards as sufficiently serious to report to the police in the first place (Mayhew et al., 1989).

Policing in an Adversarial System

The Royal Commission on Criminal Procedure of 1981 (Philips Commission, 1981) pointed out that the adversarial nature of the criminal trial largely determines the nature of the pre-trial procedures. The essence of the adversarial system is that the trial takes the form of a contest between prosecution and defence which is governed by strict rules of evidence and which alone determines whether the accused committed the crime charged. The pre-trial stages merely represent the collection of evidence and preparation of cases by each side. Lustgarten also stresses the importance of the adversarial nature of the criminal trial for the style of policing and provides a useful contrast with criminal procedure in inquisitorial systems (Lustgarten, 1986).

The key point is that in an adversarial system convictions are secured in one of two ways. First, the prosecution may succeed in adducing admissible evidence which persuades the magistrates or jury beyond all reasonable doubt that the accused committed the act constituting the offence with the requisite intent. Secondly, the accused may plead guilty, bypassing completely the necessity for proof of commission of the offence. It is small wonder that the police go to considerable lengths to secure a criminal trial of the second type. There is no uncertainty as to outcome; and the result will be seen by the police to accord with what they know rather than what they can prove. The evidential burdens of the adversarial system invariably mean that the police will 'know' more than they can prove. The adversarial system also leaves the pre-trial stages of the process in the hands of the police, largely uncontrolled by outside interference until the point at which the police decide to put a case forward for consideration by the criminal courts.

By contrast, the criminal process under the inquisitorial system is more in the nature of a continuing office enquiry. The police are subject to much closer scrutiny by the courts and by supervising judges throughout the process, especially where more serious offences are at issue. The dossier builds up over a period of time, and is not necessarily directed at a single individual. The trial is the culmination of a process rather than the single showcase event of the adversarial process. Crucially, under the inquisitorial system, a defendant cannot plead guilty and avoid the necessity for formal proof of the commission of the offence charged. The inquisitorial system is not, though, without its critics. It has been argued that convictions can be secured on flimsy evidence because the evidentiary burden is not as high as in the adversarial system and because the inquisitorial process is ill-suited to testing the credibility of witnesses and defendants, where the issue is whom to believe.

The Great Reform of Police Powers

The Climate for Reform

The 1950s had been the golden age of public acceptance of the police. Policing by consent was achieved to the greatest extent then. A survey conducted in 1960 for the Willink Commission revealed that eight out of every ten citizens had great respect for the police; the survey results represented a massive vote of confidence in the police.

The positive relationship between the community and the police came to be known as 'the British police advantage' and was envied by many other countries (Benyon, 1986). By the middle of the next decade, this advantage was slipping away. Some put this down to the dramatic increase in car ownership, which not only made the police more remote from the citizen, but also provided increased opportunities for negative contacts between the public and the police as they dealt with motoring and other traffic related offences. The transformation of policing into a professional specialist activity also produced an alienating influence.

There was considerable debate on the style of policing with some emphasis placed on the need for the consent and general support of the community for police activity. By contrast others favoured 'hard' policing and saw the overriding model as being conflictual: tough measures were seen as essential in the fight against crime. There was also debate about the extent to which the police themselves unearth crime. Some argued that the police should be principally reactive, responding to reports of offences from victims or others affected by criminal conduct. Others saw a role for proactive policing where the police actively seek out crime. This approach is particularly controversial in the context of the so-called 'victimless' crimes involving drugs or pornography.

In their various roles, the police are given special powers to stop, detain and question persons suspected of having committed criminal offences. Often what results from this initial interaction between suspect and the police forms the basis of the case against the suspect. Because at this stage the suspect is deemed innocent, there is a careful balance to be struck between the liberties of the individual and the protection of society. In the mid-1970s there was serious concern that the balance had been lost. Some argued that the increasing incidence of serious crime was partly caused by the restraints of criminal procedure preventing the police from proceeding against persons known to have committed offences. Others argued that a serious gap had arisen between the formal protection provided for suspects by the rules of criminal procedure and the actual practice of those rules. The formal protection was, it was argued, illusory.

Matters were brought to a head by the wrongful conviction of three youths for the murder of Maxwell Confait. The subsequent enquiry into this case revealed improprieties in the police conduct of the investigation of the offence (Fisher Inquiry, 1977). The response to these concerns was the establishment in June 1977 of the Royal Commission on Criminal Procedure – 'the Philips Commission' – which reported in 1981 on the processes of investigation of crime and the prosecution of offenders (Philips Commission, 1981).

The Philips Commission's 'fundamental balance'

The Philips Commission was noteworthy for the volume of original research which it commissioned in order to provide a sound empirical basis on which its recommendations could be based. The research studies were published under the aegis of the Philips Commission and provide valuable information about the operation of the criminal process. The Report of the Philips Commission has as its philosophical base the concept of a fundamental balance between the interests of the community in bringing offenders to justice and the liberties of persons suspected of crime. The Report recognizes the difficulty of identifying the central features of this fundamental balance. Ultimately the Report concludes that it is the responsibility of Parliament to load the scales in order to strike the fundamental balance, and to keep that balance under regular review. But throughout the Report it is clear that the Commission considered that individual rights and community interests should be carefully balanced and that this would provide the litmus test for determining the coherence and effectiveness of the pre-trial criminal process. The choices made should manifest qualities of fairness, openness and workability.

The Philips Commission considered that it had produced a carefully constructed package which clarified police powers, but in each case balanced them with safeguards designed to protect the citizen. It was a powerful and challenging report that generated discussion and debate on policing. It was the kind of report which cannot be shelved. The government's response was to base new legislation on its recommendations.

PACE and the Codes of Practice

The legislation was so controversial that the first attempt to secure a new statute was a casualty of the calling of the 1983 general election. During the Parliamentary session before the 1983 election, the major report on policing in London which had been commissioned by Sir David McNee, the Metropolitan Police

Commissioner, was published. This provided further evidence of the failure of existing safeguards to protect the citizen. The study presents a picture of the police a world away from the cosy comfort of the 'Dixon of Dock Green' image of the 1950s. Following their return to power, the Tory government returned to Parliament with substantially the same bill. In due course this became the Police and Criminal Evidence Act 1984 (PACE). This Act and its counterpart, the Prosecution of Offences Act 1985, have been described by Lord Scarman as follows:

> The two Acts will in due course work great changes in the way the criminal law is enforced. They will restructure the whole criminal process from arrest or summons up to the moment at which the trial begins. Our police and prosecution services will be changed irreversibly; the old pattern will fade into history. (Benyon and Bourn, 1986 p. xix)

PACE itself contains a core of rules dealing with the pre-trial criminal process from stop and search on the street to charge at the police station. It also makes changes to the rules of evidence and updates the police complaints procedure. PACE adopts the device of coupling rules in the primary legislation with detailed guidance contained in codes of practice, which the Home Secretary is required to prepare and submit to Parliament for approval under ss.66 and 67 of PACE.

There are now five codes of practice: Code A on the exercise by police officers of statutory powers of stop and search; Code B on the searching of premises by police officers and the seizure of property found by police officers on persons or premises; Code C on the detention treatment and questioning of persons by police officers; Code D on the identification of persons by police officers; and Code E on tape recording of police interviews with suspects. These codes are of enormous significance. Though not technically subordinate legislation, they have much the same effect. A number of subsections of the seemingly innocuous s.67 of PACE spell out the status of the codes.

Failure to comply with the codes will render a police officer liable to disciplinary proceedings within the force. But a failure to comply with the provisions of any code 'shall not of itself render [the police officer] liable to any criminal or civil proceedings'. This means that a police officer ignoring the provisions of a code only commits a criminal offence if the conduct would otherwise amount to a crime. Beating up a suspect in a police cell is a breach of a number of provisions of Code C, but it will only be a crime because the constable's conduct will almost certainly amount to an offence against the person under the criminal law. Equally, a failure to comply with Code A in stopping and searching a person will not, of itself, render the constable liable in damages for trespass to the person. The aggrieved individual will have to establish such a claim under the ordinary rules of the law of tort.

In each of the above two examples, the person complaining about police conduct can adduce in evidence the requirements of the relevant code's provisions. Section 67(11) of PACE provides that 'if any provision of such a code appears to the court or tribunal conducting the proceedings to be relevant to any question arising in the proceedings it shall be taken into account in determining that question.'

Police Choice

The police have considerable discretion in the investigation and prosecution of criminal offences. Obviously with something in excess of 8000 different criminal offences, the criminal justice system would soon grind to a halt if the police relentlessly and inexorably pursued to prosecution every infringement which came to their knowledge. There is neither sufficient staff in the police force, in the legal profession and in the courts for such action, nor is there a public demand for such intensive policing. Four distinct areas of police discretion can be identified:

> the chief constable's discretion in allocating the resources of his force;
> the allocation of resources to the solving of a particular crime;
> choice on the street;
> choice over whether or not to charge an offender.

Allocating the Resources of the Force

The first area of discretion is that vested in each chief constable to determine the general allocation of resources to particular operational tasks. The courts will not interfere with the judgment of chief constables in determining priorities for their forces. The classic statement of this discretion is by Lord Denning in *R* v. *Commissioner of Police for the Metropolis, ex parte Blackburn* ([1968] 2 QB 118):

> It is for . . . the chief constable . . . to decide in any particular case whether enquiries should be pursued, or whether an arrest should be made or a prosecution brought. It must be for him to decide on the disposition of his force and the concentration of his resources on any particular crime or area. No court can or should give him directions on such a matter. He can also make policy decisions and give effect to them. . . . But there are some policy decisions with which, I think, the courts in a case can, if necessary, interfere. Suppose a chief constable were to issue a directive to his men that no person should be prosecuted for stealing any goods less than £100 in value. I should have thought that the courts could countermand it. He would be failing in his duty to enforce the law. (p. 136)

This principle has been restated with approval in *R* v. *Commissioner of Police for the Metropolis, ex parte Blackburn* (No. 3) ([1973] QB 241) and in *R* v. *Chief Constable of Devon and Cornwall, ex parte Central Electricity Generating Board*, ([1982] QB 458). In the latter case the Court of Appeal refused to interfere with a policy decision by John Alderson, the architect of community policing, not to use the police to remove objectors whose presence was interfering with a CEGB survey of a potential site for a nuclear power station. These cases make it clear that chief constables may not re-write the law by, for example, making a general policy decision not to prosecute cases of theft involving less than £100, but may make decisions on issues involving the allocation of police resources.

Allocating Resources to Particular Crimes

The second area of discretion involves a police officer's decision as to the resources to be devoted to the investigation of a particular crime. Again it is clear that the police are under no duty to investigate to the limit of their resources every complaint of an alleged offence which is reported to them. As noted above, cases where the chances of apprehending the offender seem slim receive only minimal attention.

Choice on the Street

The third area of discretion is that enjoyed by a police officer in deciding how to respond to some incident in which he or she becomes involved. The classic example is the minor motoring offence. A driver is observed by the police driving a car with a defective brake light. There has clearly been an offence, but the police may choose whether or not to stop the car and, if they do so, whether or not to press charges. If the driver is stopped, the police may simply advise the driver to have the light repaired as soon as possible. This is a fairly uncontentious example.

More contentious are the decisions made by police officers as to whether to stop, to stop and search or to arrest individuals, all of which involve an exercise of discretion by the police. The exercise, and control, of discretion in these types of cases obviously has an impact on the style of policing. In this area research has suggested that stereotyping of individuals plays an important role (McCabe and Sutcliffe, 1978; Smith, D. et al., 1983, vol. I). One guide for police officers even lists indications of suspiciousness, which suggests that young people, anyone unconventional in appearance, or people in old cars should be regarded as suspicious (Powis, 1977). The Policy Studies Institute's Report found that Afro-Caribbean men between the ages of 15 and 24 were likely to be stopped with considerable frequency, and with much greater frequency than white or Asian males in the same age group (Smith, D. et al., 1983, vol. I).

One justification put forward for the use of stereotypes is that they are the product of experience, but it should be noted that the use of stereotypes can lead to self-fulfilling prophecies. If more members of a particular group are stopped, then it is likely that offences by that group will take on a prominence quite independently of the accuracy of the stereotyping. Equally even where statistical evidence provides some basis for the stereotype, it is inaccurate in relation to the majority of persons within that group. Stops of individuals in London result in the discovery of some offence in only about one in eight cases, which, of course, means that seven innocent individuals have been stopped. The solution to the problem of the appropriate exercise of discretion in this area would seem to depend on the existence of effective human awareness training as part of police training. Some efforts are made to do this, but there still seem real problems over the existence of a 'police culture' inside police stations where group norms operate very powerfully to ensure compliance with the prevailing culture which may be at variance with that put forward in training (Smith, D. et al., 1983, vols I and IV).

Choice on the street is, however, not wholly personal. Police officers are subject to instructions contained in detailed standing orders. There will be force expectations about the appropriate response to particular incidents. A decision to stop and search, or to arrest an individual, is subject to effective supervision by decisions taken by superior officers, who may require particular action consequent upon the constable's initial action. For example, a more senior police officer may require that a suspect be charged, where the arresting officer proposes only a caution. Where police discretion is greatest, because it is not susceptible to hierarchical decision-making, is where a constable chooses *not* to take action. In most cases, that will be the end of the matter.

Charging Offenders

The final discretion residing with the police is whether or not to charge or summons when they have clear and credible evidence that the suspect has committed the alleged offence. The advent of the Crown Prosecution Service has not altogether removed this area of discretion; it still remains for the police to start the ball rolling by charging a suspect or issuing a summons. If they do not, there appears to be no power in the Crown Prosecution Service to direct that a prosecution be started. The power of the Crown Prosecution Service is the power to end proceedings started by the police.

Evidence given by the Metropolitan Police Commissioner to the Philips Commission provided some valuable insights into this area of decision making, which appears to be largely unchanged following the introduction of the Crown Prosecution Service. The decision to prosecute involves initially an assessment of the case against the suspect. The requirements for prosecution are that there is credible evidence available to prove all the essential elements of the offence. Only in such cases can it be said that the police exercise a discretion to prosecute. Given that these conditions are satisfied, enquiry will be made into the nature of the offence and the circumstances of the offender and of the persons affected by the offence in considering whether or not to proceed. The more serious the offence, the more compelling must be the case for not proceeding. By contrast, for very trivial offences there must be some reason for proceeding, such as the need to curb an outbreak of similar offences. In looking at the circumstances of the offender, age, health, likely punishment and the overall effect of a prosecution on the particular offender are relevant considerations. Finally the wishes and interests of the victim of the crime will be considered. Important considerations will be the possible benefits of prosecution to the victim who may be able to seek a restitution order or compensation order in the criminal proceedings thus avoiding the need to bring separate civil proceedings.

In deciding whether to proceed the police will also consider whether a caution would be appropriate. Cautions are of greater significance where the offender is under 17 years of age. The cautioning of adults has no statutory or common law basis; the practice is purely customary (Bartle, 1990). It involves a formal warning by the police which is recorded for future reference. Its use with adults is largely confined to minor motoring offences and practice varies considerably in its use from area to area.

An earlier study identified similar factors taken into account in deciding whether or not to prosecute (Wilcox, 1972). Occasionally the opportunity will arise for a lawyer or other person to make representations to the police concerning the decision to prosecute, but the process is largely private.

So the police remain in almost exclusive control of the pre-trial stages of the criminal process from initial interaction on the street to the point of charge or the issuing of a summons. At many points they will exercise choices as to how they should tackle the issue facing them.

Stop and Search

The Problem

The Philips Commission noted the confusing state of the law relating to the police's powers of stop and search, which formed a mosaic of local and national provisions. The position was sufficiently complex that few could have any certainty that they knew the law applying in the place they were and consequently few were in a position to challenge action taken by the police.

Some argued that the existence of stop and search powers was a source of friction between the police and the public. A minority of those giving evidence to the Philips Commission argued that specific powers were not needed, because a power of personal search existed on arrest; interference with an individual's civil liberties should not arise unless there was a level of suspicion sufficient to justify an arrest. The majority of submissions, however, merely called for rationalization of the powers of stop and search, and improved remedies for those against whom such powers are used unlawfully.

The exercise of a power to stop and search has always been triggered by a requirement of reasonable suspicion that the constable will find on the person, or in the vehicle, searched, a specific article evidencing the commission of an offence to which the power attaches. The courts have never required a high level of suspicion to justify a stop and search. Mere suspicion was enough. This led to stops being based on appearance and, it seems, racial group rather than satisfaction of some objective test. Empirical evidence bears this out.

The Policy Studies Institute's Report found that the requirement of reasonable suspicion was not an effective constraint on police officers in their decisions whether or not to stop and search. The Report also finds that the choice of person to stop is not random, but is based on stereotypes of persons thought likely to be offenders. The study estimated that the police in London stopped 1.5 million people or vehicles each year and that this resulted in the discovery of about 100,000 offences. Only one person in 20 was arrested as a result of the stop and search. In one-third of the cases observed the survey could see no good reason for the stop (Smith, D. et al., 1983, vol. IV). In giving evidence to the Philips Commission, a number of police forces admitted stopping and searching individuals where there was no authority to do so. The justification put forward was that the use of stop and search was a valuable tool in the fight against crime and that in almost all cases the person stopped 'consented' to the stop and search. This, of course, begs the question. There may have been no objection raised, but this absence of protest is likely to have been based on the assumption that the police had a power to stop and search. In such cases the consent is illusory because it is not informed. The survey notes that about four in five stops are fairly relaxed and amiable affairs, but nevertheless concludes that 'stops tend to have a poor effect on people's relations with the police even where . . . they are fairly relaxed and amiable encounters.' (Smith, D. et al., 1983, vol. IV, p. 323).

The Philips Commission recommended a consolidation and rationalization of the powers of stop and search available to the police. Part I of PACE does not contain a comprehensive code on the powers of stop and search, because it does not re-enact specific powers given in other legislation. The most significant of these is the power to stop and search persons suspected of being in possession of controlled drugs under the Misuse of Drugs Act 1971.

The Solution

Section 1 of PACE enables a police officer to stop and search any person or vehicle in a public place or a place to which the public has access, if the police officer has reasonable grounds for suspecting that the person is in possession of, or the vehicle contains, stolen goods or other prohibited articles. Prohibited articles include offensive weapons (articles made, adapted or intended to be used, for causing injury) or articles made or adapted for use in connection with a burglary, theft, taking of a motor car or the obtaining of property by deception.

The crucial trigger justifying the stop and search is reasonable suspicion of possession of stolen goods or prohibited articles. Reasonable suspicion was originally explained in Annex B of Code A, which applied to all stop and search powers whatever their authority. The test laid down in Annex B was much tougher than that applicable before the implementation of PACE. The level of suspicion required was the same as that required for arrest. The exercise of the lesser intrusion into a person's civil liberties of stop and search rather than arrest is preferred because it may obviate the need for an arrest. Mere suspicion, hunch or instinct will not be sufficient justification. The test required the existence of material susceptible to objective evaluation. A good way of looking at the test was to consider whether an impartial third party, presented with the specific observations of the constable in the face of a particular incident together with any other information known to the constable, would agree that there were reasonable grounds for suspecting possession of the specific article sought by the person in question. Reasonable suspicion must exist before a person is stopped. Questioning following a stop cannot provide reasonable suspicion, though naturally it may confirm or dispel it. Code A has now been substantially rewritten in the face of complaints from the police that the original version was difficult to follow and apply. The definition of reasonable suspicion has been changed by the removal of the requirement that the facts upon which the reasonable suspicion is based are particular to the individual to be searched. The test is no longer as tough as it was in the first version. The code now reads:

> 1.6 Whether reasonable grounds for suspicion exist will depend on the circumstances in each case, but there must be some objective basis for it. An officer will need to consider the nature of the article suspected of being carried in the context of other factors such as the time and the place, and the behaviour of the person concerned or those with him. Reasonable suspicion may exist, for example, where information has been received such as a description of an article being carried or of a suspected offender; a person is seen acting covertly or warily or attempting to hide something; or a person is carrying a certain type of article at an unusual time or in a place where a number of burglaries or thefts are known to have taken place recently. But the decision to stop and search must be based on all the facts which bear on the likelihood that an article of a certain kind will be found.
>
> 1.7 Reasonable suspicion can never be supported on the basis of personal factors alone. For example, a person's colour, age, hairstyle or manner of dress, or the fact that he is known to have a previous conviction for possession of an unlawful article, cannot be used alone or in combination with each other as the sole basis on which to search that person. Nor may it be founded on the basis of stereotyped images of certain persons or groups as more likely to be committing offences.

PACE and Code A also contain rules on the conduct of the search. Embarrassment to the person must be kept to a minimum. Force may only be used as a matter of last resort, but s.117 of PACE authorizes the use of reasonable force where necessary in exercise of powers given by PACE. The Code indicates that most searches should take no more than a few minutes.

Where a search takes place in public, the person searched may not be required to remove more than an outer coat, jacket and gloves (s.2(9)(a), PACE). The omission of reference to headgear may be an oversight, though the Code suggests, rather confusingly, that removal of footwear and headgear may be required 'in a police van or a nearby police station if there is one'. Since removal of the person under compulsion to a police station would constitute an arrest, it is difficult to see what the code is envisaging here.

The omission of any reference to searching bags has also given rise to academic argument as to whether the power extends to such searches. It probably does, because s.2(9)(a) of PACE is concerned with the reduction of embarrassment and the search of a bag is not cognate with requirements that a person removes items of clothing.

The requirement of reasonable suspicion is the main safeguard against arbitrary use of powers of stop and search. However, ss.2, 3 and 5 of PACE impose the further safeguards of notification, recording and supervision of records in respect of all stop and search powers, whatever their authority. The requirements only apply where a search follows a stop. If the questions asked following a stop make it apparent that no search is needed, no record need be made of the stop. Under the notification requirements, the police officer must give his or her name, state the purpose of the stop and search and the grounds for making it. Police officers not in uniform must also produce documentary evidence that they are police officers. The police officer must as soon as is reasonably practicable after the completion of the search make a record of the search which states the name of the person searched, the object of, and grounds for, the search, the date and time of the search and the identity of the officer making the search. If a vehicle is searched, a note describing the vehicle must be made. This record is known as the national search record. The police officer need not make a record if it is impracticable to do so. An example would be where multiple searches are made of persons attending a football match where the need to make notes would interfere with the purpose of the searches. Within 12 months of the date of the search, the person searched is entitled on request to a copy of any record made of the search. In most cases a copy of the national search record is handed over on the spot.

The annual reports of police authorities must contain information about searches carried out within their areas. Though information about specific searches is not required, a monthly breakdown of searches for stolen goods, offensive weapons and for other prohibited articles and the total number of arrests each month resulting from such searches must be given.

Has the New Law Made any Difference?

It is open to question whether these safeguards are effective. The powers given by the Act are sweeping and it seems that the requirement of reasonable suspicion is not an effective constraint. Much therefore depends on the response to the monitoring of stops and searches. No specific sanctions are provided in the Act for failure to follow the required procedures, though such matters will be governed by internal police disciplinary codes.

Some statistical information on the incidence of stop and search since the implementation of PACE is now available. This shows a sharp reduction in the numbers of stops and searches. Nationwide there were 202,800 stops and searches in 1989, which represented a 36 per cent increase over the number in 1988 and an 85 per cent increase in the 1986 figure (Home Office Statistical Bulletin 18/90). Arrests followed in 32,800 cases, that is, following about one in six stops.

In the Metropolitan Police District there were approximately 420,000 stops of persons in 1979, but in 1988 there were only 79,872, though this was a 47 per cent increase over the number of searches conducted in 1987. The rate at which stops and searches has produced results has, however, not markedly increased. In 1979 around one in eight stops resulted in an arrest; by 1989 that figure had only improved to one in six. The success rates vary considerably. The best results relate to stops for offensive weapons, where the strike rate is one in four. But searches for stolen goods were only successful in one in eight cases. Even worse were stops and searches relating to going equipped for stealing, that is, a search on reasonable suspicion of possession of some article for use in the course of or in connection with any 'burglary, theft or cheat'. Only one in twelve of such stops discovered items of interest to the police.

Figures outside London show a similar pattern. The Leicestershire Constabulary searched 1430 persons in 1988 which resulted in 194 arrests; this is a strike rate of one in seven (Leicestershire Constabulary, 1989). Corresponding figures for the Nottinghamshire Constabulary were 1335 searches producing 233 arrests; this is a strike rate of one in six. In both force areas, there are considerable variations in the strike rate for different types of search. For example, in Leicestershire 140 searches for offensive weapons resulted in only 13 arrests, whereas in Nottinghamshire 134 searches resulted in 31 arrests (Nottinghamshire Constabulary, 1989).

Despite these figures, the police complained that the guidelines on reasonable suspicion in Code A were too severe and were hampering the prevention of crime. The revisions to Code A described earlier in this chapter have relaxed the requirements for making stops and searches, and from April 1991, it has been easier for the police to exercise these powers.

Entry, Search and Seizure

On occasion, the police will need to enter premises to search for evidence. The general rule is that, unless some affirmative justification exists, a constable may not enter premises without the consent of the occupier. There are, however, innumerable statutory rights of entry given to the police and various other officials (Philips Commission, 1981; Stone, R. 1989). We are here concerned only with those general powers available to the police for the purpose of the investigation of suspected criminal activity.

Search with a Warrant

PACE leaves unaffected most rules concerning the obtaining of search warrants. There are many statutes, such as the Theft Act 1968 and the Misuse of Drugs Act 1971, empowering magistrates to issue warrants authorizing entry to, and search of, premises for specific purposes. Magistrates have a duty to satisfy themselves that it is right to issue a warrant and may question the person swearing the information requesting the warrant. Where the information is based on a tip-off from an informer, there is no obligation to disclose the identity of the informer, though the magistrate may ask questions to assess the likely truth of the tip-off. The Philips Commission noted the criticisms raised by some who gave evidence 'that magistrates may exercise insufficient care in ensuring that a warrant is necessary; and that too often they merely rubber stamp police requests'. (Philips Commission, 1981, para. 3.37).

Prior to PACE the police had no *general* power to seek warrants to search for evidence. Specific powers had to be exercised. The absence of a general power gave rise to anomalies. The Philips Commission noted that there was no power of entry to search the scene of a kidnap or murder. Section 8 of PACE remedies this deficiency by allowing the issue of a warrant to search for evidence where there are reasonable grounds for believing that a *serious arrestable offence* has been committed. Section 116 of PACE contains a rather tortuous definition of serious arrestable offences. This is an important category of offences, because additional police powers are available where such offences are involved. In very broad terms serious arrestable offences include murder, manslaughter, rape, kidnapping, serious sexual offences and offences involving the use of firearms or explosives. Also included are any offences whose *consequences* are likely to be serious as a threat to national security or public order, or because they involve a risk of death or serious injury or serious financial loss to any person. In *R* v. *Samuel* ([1988] 2 All ER 135) the Court of Appeal agreed that a burglary involving theft of property worth £1135 was elevated to the category of serious arrestable offences because of the serious financial loss caused to the householder. There is no consideration in the case of whether the householder was insured against such loss.

Once it is established that a serious arrestable offence is involved, it is necessary to show reasonable grounds for believing that there is admissible evidence relating to that offence on any premises and that at least one of the following conditions applies:

> it is not reasonably practicable to communicate with any person who would be entitled to grant permission to enter the premises;
> such a person has unreasonably refused access to the premises or to the evidence;
> the evidence is likely to be concealed, removed or destroyed if access is sought without a warrant.

Objections have been made to these provisions on two grounds. First they have the potential for authorizing the police to go on 'fishing trips' for evidence, and, secondly, the stringent safeguards recommended by the Philips Commission have been largely ignored. The Philips Commission had recommended authorization by a Circuit judge rather than by a magistrate; the fear was that magistrates might rubber stamp these types of warrant as they are alleged to do with other types of search warrant. The case of *R* v. *Guildhall Magistrates, ex parte Primlaks* (*The Times*, 30 December 1988) supports this view. The Divisional Court quashed an order given on an *ex parte* application in relation to the premises of reputable solicitors, because the magistrates could not have been satisfied that the material sought was not covered by legal professional privilege nor that the conditions set out above were satisfied. The Philips Commission had also recommended the adoption of similar safeguards to those applying to excluded or special procedure material discussed below.

Sections 9 to 14 of PACE contain special rules relating to material held in confidence, which is called 'excluded material' and 'special procedure material' in PACE. These special rules encompass privileged communications between solicitors and their clients, personal records as part of business or professional information held in confidence, body samples held in confidence for medical diagnostic or treatment purposes and journalistic material held in confidence or acquired or created for the purposes of journalism. To get at such material a warrant must be obtained from a Circuit judge and the holder of the evidence is entitled to be heard on the application for the warrant. To obtain a warrant the police must satisfy the Circuit judge that:

there are reasonable grounds for believing that the evidence is on the premises and would be of substantial value in the investigation of a serious arrestable offence which has already been committed;

other efforts to obtain the evidence have failed or have not been tried because they are certain to fail;

it is in the public interest that the evidence is handed over.

If so satisfied, the Circuit judge will grant an order addressed to the holder of the evidence requiring its delivery to the police. Only on a failure to comply with such an order, or where the police can show that the issue of an order for delivery of the evidence would seriously prejudice the investigation, will the Circuit judge issue a warrant authorizing entry to, and search of, the premises for the evidence.

The significant differences between the safeguards attaching to this material and those applicable in the case of the general warrant to search for evidence will now be obvious.

Search without a Warrant, other than on Arrest

Search on arrest is considered below. Section 17 of PACE lists the situations in which the police may enter premises without a warrant. These are limited to constables in uniform who are seeking to effect an arrest, or to recapture a person unlawfully at large and who is being pursued, or to save life and limb, or to prevent serious damage to property.

Entry to Prevent a Breach of the Peace

Section 17 of PACE abolishes all common law powers of entry save that relating to a breach of the peace. The power of entry to deal with a breach of the peace was established in the early nineteenth century, though it was not until the case of *Thomas* v. *Sawkins*, ([1935] 2 KB 249) that it was made clear that the power extended to entry to prevent a breach of the peace. This power raises problems similar to those discussed below in relation to the common law power of arrest for breach of the peace.

Seizure of Evidence

Section 19 of PACE replaces the rules on what may be seized in consequence of any lawful search previously laid down in the case of *Ghani* v. *Jones*, ([1970] 1 QB 693). Police officers may seize any items other than those to which legal privilege attaches which they reasonably believe to be evidence in relation to the offence under investigation, or to any other offence, or to have been obtained in consequence of the commission of an offence; it must also be necessary to seize the items to prevent their removal, concealment or destruction. The power is considerably broader than that proposed by the Philips Commission which would have limited the seizure of items not directly related to the offence under investigation to evidence in relation to some 'grave offence', a group of offences broadly similar to serious arrestable offences under PACE.

General Safeguards

Searches are only lawful to the extent that they are required for the purpose for which the power to search arose. This is intended to preclude excessive vigour in the execution of searches; it will be unlawful to rip furniture apart on a warrant to look for stolen video recorders. There are also notification and recording safeguards. Warrants must contain information as to the name of the person applying for them, the date of issue, the authority under which they are sought, the articles sought and the premises to be searched. Occupiers of premises searched must be given a copy of the warrant and, on request, a list of items seized. Warrants must be endorsed with the results of the search and a list of items seized. Similar requirements for recording the outcome of searches apply to searches and seizures without warrants.

Arrest

Part III of PACE has not clarified matters as much as it might have done and the law on arrest remains a mixture of statute and common law. Arrest is essentially a deprivation of the liberty to go where one pleases. Lord Parker CJ described arrest as follows in *Alderson* v. *Booth*, ([1969] 2 QB 216):

> There are a number of cases both ancient and modern as to what constitutes an arrest . . . .. There may be an arrest by mere words, by saying 'I arrest you' without any touching, provided of course that the defendant submits and goes with the police officer. Equally it is clear, as it seems to me, that an arrest is constituted when any form of words is used which in the circumstances of the case were calculated to bring to the defendant's notice, and did bring to the defendant's notice, that he was under compulsion and thereafter he submitted to that compulsion. (p. 220)

The arrest may be lawful or unlawful. There are three kinds of lawful arrest: arrest under warrant; arrest without a warrant under statute; and arrest without warrant under common law. All arrests which do not meet the conditions for a lawful arrest are unlawful.

Helping the Police with their Enquiries

Individuals frequently attend at the police station at the request of the police 'to help them with their enquiries'. Such individuals sometimes find it harder to leave the police station, though as a matter of law they are free to leave at any time unless placed under arrest. Again ignorance of the legal position and equivocation by the police about their status can operate to deny such persons the freedom to leave. Section 29 of PACE clarifies the position by specifying that persons attending voluntarily at a police station shall be entitled to leave unless arrested and by requiring them to be informed at once of the fact of their arrest if they are prevented from leaving. There is no specific sanction in the Act for failure to comply with these requirements.

Arrest under Warrant

PACE leaves the power of arrest under warrant largely unaffected. The usual procedure is governed by s.125 of the Magistrates' Courts Act 1980 whereby the police present and swear an information to a magistrate that a particular person has, or is suspected of having, committed an offence and on the basis of that information the magistrate issues a warrant for the arrest of the person. Warrants for arrest are not normally available unless the offence is one triable either way or the address of the person is not sufficiently established for a summons to be used to secure attendance at court. The magistrate has an unreviewable discretion as to whether or not to issue a warrant. A police officer may use reasonable force to enter premises where the suspect is known to be to effect the arrest.

Arrest without Warrant under Statute

For arrestable offences Except for the 19 statutes listed in Sched. 2 of PACE, the rules contained in Part III of PACE replace the existing statutory powers of arrest without warrant. Under s.24 of PACE a police officer may arrest without warrant any person who is in the act of committing, or who is reasonably suspected to be committing or to have committed, an *arrestable offence*. A police officer may also arrest someone about to commit or reasonably suspected to be about to commit an arrestable offence. The power of arrest extends to persons conspiring or attempting, or inciting, aiding, abetting, counselling or procuring the commission of an arrestable offence. The definition of arrestable offence is very important because it delimits the scope of the power. Arrestable offences are (1) those for which the sentence is fixed by law (the best example is murder which carries a statutory penalty of life imprisonment); (2) those for which persons aged 21 or over may be sentenced to a term of imprisonment of five years or more; and (3) those offences specifically listed in s.24(2), of which the most notable are official secrets offences and various sexual offences.

Whether a police officer has reasonable grounds for suspecting that a person is guilty of an offence before that person is arrested is to be determined objectively from the information available to the arresting officer. More than an honest belief founded on reasonable suspicion is required (*Castorina* v. *Chief Constable of Surrey*, New Law Journal, 24 June 1988, p. 180).

For any offence   Section 25 of PACE lays down general grounds for arrest where one or more of what are called *general arrest conditions* is satisfied. The power applies where a police officer has reasonable grounds for suspecting that *any* offence has been committed or attempted if one of the following general arrest conditions is satisfied:

> the suspect's name and address are not known to and cannot be ascertained by the police officer;
> the police officer has reasonable grounds for believing that the name and address supplied by the suspect are false;
> arrest is reasonably thought necessary to prevent suspects from causing (1) physical harm to themselves or others; (2) loss of or damage to property; (3) an offence against public decency; or (4) an unlawful obstruction of the highway;
> arrest is reasonably thought necessary for the protection of a child or other vulnerable person from the suspect.

The Philips Commission had by majority recommended the creation of the above powers but envisaged that their use would be 'a very rare occurrence'. The minority did not consider the problems covered by the section to be such as to justify the creation of a power of arrest, which they considered would be a source of friction between the police and members of the public.

For fingerprinting   On conviction for a *recordable offence* and where fingerprints have not previously been taken, s.27 of PACE enables a police officer within one month of the date of conviction to arrest without warrant a convicted person to secure attendance at a police station for fingerprinting. Recordable offences are defined by the National Police Records (Recordable Offences) Regulations 1985 (SI 1985 no. 1941) as offences punishable with imprisonment, offences under s.1 of the Street Offences Act 1959, under s.43 of the Telecommunications Act 1984, and under s.29 of the Road Traffic Act 1972.

Arrest without Warrant under Common Law

The common law power of arrest without a warrant was neatly summarized by Lord Diplock in *Albert* v. *Lavin*, ([1982] AC 546):

Every citizen in whose presence a breach of the peace is being, or reasonably appears to be, committed has the right to take reasonable steps to
make the person who is breaking or threatening to break the peace refrain
from doing so; and those reasonable steps in appropriate cases will include
detaining him against his will. At common law this is not only the right of
every citizen, it is also his duty, although, except in the case of a citizen
who is a constable, it is a duty of imperfect obligation. (p. 565)

The concept of a breach of the peace which triggers the power of arrest is
notoriously difficult to define. In 1981 the criminal division of the Court of
Appeal confirmed that the presence or threat of violence was required (*R* v.
Howell, [1982] QB 416), but in *R* v. *Chief Constable of Devon and Cornwall,
ex parte* CEGB, ([1982] QB 458), the civil division of the Court of Appeal
intimated that 'passive resistance' in the form of a non-violent campaign of
obstruction which might provoke a violent response by a third party would
amount to a breach of the peace even before any resort to force was imminent.

The Power of Search following Arrest

Prior to PACE it was uncertain what powers of search arose on the arrest of a
person, though it was common police practice both to search the person and his
or her home immediately following arrest. There was authority allowing the
room in which a person was arrested to be searched (Dillon v. O'Brien, [*1887*]
16 Cox CC 245), though a search of premises is unlawful where there is no
connection between the search and the offence for which the arrest was made.
Thus in *Jeffrey* v. *Black*, ([1978] 1 QB 490) it was held to be unlawful to have
searched the flat of a suspect following his arrest by members of the drug squad
for the theft of a sandwich from a public house. The search discovered cannabis
in the flat. Though the search was unlawful, the evidence so obtained was nevertheless admitted at trial on a drugs charge. The law is now clarified in ss.18 and
32.
   Section 32 of PACE deals with searches of persons and premises where the
arrest took place or where the suspect was immediately prior to arrest. Under
s.32 of PACE arrested persons may be searched if a police officer has reasonable
grounds for believing that they may present a danger to themselves or others, or
may be in possession of articles which might be used to escape from police custody, or might be evidence relating to an offence. The constable may enter and
search any premises in which the arrested persons were immediately prior to the
arrest. The power is limited to a search reasonably required for the purpose of
discovery of such articles or evidence. In conducting all these searches the police
may use such force as is reasonably necessary. The police may, under s.32 or the
general power in s.19, seize other articles found on a search of individuals
or premises if the constable reasonably believes them to be evidence of any
offence and that their seizure is necessary to prevent their concealment, loss or
destruction.
   Section 18 of PACE permits the search of any premises occupied or controlled

by suspects *following their arrest for an arrestable offence* where the police have reasonable grounds for believing that they will find evidence relating either to the offence for which the suspect was arrested or to some other arrestable offence connected with, or similar to, that offence. The power may be exercised without authorization if the search is made before the suspect is taken to the police station 'if the presence of that person at a place other than a police station is necessary for the effective investigation of the offence'. But after the suspect has been taken to the police station, the written authorization of a senior police officer not below the rank of inspector is required.

Searches without prior written authorization must be notified as soon as reasonably practicable to a senior police officer not below the rank of inspector. In either case a record of the search must be kept including a note of the grounds for it and the nature of the evidence sought.

General Duties following Arrest

Section 28 of PACE lays down certain general duties to be complied with on the arrest of a person whatever the basis of the power of arrest. Failure to comply with the requirements renders the arrest unlawful. Unless it is impracticable to do so because the suspect has escaped from custody and unless the suspect has been arrested by being informed that he or she is under arrest, the police officer must inform the suspect as soon as practicable that he or she is under arrest and of the grounds for the arrest, and must do so even though the fact of the arrest is obvious. This statutory formula replaces the narrower requirements formerly laid down in the famous case of *Christie* v. *Leachinsky*, ([1947] AC 573). Section 30 requires a person arrested elsewhere than at a police station to be taken to a police station as soon as practicable after the arrest unless a police officer is satisfied that there are no grounds for keeping the suspect under arrest. In this case a record of the release from arrest must be made. A delay in taking a suspect to the police station will be justified 'if the presence of that person elsewhere is necessary in order to carry out such investigations as it is reasonably necessary to carry out immediately.' If such a delay occurs, its existence and the reasons for it must be recorded.

The normal procedure on arrest (after making any searches deemed necessary) will be to take arrested persons to the police station where they will be subject to the standard procedure for the reception of arrested persons. It is likely that they will enter the police station from a rear yard through one or more locked doors. They will then be presented to the custody officer, normally a uniformed police sergeant, who will determine whether the person's detention for question is required. The process is humiliating; even where the police follow all the rules contained in PACE and the codes, reception into custody at the police station is necessarily a degrading and oppressive experience (Irving, 1980; Irving and Hilgendorf, 1980; Softley, 1980b; Irving, 1986).

4

Policing: In the Station and into Court

Detention and Questioning of Suspects

General Principles

The explanation of the provisions of PACE which follows covers only the questioning of persons aged 17 or over; there are special rules which apply to juveniles. The general principle infusing the exercise of all police powers is that of minimum interference with the civil liberties of the citizen. PACE requires the duration of detention to be as short as is consistent with the proper exercise of police investigation of crime.

The rules in Part IV of PACE and Code C on the detention treatment and questioning of persons by police officers replace the Judges Rules and Administrative Directions and will be the 'bible' in the police station. Provided that the provisions of PACE and Code C are routinely applied in police stations, these provisions represent a new deal for suspects in police stations. There are two main concerns running through the Code: keeping the duration of detention as short as possible and ensuring that the questioning of suspects is fairly conducted. Such controls are very necessary because the police have overwhelming powers over suspects in the station. They have absolute physical control over their movements and contacts with others at the initial stages of their enquiries. A number of provisions of the Code are designed to reduce the effects of isolation and disorientation which inevitably accompany incarceration in a police station, and which can lead to unreliable information being provided by suspects in their desire for release.

The Custody Officer

On arrival at the police station, the suspect must be presented to the custody officer. The role of this officer is central to the scheme in the Code for the protection of those detained in the police station. Crucial decisions about the detention and treatment of the suspect are primarily in the hands of this quasi-independent officer who is charged with the care of suspects while at the station. The custody officer cannot be directly involved in the investigation of the offence and applies an element of impartial decision making. The custody officer must keep a detailed chronicle of events while the suspect is in police custody; this chronicle is known as the custody record. Suspects and their legal advisers are entitled to a copy of the custody record. Any disagreement between the custody officer and the investigating officers must be referred for resolution to an officer of the rank of at least superintendent (s.39(6), PACE).

The very first duty of the custody officer under s.37 of PACE is to determine whether there are sufficient grounds for keeping the suspect in custody at all. The custody officer must proceed immediately to charge if there is sufficient evidence for a charge to be preferred. If the custody officer decides that there is insufficient evidence for a charge to be preferred, the suspect must be released with or without bail unless there are reasonable grounds for believing that the suspect's detention is necessary:

to secure or preserve evidence of, or relating to, the offence for which the arrest was made; or

to obtain such evidence by questioning the suspect.

If the custody officer decides that there are grounds to keep the suspect in custody, the suspect must be told this and the grounds for detention.

The custody officer must also tell suspects of the rights not to be held incommunicado, to free legal advice, to consult the codes of practice and to receive a copy of the custody record. The right to legal advice is a continuing one and suspects must be told they can exercise it at any time. Suspects must be given written notice setting out these rights and will be asked to sign the custody record to acknowledge receipt of this notice. The custody officer also gives suspects at this time written notice of the arrangements effective at the police station for obtaining legal advice there and a notice summarizing their entitlements while in custody.

The next decision for the custody officer is whether to subject the suspect to a personal search. It is normal for suspects to hand over all their property to the custody officer for safekeeping. The custody officer has a statutory duty to ascertain all property in the suspect's possession and may search the suspect for this purpose under s.54 of PACE. Even if no search is conducted at this time, it is possible to conduct such a search at any time while the suspect is in custody (s.54(6A), PACE).

In rare instances, a strip search or an intimate search may be ordered. Annex A of Code C summarizes the grounds for these. Section 55 of PACE permits a superintendent to authorize an intimate search, that is, a physical search of the body orifices, by a medical practitioner or police officer if there are reasonable grounds for believing that the suspect may have concealed an article which could be used to cause physical injury and might be so used while in custody. Such searches are rarely made in practice and are invariably unpleasant affairs. The medical profession has indicated that it will only carry out such searches with the informed consent of the suspect.

Fifty intimate searches (23 for drugs and 27 for harmful articles) were carried out nationwide by the police in 1989. All but eight were conducted by doctors. Three were positive. In 1988 neither the Leicestershire nor the Nottinghamshire Constabulary carried out any intimate searches. Strip searches are not specifically provided for in PACE and statistics of their incidence are not made publicly available. In one study of 5519 arrests, there were 59 strip searches and seven intimate searches (Brown, D. 1989).

Reception into custody takes about 15 minutes. Once completed, the suspect will be escorted to a single cell and left their to await the attentions of the investigating officers. Suspects may have been required to hand over any belt or braces if the custody officer believed that they might use them to cause injury to themselves or others, or to assist in an escape. They will probably be required to leave their shoes outside the cell. A period of total isolation usually follows.

The Right not to be Held Incommunicado

Suspects detained at a police station have a right under s.56 of PACE to have a person known to them who is likely to take an interest in their welfare informed as soon as practicable and at the public expense of their whereabouts. Code C, para. 5.1, provides that up to two alternatives may be chosen if the first person named cannot be contacted. The custody officer has a discretion to allow further attempts to contact someone to be made. The person contacted may visit or telephone the suspect at the custody officer's discretion. The suspect may also make one telephone call for a reasonable time. The police will listen to any such conversations. Friends or relatives telephoning to enquire about suspects should be told their whereabouts.

Annex B of Code C restates the rules in s.56 of PACE which permit delay in the exercise of this right. The right may only be denied or delayed in cases involving *serious arrestable offences* and only on the authority of a police officer not below the rank of superintendent. There must be reasonable grounds for believing that the exercise of the right will interfere with the proper investigation of the offence. In no circumstances may access be delayed beyond 36 hours.

David Brown's study of the operation of the detention and treatment provisions of PACE (Brown, D. 1989) showed that one in five suspects exercise the s.56 right. There is, however, wide variation in take-up rates between police stations. In some, one in three exercise the right, while in others, only one in twelve do so. The variation is largely unexplained, but one relevant factor suggested is the way in which custody officers outline the rights to suspects. In most cases contact was made with the person named within half an hour; only one in four cases took longer.

By contrast only one in seven suspects elected to make a telephone call. One in 20 received a visit from a friend or relative, though no figures are available for refusals of visits.

The Right to Legal Advice

The right of suspects to legal advice while in custody received formal recognition for the first time in s.58 of PACE. The right is additional to the right not to be held incommunicado in s.56 of PACE, and consists of the right at any time to consult and communicate privately, in person, in writing or by telephone, with a solicitor. The right extends to a solicitor's clerk authorized to provide advice on behalf of the solicitor unless an officer of the rank of at least inspector considers that such a visit will hinder the investigation. If the clerk is refused access, the solicitor must be notified immediately so that alternative arrangements can be made (Code C, paras. 6.12–6.14 and see *R* v. *Chief Constable of Avon and Somerset, ex parte Robinsons*, [1989] 2 All ER 15).

The police can only delay access to legal advice under s.58 in cases involving serious arrestable offences; the rules are similar to those governing delay in notifying a person reasonably named of the suspect's whereabouts and are also covered by Annex B of Code C. In *R* v. *Samuel* ([1988] 2 All ER 135) the police were sharply criticized by the Court of Appeal for delaying access to a solicitor allegedly for fear that the solicitor would inadvertently warn others involved in the offence under investigation. Hodgson J said of the test permitting delay in allowing access:

> The task of satisfying a court that reasonable grounds existed at the time the decision was made, whether in respect of intentional or inadvertent conduct, will, we think, prove even more formidable. Any officer attempting to justify his decision to delay the exercise of this fundamental right will, in our judgment, be unable to do so save by reference to specific circumstances, including evidence as to the person detained or the actual solicitor sought to be consulted.

Though not dissenting from the conclusion in the case, a differently constituted Court of Appeal in *R* v. *Alladice* ([1988] 87 Cr App R 380) did not share the earlier Court's scepticism about solicitors being used as unwitting channels of communication between rogues.

Any scheme which establishes a right to legal advice will only be as good as the system for delivering that advice. One response to ensure the ready availability of legal advice has been the introduction of statutory 24 hour duty solicitor schemes. The operation of these schemes is now governed by the Legal Aid Board Duty Solicitor Arrangements 1990. Schemes now cover four out of every five police stations. Where a scheme is in operation, a suspect may call on the services of the duty solicitor on call on that day or night. The service is provided as part of the legal aid scheme, but there is no means or merits test. The duty solicitor is normally paid up to £90 for work done, though this may be extended if it can be shown that more work needed to be done as a matter of urgency.

Since the new right was introduced, about one in four suspects asks at some time during the period in custody to see a solicitor; one in five exercise the right on arrival at the police station. As with the right not to be held incommunicado, there are significant regional variations with the greatest variations surprisingly clustering around the more serious offences (Brown, D. 1989).

In most cases a legal adviser attended the police station within 90 minutes; around half arrived within 50 minutes after contact, which in turn seldom took more than half an hour. But personal attendance by a solicitor at the police station only occurred in around three quarters of cases where a solicitor is contacted. At Leicester, where tape recording of interviews has been in operation since 1984, attendance followed only one in four requests for assistance. In one in 15 cases there was no direct contact with the solicitor, but in most cases where the solicitor did not attend, advice was given directly by telephone.

Relating outcome to receipt of legal advice in the police station shows that there is little difference between the treatment of those who have received legal advice and those who have not. There is certainly nothing in the figures to justify the howls of anguish once heard from the police that the presence of solicitors in the police station so hampers police enquiries that large proportions of those held at the police station would have to be released without charge. The level of penetration of advice in police stations is confirmed by the Birmingham University study (Sanders et al., 1989), which found that over one third of all advice at the police station came from duty solicitors. Though there is no evidence of widespread denial of access to legal advice by the police, there was evidence of incomplete notification of the right to legal advice and the use of ploys designed to discourage requests for legal advice. An example is the stressing of the delays that might be entailed if legal advice is requested. Half those requesting advice did not get to see a solicitor; they received telephone advice or no help at all. The study comments:

> The police would have us believe that defence solicitors saw their main role in life as being to persuade suspects not to co-operate with them, and to defend suspects unreservedly – which is, after all, the theory of the adversary system. On closer questioning the police divide solicitors into two types, of which only one adheres to that model. And, indeed, some solicitors do, while others do not, adopt a combative adversarial stance. What is surprising is how many do not do so. And also that there is a third category which is either anti-suspect or uncaring about suspects, in that the advice they give is either perfunctory or doomed to being ineffective. (Sanders et al., 1989, p. 191)

Monitoring the Length of Detention

PACE makes continuing detention at the police station subject to formal review after set periods of time. The time limits specified in PACE are approximate (s.45(2), PACE); this is designed to allow some flexibility and to avoid argument over legality if the police are over the limits by a small margin. Each review of detention which takes place must be fully documented in the custody record. The overriding principle is that detention should end as soon as possible. Code C also contains detailed rules about the treatment of those in custody, which it is the responsibility of the custody officer to ensure are observed.

The first formal review of detention is required not later than six hours after the detention was authorized, though postponement of the review is permitted where it is not practicable to carry out the review at that time and it is specifically stated that it may be postponed if it would mean interrupting the questioning of a suspect which would 'prejudice the investigation'. Thereafter reviews take place after a further nine hours and at subsequent intervals of not more than nine hours. The custody officer carries out the review in the case of suspects already charged, while a police officer not below the rank of inspector, who is not directly involved in the investigation, reviews the cases of suspects who have not been charged. The purpose of the review is to establish whether continued detention is justified.

Twenty-four hours after arrest a special review by a police officer not below the rank of superintendent takes place. At this point the suspect may be detained further until 36 hours from the time of the arrest on the authority of the superintendent only:

   if the investigation is into a serious arrestable offence;
   if the investigation is proceeding with due diligence and expedition; and
   if the continued detention is necessary to secure or preserve evidence or to question the suspect further.

Detention beyond 36 hours may only be authorized by a magistrates' court (defined for this purpose as two magistrates sitting otherwise than in open court). The suspect is entitled to be heard on the application for further detention. Applying the same criteria as the police at the earlier review, the magistrates must decide whether further detention is justified and if so for what period up to a maximum of a further 36 hours ending not later than 96 hours after the time of the arrest or arrival at the police station whichever was earlier. Thus in order to detain a suspect for the full 96 hours, two applications to the magistrates are required, as well as a number of reviews at the police station by senior police officers.

Under the PACE provisions, the mean period of detention in one survey was just over five hours, while the median period of detention was three hours and 19 minutes. By six hours just over three-quarters of suspects had been dealt with. It appears that the first review at six hours concentrates the minds of police officers and forces decisions to be made about the continued detention of suspects. By the end of 24 hours, when the limit of detention for ordinary offences arrives, 99 per cent of suspects have been dealt with, including half of the two per cent of those in custody in connection with serious arrestable offences. Warrants for detention beyond 24 hours were obtained in 46 of the 5519 cases in the sample, and beyond 36 hours were sought from magistrates in 14 cases and obtained in 11 (Brown, D. 1989).

National figures for 1989 show that 597 defendants were detained for more than 24 hours and subsequently released without charge. There were 287 applications to magistrates for warrants of further detention; all but five were successful (Home Office Statistical Bulletin 18/90).

The new provisions do not appear to have reduced dramatically the time suspects spend in the police station, but they are now better protected. Indeed the procedures required by PACE themselves account for some of the time spent in the police station. The time spent being questioned will only be part of the time spent in custody, which involves a considerable amount of time waiting in a cell.

Monitoring the Questioning of Suspects

It is, of course, the police's power to question suspects which is regarded as one of their most important powers. Suspects, however, enjoy the right to silence; the suspect can refuse to answer any questions with impunity. Under the adversarial system is it for the police and prosecution to adduce admissible evidence of guilt unassisted by the suspect. Despite the right to silence, few suspects remain silent at the police station. Various research studies of questioning at the police station have shown that only about one in 25 suspects exercise the right to silence. Yet the right is currently under review by the Home Office which has made little secret of its wish to see magistrates and juries permitted to draw adverse inferences from the exercise of the right at the police station.

Very many suspects make statements, admissions and confessions in the face of police questioning. The research studies carried out for the Royal Commission had shown that the making of statements was common; anything between one in three and one in five suspects make incriminating statements to the police. It is therefore important that questioning is fair and that the statements made by suspects are reliable and freely given. Before being questioned every suspect must be cautioned. This is a reminder of the right to silence. Under Code C the caution is issued in the following form:

> You do not have to say anything unless you wish to do so, but what you say may be given in evidence.

PACE upgrades the requirements for the recording of interviews with suspects. Code C contains detailed rules relating to interviews with suspects, and stresses the prohibition on interviews away from the police station save in exceptional circumstances. The amendments to the code also contain a worryingly narrow definition of what amounts to an interview. This corrects an oversight noted in R v. *Absolam* ([1989] 89 Cr App R 332) and is broadly in line with the definition offered in that case and in R v. *Maguire* ([1990] 90 Cr App R 115). *Notes for Guidance* IIA of Code C reads:

> An interview is the questioning of a person regarding his involvement or suspected involvement in a criminal offence or offences. Questioning a person only to obtain information or his explanation of the facts or in the ordinary course of the officer's duties does not constitute an interview for the purpose of the code.

Where no tape recording of the interview takes place, the record of the interview must normally be made during the course of the interview (Code C, para. 11.5) and should be as nearly as possible a verbatim account of the interview. Incidents occurring during the course of the interview must be fully documented. The Philips Commission recommended better training in interview techniques; it ascribed some common irregularities to lack of proper skills in the task. Most suspects are interviewed only once while in custody and most interviews last between 20 minutes and two hours. Taped interviews tend to be shorter by one-third than non-taped interviews (Brown, D. 1989). Suspects must be asked at an appropriate point whether they have said all they wish and the interview must stop if they indicate that they have.

The tape recording of interviews is the main safeguard provided by PACE against oppressive interviewing in police stations. Research carried out for the Philips Commission showed that such tape recording was feasible and effective (Barnes and Webster, 1980), but the Philips Commission itself proposed a rather modest, partial and gradual introduction of the tape recording of the whole of police interviews of suspects. Section 60 places a statutory duty on the Home Secretary to make an order requiring the recording of police interviews with suspects and requires him to issue a code of practice for the tape recording of interviews. Field trials in six police divisions ran for two years from 1984 and proved to be a success (Willis, 1984; Willis et al., 1988). Tape recording of interviews is now being introduced nationally and Code E containing detailed guidance on the procedures to be followed has been approved by Parliament. One concern which has been expressed is that tape recording of interviews at the police station may lead to the higher incidence of incriminating statements made away from the police station. This appears to have happened in Scotland (McConville and Morrell 1983; Mirfield, 1984). The revisions to Code C remind the police of the impropriety of conducting interviews away from the police station save in the most exceptional circumstances. Even then a full record of the interview must be made.

The Next Stage

At the end of questioning, a number of things may happen. To understand these, it is necessary to appreciate that there are two ways the police may put the matter in the hands of the criminal courts, which also triggers the transfer of the file to the Crown Prosecution Service. The first is by way of charge, which is a procedure which takes place at the police station. The suspect is brought before the custody office and the investigating officer proffers the charge which the custody officer accepts if satisfied that there is sufficient evidence to justify the charge. The case comes within the jurisdiction of the courts when the charge sheet is delivered to the magistrates' court.

The second method is to proceed by way of summons. To obtain a summons a constable must attend before a magistrate to swear an information. If the summons is granted, it must then be served on the defendant. This can be done personally or by using the postal system. Proceeding by way of summons involves more paperwork, but is frequently used for less serious offences. National figures show that 65 per cent of defendants are brought before the courts by means of summons. Thirty per cent are arrested but subsequently bailed pending first appearance in court, while five per cent (about 90,000 people a year) are arrested and held in custody pending first appearance. For either way offences, four out of every five defendants are arrested and charged, rather than summonsed to attend court.

At the end of detention, the suspect may be released without charge. This may mean an end of the matter, or the suspect may be advised that the question of prosecution will be considered. In the latter case, the police would normally bring the matter to court by means of information and summons. Alternatively, the suspect may be released without charge, but be bailed pending further enquiries. The final possibility is that the suspect may be charged and held in custody pending appearance before the magistrates.

Once persons are charged, the normal rule is that they may not be subjected to further questioning. It is therefore necessary to consider the police powers to grant bail and the decision to prosecute.

Police Bail

The police's powers to grant bail are separate from those enjoyed by magistrates, which are discussed in the next chapter. The refusal of bail by the police only triggers a detention in custody for a short time; the person must be brought before a magistrates' court as soon as practicable, and normally within 24 hours.

Bail Pending Further Enquiries

When the custody officer decides that there is insufficient evidence to charge a person arrested and brought to the police station, that officer may release the suspect on bail (s.37(2)). This is bail pending further enquiries. The suspect is released but is under a duty to return to the police station when required to do so. Failure to attend is an offence under s.6 of the Bail Act 1976. A good example of this type of bail would be the arrest of a person on suspicion of possession of controlled drugs after a packet of what appears to be cocaine is found on him or her. Normally a charge cannot be brought until the substance has been analysed. Pending the outcome of the analysis, the suspect will be bailed. If the analysis confirms that the substance is a controlled drug, the suspect will be charged on return to the police station. A person so bailed need not return to the station if advised in writing by the police that there is no requirement to do so.

The power to grant bail may also be used if the police want time to decide whether or not to proceed against the suspect (s.37(7), PACE), though equally the suspect can be released without bail and the matter proceed by way of summons if the police decide to proceed.

Bail following Arrest under a Warrant

Where a person has been arrested on a warrant, the warrant will normally deal with the question of the detention of the suspect. In other words the magistrate makes the decision rather than the police. The decision is endorsed on the warrant and the police must comply with its terms on charging the suspect.

Bail following Arrest without a Warrant

Where a person is charged with an offence following arrest without a warrant, the custody officer determines whether the suspect is to be detained in custody or bailed under s.38 of PACE. Such a person may only be kept in police custody pending first appearance before a magistrates' court in the following circumstances:

  if the police cannot ascertain the suspect's name and address or reasonably believe a name and address given is false;
  if the police reasonably believe that detention is necessary for the suspect's protection or to prevent the suspect from causing harm to any other person or from causing loss of, or damage to, property;
  if the police reasonably believe that the suspect will fail to attend at the required time or might interfere with witnesses or otherwise obstruct the course of justice.

The person charged and kept in custody must be brought before the magistrates' court as soon as is practicable.

The new rules on police bail are a considerable improvement on the existing law which gave too wide a discretion to the police to detain charged persons in custody. The tightening of the rules on police bail is also welcome because evidence has shown that there is a correlation between detention in custody by the police and the decisions of magistrates on custody or bail with magistrates following the decisions of the police, even when the tests were very different (King, 1973).

Refusal of Police Bail

If the custody officer refuses bail, there is little that can be done prior to the hearing before the magistrates, though the decision to refuse bail and the reasons for the refusal must be entered on the custody record. An approach to a senior police officer with representations on behalf of the detainee may result in a review of the initial decision.

Controlling Police Misconduct

There are four approaches that can be taken in the face of police misconduct. The first is self-help. Constables only enjoy special powers where the conditions for the exercise of those powers are met. If they are not, a citizen is not required to submit to the intrusion in his or her civil liberties. The second remedy is to challenge the admissibility of evidence obtained in breach of the provisions of PACE or the codes. The third is to pursue a civil action against the police, who enjoy no immunity from civil suit if they overstep their powers. Finally, a complaint can be made about the constable's conduct which may result in internal disciplinary proceedings against the constable.

Self-help

A citizen is only required to submit to a search, or to arrest, where the conditions for the exercise of the power are met. So a person stopped on the mere whim of a constable need not submit to a search, and may lawfully resist any attempt by the constable to conduct the search using force. Equally, a person whose arrest is unlawful need not accompany the constable to the police station.

The difficulty, of course, is one of the balance of knowledge. Only the most knowledgeable and the most confident will feel able to stand up to a constable purporting to exercise statutory or common law powers. There is also the risk that the person resisting the exercise of the powers will be charged with obstructing the constable in the execution of his duty. Avoiding conviction for this offence will involve persuading the criminal courts that the constable was acting unlawfully, and so was not acting in the execution of his duty.

Self-help is a remedy only for the brave or the foolhardy.

Challenging the Prosecution Evidence

This is an important area. There are a number of provisions of PACE designed to ensure compliance with the provisions of the Act and the codes by rendering evidence obtained other than wholly in compliance with the new rules liable to be excluded from any subsequent trial. There are three principles which might apply in deciding to introduce rules which provide for the exclusion of evidence. First, there is the 'reliability principle': evidence of certain kinds is or may be so unreliable as to preclude its use in a criminal trial. Second, there is the 'disciplinary principle': exclusion of unfairly obtained evidence compels police compliance with rules on the collection of evidence. And third, there is the 'protective principle': citizens have a right to protection against failure by the police to meet the standards required of them and, if they are not afforded that protection, they should not be put at risk, nor should the prosecutor gain an advantage. The courts have shown little favour towards the disciplinary principle; existing rules are based upon a combination of the reliability principle and the protective principle.

Confessions, including incriminating statements falling short of full confessions, are admissible against defendants without any corroborating evidence unless the defendant challenges the statement. When this happens, there must be a trial within a trial as to the admissibility of the evidence. Section 76 of PACE conditions the admissibility of confession on the concept of reliability. Where a

confession is challenged, the prosecution must prove beyond reasonable doubt
that the confession, notwithstanding that it may be true, was not obtained:

> by oppression of the person who made it; or
> in consequence of anything said or done which was likely in the circumstances
>   existing at the time to render the confession unreliable.

Oppression *includes* torture, inhuman or degrading treatment and the use or
threat of violence, whether or not it amounts to torture (s.76(8), PACE).

Section 76 is concerned solely with confession evidence. Section 78 of PACE
is rather wider. It is poorly drafted and the explanation for this is horse-trading
during the Parliamentary stages of the legislation (Sieghart, 1986). The section
gives the courts a *discretion* to refuse to allow evidence to be admitted on which
the prosecution proposes to rely, if it appears that, having regard to all the circumstances, including the circumstances in which the evidence was obtained, the
admission of the evidence would have such an adverse effect on the fairness of
the proceedings that it ought not to be admitted. Section 78 is so opaque that
no one is quite sure of its scope and effect. In the pre-PACE case of *R v. Sang*
([1980] AC 402), which was concerned, in part, with evidence other than
admissions, the House of Lords had held that, although the courts had a discretion to exclude evidence the prejudicial effect of which outweighed its probative
value, they lacked any general discretion to refuse to admit relevant admissible
evidence because it was obtained unfairly. As long ago as 1949 in *Noor
Mohammed* ([1949] AC 182) Lord du Parcq sitting in the Privy Council had
given guidance on the application of the weighing of prejudicial effect against
probative value:

> The judge ought to consider whether the evidence is sufficiently substantial,
> having regard to the purpose to which it is professedly directed, to make
> it desirable in the interests of justice that it should be admitted. If, so far
> as that purpose is concerned, it can in the circumstances have only trifling
> weight, the judge will be right to exclude it. To say that is not to confuse
> weight with admissibility. The distinction is plain, but cases must occur in
> which it would be unjust to admit evidence of a character gravely preju-
> dicial to the accused even though there may be some tenuous ground for
> holding it technically admissible. (p. 192)

There has been a flurry of case law on the meaning of s.78, but this does not
answer all the questions raised by the poor drafting of the section, especially
when s.82(3) of PACE tucks in a provision that nothing in Part VIII of PACE
'shall prejudice any power of a court to exclude evidence . . . at its discretion.'
No case has yet given detailed consideration to the scope and meaning of the
section (Birch, 1989).

In *Matto* v. *Wolverhampton Crown Court* ([1987] RTR 337) Woolf LJ
considered that the section did not replace any common law discretion which
existed, but gave new guidance on how to exercise it. It seemed that the princi-

ples set out in *Sang* lived on. This was the view taken in *R* v. *Mason* ([1987] 3 All ER 481), which also established that s.78 could be used in the context of confession evidence which was not excluded under s.76. In *Mason* a fabricated story by detectives which had induced the defendant to confess and which had been proffered to his lawyer as the truth resulted in the quashing of a conviction for arson. In so doing, Watkins LJ repeated the point made frequently by the courts that criminal trials and appeals against criminal convictions are not the place to discipline the police. In *R* v. *Delaney* ([1989] Cr App R 338) the Court of Appeal affirmed that evidence obtained unlawfully should not be ruled inadmissible merely because of the breach in order to punish the police. The evidence should only be excluded if the breach made it unreliable.

In *R* v. *Samuel* ([1988] 2 All ER 135) the Court of Appeal quashed a conviction for robbery in circumstances where Samuel had been unlawfully denied access to a solicitor at the police station. The confession made by Samuel had to be excluded from the court's consideration. *R* v. *Alladice* ([1988] 87 Cr App R 380) also concerned a failure to comply with the suspect's right to legal advice under s.58 of PACE. Alladice was not as lucky as Samuel. His appeal failed. The Court of Appeal concluded that, had the trial judge considered the matter, he would have concluded that there had been a serious breach of s.58, but having regard to answers given by Alladice during the trial within a trial in the Crown Court to the effect that the presence of a solicitor would only have reinforced what he already knew, namely that he was not obliged to answer any further questions, the trial judge would have been free to conclude that the breach of s.58 of PACE did not prejudice the accused and so the evidence might well not have been excluded.

In *R* v. *Hughes* ([1988] Crim LR 519) the Court of Appeal considered that the fairness at which s.78 aims is in the nature of a balance between the interests of the prosecution and the defence, and not simply the protection of the accused against the admission of prejudicial evidence. The Court of Appeal has also stressed that the effect of the evidence on the fairness of the trial is the governing consideration (*R* v. *O'Leary*, [1988] 87 Cr App R 387). In *R* v. *Keenan* ([1989] 3 WLR 1193) Hodgson J sitting in the Court of Appeal considered that significant and substantial breaches of the Code of Practice relating to admissions and other incriminating statements were likely to lead to exclusion of the evidence, but he stressed the need for significant and substantial breaches of the provisions if the exclusion of evidence was not to amount simply to punishing the police for failure to observe the Codes.

In so far as it is possible to make any general conclusions on s.78 of PACE, it seems that it introduces no new test for the exclusion of evidence, but that it is now legitimate in operating the test to consider all the circumstances, including the circumstances in which the evidence was obtained. This is a change to the *Sang* test, since under that test, the circumstances in which the evidence was obtained were irrelevant except where the evidence consisted of admissions made by the accused. It may be, as Professor Smith predicted (Smith, J. 1986), that s.78 will be applied to exclude evidence obtained in circumstances which shock the conscience.

The bottom line is that the discretion in s.78 of PACE will be exercised by the 1000 judges regularly sitting in the Crown Court. Until someone is able to conduct a major piece of empirical research on this area of judicial discretion, we will not *know* how the discretion is exercised nationwide where it matters most. That is, at trial rather than review of the discretion on appeal. For defendants, reliance on exclusion of evidence is something of a lottery.

Suing the Police

There are a growing number of civil actions against the police. This is partly because it is a remedy which delivers compensation and the case remains in the control of the complainant, and partly because of some disillusionment with the police complaints procedure. Of considerable significance is the difference in the burden of proof. In the civil courts the burden of proof is on the balance of probabilities; to sustain a complaint against the police the criminal standard of proof beyond reasonable doubt applies.

A constable is susceptible to civil action because constables enjoy no immunity from suit where they overstep their powers. If the constable had no lawful justification for his or her actions at the time of their exercise, the constable will almost certainly commit a tortious act, which cannot be made lawful by subsequent events (*Chic Fashions (West Wales)* v. *Jones*, [1968] 2 QB 299, p. 313). The torts most likely to be involved in police misconduct are (Clayton and Tomlinson, 1987; Harrison, 1987):

> assault and battery, where someone is hurt or searched;
> false imprisonment, where someone is stopped, detained or arrested;
> malicious prosecution, where a person is prosecuted even though the police know they did not commit the offence charged;
> trespass to property, where a constable enters premises without lawful authority;
> trespass to goods, where the police take or damage property without lawful authority.

Where a civil action is being pursued, it is recommended that no complaint against the police be filed at the same time and that no co-operation is offered in connection with any police internal disciplinary enquiry (Harrison, 1987 pp. 19–20).

The total amount paid out by the Metropolitan Police has been increasing dramatically in recent years: in 1976 a mere £7251 was paid out in damages and settlements; by 1986 this had increased to £377,169 (Clayton and Tomlinson, 1987). The 1989 total was £479,000 and the 1990 out-turn is likely to be double this figure (the *Guardian*, 28 May 1990). The upward trend is partly explained by the diminishing public confidence in the complaints machinery and a preference for civil action. Though more modest sums are involved, a similar pattern emerges in relation to provincial forces.

Making a Complaint

The procedure for making a complaint is simple and cheap, but once made the matter is largely out of the hands of the complainant. No compensation will be paid as a result of the complaint. A person can complain about any matter within the Police Discipline Code, which lists large numbers of matters of police discipline. The list extends far beyond the limited range of complaints which can be dealt with by the civil courts. Rudeness, racist comments or even conducting a search without good cause (a species of abuse of authority) are included. The downside is that there is still little confidence in the process (Brown, 1987); the chances of success are slim at less than one in ten complaints upheld.

The system for dealing with police complaints has long been a matter of concern. The Government was concerned to ensure that there was seen to be effective independent review of the process of investigation as well as of the results of investigations. There was also room for better matching of resources applied to the investigation of complaints depending on the seriousness of the allegation. Overall, the Government's aim is to persuade the public that complaints are fully and properly dealt with and to assure police officers that they will be treated fairly in the investigation of complaints against them. Calls by both the National Council for Civil Liberties (NCCL) and the Police Federation for the introduction of an independent investigating agency for complaints were rejected as impracticable. The new scheme is described in Part IX and Sched. 4 of PACE. The Police Complaints Board is upgraded to a Police Complaints Authority, which is given power to supervise the investigation of complaints. Indeed the Authority is required to supervise the investigation of the most serious cases and has power to call in other investigations for supervision. In these cases the police investigation of the complaint is answerable to the Authority. Serious cases include those involving death or serious injury. Regulations have been made requiring the reference of all cases involving allegations of corruption, assaults occasioning actual bodily harm and other complaints adversely reflecting on the reputation of the police service so that the Authority can determine whether or not to supervise their investigation. On the conclusion of these investigations the Authority will have to certify that they are satisfied with the conduct of the investigation.

In all cases the Authority retains the power to order or advise on particular disciplinary action, or on the referral of the case to the Director of Public Prosecutions for consideration of the prosecution of any police officer. The Authority also retains the Board's powers to sit with the chief constable on certain disciplinary hearings.

Apart from these serious cases, it is the responsibility of the chief constable, or his deputy, on receipt of a complaint to determine whether it should be resolved formally or informally (s.85, PACE). Cases suitable for informal resolution are those complaints which, if true, are unlikely to result in criminal or formal disciplinary proceedings against the police officer concerned. Informal resolution requires the consent of the complainant. In such cases the investigating officer may direct that an apology is made to the complainant or may advise the complainant that he or she has 'had a word' with the officer against whom the complaint has been made. Independent oversight of such cases is left in the hands of the local police authority and HM Inspectorate of Constabulary.

Formal resolution of complaints requires investigation by an officer not below the rank of chief inspector and not connected with the case appointed by the chief constable from his or her own or some other force. On receipt of the report of an investigation the chief constable, or his deputy, must consider whether or not a criminal offence appears to have been committed, in which case the file must be referred to the Director of Public Prosecutions (DPP) for consideration of prosecution. If no criminal offence appears to have been committed, the chief constable must consider whether disciplinary proceedings should be instituted. In both these matters, the chief constable is subject to directions from the Authority. Minor matters are heard by the chief constable, or his deputy, alone, but more serious matters are heard by a disciplinary tribunal consisting of the chief constable, or his deputy, sitting with two members of the Authority. The police officer against whom such proceedings are taken is entitled to be legally represented and the penalties available are formidable, ranging from a caution to dismissal from the force and loss of pension rights. There is an appeal following a decision at first instance to the Secretary of State, who will appoint a tribunal to hear the appeal.

The Crown Prosecution Service

The Crown Prosecution Service (CPS) now provides the bridge between the police investigation of cases and the determination of guilt or innocence by the criminal courts (Hall Williams, 1988). On charge or the obtaining of a summons, the police file passes into the hands of the CPS, who have the power to discontinue the matter if they are not satisfied that the case is strong enough to put before the courts. To understand this dramatic development, some historical background is needed.

Historical Introduction

Prior to the implementation of the Prosecution of Offences Act 1985, there was no public system of prosecution. In ancient times all prosecutions were private prosecutions. It was custom which resulted in chief officers of police becoming the person primarily responsible for the decision to institute criminal proceedings. As a consequence of this, the practice of police officers conducting the prosecution of minor cases in the magistrates' court also became widespread. Yet from time to time, the essentially private nature of the prosecution of offences has been brought home vividly. In 1974 PC Joy stopped a motorist and reported him for a motoring offence. That motorist was a Member of Parliament and PC Joy's superiors refused to pursue the case. PC Joy thought this unjust and successfully brought a private prosecution.

Two developments prior to the 1985 Act modified the position. In 1879 the office of Director of Public Prosecutions was established. The prosecution of certain, usually very serious, offences, the importance, difficulty or other characteristics of which made prosecution by a central authority appropriate, were reserved for the DPP. The second development was the requirement in a number of statutes which created offences that the consent of the Attorney-General, DPP or some other designated authority be obtained as a prerequisite to the starting of a prosecution for that offence. These are not always the most serious offences. They are generally those where there is a risk that local decision making may result in regional variations in the prosecution of the offences. Good examples are the offences of incitement to racial hatred under the Race Relations Act 1976 and the dissemination of comics harmful to children under the Children and Young Persons (Harmful Publications) Act 1955.

The police discretion over the charging of offenders was referred to in the last chapter. The police have never been precluded from seeking legal advice in making a decision on the starting of criminal proceedings, and for many years the police have instructed solicitors and counsel to advise them and to act for them in serious cases. The Willink Commission in 1962 addressed this issue and recommended that the provision of legal advice to the police should be institutionalized (Willink Commission, 1962). As a result of these recommendations most, but by no means all, police authorities established prosecuting solicitors departments (Weatheritt, 1980). The significant feature of the relationship between the chief constable and the prosecuting solicitor is that it was one of solicitor and client. The prosecuting solicitor was subject to the instructions of the chief constable. Thus, in theory at least, a chief constable could instruct a prosecuting solicitor to undertake a prosecution against the advice of the solicitor. Only if the prosecution would be unconscionable in the sense that it would conflict with the solicitor's duty to the court could a solicitor refuse to follow the chief constable's instructions.

Not surprisingly, there were suggestions that there was no independent and impartial consideration of the police case prior to the matter being brought before the courts. A further filter to weed out weak cases was required.

The JUSTICE Report

The modern campaign for the creation of an independent prosecution service started in 1970 with the publication of the JUSTICE report, *The Prosecution Process in England and Wales*. This report argued cogently for a complete separation of the responsibilities for the investigation of crime and its prosecution (JUSTICE, 1970). Independence of these functions, argued the report, is the best safeguard of fairness, objectivity and impartiality in the investigation and prosecution of offences. JUSTICE claimed that practice in England and Wales was out of line with practices adopted in other countries with a common law tradition.

JUSTICE recommended the introduction in England and Wales of a system similar to that in operation in Scotland. There the decision to prosecute is undertaken by agencies independent of the police. Prosecutions at local level are supervised by Procurators-Fiscal appointed by the Lord Advocate. The police are required to report all cases to the fiscals who must examine each file and mark it with the decision whether or not to proceed. Fiscals have the power to direct the police to obtain fuller evidence if they consider this necessary. They also conduct the prosecution of all lesser criminal offences; more serious offences are prosecuted by one of the Law Officers or an Advocate-Depute (one of six deputies to the Lord Advocate). JUSTICE argued that such a system would be convenient, economic, efficient and productive of greater uniformity of practice and procedure.

The Philips Commission: Proposals and Second Thoughts

The Philips Commission recognized the capacity of the present arrangements in England and Wales to give rise to a conflict of interest when the police become convinced of the guilt of a person charged and are also responsible for the selection of evidence and the presentation of the prosecution case in court. The Philips Commission also found that the various arrangements operating in each of the 43 police areas defied 'simple and unqualified description'. Those arrangements precluded any move towards a consistent national prosecution policy. It was accepted that existing prosecuting arrangements should be replaced by an independent prosecution service. There was less agreement about the form that service should take. The DPP and the Prosecuting Solicitors Society argued for a regional system, which would, in essence, have converted and enlarged existing prosecuting solicitors departments into independent units. The Philips Commission recommended the adoption of this model, but there was considerable criticism subsequently expressed about its feasibility.

The overall result of the recommendations of the Philips Commission was to split the decision to prosecute between the police and the new prosecution service. The initial decision to proceed would be taken by the police, but this would be subject to examination by the new prosecution service which would be free to alter or drop the charges.

One early response to the charge of lack of openness was the publication by the Attorney-General of criteria for prosecution, which were commended by the Home Secretary as valuable guidelines for making the decision to prosecute. There were no surprises in these guidelines. A second response was the setting up of a working party to consider views of interested parties on the viability of three models:

an integrated national service;
a decentralized national service; and
a locally based service.

In 1983 the Government produced a White Paper, *An Independent Prosecution Service for England and Wales* (Cmnd 9074) containing its proposals. The Government came down in favour of an integrated national model with local Crown Prosecutors having responsibility for the conduct of all cases now prosecuted by the police. The White Paper agreed with the Philips Commission's conclusion that the police would continue to make the initial decision on whether or not to prosecute, though they would remain free to seek the advice of the Crown Prosecutor before doing so. Once a decision to prosecute had been made by the police, the matter would pass into the jurisdiction of the Crown Prosecutor who could decide whether the charges should proceed, be amended or be dropped.

The Crown Prosecution Service is Born

Part I of the Prosecution of Offences Act 1985 establishes a Crown Prosecution Service (CPS) which consists of the DPP as head of the service and of Chief Crown Prosecutors for areas based on existing police force areas, though some areas share a Chief Crown Prosecutor. The DPP is henceforth to be appointed by the Attorney-General. This is an important change which removes the anomaly of appointment of the DPP by the Home Secretary, even though the Attorney-General has ministerial responsibility for the duties and acts of the DPP.

Section 3 of the Prosecution of Offences Act 1985 spells out the functions of the DPP:

the conduct of all criminal proceedings other than proceedings specified by order made by the Attorney-General instituted by or on behalf of a police force, including all binding over cases;

to institute and have the conduct of criminal proceedings the importance or difficulty or other characteristics of which make it appropriate for the proceedings to be instituted by the DPP;

to take over proceedings concerning the forfeiture of obscene articles under s.3 of the Obscene Publications Act 1959;

to appear for the prosecution on all criminal appeals;

to discharge such other functions assigned from time to time by the Attorney-General.

Barristers and solicitors employed by the CPS are known as Crown Prosecutors and a Chief Crown Prosecutor has been appointed for each area. Without prejudice to the functions assigned to them in their capacity as members of the CPS, every Crown Prosecutor 'shall have all the powers of the Director as to the institution and conduct of proceedings but shall exercise those powers under the direction of the Director' (s.1(6), Prosecution of Offences Act 1985).

The distribution of functions between headquarters and the local offices was spelled out in a further White Paper, *Proposed Crown Prosecutions Service* (Cmnd 9411). These involved a shareout of the current consent requirements and intervention provisions applicable to the DPP and Attorney-General between headquarters and the local offices. Most decisions are taken in local offices under guidelines provided by headquarters. Crown Prosecutors, regardless of whether they are solicitors or barristers, will enjoy the rights of audience enjoyed by solicitors holding practising certificates including those rights granted by direction of the Lord Chancellor extending the normal right of audience of solicitors.

These directions allow solicitors rights of audience in the Crown Court in those areas where there are insufficient barristers locally to cover the case load.

Accountability for decisions involves supervision of the operation of any system and may involve some system either for vetoing decisions inconsistent with established policy guidelines or for providing an explanation of the basis of decisions. The only formal accountability of the CPS is the requirement that an annual report be presented to the Attorney-General, which he is obliged to lay before Parliament. It will not be open to any Member of Parliament to raise any specific case in any debate on the report. It is difficult to see this system providing any real control of decision making.

The CPS was in operation nationally by October 1986. Throughout its short life to date the CPS has had a problem recruiting enough lawyers. For most of the time it has been about one-quarter under its establishment of 1500 lawyers, with the problem being most acute in London (National Audit Office, 1989). The National Audit Office's *Review of the Crown Prosecution Service* reported on the chronic shortage of staff experienced by the CPS since its establishment and that the Home Office had seriously underestimated the resource require-ments of the new service (National Audit Office, 1989). Other conclusions were that some 7.5 per cent of cases finalized in the magistrates' courts in 1987–8 had been dropped by the CPS, and in two-thirds of these cases this had occurred at the time of the first hearing. The CPS is criticized for not having introduced any systematic analysis of the reasons for the discontinuance of proceedings (see below).

The Operation of Discretion

The DPP has issued a *Code for Crown Prosecutors* under s.10 of the Prosecution of Offences Act 1985. The purpose of the Code is to promote efficient and consistent decision making in order to develop and maintain public confidence in the CPS. The guidelines are, not surprisingly, based on the Attorney-General's criteria for prosecution.

The Code stresses that the first consideration in any decision to continue pro-ceedings is the sufficiency of the evidence against the accused. The Code refers to the need for 'admissible, substantial and reliable evidence' (para. 4) which pro-vides a realistic prospect of securing a conviction. In evaluating the evidence in the police file, the Crown Prosecutor should consider, among other issues:

whether any evidence might be excluded under Part VIII of PACE;
whether any witness is exaggerating, has a faulty memory, is hostile or friendly to the accused, or otherwise unreliable;
what sort of impression a witness will make, and how that witness is likely to stand up to cross-examination;
the availability of witnesses.

Once all these factors are considered, there should remain a realistic prospect of being able to secure a conviction. Only if this is so, should the case proceed.

Next the Crown Prosecutor should consider the 'public interest criteria' (Ashworth, 1987). The general test is whether it appears that the offence or the circumstances of its commission are of such a character that a prosecution is required in the public interest. In determining the outcome of this test, Crown Prosecutors are directed to consider:

the likely penalty for the offence; the lighter the likely penalty, the stronger the case for considering an alternative to prosecution;

the staleness of the offence; if the offence is three or more years old by the probable date of trial, there should be special reasons for proceedings;

the youthfulness of the offender; it is in the public interest to avoid as far as possible the conviction of a young adult if there are other appropriate means for dealing with him or her;

the older and more infirm the offender, the more reluctant should the Crown Prosecutor be to proceed;

careful consideration should be given to the decision to proceed where there is evidence of mental instability, mental illness or stress; the Code acknowledges that decisions in this area are particularly difficult;

it will seldom be the case that it is not in the public interest to proceed against a person charged with sexual assault;

in some cases, it will be appropriate to consider the complainant's attitude;

proceedings against peripheral defendants should be carefully considered; it is most important to proceed against those whose involvement goes to the heart of the issues;

in cases where doubt remains after considering all these issues, the scales should normally be tipped in favour of prosecution, since the court can then be the final arbiter of the matter.

Where a Crown Prosecutor decides not to proceed, then the proceedings will be discontinued under s.23 of the Prosecution of Offences Act 1985. Where a defendant has been charged after being taken into custody without a warrant but no magistrates' court has been informed of the charge, the notice of discontinuance ends the matter there and then. Once a court is seised of the matter, the procedure is more complex. Reasons for discontinuance must be given to the court, but need not be given to the defendant. The defendant on receiving a notice of discontinuance of proceedings in this instance may nevertheless elect to have the case proceed by serving a counter-notice. This requires the matter to be brought before the court, where, of course, the prosecution may be called to account for the decision and orders for costs can be made.

Service of a notice of discontinuance does not prevent the institution of fresh proceedings for the same offence, if further evidence against the defendant subsequently comes to light. Some commentators feel that the process of 'uncharging' is inappropriate, and that it would have been better to have the file passed to the CPS when the police felt there was enough evidence to charge. This would have placed the decision to prosecute solely in the hands of the CPS. Under the system adopted, the ball is firmly rolling by the time the Crown Prosecutor sees the file; this is too late to be an effective safeguard against weak and inadequate prosecutions (Sanders, 1985; Sanders, 1986). Unless Crown Prosecutors are bold in their decision making and examine with some vigour the papers passed to them by the police, there is a risk that they will simply rubber stamp decisions made by the police. There is some evidence that prosecuting solicitors did just that (Sanders, 1985) and most Crown Prosecutors are former prosecuting solicitors. There is no evidence yet that they are taking a bold stance and providing a new deal for defendants. They do not appear to have taken up the challenge of policing the police (White, Robin 1986).

The private prosecution has not been abolished by the new legislation. It remains open to any citizen to bring a private prosecution, though such prosecutions are automatically referred to the CPS to determine whether they wish to take them over. There would seem to be nothing to prevent such a prosecution being taken over solely with a view to the discontinuance of the proceedings.

The CPS is markedly different from the much praised Scottish system. Yet even there research has shown that there is a gap between the rhetoric of the system and the protection it affords to defendants (Moody and Tombs, 1982). The research study showed that there is almost a presumption of prosecution which is only rebutted in a small number of cases. Furthermore the existence of fiscals does not seem to have resulted in any clearer understanding of the basis of decision making in the exercise of the discretion to prosecute. Most decisions not to proceed are based on an insufficiency of evidence or on the triviality of the offence. Decision making is based on received wisdom learned in post rather than from the formulation and revision of prosecuting guidelines.

A significant aspect of the decision to prosecute is that it is an essentially private process seldom open to any kind of public scrutiny. Internal checks and monitoring are therefore the only means of ensuring that in every case full and thorough consideration is given to the circumstances of the case before a decision to proceed is taken. In some areas, notably the acceptance of pleas of guilty to lesser offences, the Code is somewhat opaque. The Code says:

> The over-riding consideration will be to ensure that the Court is never left in the position of being unable to pass a proper sentence consistent with the gravity of the defendant's actions. (para. 11)

The pressure of work in the CPS led to the introduction of case screening by Executive Officer grades, who are not lawyers. Two days special training was given and a special manual prepared for their use. Case screeners could decide that a case was to proceed, but any consideration of discontinuance had to be referred to a Crown Prosecutor. Case screeners were also encouraged to refer to Crown Prosecutors any cases where they felt unsure as to the correct decision to make. The first annual report of the DPP states that the function of the case screener is to act as a first filter under the supervision of a senior Crown Prosecutor to ensure the efficient and effective consideration of all files referred to the CPS. In May 1988 the Divisional Court declared this practice *ultra vires*

(*R v. Director of Public Prosecutions, ex parte Association of First Division Civil Servants, The Times*, 24 May 1988). Watkins LJ declared that the DPP had acted unlawfully in setting up the scheme:

> We do not regret arriving at such a conclusion seeing that one of the main purposes for which the Prosecution of Offences Act was enacted was to bring an independent legal mind to bear on each prosecution. If an executive officer can decide to allow a prosecution to continue with the result that because the accused pleads guilty the case never goes to a Crown Prosecutor, that, in our view, frustrates that very important purpose of the Act, and although in the context of the Crown Prosecution Service's workload that case may be insignificant, it is to the individual who is accused a matter of great concern.

The Conduct of the Prosecution

Where, as will be the usual case, the decision of the CPS is to proceed with a prosecution, the CPS has the responsibility to arrange for a lawyer to present the case in court. All Crown Prosecutors have rights of audience in the magistrates' courts, and it will usually be one of them who deals with such cases. But the workload is such that the CPS still spends significant sums of money on the employment of solicitors in private practice to act as agents for them in court proceedings.

It is the work of the CPS in magistrates' courts which has caused greatest criticism. Delays, missing files, and confusion over who is to handle the case have all given rise to complaints about the service. In a number of cases, prosecutions have been dismissed by magistrates because the prosecution was in such a state of disarray.

Where the case is sent to the Crown Court for trial, the CPS must instruct a barrister to appear for them, since Crown Prosecutors have no rights of audience in the Crown Court. The Prosecution of Offences Act 1985 enables the Lord Chancellor to make a direction extending rights of audience to them, but this has not yet happened. It is certain to come in due course, because there is little beyond the Bar's self-interest to justify the expense of instructing counsel, for example, for at the very least the many guilty pleas which take place in the Crown Court.

Barristers appearing in the Crown Court rather oddly enjoy a degree of independence from the CPS which instructs them. Despite the scrutiny to which the case has been put by the CPS, it remains open to a barrister to conclude on the day that the case is not strong enough to proceed and to offer no evidence, or to accept a plea of guilty to a lesser offence (Farquharson, D. 1986).

The Serious Fraud Office

In one area the investigation of offences and the decision to prosecute are integrated. This is in the area of serious fraud. There was growing concern about the ability of the police to investigate serious frauds efficiently and to secure convictions in such cases. The whole area was considered by the Roskill Committee on Fraud Trials (Roskill Committee, 1986). The recommendations made in the report were implemented in the Criminal Justice Act 1987. Now a staff of lawyers, accountants and police officers working together in the Serious Fraud Office is responsible for the investigation and prosecution of serious frauds. The Serious Fraud Office is responsible to the Attorney-General. There is no right to silence in the face of an investigation by the Serious Fraud Office, though some protection is afforded to statements made in the course of an investigation (Wood, 1989).

5

The Defendant in the Magistrates' Court

Protecting the Interests of Defendants

Every case concerning an adult charged with a criminal offence will be considered by magistrates. In dealing with defendants, magistrates exercise a variety of functions. As was noted in the previous chapters, much of the police investigation of offences is unregulated by the courts, though there are key areas where authorization from magistrates is required. Examples are the obtaining of warrants for arrest or for search, or for further detention in police custody beyond 36 hours. In such cases magistrates are clearly exercising a supervisory function, designed to protect the liberty interests of defendants.

The protection of the liberty interests of defendants continues once magistrates have jurisdiction over the case, which occurs when the charge sheet is delivered to the court or where a summons is issued on the swearing of an information. In the time leading up to the trial and sentencing of the guilty, there are a number of important issues which come before magistrates. This chapter is as much concerned with these issues as with trial in the magistrates' courts. Magistrates determine, among other things, whether defendants are represented at the public expense; remain at liberty pending their trial; and are tried in the magistrates' court or the Crown Court.

In more serious cases, magistrates act as a filter to determine whether there is adequate evidence to justify sending the defendant for trial in the Crown Court. Finally, magistrates sentence those found guilty before them. If they feel their sentencing powers are inadequate, they may, in either way cases, commit the defendant for sentence to the Crown Court.

The effective performance of this variety of tasks involves a variety of skills. In making bail decisions, magistrates will be assessing the personality of defendants in order to make a prediction about their future conduct. In making decisions on legal aid, magistrates will be assessing the likely consequences of the prosecution for defendants and whether they will be able effectively to argue their own case. Inevitably, magistrates have broad discretionary powers, but these are increasingly being placed within a statutory framework for decision

making. The requirement of giving reasons for, and recording, decisions is often
used to check that the formalities have been observed.

The material in this chapter should not be isolated from the processing of
defendants by the police, nor should the textbook separation of the various tasks
detract from the important interrelationship between every stage of the criminal
process. Often what has gone before is the major determinant of later decisions.

Getting Legal Help

The Problem

At a multitude of points in the pre-trial criminal process, the suspect or
defendant will look to others for advice on how to act or respond. Those to
whom suspects and defendants turn are the police, their families and friends, and
lawyers. Once it is clear that the case is to proceed to court, defendants' needs
for legal advice become compelling. In 1988 over £250 million was spent on
publicly funded legal help for those at the police station and before the criminal
courts (Lord Chancellor's Department, 1989). Yet the provision of help is neither
systematic nor comprehensive; it is a mixture of basic emergency cover, some
advice in the lawyer's office and representation on a significant scale only for
those charged with the most serious offences.

If the offence is very serious, then virtually all defendants will be represented.
These cases will be tried in the Crown Court. For less serious offences dealt with
in the magistrates' courts, the proportion of defendants who will be unrepresented remains substantial. Early studies suggested that fewer than a quarter of
defendants dealt with in the magistrates' courts are represented (Zander, 1969;
Zander, 1972a). These studies are now very dated. The proportion of defendants who are now unrepresented when they appear in court is probably very
much lower. No precise figures are available, which is itself surprising. In one
recent study of 909 cases triable either way where the sample was weighted in
favour of cases committed to the Crown Court for trial, one in five defendants
was unrepresented when their cases came to court (Riley and Vennard, 1988).

A question which is often asked is why defendants need representation if they
are pleading guilty. The assumption that such defendants can be dealt with
unassisted by a representative fails to recognize the important role of the representative in guiding defendants through the complex and mysterious process in
the criminal courts, which often leaves defendants confused. Even a guilty plea
requires the skills of marshalling fact and argument, so that the magistrates are
fully informed when they consider the sentence to be imposed. Advocates are the
articulate spokespersons of often inarticulate clients; the client provides the script
and the advocate ensures that everything that can be, and needs to be, said for
the defendant is presented to the court in a manner which is efficient, effective
and directed to the issues the magistrates will need to consider.

Assistance to defendants at the public expense may be provided on an
emergency basis under the court duty solicitor scheme, or on a more planned

basis under the Green Form scheme, or under legal aid for representation in criminal proceedings. The range of schemes is impressive, but remains haphazard in coverage. The duty solicitor scheme only provides limited help, while the tests for full representation at the public expense are tough and, in practice, help mainly those whose cases are tried in the Crown Court.

The Benson Commission in 1979 argued for a massive extension of the criminal legal aid scheme. Under their proposals there would be a statutory right to legal aid for bail applications, committal proceedings, and trial of offences triable on indictment or triable either way. For offences triable only summarily there would be a statutory presumption in favour of the grant of legal aid which could only be rebutted if the court was satisfied both that there would be no likelihood of a custodial sentence or substantial damage to the defendant's reputation, and that adequate presentation of the defendant's case, including a plea in mitigation, did not require legal representation (Benson Commission, 1979). It is clear from the recent legislation and from the official response to the Benson Commission's recommendations (Government Response to Benson, 1983) that the Government has firmly rejected these recommendations.

Duty Solicitor Schemes

The 24-hour or police duty solicitor scheme was discussed in the last chapter. Those who see a solicitor in the police station may well continue to use the services of that solicitor at a later stage of the criminal process under another part of the legal aid scheme. The police duty solicitor scheme grew out of the voluntary court based schemes, which were a response to the problem of defendants appearing in the magistrates' courts bewildered and with little understanding of what was happening to them. Duty solicitor schemes operating in magistrates' courts offer a safety net to catch those who appear without having obtained any legal advice.

The Benson Commission was impressed with duty solicitor schemes and recommended their extension to provide coverage in all the busy courts (Benson Commission, 1979). As a result duty solicitor schemes were placed on a statutory footing in 1982 and are now governed by Part III of the Legal Aid Act 1988 and regulations made under the Act. The detailed organization of the scheme is laid down in the non-statutory Legal Aid Board Duty Solicitor Arrangements 1990.

The administrative scheme established by the Legal Aid Board Duty Solicitor Arrangements 1990 provides for a three-tier committee structure. A national Duty Solicitor Committee is appointed by the Legal Aid Board to oversee the operation of the scheme nationally. Beneath them is a network of regional duty solicitor committees, which determine the needs for duty solicitor schemes in their regions. These committees must contain a majority of solicitor advocates, and must have a representative from each local duty solicitor committee in the region plus a magistrate, a justices' clerk and two lay members. There may also be representation of the probation service and the Crown Prosecution Service, and in London a stipendiary magistrate. The regional committees decide in which courts schemes are to be set up and generally supervise the operation of schemes in their region, ensuring that they operate effectively. Beneath regional committees are local duty solicitor committees for each operational scheme. It is the local committee which is initially responsible for the selection of duty solicitors, but any solicitor who is excluded has an appeal to the appropriate regional committee. The scheme contains detailed rules on the experience required to qualify a solicitor for selection as a duty solicitor, designed to ensure that duty solicitors have sufficient experience of criminal advocacy to be able to take instructions from, and act effectively for, a number of defendants at short notice.

The Arrangements also set out the service to be offered by duty solicitor schemes. Duty solicitor schemes usually operate as follows (Blake et al., 1988). The duty solicitor will be a local solicitor from private practice who has agreed to be 'on call' at the court on certain days on a rota basis. The duty solicitor is there to help any defendant who is without representation, and will see both defendants in custody and those arriving at court from their homes. The co-operation of court personnel and the police is also sought to ensure that the presence of the duty solicitor is widely known.

The duty solicitor obviously cannot do more than provide 'first aid'; he or she will, after all, not have seen the defendants until that morning. What the duty solicitor usually can do is to give general advice, to oppose any police objections to bail where appropriate, and to make straightforward pleas in mitigation where the defendant is pleading guilty. If the defendant is intending to plead not guilty or if the duty solicitor needs more time to represent the defendant adequately, the duty solicitor will apply for legal aid and seek an adjournment. If the defendant wishes, the solicitor will continue to act for the defendant, but representation on any future occasion will be on the traditional solicitor–client basis. There is an embargo on a duty solicitor acting, as duty solicitor, for a defendant who has previously been assisted by a duty solicitor, unless a failure to do so may lead to the defendant being at risk of imprisonment. This rule is designed to avoid repeated representation by a duty solicitor being used by courts as a substitute for the grant of criminal legal aid. It is also made clear that duty solicitors cannot act for defendants pleading not guilty or in committal proceedings. Duty solicitors are only in exceptional circumstances to assist persons charged with non-imprisonable offences; this will narrow the scope of service offered by some existing duty solicitor schemes. The scheme makes provision for the remuneration of duty solicitors, who are paid a modest hourly rate for their attendance at court.

Research comparing a court with a duty solicitor scheme with a neighbouring court without such a scheme, but served by the same clerk and magistrates, showed that the duty solicitor scheme resulted in more defendants released on bail and more defendants being granted legal aid (King, 1977). But other research has suggested that the presence of duty solicitors leads to a higher proportion of guilty pleas (Bridges et al., 1982). Duty solicitor schemes have only a limited potential in ensuring that defendants are treated fairly by the criminal justice system. This was recognized by the Benson Commission which coupled its recommendation for the continuation of duty solicitor schemes with a recommendation for a massive increase of spending on criminal legal aid.

Solicitors' participation in the scheme is not wholly altruistic. It is a means of developing a criminal legal aid practice. The introduction of voluntary schemes coincided with a period when competition in the conveyancing sector of legal practice meant that solicitors were feeling the need to diversify. At that time criminal legal aid was seen to pay well if the work could be done on a sufficient scale. Now there is something of a crisis, because many solicitors are giving up poorly paid legal aid work in favour of other more remunerative work. This is an issue which is discussed in the latter part of this book in the delivery of legal services.

The Green Form Scheme

Assistance from a duty solicitor, whether at the police station or in court is neither means tested nor merits tested. Those defendants who consult a lawyer *before* reaching court are likely to receive initial assistance under the advice and assistance scheme (Part III, Legal Aid Act 1988). This has come to be known as the Green Form scheme from the colour of the application form. Eligibility for advice under the Green Form scheme is means tested but not merits tested. It is available for advice on any point of law except one arising in connection with conveyancing or the making of a will. It does not include representation in any court or tribunal. The initial limit is two hours of the solicitor's time, though this can be extended on obtaining authorization from the legal aid area committee.

The means test is a simple one conducted by the solicitor providing the advice. It takes no more than a few minutes to determine whether applicants are eligible for free help, will have to pay a contribution, or have sufficient capital and income to take them outside the scope of the scheme. Although the scheme provides no help from a lawyer in court, there is much that can be done to assist a defendant outside the courtroom. It can cover the cost of taking a statement from the defendant and any potential defence witnesses, or applying for criminal legal aid for representation, and of obtaining advance disclosure of the prosecution case. Discussion and consideration of any choices open to the defendant on the mode of trial and on intended plea also take place in the solicitor's office rather than in court.

If representation is needed, defendants must either pay the solicitor from their own resources, or succeed in an application to the magistrates' court for criminal legal aid.

Criminal Legal Aid

Criminal legal aid for representation before the criminal courts is both means tested and merits tested and is governed by Part V of the Legal Aid Act 1988. Merits testing requires the defendant to satisfy the 'competent authority' (in most cases, the magistrates' court) that there are features of the case which make representation necessary. There are statutory tests to be applied in determining the answer to this question. Applications are usually made by completing an application form and submitting it to the clerk to the justices, who will consider the application. The clerk may choose to refer difficult cases to the magistrates, but now decides most cases without reference to them. It is possible to apply for legal aid orally before the magistrates, but invariably the magistrates will require an application form to be completed.

In place of the old fairly flexible financial limits, there is now a formal assessment of the disposable income and capital of the defendant by staff in the magistrates' court. This is similar to that which has operated for many years for civil legal aid. Following the calculation of disposable income and capital, weekly contributions may be required and a lump sum payment of all disposable capital in excess of £3000 by way of contribution towards the lawyer's fees. Any culpable failure to pay any weekly contribution may result in revocation of the legal aid order. The contribution system goes directly against the recommendation of the Benson Commission that contribution orders under criminal legal aid in the magistrates' courts should be abolished (Benson Commission, 1979).

The only defendants who *must* be granted legal aid if they apply and are within the financial limits are:

> those committed for trial on a charge of murder, for the trial (s.21(3)(a), Legal Aid Act 1988);
> those applying for bail after having been kept in custody following a remand hearing at which they were unrepresented, for the bail hearing (s.21(3)(b), Legal Aid Act 1988);
> those to be kept in custody after conviction but before sentence pending the obtaining of a report or pending an enquiry, for the sentencing hearing (s.21(3)(d), Legal Aid Act 1988);
> those about to be sentenced to a term of imprisonment provided that they have not been in prison before, for the sentencing hearing (s.21, Powers of Criminal Courts Act 1973);
> those about to be sentenced to a period of youth custody or to receive a detention centre order, for the sentencing hearing (s.2, Criminal Justice Act 1982).

For the rest it will be the application of the notoriously vague merits test that determines whether legal aid will be granted. The merits test provides that legal aid for trial proceedings should be granted when it is 'desirable to do so in the interests of justice.' Non-statutory criteria, widely known as the 'Widgery criteria', have since 1966 (Widgery Committee, 1966) guided magistrates in determining when the grant of legal aid will be in the interests of justice. These have now been given statutory form in s.22 of the Legal Aid Act 1988 where they are described as follows:

> the offence is such that if proved it is likely that the court would impose a sentence which would deprive the accused of his liberty or lead to loss of his livelihood or serious damage to his reputation;
> the determination of the case may involve consideration of a substantial question of law;
> the accused may be unable to understand the proceedings or to state his own case because of his inadequate knowledge of English, mental illness or other mental or physical disability;

the nature of the defence is such as to involve the tracing and interviewing of witnesses or expert cross-examination of a witness for the prosecution;

it is in the interests of someone other than the accused that the accused should be represented.

The Widgery criteria gave as an example of the last head, the trial of a charge of sexual assault against young children where it is undesirable that the defendant should cross-examine the witness in person. The list in s.22 is not exhaustive, but magistrates must consider each of the factors listed there. The Lord Chancellor has taken power to modify the factors either by amendment or addition of factors to be taken into account (s.22(3), Legal Aid Act 1988).

Many of the questions on the application form are directed at obtaining information to show whether any of the criteria for the grant of representation for trial proceedings is met. Some can only properly be answered with advice from a solicitor and the form itself recommends consulting a solicitor. Green Form money can be used for this purpose. The broad effect of the application of the criteria is that virtually all those who are to be tried in the Crown Court will obtain legal aid, but for those who are to be tried in the magistrates' court, there is less chance.

One continuing concern about the operation of the criminal legal aid scheme has been the wide variations in the rates of refusals for criminal legal aid among the country's magistrates' courts (Benson Commission, 1979, Levenson, 1981). The chances of obtaining criminal legal aid can be many times better at one court than its neighbour a few miles away. Between 1978 and 1988 the national refusal rate dropped from 14 per cent to 9 per cent of applicants. But wide local variations have remained and some courts have steadily increased their refusal rates. In 1988 a defendant had only a one in a hundred chance of being refused criminal legal aid by the Reading magistrates; a few miles away in Slough, one in ten applicants were refused. Similarly the South Sefton magistrates on Merseyside refused one in a hundred applicants, while the St Helens bench refused one in six. The Lord Chancellor's Department has in the past attributed the variations to differential application of the Widgery criteria, which have been incorporated in the Legal Aid Act 1988 in only slightly modified form.

Appeal against a Refusal of Criminal Legal Aid

Concerns about regional variations in the grant of legal aid resulted in the introduction in 1982 of a system of review of magistrates' decisions in this area, known as a 'right of recourse' designed to secure greater uniformity in decision making. The review is now governed by regulations made under s.21(10) of the Legal Aid Act 1988.

Those defendants who are refused legal aid by a magistrates' court may apply to the criminal legal aid committee for a review of the refusal. But they can only do so if the offence with which they are charged is one triable on indictment or either way. There is still no appeal against a refusal of legal aid for representation in a case triable only summarily. The members of the criminal legal aid committee are solicitors and barristers in private practice. Where a defendant applies for a review, the committee will consider the application in the light of the statutory test. For the first time, there is now an independent review of legal aid decision making by magistrates. Since criminal legal aid committees are based on legal aid areas, they will draw cases from a number of magistrates' courts and their influence should operate to secure greater uniformity in legal aid decisions by magistrates.

In 1988 one in eight refusals were referred to criminal legal aid committees, though rates of referral differed dramatically among the legal aid regions. Two out of every three such reviews resulted in the grant of criminal legal aid. Despite the introduction of these additional safeguards, some defendants are still denied representation for their criminal trial by accident of geography rather than the merits of their claims to legal aid.

Bail in the Magistrates' Court

The Importance of Bail

For those defendants remanded in custody by the police, the first appearance before the magistrates' court will concern the important question of whether they are to be kept in custody pending their trial. This is known as a *remand hearing*; a remand is technically continuing authorization of the defendant's status as an arrested person. Even if released on bail, the defendant remains under arrest. Only very straightforward cases where the defendant is pleading guilty will be disposed of by magistrates' courts at the first appearance of the defendant.

A remand in custody is imprisonment without trial and flies in the face of the presumption of the criminal process that a person is innocent until proved guilty. At any given time, one in four of the prison population is a remand prisoner. A feature of recent years has been the sharp increase in the growth of the remand population despite the relative stability of the numbers passing through the magistrates' courts (Morgan, 1989). The growth has been so great that a number of remand prisoners have had to be accommodated in police cells, which are only designed for very short term detention. They are quite inadequate for the longer-term prisoner. In 1980 the average remand population, that is, the typical number of prisoners awaiting trial on any given day, was 6600; by 1987 it had risen to 11,200 (Home Office Circular 25/1988). One in fifty of those tried in the magistrates' court is kept in custody pending trial, but one in five of defendants tried in the Crown Court is kept in custody.

The presumption of innocence until proof of guilt requires a clear justification for depriving a person of their liberty before conviction. There are generally seen to be three reasons which might justify so drastic a step:

> to protect the public from those considered dangerous or likely to commit further serious offences unless kept in custody;
> to secure the attendance at their trial of those who are considered likely to abscond;

to prevent defendants from interfering with the administration of justice by, for example, threatening witnesses.

Those remanded in custody will have greater difficulty in preparing a defence. Apart from the obvious restriction on their freedom to come and go, access to their lawyers will be subject to the administrative arrangements made by the prison where they are held. The conditions of detention are a national disgrace. Remand prisoners may well be locked three to a cell built for one with only a bucket each for a toilet for 23 hours a day. A defendant is likely to spend between seven and sixteen weeks in prison awaiting trial. Yet between one half and three-quarters of decisions to remand in custody are not contested (Brink and Stone, 1988).

Prior to the Bail Act 1976, the grant of bail was a matter for the discretion of magistrates (King, 1973). The Act controls this broad discretion and aims to secure the release of more defendants while awaiting trial. Section 4 of the Bail Act 1976 creates a right to bail, which can only be displaced if one of the statutory exceptions applies. The thrust of the legislation is that bail is to be granted unless there are compelling reasons for keeping a defendant in custody pending trial. What seems to have happened in practice is that a defendant has an uphill struggle to establish reasons why he or she should be released when the Crown Prosecution Service raise objections to the right to bail.

Before the establishment of the CPS, it was the police who put objections to bail before the courts. The process lacked uniformity since hundreds of police officers made objections to bail without any central supervision. There was little screening of police objections to bail even where police forces maintained their own prosecuting solicitors departments. The responsibility for making objections to bail now lies with the CPS; this has had the beneficial effect of providing a focal point for the screening of bail decision making. Many CPS offices have reserved the handling of custody cases on first appearance to a small number of in-house lawyers. This should, in turn, produce greater consistency in the formulation and presentation of objections to bail. It also makes it easier to operate bail information schemes because information is channelled to a single source (Stone, C. 1988). In future the Crown Prosecution Service will be represented at some bail hearings by staff of the CPS who are not lawers. New s.7A of the Prosecution of Offences Act 1985, inserted by s.114 of the Courts and Legal Services Act 1990, permits designated staff of the CPS who are not Crown Prosecutors to appear on behalf of the CPS in relation to any application for, or relating to, bail in criminal proceedings. The independence of action enjoyed by designated staff is not the same as that of Crown Prosecutors, since designated staff must act strictly in accordance with instructions given either particularly or generally in relation to such applications. Since the decision that the general right to bail is displaced is one for the court in the light of information it gathers from both parties, there is probably no great objection to be made to this provision. The function of the CPS in such matters is not adversarial, though there will be many occasions when the CPS wishes to place information before a court which suggests that one of the grounds on which bail can be refused is present.

Exceptions to the Right to Bail

In spelling out the reasons which will justify a refusal of bail, the Act divides offences into two groups: *imprisonable offences* and *non-imprisonable offences*. For the purposes of the Bail Act any offence which carries the possibility of punishment by imprisonment is an imprisonable offence. All restrictions on imposing custodial sentences arising as a matter of sentencing law and policy are to be ignored. This means that the category of non-imprisonable offences contains only the most trivial types of offence where magistrates would usually proceed by way of adjournment rather than remand in custody or on bail.

The very first question to which magistrates must address themselves will always be: is the offence charged an imprisonable offence or a non-imprisonable offence? Where the offence is non-imprisonable, the magistrates can only withhold bail from a defendant who has previously failed to surrender to custody and who, in the light of that failure, is believed to be likely to abscond. If the defendant does not fall within this exception to the right to bail, bail can only be denied if one of the general, and rather limited, exceptions mentioned below is established.

Where the offence is an imprisonable offence, as will usually be the case where there is a serious issue about entitlement to bail to be considered, a much more complicated enquiry must take place. The magistrates may, *at their discretion*, remand a defendant in custody if they are 'satisfied that there are substantial grounds for believing' that the defendant will, if released on bail:

> abscond; or
> commit further offences; or
> interfere with witnesses or otherwise obstruct the course of justice.

The magistrates' task here is to make a prediction about the way the defendant will behave while awaiting trial. On what basis do they make this prediction? Schedule 1 of the Act requires magistrates to have regard to a number of matters, which seek to ensure that they obtain a good picture of the defendant. They must have regard to:

> the nature and seriousness of the offence;
> the defendant's character, previous convictions, employment record, associations and community ties;
> the defendant's previous record as regards past grants of bail;
> the strength of the case against the defendant; and
> any other factor which appears to be relevant.

The relevance of these factors is largely self-explanatory. The more serious the offence, the greater will be the incentive to abscond; the less serious the offence, the less likely it will be that the defendant will fail to appear for trial. The defendant's previous convictions will need to be considered with some care. A defendant with a long string of convictions for minor offences should not automatically be remanded in custody, especially if he or she has always turned up for his or her trial in the past. The defendant's home circumstances and employment record are of very great significance. A defendant in employment with a stable home environment is likely to be regarded as a good bail risk even on a serious charge, while a defendant without employment or an established home is likely to be regarded as a poor bail risk. Where magistrates feel that bail could be granted if suitable accommodation were available for the defendant, Home Office Circular 25/1988 stresses the important role the probation service have in ensuring that the court is advised of the provision of places in bail hostels and other supported or supervised lodging arrangements. Consideration of a defendant's having answered to bail on previous occasions includes grants of bail prior to the implementation of the Bail Act 1976. The strength of the evidence against the defendant is relevant, because a defendant likely to be convicted on a serious charge which will lead to the virtual certainty of a substantial custodial sentence is a defendant with a considerable incentive to avoid trial. An example of 'any other factor which appears to be relevant' is the practicality of obtaining a medical report on a person on remand on a charge of murder (*R v. Vernege*, [1982] 1 WLR 293).

None of the above considerations should operate as a bar to bail; they are merely matters to be considered in determining whether there are substantial grounds for believing that one of the three grounds for denying bail is established. Information about the defendant is central to the prediction about future behaviour. It is therefore somewhat surprising that the Act does not place any obligation on anyone in the criminal process to obtain relevant information about the defendant.

There are two other limited grounds on which magistrates can withhold bail from a defendant charged with an imprisonable offence. First, where there is an adjournment for enquiries or a report, the magistrates can remand in custody if it appears impracticable for the enquiries or report to be completed without the defendant's being in custody. This will usually be after a finding of guilt but where the magistrates need more information about defendants before sentencing them. Secondly, the magistrates can remand in custody where it has not been practicable to obtain sufficient information for want of time to enable a proper decision to be made. This is an objectionable exception to the statutory right to bail. In such cases sufficient enquiry can be made of the defendant in person to enable a decision to be made. If it is felt necessary to verify information given by the defendant, this could be done by the court or a probation officer and will normally take no more than an hour or so. The court should not rise until decisions in such cases have been made. The incidence of the use of this ground for refusing bail is not known.

Finally, there are three general exceptions which apply regardless of whether the offence charged is imprisonable or non-imprisonable. First, the magistrates may withhold bail if satisfied that defendants need to be kept in custody for their own protection. Secondly, defendants already in custody following sentence and before the court for some other offence will not be granted bail. Thirdly, those who abscond lose the statutory right to bail.

Conditions, Security and Sureties

Where after careful consideration the magistrates are left with some doubt as to the safety of releasing a defendant on bail, they may be able to resolve those doubts by attaching conditions to the grant of bail, by requiring security to be provided, or by requiring sureties. These qualifications should only be added where strictly necessary. Conditions are straightforward; a common condition of bail is a requirement to report to a police station at specified intervals or to keep away from a place or person. During the 1984 miners' strike, a number of those charged with offences while picketing, were granted bail subject to the condition that they did not engage in further picketing. The legality of the condition was challenged by way of judicial review in *R* v. *Mansfield Justices, ex parte Sharkey and others*, ([1985] QB 613) but was upheld as lawful.

Security can only be required by or on behalf of a defendant where it appears that he or she is likely to leave Great Britain before trial. It involves the actual deposit of something of value likely to preclude the possibility of departure from Great Britain.

Sureties are persons acceptable to the court who know the defendant and are prepared to risk a sum of money, known as a *recognisance*, against default of the defendant. No money is actually deposited with the court. A surety is expected to do everything reasonably practicable to ensure the compliance of the defendant with the requirements of bail. If the defendant defaults, the surety will be brought before the court to determine whether the whole or a part of the recognisance should be forfeited.

Giving Reasons for Decisions

The principal device adopted to ensure compliance with the complex statutory code for making bail decisions is the requirement that decisions be recorded and reasons given for adverse decisions. There can be no doubt that this has increased the workload of magistrates' clerks upon whom this task falls. Whether the device achieves its purpose is another matter; it would be a poor clerk who could not formulate a reason falling within the terms of the Act and it would be a foolish magistrate who insisted on recording a personal prejudice as the reason for the decision.

One objective of the Bail Act 1976 was to move away from the notion that operated in some magistrates' courts that entitlement to bail depended on the offence charged. So it was common before the implementation of the Bail Act 1976 to find bail routinely refused if the offence charged was burglary. Given this objective, it is unfortunate that s.153 of the Criminal Justice Act 1988 has amended the Bail Act 1976 to require magistrates to give reasons for *granting* bail where the offence charged is murder, attempted murder, manslaughter, rape and attempted rape.

Bail Information Schemes

The vital importance of information about the defendant was acknowledged in the Report of the Home Office Working Party in 1974 on *Bail Procedures in Magistrates' Courts*, whose recommendations were largely implemented in the Bail Act 1976. Research prior to the Bail Act highlighted the speed with which bail decisions were made and the paucity of information available about defendants (King, 1973). It has been suggested that the Bail Act is an example of 'lawyers' law' which will not result in any significant change of practice (White, Robin, 1977). Studies and statistics since the Act came into force in 1978 would seem to confirm this prediction (Zander, 1979a; *see also* Cutts, 1982; East and Doherty, 1984).

The points system used in the Manhattan Bail Project run by the Vera Institute of Justice (King, 1973) seems to offer an effective aid to making the bail decision. Under the scheme consenting defendants are asked by 'bail investigators' employed by the probation service to provide basic information about themselves which after verification is used to establish a points score which determines the type of bail risk the defendant presents. The information is available to judges on the defendant's first appearance, but is not binding on them. The scheme has worked well in the United States and has been widely adopted. Typically, on its introduction more persons have been released on bail and fewer have defaulted. The success of such schemes shows that bail decisions can be made objectively and that careful screening does seem to identify successfully those who can safely be released on bail.

With Home Office approval, the Vera Institute advised the Inner London Probation Service on the introduction in 1974 of a pilot scheme at Camberwell Green Magistrates' Court. This proved a considerable success. But there is a drawback. The operation of such schemes involves public expenditure and, although the Home Office recommended in a circular that similar schemes should be introduced 'where existing resources permit', available resources were so stretched that the use of the system fell into complete disuse. But in the face of increasing numbers of remands in custody, the use of such schemes has been resurrected and eight pilot schemes have been set up, again with encouraging results (Home Office Circular 25/1988; Stone, C. 1988). Other similar experiments have enjoyed success, such as the bail action project run by the Inner London Probation Service at HM Prison Wormwood Scrubs (Mair, 1988). About 100 courts are expected to be operating such schemes by 1992 (Home Affairs Committee, 1990). But in the majority of courts, such schemes are not in operation, and it is left to defendants and their advisers to ensure the availability before the court of relevant information. Naturally, when the prosecution seeks to persuade magistrates to refuse bail, they will have collected certain information about the defendant, but there is no obligation on them to obtain and present general information about the defendant.

Challenging an Adverse Bail Decision

The normal effect of a remand pending trial in the magistrates' court or committal for trial in the Crown Court is to authorize the defendant's detention in custody for eight clear days (s.128, Magistrates' Courts Act 1980). The requirement to return to court every eight days resulted in large numbers of prisoners being moved from prison to court for very short hearings. Now the normal rule can be displaced and a remand can take place in the absence of the defendant if both the defendant and the prosecutor consent. Defendants cannot consent unless they have a solicitor acting for them. Remands in the absence of the defendant can only take place on three successive occasions, unless the court decides to exercise its discretion to remand in custody for a longer period not exceeding 28 days under s.128(A) of the Magistrates' Courts Act 1980 which has been inserted by s.155 of the Criminal Justice Act 1988.

The repetition of remand hearings every eight days was once thought to be an effective way of having a decision to remand in custody reviewed. But this was foreclosed by the decision of the Divisional Court upholding the practice of the Nottingham justices. That bench had adopted a policy, the effect of which was that on a third or subsequent remand hearing, full argument would only be heard if there was a change of circumstances such as to justify a full hearing. Two full hearings were permitted, since, on a first appearance, the defendant may have been represented by a duty solicitor who would only have had a limited chance to take instructions. Full argument might only have been possible on a second hearing, when the defendant's solicitor would have had plenty of time to take detailed instructions. In *R* v. *Nottingham Justices, ex parte Davies*, ([1981] QB 38) an order of *mandamus* was sought to compel the magistrates to hear full argument every time the defendant was remanded. Donaldson LJ (as he then was) upheld the policy of the Nottingham justices characterizing the finding of the magistrates that there were substantial grounds for believing that the defendant would default as a finding of fact that could only be overturned on appeal or if it could be shown that the facts underlying the decision had changed necessitating a reconsideration. He recommended the use of the following question on third and subsequent remands: 'Are there any new considerations which were not before the court when the accused was last remanded?' If there are none, there will be a further remand in custody; the hearing is a mere formality. It was to deal with this type of case that the remand hearing in the absence of the defendant was introduced.

Section 154 of the Criminal Justice Act 1988 has introduced an addition to Schedule 1 to the Bail Act 1976 codifying this practice. Section 5(6A) of the Bail Act requires the magistrates to issue a certificate that the court has heard full argument on the application before refusing bail, where it has not previously heard such argument or where there has been a change of circumstances justifying the hearing of full argument on the matter in the light of the changed circumstances.

The standard avenue of appeal against a refusal of bail is the right of appeal to the Crown Court introduced in 1983 (s.60, Criminal Justice Act 1982). The appeal does not lie against a decision to impose a condition or to require surety. Legal aid is readily available to cover such applications, because a criminal legal aid order granted for representation in the magistrates' court automatically extends to cover the costs of an appeal to the Crown Court against a refusal of bail. The defendant is not entitled to be present at the hearing without the leave of the Crown Court. The decision will be made after hearing argument from counsel for each side; solicitors enjoy a right of audience for these appeals. For those denied legal aid, the Official Solicitor will act. The Official Solicitor is a government lawyer who has as one of his or her duties the safeguarding of the rights of prisoners.

There will need to be careful consideration given to when it will be appropriate to seek to persuade magistrates that there has been a change of circumstances justifying the grant of bail, and when it will be appropriate to exercise the right of appeal. The difficulty is that an unsuccessful appeal will render it extremely difficult to persuade the magistrates on any later remand hearing that there has been a change of circumstances. Practitioners often advise that, except in the most urgent or convincing cases, it is not wise to apply elsewhere until all possibility of reconsideration in the magistrates' court has been exhausted (Hall, 1984).

The new remedy of appeal to the Crown Court has not entirely replaced the old remedy of application to a High Court judge in chambers under s.22 of the Criminal Justice Act 1967. Indeed this procedure is the only means of challenging at higher level the imposition of a condition or the requirement of surety. Under the procedure, defendants are not present at the hearing of their applications; their cases will be put by counsel who relies on an affidavit setting out the relevant facts which will have been prepared by defendants' solicitors. This procedure at one time applied only to those who could afford the services of solicitor and counsel, for, although legal aid was technically available, it was never granted. This was because application through the Official Solicitor is available to defendants unable to afford private representation. Unfortunately applications processed through the Official Solicitor are less thoroughly prepared, take longer to deal with and are markedly less successful than those submitted privately (King, 1973; Bases and Smith, 1976). In 1980 there were 522 private applications of which 364 were successful (69 per cent); by contrast there were 5275 applications processed through the Official Solicitor of which 473 (9 per cent) were successful. Repeat applications are not permitted. Increasing concern over the inequities of the system led the Council of the Law Society to issue a statement in November 1981 to the effect that legal aid was in fact available for applications to the High Court, though it was also stated that as far as possible the Official Solicitor procedure should continue to be used. This remains officially the position, though the Legal Aid Board will require convincing that the appeal to the Crown Court is inappropriate before granting legal aid for an application to a judge in chambers.

Bail at Committal

Where the magistrates' court commit a defendant for trial, consideration is given to whether the defendant should be kept in custody pending trial in the Crown Court (s.6(3), Magistrates' Courts Act 1980). Once remanded in custody on committal, there is no requirement of repetition of remand hearings every eight days. The decision lasts for the duration of the detention, subject to applications made by the defendant and the time limits considered below. For defendants already granted bail, the decision is likely to be a formality with the magistrates renewing the grant of bail or any conditions applied at the earlier stage. If the defendant is in custody, the question arises as to whether the remand hearing should be an occasion on which to hear full argument. The decision of the Divisional Court in *R* v. *Reading Crown Court, ex parte Malik*, ([1981] 2 WLR 473) suggests that a full hearing should take place since the committal papers will enable the court for the first time to make a truly informed assessment of the strength of the evidence against the defendant.

Appeal to the Crown Court is available if the magistrates refuse bail following committal, but it is also possible to make application to the Crown Court for bail after committal. Theoretically, this can be done even after an unsuccessful appeal against the magistrates' court's decision. This is because on committal, the Crown Court gains jurisdiction over the defendant, and the court with jurisdiction over the defendant always has power to grant bail (*ex parte Malik*, [1981] 2 WLR 473). The statutory framework for decision making contained in the Bail Act 1976 applies to bail decision making in the Crown Court.

Adjournment as an Alternative to Remand

An alternative to remand is simple adjournment. Some cases where attendance at court has been secured by charge are not at all serious and in these cases the magistrates may well not remand in custody or on bail, but will simply adjourn the case until a specified day and time or to a day to be fixed later, which is called adjournment *sine die*. Simple adjournments are used when it is not considered necessary to take any special precautions to ensure that the defendant attends court on some future occasion. The requirement to remand the defendant rather than to deal with the case by adjournment arises where the defendant is charged with an offence triable only on indictment (s.5, Magistrates' Courts Act 1980) or where the defendant is charged with an offence triable either way and was initially arrested by the police (s.18(4), Magistrates' Courts Act 1980). Where the defendant is brought before the court by summons for an offence triable either way, the magistrates have a discretion as to whether or not to proceed by remand or simple adjournment. The same is true of offences triable only summarily, though there would usually need to be some special feature to the case before the magistrates would decide to proceed by way of remand.

Custody Time Limits

Scotland has long operated a system of time limits in criminal cases. In summary cases, if a defendant in custody is not brought to trial within 40 days, the prosecution lapses and the defendant must be freed. Where committal for trial is involved, there is a similar custody time limit of 110 days between committal and the start of the trial. In rare cases having exceptional features, extensions of these time limits are available on application to the courts (s.101, Criminal Procedure (Scotland) Act 1975; Renton and Brown, 1972).

A timid and excessively cautious system of custody time limits has been introduced in most of England and Wales by s.22 of the Prosecution of Offences Act 1985 to combat the grave injustice of long remands in custody pending trial. There is no absolute time limit; generous provision is made for courts to extend the time limits specified in the regulations. There is no appeal against the extension of time limits. One or more extensions may be granted provided that the prosecution can show that there is good and sufficient cause for doing so and that the prosecution has acted with all due expedition. The legislation introduces two types of time limit: *custody time limits* and *overall time limits*.

A custody time limit restricts the period a defendant can be kept in custody:

pending the start of summary trial;

in cases of trial on indictment, between first appearance in court and committal for trial;

in cases of trial on indictment, between committal for trial and the start of the trial.

All periods in custody for the same offence are aggregated. Expiry of a custody time limit triggers automatic release on bail, though the case may proceed to trial provided that it remains within any overall time limit.

The clock can be stopped by conduct of the defendant. Escape from custody and failure to surrender to custody stop all time limits. Arrest for breach of a condition of bail stops custody time limits. The custody time limits set out in the regulations made under the section are 70 days (84 in Birmingham) between first appearance and summary trial or committal to the Crown Court for trial. But if the court determines within the first 56 days of detention that the defendant is to be tried summarily, the custody time limit becomes 56 days. The custody time limit following committal is 112 days. So, for example, the aggregate custody time limit for a defendant committed to the Crown Court on a charge of burglary is a generous 182 days (196 in Birmingham).

In *R* v. *Sheffield Magistrates Court, ex parte Turner* (New Law Journal, 30 November 1990, p. 1681) the Court of Appeal held that the custody time limits arising before and after committal are independent custody limits. Once a custody time limit has expired and the prosecution, for whatever reason, has failed to obtain an extension of time under the Act, magistrates have no power to grant an extension of time and bail must be granted. However, when the defendant is committed for trial, the committing magistrates have power to remand the defendant in custody pending trial even though he or she has earlier been released on bail on the expiry of the first custody time limit.

An overall time limit restricts the overall length of time, whether in custody or not:

pending the start of summary trial;

in cases of trial on indictment, between first appearance in court and committal for trial;

in cases of trial on indictment, between committal for trial and the start of the trial.

Expiry of an overall time limit results in the release of the defendant, who is to be treated for all purposes as having been acquitted of the offence. Regulations have yet to be made specifying overall time limits.

Advance Disclosure of the Prosecution Case

Under s.48 of the Criminal Law Act 1977 and The Magistrates' Courts (Advance Information) Rules 1985 (SI 1985 no. 601) a defendant charged with an either way offence is entitled on application to advance disclosure of the prosecution case. Those charged with either way offences are given a notice by the prosecution advising them of their entitlement under the section. Disclosure of the prosecution case takes the form either of copies of the written statements of witnesses whose evidence will be adduced against the defendant or of a summary of the facts and matters of which the prosecution proposes to adduce evidence in the proceedings. If the prosecutor believes that disclosure of the information might lead to the intimidation of a witness or to any other interference with the course of justice, the information may be withheld. A notice must then be served on the defendant to alert him or her to the withholding of information. Before enquiring into issues relevant to the determination of the appropriate mode of trial, the magistrates' court must satisfy itself that the defendant has had the benefit of advance disclosure of the prosecution case.

One contentious issue is the form of disclosure. The Home Secretary in 1986 indicated that all disclosures would take the form of copy statements rather than summaries when the Crown Prosecution Service took responsibility for advance disclosure. This has not yet happened, largely because of the burden it would impose on the CPS. It seems that summaries are the most common form of disclosure. Summaries are, of course, bound to contain some element of subjectivity and may disguise a weakness in the prosecution case. Everything will depend on the quality of the summary (Feeney, 1984; Feeney, 1985; Baldwin and Mulvaney, 1987a). One study has criticized some summaries as a 'misguided attempt by the compilers to construct a single reality where none exists' (Baldwin and Mulvaney, 1987b).

Proper advice to defendants and preparation of their cases would suggest that solicitors who failed to seek advance disclosure were acting negligently. Yet one survey showed that only around half the defence solicitors sought advance disclosure of the prosecution case, though the use of summaries rather than copy statements, a clear intention to plead guilty before the magistrates, or an intention to fight the case in the Crown Court where full disclosure would be made on committal, may account for these figures (Riley and Vennard, 1988). Despite these figures, the Home Office has complained that delays are being caused by the frequency with which defendants seek advance disclosure. The Law Society's criminal law committee has responded with guidance indicating that solicitors will meet their professional responsibilities to their clients if they do not seek advance disclosure where the defendant indicates an intention to plead guilty in the magistrates' court or to fight the case in the Crown Court (*Law Society's*

Gazette, 30 August 1989, p. 3). Many solicitors will properly continue to seek advance disclosure in all cases; advice given following study of information provided by advance disclosure must be better informed than that which is given without such information.

Determining which Court is to Try the Case

The Classification of Offences

The importance of the system of classification of offences for the purposes of determining the mode of trial in the relationship between the magistrates' courts and the Crown Court was referred to at the end of chapter 2. There are only three classes of offence for this purpose. First, there are offences triable only on indictment, which must be tried in the Crown Court. Such offences are all common law offences, such as murder and manslaughter, together with those offences created by statutes which provide for a penalty to be imposed only on indictment. Examples are robbery, and wounding with intent contrary to s.18 of the Offences against the Person Act 1861.

Secondly, there are offences triable only summarily, which can be tried only in the magistrates' courts. Such offences are those created by statutes which provide for a penalty to be imposed only on summary conviction. Thirdly, there are offences triable either way, which may be tried either in the magistrates' courts or in the Crown Court depending on their seriousness. Such offences are those listed in Sched. 1 to the Magistrates' Courts Act 1980, and those offences created by statutes which provide for a penalty to be imposed following conviction on indictment or summarily.

The choice of venue where an offence is triable either way is a matter for decision by the magistrates' court. It is for them to determine which mode of trial is more suitable having regard to all the circumstances of the case. Defendants always have a right to elect to be tried in the Crown Court, though they have no corresponding right to elect to be tried in the magistrates' courts. All they can do is to make representations and hope that the magistrates agree that trial in the lower court is appropriate.

The first task of magistrates is to determine the classification of the offence charged. This will be determined by looking at the statute creating the offence or at the Sched. 1 to the Magistrates' Courts Act 1980.

The Special Case of Criminal Damage

There is one offence which has a hybrid character. The offence of criminal damage contrary to s.1 of the Criminal Damage Act 1971 is triable either way, but in some circumstances it is treated as an offence triable only summarily. Where the value of the property damaged or destroyed is clearly less than £2000, the offence is triable only summarily. But if the value of the damage clearly exceeds £2000, the offence retains its character as an offence triable either way.

Where it is unclear whether the value of the damage is more or less than £2000, the defendant can choose how the offence is to be classified.

There are therefore only three possibilities and the magistrates do not enter into lengthy considerations of the value of the damage caused. They will hear representations, but will not take evidence (*R v. Canterbury Justices, ex parte Klisiak*, [1982] QB 398). First, the value of the damage involved is clearly less than £2000. The offence is triable only summarily and the restricted sentencing powers set out in s.22 of the Magistrates' Courts Act 1980 will apply. Secondly, the value of the damage clearly exceeds £2000. The offence is triable either way and the magistrates will proceed in exactly the same manner as for any such offence. Thirdly, it is unclear whether the value of the damage is more or less than £2000. In these cases, the defendant can choose whether the offence is treated as triable only summarily or as triable either way, and the offence must be so treated.

Where the defendant has caused damage to two objects in the same spate of violent activity, he or she has committed two offences, but the value of the damage for the purpose of classifying the offence is the aggregate of the damage caused.

Dealing with Either Way Offences

Where the offence is triable either way, the magistrates conduct an enquiry to decide which mode of trial is more suitable in the particular circumstances of the case before them. Sections 18–21 of the Magistrates' Courts Act 1980 lay down the procedure to be followed. In essence the magistrates' court has to decide whether it would be more appropriate to try the case summarily, and the defendant has to consent to the case being so tried. Before considering this issue the magistrates must satisfy themselves that the defendant knows of the right to advance disclosure of the prosecution case. If a request has been made to the prosecution which has not yet been complied with, the court must usually adjourn the hearing.

The magistrates' court then turns its attention to the issue of the mode of trial. The prosecution and the defendant, in that order, are given the opportunity to make representations as to the appropriate mode of trial. It is rare for magistrates to disagree with the representations made by the prosecutor; in a study carried out in 1986 the magistrates disagreed with the prosecutor's proposal that the case was suitable for trial summarily in only 23 out of 663 cases (Riley and Vennard, 1988). The preference expressed by the prosecutor is in no way binding on the court, unless the Attorney-General, Solicitor-General or DPP is prosecuting. In these cases the court is bound by an election that trial in the Crown Court is more suitable. These binding elections relate only to the decision to go to the higher court. Where no binding election is made, the magistrates must decide which court is more appropriate and the Act directs them to consider:

the nature of the case;
whether the circumstances make the offence one of a serious character;

whether the magistrates' sentencing powers are adequate having regard to the nature of the offence, and disregarding at this point the defendant's previous record;

any other circumstances relevant to determining the suitability of the offence for trial one way or the other, such as the complexity of issues of fact or law involved or the public importance of some issue raised by the case.

The court has a clear duty to consider the mode of trial and to decide which will be more suitable, though there is no requirement here to give reasons for the decision. In order to help magistrates decide whether or not to commit either way offences for trial in the Crown Court, the Divisional Court of the Queen's Bench Division issued national mode of trial guidelines on 26 October 1990 (*Practice Note (Mode of Trial: Guidelines)* [1990] 1 WLR 1439). These made a number of general and specific observations. Seven general points were made:

decisions should not be grounded on reasons of convenience or expedition;

the magistrates should assume for this purpose that the facts put forward by the prosecution are correct;

the defendant's antecedents and any mitigation are not relevant to the mode of trial decision;

the fact that the charges are specimen charges is relevant, but the fact that the defendant will be asking for other offences to be taken into consideration (see below) is not;

the presence of complex questions of law or difficult questions of fact should lead the magistrates to consider committal for trial;

jointly charged defendants should be kept together, so that if one of a group of defendants elects to be tried in the Crown Court, the magistrates should deal with all of them as examining justices;

in general, the presumption should be that summary trial is adequate unless one of the specific factors referred to in the guidelines is present *and* the magistrates feel their sentencing powers would be insufficient to deal with the defendant. For certain specified cases the presence of a specific factor alone would justify committal for trial without the need for the magistrates to consider their sentencing powers.

There follows guidance on a number of specific offences. These suggest, for example, that if the magistrates believe their sentencing powers will be inadequate in a case of burglary of a house during the daytime when the occupier is present, they should commit for trial. In criminal damage cases, specific factors which, coupled with the sentencing difficulty, would lead to committal for trial are deliberate fire-raising, offences committed by groups and damage of high value, which is defined as a figure equal to or exceeding twice the limit imposed on a magistrates court when making a compensation order (£2000 at the time of writing). However, a case of unlawful sexual intercourse with a girl over 13 but under 16 where there was a wide disparity in age should generally be tried on indictment.

If the magistrates think summary trial is more appropriate, they must tell the defendant so and also tell him of their power to commit him to the Crown Court for sentence if at the end of the case they decide that the more severe penalties available in the Crown Court should apply. The defendant is then asked whether he consents to summary trial. The defendant always has the right to elect to be tried in the Crown Court. Neither prosecution nor defendant can elect as of right to be tried in the magistrates' court. If the defendant consents, summary trial will follow there and then or at some later date. If the defendant does not, committal proceedings will follow there and then or at some later date.

If the magistrates decide that trial on indictment is more appropriate, they tell him of their decision which is conclusive. Committal proceedings will follow either immediately or at some later date.

Six out of every ten defendants tried in the Crown Court have exercised their right to be tried there; the remaining four in ten have been committed there at the discretion of the magistrates. Four in every ten of those committed by decision of the magistrates would have consented to summary trial (Riley and Vennard, 1988).

Electing Trial in the Crown Court

This rather technical account of determination of the mode of trial conceals the very important influence the mode of trial has on the way in which the defendant will be treated. The reasons defendants choose to exercise their right to be tried by judge and jury in the Crown Court reveal much about perceptions of the different processes. A very important aspect of trial in the magistrates' court that often accounts for a defendant not choosing trial in the Crown Court is that the sentencing powers of magistrates are restricted. Generally, magistrates cannot impose fines in excess of £2000 nor sentence to imprisonment for more than six months for a single offence or a total of more than twelve months for two or more offences.

Magistrates' courts deal with cases in bulk and so an element of 'routinization' inevitably exists in its processes. In the Crown Court, where trial is slower and consequently more expensive, a greater proportion of defendants contest cases. The Crown Court is a professional court dominated by lawyers, while the magistrates' courts are run by lay magistrates. There are significant differences in the number of defendants represented by lawyers: almost all defendants in the Crown Court are represented, whereas for offences triable either way in the magistrates' courts about six in every ten defendants are represented. There is also a widespread belief that trial in the Crown Court is a superior procedure (James Committee, 1975).

It is a truism to say that not every defendant views his or her involvement with the criminal courts in the same way. But research has identified four typical approaches to the process (Bottoms and McClean, 1976). There are the 'rights-assertive' defendants, who are likely to have considerable experience of the criminal process. They are fully aware of their rights and typically exercise all available rights and privileges. They are not as clever as the 'strategists' who again will normally have considerable experience of the criminal process and be aware of all the rights and privileges available to them. But they elect only to exercise those rights which might result in some advantage. A third group is the 'remorse-dominated' who readily acknowledge their guilt; they are typified by their wish to make expiation for their wrongdoing by co-operating fully with the criminal process which will bring them their *just deserts*. Finally, there is a group which comprises about one-third of all defendants: the 'passive'. These defendants take the easy option of letting the whole process happen around them. Such defendants plead guilty, do not opt for trial on indictment, do not apply for legal aid and do not seek any legal help. Some will be sent to prison. They will probably not understand much of what is happening to them.

It is against this categorization of defendants that most can perhaps be gleaned from the two surveys which have been carried out into the views of defendants as to choice of venue (Bottoms and McClean, 1976; Gregory, 1976). In looking at the reasons discovered in each of these surveys, care should be taken to remember that the choice of venue can never be isolated from other aspects of the process, of which perhaps the most important are bail, representation and intended plea.

The two surveys agree that the major reasons for not electing to be tried in the Crown Court are the avoidance of delay, the better chance of a lighter sentence from the magistrates and the view that the case is too trivial for the Crown Court. When views as to the reasons for electing trial on indictment are compared, the principal reasons differ under each survey. Bottoms and McClean's findings show a belief that trial on indictment is fairer, the following of solicitors' advice and a belief that there is a better chance of acquittal as the principal reasons. Gregory lists as principal factors the more thorough consideration of the case, the fact that the jury decides guilt or innocence, the following of solicitors' advice and a fear that magistrates' courts are biased in favour of the police. A more recent survey has broadly confirmed the findings of these surveys. Defendants who want to plead not guilty saw the Crown Court as offering a better prospect of acquittal and were not deterred by the longer waiting times or the chance of a heavier sentence if convicted (Riley and Vennard, 1988). The predominant factor determining whether a defendant elects to be tried in the Crown Court is intended plea.

Lurking behind all these reasons is the issue of routinization, which is the hallmark of justice in the magistrates' courts, compared with the slower more careful examination of cases that takes place in the Crown Court. But it is certain that without a speedy and relatively cheap forum for processing large numbers of minor offences, the criminal justice system would soon grind to a halt. At present the concern is that the need for speed has routinized magistrates' justice too much. There would seem to be some justification for the view that magistrates' courts work best when dealing with guilty pleas and do not offer an adequate system for dealing with contested cases. There is indeed some research to suggest that magistrates tend too readily to accept prosecution evidence, though the same research also suggested that most convictions in contested trials in magistrates' courts were in accord with the weight of the evidence. One explanation for the ready acceptance of prosecution evidence may well be the reluctance of defence lawyers to challenge it sufficiently forcefully, for when prosecution evidence is challenged it seems that there is a far better chance of acquittal (Vennard, 1982).

Committal for Trial

When dealing with cases to be tried in the Crown Court, the magistrates must examine the case against the defendant to determine whether there is sufficient evidence to put before a jury in the Crown Court. This process is known as *committal for trial*. The purpose of committal proceedings is to act as a filter to ensure that only those against whom there is reasonable evidence are sent for trial. They also ensure that defendants know the case against them and enable an indictment to be drawn up. An indictment is the formal charge against defendants where they are to be tried in the Crown Court. It replaces any earlier charge against the defendant and will be drawn up only after committal.

There are basically two types of committal proceedings. The first is known as 'full committal' and is full consideration of the prosecution case. The prosecution evidence is given in full, though some written statements may be accepted by the defence and these are simply read out. Prosecution witnesses are cross-examined on behalf of the defendant. Though this may look like a trial, it is not. It is only a testing of the prosecution case to determine whether the case should be sent for trial. No defence need be put to the magistrates, though a strong defence case should be put where it may serve to convince the magistrates that the prosecution evidence is too weak to send the case for trial.

'Full committals' are lengthy exercises and are not always necessary. Today they are rare, accounting for no more than two per cent of all committals (Philips Commission, 1981). The defendant may well accept that there is a case to be put to the jury, or indeed may be intending to plead guilty to an offence that is triable only on indictment. To save time in such cases 'paper committals' under s.6(2) of the Magistrates' Courts Act 1980 are used. Written statements of all prosecution witnesses are sent to the defence solicitors who must read them carefully to satisfy themselves that there is enough evidence to put before a jury. If so satisfied, there will be a very brief hearing at which the written statements are submitted to the court and at which the defendant is formally committed to the Crown Court. Where the defence rests on an alibi, notice of that defence must be given to the prosecution at committal proceedings or within seven days of committal. This is to enable the prosecution to check it out. At the end of the proceedings, the magistrates must either commit the defendant to the Crown Court for trial or discharge him or her. This is not, of course, the same as an acquittal.

The main safeguards against abuse of the paper committal procedure are that both sides must agree to the use of the procedure and that the defendant must be represented, though under s.61 of the Criminal Justice Act 1982 the solicitor need not be present in court at the committal. But the ultimate safeguard is the careful consideration of the statements by the defendant's solicitor or counsel. The whole procedure becomes a farce if the defence fails to consider in detail the prosecution case. In recent years there have been suggestions that the safeguards are not working well. Late delivery of statements or delivery of additional statements at the eleventh hour also seem common (Philips Commission, 1981). A pilot study carried out by Baldwin and McConville in the early 1970s showed that in a majority of cases dealt with by 25 Coventry solicitors there was inadequate examination of the evidence prior to a paper committal. Clearly there is severe injustice to a defendant who may have spent three months or more in prison awaiting trial if the prosecution case collapses because it is too weak to sustain a verdict of guilty.

The Philips Commission made some controversial recommendations concerning committal proceedings, which have not been implemented. The Philips Commission recommended that there should be a procedure of application for discharge to replace committal proceedings, which they felt to be unnecessary. Defendants who, on receipt of the prosecution evidence, felt that there was insufficient evidence against them to justify a trial in the Crown Court would be able to apply to the magistrates for a discharge on the basis that there was no case to answer. If successful the defendant would be discharged. The procedure was criticized as requiring action by defendants to consider the case against them.

There are currently proposals from the Home Office and Lord Chancellor's Department which would abolish committal proceeds and affect the way courts dealt with either way cases. The favoured option put forward in a joint consultation paper (Home Office, 1989) would involve the prosecution serving a notice on the defendant of its intention to proceed to trial within a stated period and indicating whether it proposed to proceed in the magistrates' court or in the Crown Court. Defendants would receive advance disclosure of the prosecution case at this stage. Where the prosecution proposed to proceed in the magistrates' court, the defendant would still be able to elect to be tried in the Crown Court. Whatever mode of trial is specified in the prosecution notice, it would be open to the defendant to serve a counter-notice challenging the sufficiency of the prosecution evidence. There would then be a hearing in the magistrates' court to consider the sufficiency of the evidence. Such hearings would be based on written statements and oral submission would be allowed only with the leave of the court. The consultation paper recognizes the difficulties that would be faced where the defendant is unrepresented and seems to have no solution to the problem. The best that is offered is the requirement that in all such cases the magistrates should always consider the sufficiency of the prosecution evidence before committal for trial.

Committal proceedings have already been abolished in serious fraud cases handled by the Serious Fraud Office established under the Criminal Justice Act 1987. In such cases the matter is placed in the Crown Court's jurisdiction by the service of a notice by the Director of the Office transferring the case to the Crown Court.

Trial

Attendance

In general, appearance by the defendant in person will be necessary, but there are important exceptions. For example, few of those charged with minor motoring offences appear in person; many choose to plead guilty by post to the written statement of facts served with the summons, and will send to the court a written statement of any mitigating circumstances. This procedure can be used for any summary offence which does not carry the possibility of more than three months' imprisonment. It is the prosecutor who decides whether or not to use it. It is most frequently used for minor motoring offences and for trivial offences like failure to have a television licence. A person represented by a solicitor or barrister need not be present in court, though they usually will be present and will inevitably need to be present in defended cases. Finally, there are special rules for companies who may appear through a solicitor, though if the case is to be contested, there will need to be company witnesses present. But there is no requirement that a director be present.

Whenever the charge is for an offence triable only summarily, the magistrates can proceed in the absence of the defendant or his representative. But there are safeguards. In such cases, the prosecution must prove both that the defendant has been served with the summons and that the defendant committed the offence charged. The case proceeds in much the same way as if the defendant had pleaded not guilty (see below), but, obviously, there will be no case for the defence put to the court.

The Guilty Plea

The procedure will be determined by the plea. The charge is read out to the defendant who is asked how he or she pleads. Where the defendant pleads guilty, the representative of the Crown Prosecution Service outlines the facts of the case, and will give details of any previous convictions. At this point the defendant can ask for any other offences to be 'taken into consideration' in assessing sentence. These are offences the defendant has committed but for which he or she has not been tried. The prosecution usually raises no objection to such a request. Sentence is limited to the maximum for the offence for which the defendant has been tried. Although not technically convicted of offences taken into consideration, no prosecution for such offences will ever take place. The advantage for defendants is that they can put all previous wrongdoing behind them safe in the knowledge that it will not return to haunt them in the form of later prosecution.

The defendant is then given an opportunity to make a plea in mitigation, which is his explanation of any circumstances surrounding the offence which explain how it came to be committed and provide some excuse for its commission. Only mitigating factors relating to the offence should be included, but the court should also have attention drawn to the defendant's conduct after the offence which indicates contrition and any factor in the defendant's personal life that suggests the appropriateness of a lenient penalty. Mitigation is not usually backed up by formal evidence. But, occasionally, to add weight to the plea, defendants will go into the witness box and explain matters on oath. They may then be cross-examined by the prosecution. Pleas in mitigation are often no more than ritual incantations of contrition delivered on behalf of the defendant by his or her solicitor. The magistrates then determine what penalty is to be imposed.

The Not Guilty Plea

When the defendant pleads not guilty, the prosecution must prove its case and the burden of proof is proof beyond all reasonable doubt. The prosecution may make an opening speech before calling witnesses who after answering the prosecutor's questions are cross-examined by the defendant or his or her lawyer. The prosecutor may re-examine to clarify any points raised in cross-examination. The purpose of re-examination is to defuse the effect of cross-examination. At the conclusion of the prosecution case, it is time for the defence case to be put. There is no obligation on the defence to put forward any case at all since the prosecution has the burden of proof. If the defendant's solicitor does not feel that the prosecution has made a case against the defendant, he or she can make a submission of no case to answer. If this is rejected, he or she can still go on to put the defence case, which may well swing matters in the defendant's favour. Often it will be the defendant's explanation which defeats the prosecution case.

Once defence witnesses have given evidence, been cross-examined and re-examined, the defence solicitor may make a closing speech if he or she has not made an opening speech or if the magistrates have agreed to let each side speak twice. Normally only one speech is permitted. At this stage, the magistrates determine guilt or innocence.

Surprisingly, a defendant who is found not guilty is not automatically entitled to costs from the prosecution. It is a matter for the discretion of the magistrates' court under s.16 of the Prosecution of Offences Act 1985. Even if an award is made, it may be for a lesser sum than the full amount of the defendant's costs. A number of commentators have suggested that the magistrates would continue to be guided by an earlier *Practice Note* ([1982] 1 WLR 1447); that guidance indicated that orders might well not be made if the defendant's conduct had brought suspicion on himself or if he had been acquitted on a technicality. This *Practice Note* has been replaced by a detailed *Practice Direction* of 26 May 1989 (*New Law Journal*, [1989] 1 WLR 625), but the terms of this apply to the Crown Court and above. It may be that the magistrates' court will follow these guidelines where they are relevant to them. The new *Practice Direction* repeats the guidance on when an order ought not to be made set out in the earlier document.

If the finding is one of guilty, the prosecutor puts any previous convictions before the magistrates and the defendant is permitted to make a plea in mitigation before the decision on sentence is taken.

The Adversarial System

Once again this technical description of the procedure disguises the realities of the processes in the magistrates' courts. Fewer than two in ten defendants before magistrates' courts contest their guilt, whereas in the Crown Court about one in three contest the issue of guilt. In both courts such information as can be gleaned from the official statistics suggests that about half of those contesting the cases will win. It is undoubtedly true that the criminal justice system encourages guilty pleas; some would argue that there is pressure to plead guilty. This encouragement takes a variety of forms. The principal encouragement is that the system co-operates with those who plead guilty. A plea of guilty will be rewarded by an early disposal of the case and it is accepted that it is legitimate to apply a sentencing discount to the defendant pleading guilty. The 'discount' may be as much as 30 per cent (Thomas, 1978; Moxon, 1988). The reasoning is that the guilty plea is a sign of contrition and this justifies a lighter sentence than in the case of a defendant who unsuccessfully fights the case and who, by inference, has wasted the court's valuable time.

In many cases defendants will have received advice from the police, family, friends and even lawyers, that a plea of guilty will get the matter over with speedily and with the minimum of publicity (King, 1981). In more serious cases there may even be suggestions by the police that an indication of a guilty plea will smooth the way to release on bail. The availability of legal aid may also influence the decision to plead guilty. Finally the widely held view that magistrates' courts will believe the police anyway can lead to the feeling that there is little point in fighting the case in the face of an inevitable conviction.

Two studies (Davies, 1970; Dell, 1971) have even shown that some defendants plead guilty even though they firmly assert their innocence. Some receive prison sentences as a result of their pleas. Though proportionately a small number, the numbers cannot be dismissed as insignificant and must raise questions about the necessity for safeguards to minimize such occurrences. While it is a very serious matter when a person who claims to be innocent pleads guilty to an offence which might result in a prison sentence, the problem also exists for minor matters including motoring offences. Anecdotal accounts by practitioners indicate that a significant number of those charged choose to plead guilty and get the matter over with quickly rather than fight the case even though there is an arguable defence. Having regard to the poor chance of obtaining legal aid for such cases and the risk of having to pay the prosecution costs in addition to a heavier fine and own legal costs if the case is lost, many practitioners are reluctant to press defendants too hard concerning a guilty plea where there might be an arguable defence.

For the minority of defendants who contest their guilt in the magistrates' court, the adversarial system is supposed to provide the most effective means of discovering the truth in what is often an argument about fact rather than law. But unless defendants are represented, they will be at a disadvantage. They are unlikely to be skilled in the advocacy techniques that are essential to the establishing of their case. It has also been argued that the adversarial system, far from being the best vehicle for establishing the truth, is inherently unreliable, since the 'suggestive' questions put in cross-examination to attack the credibility of the evidence cloud rather than clarify the issues. The amount of evidence increases, but its clarity decreases (Greer, 1971). Research has also shown that recollections of an incident will vary considerably among witnesses who will honestly but inaccurately recall what they have witnessed. Physical features such as lighting, distance and duration of the incident witnessed may lead to differing perceptions of the same incident. Add psychological factors such as emotion, interest, expectation and individual prejudice and further distortion takes place (Greer, 1971). Indeed some steps have been taken to prevent errors in identification evidence, once considered the surest indicator of guilt.

The anxiety of being subjected to the attack on one's credibility that is implicit in cross-examination leads many who have appeared as witnesses to describe the experience as an ordeal. When the scales are loaded, it seems that the prosecutor has an unfair advantage. Part of police training concerns the presentation of evidence and police witnesses are allowed to refresh their memories from their note books, which are supposed to be contemporaneous accounts of incidents, though the practice of collusive preparation of note book accounts of incidents is widely accepted. Police officers also gain experience by repeating the task of giving evidence. A research study into prosecution evidence in contested cases in magistrates' courts (Vennard, 1980) showed that there was direct evidence, often in the form of witnesses to the crime, in three-quarters of the 394 cases in the sample. In these cases conviction is highly likely. But in about 30 per cent of the cases there were admissions varying from a full written confession to 'verbals', like the alleged statement to the police, 'It's a fair cop, Guv.' In a significant number of these cases, there was an attempt to have the statements excluded as 'involuntary', that is, given in the face of unreasonable pressure from the police and so making them unreliable, or, in the case of 'verbals', as not having been made at all. It seems that magistrates are reluctant to exclude such evidence and the research study suggests that existing safeguards may not be adequate for the verification of incriminating statements.

Further research suggests that magistrates have a tendency to assume police reliability in giving evidence and are ignorant of the increasing body of evidence suggesting the fallibility of eyewitness accounts. Some of this empirical research shows that the police are likely to be susceptible to the misinterpretation of certain conduct and are more likely than civilians to be prone to errors of recall after a period of time. All this tends to suggest a willingness to convict and a reluctance to require as clear a discharge of the burden of proof as juries seem to require. But the same research also suggests that, broadly speaking, convictions following contested trials in the magistrates' courts follow the weight of the evidence. (Vennard, 1982).

Defendants will be unfamiliar with the processes; they may not be represented; they may have been advised that they are foolish to try to fight the case. Ultimately it is easy to see why some argue that the process systematically disadvantages them. Some social scientists have even suggested that trial before the magistrates, far from being the impartial weighing of each side's case and of information about the defendant, is no more than an elaborate 'game' in which those regularly participating in the game (police, lawyers, magistrates, probation officers and court officials) know the rules while the defendant stands as a 'dummy player' absorbing the gains and losses of the regular players (Carlen, 1976). Other commentators draw attention to the penitence ritual aspects of the process, which are so much to the forefront that magistrates' courts deal badly with the contested case which is a manifestation of no penitence at all (Bankowski and Mungham, 1976; King, 1976).

Ultimately the problem is one of being able to develop processes which achieve a perfect balance between the need to process minor offences speedily, cheaply and uniformly and the need to identify offences of violence and dishonesty of sufficient seriousness to warrant the slow careful consideration necessary to ensure the conviction of the guilty and the acquittal of the innocent. Fixed penalties for parking offences and minor motoring offences are an example of acceptable routinization. There have also been proposals to create separate traffic courts to deal with most motoring offences. These changes would relieve pressure on court time and allow a more measured treatment of more serious matters. But time alone may not be enough and there is a case for a more radical reorganization of processes for dealing with criminal offences.

Sentencing

General Principles

The last stage of the process in the magistrates' court will be the sentencing of the convicted offender. This process is quite separate from that of trial. Generally, the law does not prescribe fixed penalties for each offence, but offers a wide range of choices up to a maximum specified in the statute creating the offence. The most common exception is the offence of murder which carries a mandatory sentence of life imprisonment. Despite the range of choices available, for many minor offences there is a well understood tariff of fines applied by magistrates: this is a further example of routinization. These guidelines are prepared by the Magistrates' Association and approved by the Lord Chancellor and the Lord Chief Justice. But for the more serious offences, the full panoply of sentencing powers becomes relevant. Magistrates get less guidance than judges in the Crown Court, because their decisions are not subject to appeal to the Court of Appeal, but to locally based Crown Courts. Sentencing guidelines handed down by the Court of Appeal seldom have particular relevance for the day-to-day sentencing issues faced by magistrates. One of the best guides is the digest of recent sentences included in the journal *Justice of the Peace*, which is widely read by magistrates.

Sentencing has a veritable pot-pourri of objectives, not all of which are mutually consistent. There are four principal aims of sentencing. First, there is *retribution*, rooted in the Old Testament notion of 'an eye for an eye'; the more serious the offence is considered, the more severe will be the penalty. Secondly, there is *deterrence*. This is aimed at deterring the particular offender from committing further offences as well as setting a deterrent example to others. Whereas retribution looks back at the offence committed, deterrence looks forward to the likelihood of further offences being committed. Thirdly, there is *rehabilitation*, which involves the ideal of curing defendants of their criminal tendencies. Finally, there is *restitution*. This involves the provision of some compensation either to the victim or to society generally for the wrong done.

Restitution is the principal justification for restitution orders in theft cases, whereby the defendant must restore stolen goods to the owner, and compensation orders whereby a magistrates' court can order a defendant to pay up to £2000 (there is no limit in the Crown Court) to the victim of the crime who has suffered loss or injury as a result of the crime. There is research showing that courts do not use compensation orders as often as they might (Shapland et al., 1985). Courts must now give reasons where they do not make a compensation order (s.35(1), Powers of Criminal Courts Act 1973). Home Office Circular 85/1988 gives detailed guidelines on compensation in the criminal courts, including tariff awards in cases of personal injury. The principle of restitution can also be seen in the community service order, whereby a defendant is ordered to perform between 40 and 240 hours of specific unpaid work of benefit to the community.

Where magistrates feel that a social enquiry report telling them in detail about the offender would be helpful, they can have the assistance of such reports prepared by the probation service. But such reports are not mandatory in magistrates' courts, even where custodial sentences are in contemplation.

A few years ago the aim which stood foremost in many sentencers' minds was rehabilitation, but research has shown that sentences determined as a means of treatment for criminality did not succeed. The approach now stands largely discredited. At the same time a principal concern about the sentencing practices of magistrates (and also of the Crown Court) has been the wide regional variations in sentences, both in the use of fines, of imprisonment and of probation (Tarling, 1979) though a study of choices made by magistrates between certain types of sentence for offences triable either way revealed a fairly consistent pattern of sentencing (Softley, 1980a). Variations have also been shown in studies of sentences imposed in motoring cases. These were attributed to the generation of local traditions in particular magistrates' courts, labelled the 'bench effect' (Hood, 1972). While it is clearly wrong that there should be significant regional variations, too broad an extension of the tariff system subjects this part of the legal process to a routine that denies any attempt to tailor the punishment to the circumstances of the particular offender and his crime. It is probably open to the criticism of excessive rigidity. One answer may be wider adoption of sentencing guidelines, which have a flexibility missing in a strict tariff system.

Without becoming too diverted into discussions of sentencing reform, one development in the United States, which is reflected in the debate on sentencing in this country, is worthy of comment. Reaction to the failure of rehabilitation as the principal objective of sentencing and concern over disparities in sentences has led to an emphasis on retribution and the determination of sentences by reference to the criminal act rather than by reference to the likely impact of a particular sentence on the offender's future conduct. It has been labelled 'the just deserts' approach; offenders must expect a sentence of a certain severity related to the seriousness of the crime (Ashworth, 1989). This approach has been backed in the United States by sentencing guidelines, a development the United Kingdom's Advisory Council on the Penal System concluded 'should continue to be watched'. The guidelines have been described as 'summaries of the experience of all members of the bench in the particular court system and provide for the basic minimum of information necessary to indicate the usual penalty which was awarded in similar cases' (Wilkins, 1980). The guidelines permit the seriousness of the offence to be correlated with the profile of the offender in terms of prior record and other personal characteristics to produce a presumptive sentence, which may well be expressed as, say, 12 months imprisonment plus or minus three months. A sentencer wishing to depart from these guidelines is required to give reasons. If collective practice shows an overall deviation from the guidelines, the guidelines would be amended to reflect actual practice. The approach seeks to compromise between rigidly inflexible fixed sentences and too broad a discretion as to choice of sentence which produces inexplicable disparities (Wilkins, 1980; Galligan, 1981). Of course, there may be a place for fixed penalties for some offences; the move to make greater use of such penalties in 'routine' motoring cases has already been referred to as a means of saving time in the magistrates' courts.

Committal for Sentence

There will be some cases where the magistrates discover that their restricted sentencing powers are inadequate to deal with the defendant. There are two classes of case where the magistrates may conclude their deliberations on sentence by deciding that the defendant should be sent to the Crown Court for sentence. The first class of cases are those where the magistrates consider the appropriate sentence on conviction for an offence triable either way to be greater than that they can impose. There are three types of such case. First, the magistrates may commit for sentence where they decide that their sentencing powers are inadequate as a result of hearing about the defendant's previous convictions, character and antecedents (school and employment record and background). Second, they may commit an offender between 15 and 20 years of age with a recommendation for a youth custody sentence (formerly Borstal Training). And third, they may commit where they believe a hospital order with an order restricting the circumstances in which the defendant should be released is the appropriate method of dealing with the defendant.

The second class of cases covers situations where the defendant needs to be dealt with further by the Crown Court for earlier offences. This will arise where the magistrates convict a defendant who is subject to a conditional discharge or a probation order imposed by the Crown Court or where the defendant is convicted by the magistrates of an offence during a period of suspension of a sentence imposed by the Crown Court.

6

The Defendant in the Crown Court

The Features of Trial on Indictment

A Professional Court

The Crown Court is the forum for the trial of serious criminal cases. It is a professional court and its processes are generally regarded as a model of due process. The defendant is almost always represented by solicitor and counsel, and the judge is a professional judge. But the central feature of trial in the Crown Court remains the lay element: the jury. It is the jury who determine the guilt or innocence of the accused. The jury hear the evidence of witnesses which is subjected to cross-examination to test its credibility, and listen to prosecution and defence counsel's submissions and to the judge's summing up. The members of the jury then retire and deliberate in strict secrecy. They return to open court in due course to announce their verdict. They do not explain how they arrived at their decision, and attempts by judges to elicit reasons for a particular verdict have met with sharp rebukes from the Court of Appeal. If the verdict is an acquittal, it cannot be overturned. Even a conviction carries a degree of finality to it. The process of appeals following trial on indictment does not readily allow a jury's decision to be impugned. It is very difficult to adduce fresh evidence on appeal and the ordering of a retrial is a rare event. Most successful appeals are based on some error in the judge's summing up or upon the existence of some irregularity in the course of the trial, which will again be the judge's responsibility.

The Voluntary Bill of Indictment

Almost all defendants tried in the Crown Court will have been committed for trial by magistrates sitting as examining justices. But there are two alternative routes to the Crown Court. Those charged with serious fraud offences will be placed within the Crown Court's jurisdiction by transfer direction issued by the Director of the Serious Fraud Office. There is also a comparatively rarely used procedure, known as the *voluntary bill of indictment*, which may be used as an alternative to committal or after a refusal by magistrates to commit for trial. The Lord Chief Justice has directed that the procedure should only be used where good reasons for departing from the normal procedure of committal for trial can be shown and only where the interests of justice, rather than considerations of administrative convenience, require it (*Practice Direction: Voluntary Bills*, [1990] 1 WLR 1633). Under this procedure, the written statements of evidence for the prosecution are submitted to a High Court judge, who considers the papers and decides whether or not to permit an indictment to be drawn up on such evidence. The defendant has no opportunity to make representations or to challenge the evidence, though in the *Practice Direction* referred to above the Lord Chief Justice directed that, in exceptional circumstances, the judge may invite written submission on behalf of any defendant affected if, in his judgment, the interests of justice so require. The procedure has been criticized as a method of bypassing the protection to the defendant of committal proceedings. The defendant certainly loses the advantage of knowing the case against him or her. There is a risk of abuse of the procedure, but it is used most often to cure some formal defect; for example, it will avoid delay where there is a technical defect in the indictment, or will enable a defendant to be added to a trial or a charge to be added to the indictment. More contentious is the use of the procedure following a refusal of magistrates to commit for trial. There have also been cases where the voluntary bill procedure has been used to avoid a long and expensive committal, usually in cases with political overtones (Lewis, 1981). Such cases are, of course, likely to be particularly sensitive, and it is difficult to counter the charge that the voluntary bill procedure is used to deny defendants the essential safeguard of careful consideration of the prosecution evidence by lay magistrates at committal proceedings.

The Indictment

Trial in the Crown Court is called trial on indictment because on committal, a formal document called an *indictment* is prepared. This replaces the original charge or charges and the defendant is tried on the basis of the accusations made in the indictment. The indictment should be drawn up and preferred within 28 days of committal unless a judge grants an extension. The time-limit is directory and not mandatory; failure to comply with it will not be a ground for seeking to have any conviction based on it quashed (*R v. Sheerin*, [1977] 64 Cr App R 68; *R v. Soffee*, [1982] 75 Cr App R 133). Preferring the indictment merely involves delivery to, and signature by, an officer of the Crown Court. Indictments are prepared by officers of the CPS, or in complex cases by counsel, on the basis of the committal documents. Indictments may contain accusations of more than one offence; each separate offence is called a 'count' on the indictment and is recited in a separate paragraph. Indictments must contain three parts: the commencement, the statement of offence and the particulars of the offence. An example of a simple single count indictment is shown in figure 5.

THE CENTRAL CRIMINAL COURT
THE QUEEN -v- ABEL BAKER

ABEL BAKER is charged as follows:

Statement of Offence

Theft, contrary to section 1 of the Theft Act 1968

Particulars of Offence

Abel Baker, on the third day of March, 1990, in the City of London stole £500 in money, the property of Sterling Limited

---

Figure 5   Sample Indictment

Distributing Work among Crown Court Centres

There is a national network of Crown Court trial centres. Distributing work among them is based on the principle that the more senior and experienced judges try the more serious cases. The distribution of the business of the Crown Court to ensure that time spent awaiting trial is kept to a minimum is an important aspect of the criminal process. The organization of the Crown Court into tiers helps. There are three tiers and the tier of the court indicates its importance as a trial centre. First-tier centres, like all Crown Court centres, are staffed by Circuit judges, and are regularly visited by High Court judges. They will be the centres most likely to deal with very serious cases. Second-tier centres will be visited less often by High Court judges. Consequently there will be fewer very serious cases tried at second-tier centres. Third-tier centres will only rarely be visited by High Court judges; the mundane work of the Crown Court goes on at such centres. Magistrates commit defendants to the most convenient appropriate trial centre, having regard to the classification of offences for this purpose.

There is a *Practice Direction* ([1987] 1 WLR 1671) which classifies offences into four categories for the purpose of allocation both among Crown Court centres and among the judiciary of the Crown Court:

Class 1 offences (examples: murder and treason) must be tried by a High
  Court judge.
Class 2 offences (examples: manslaughter and rape) must normally be tried by
  a High Court judge unless the High Court judge presiding over the circuit
  assigns the case to a Circuit judge or Recorder. Rape cases may only be
  released for trial before a judge approved by the Lord Chief Justice to try
  such offences.

Class 3 offences (examples: arson and robbery) may be tried by either a High
   Court judge, Circuit judge, or Recorder.
Class 4 offences (example: burglary) will normally be tried by a Circuit judge
   or Recorder.

The system appears to work well in ensuring that the most experienced judges
hear the most serious and most complex cases.

Legal Representation in the Crown Court

Legal Aid

The process of applying for criminal legal aid was explained in the last chapter.
Virtually all defendants in the Crown Court are represented under the criminal
legal aid scheme. This involves representation by a solicitor and barrister. It is
an essential element of the legal aid schemes that assisted persons have a free
choice of solicitor. Once the solicitor has been chosen, it will normally be the solicitor who chooses the barrister who will act in the case. Most barristers do both
prosecution and defence work in their careers. For the most serious cases a legal
aid order will pay for the services of two barristers, a senior barrister, known
as a 'silk' or Queen's Counsel, assisted by another barrister, known as a 'junior',
who may, despite the appellation, be a very experienced barrister. A barrister
receiving instructions (known as a 'brief') from solicitors is required to accept the
instructions at a proper professional fee unless the barrister is already engaged
in another case on the day of trial or there are other 'special circumstances' which
justify a refusal of a particular brief. This is known as the 'cab-rank' rule. It
ensures that representation is readily available for all defendants, especially those
charged with crimes to which considerable notoriety attaches. The limited
freedom to refuse instructions protects members of the Bar from general unpopularity because they have, for example, defended those charged with offences
arousing a general sense of revulsion. But in practice it is not difficult for a
barrister to decline to act in a case. The fee for any brief will be determined either
by negotiation with the barrister's clerk, or in the case of a defendant with
criminal legal aid in accordance with the legal aid regulations.

Duties to the Court

Solicitors and barristers are officers of the court and consequently owe duties to
the court as well as to their clients. The lawyer's duty not to mislead the court
places the advocate in very real difficulties where a defendant admits his or her
guilt but nevertheless still wishes to enter a plea of not guilty. Provided that the
lawyer is not called upon to do more than test the prosecution evidence, the
lawyer may continue to act. But the lawyer cannot put any question to a prosecution witness suggesting that the defendant did not commit the acts which
amounted to the criminal conduct, nor can the lawyer call any evidence for the

defence which suggest that the defendant did not commit the offence. If the defendant requires any such action to be taken, the lawyer must refuse those instructions and cease to act for the defendant.

The situation is different where the lawyer does not know the defendant to be guilty, but believes that he or she is. So long as the lawyer does not know that the defendant is guilty, it does not matter that the lawyer may believe him to be guilty. For this reason articled clerks and pupil barristers are trained never to ask the direct question to the defendant, 'Are you guilty?' Provided that guilt has not been admitted, the lawyer is supposed to set aside all personal impressions and to act in the best interests of the client.

The role of prosecuting counsel is not, as is sometimes supposed, to secure a conviction at all costs. The duty to the court requires prosecuting counsel to prosecute fairly (Farquharson, 1986). This means that prosecuting counsel must be ready to acknowledge any weaknesses in the prosecution case and must not seek to hide evidence tending to contradict that put to the court. Indeed prosecuting counsel should disclose to defence counsel evidence known to the prosecution which might be helpful to the defence. Whether it will be depends entirely upon the discretion of counsel, always, of course, assuming that the evidence in question has been included in the instructions. There have been well documented cases in which such evidence has not been disclosed where miscarriages of justice have resulted (Fisher Inquiry, 1977).

The Dangers of Annoying the Judge

The concerns which have been expressed about the system of representation often centre on the increased expense of having a solicitor do the paperwork preparation of the case while the barrister does the advising and advocacy. It may also be very late in the case that the defendant meets the barrister for the first time. It is not uncommon for this to be on the first day of the trial itself. These are issues concerning the organization of the profession which are not restricted to criminal cases. They are discussed later in this book. One other issue which is mentioned below in the consideration of plea bargaining is the possibility of divided loyalties for barristers, and to some extent solicitors. Because the higher judiciary has been chosen from among the ranks of barristers and because judges pass on comments about particular barristers to the Lord Chancellor who refers to this information when judicial vacancies occur, ambitious barristers may have too much of an eye to ensuring a good record with the Lord Chancellor. This may sometimes conflict with the need to present a defendant's case with all the vigour it requires, particularly when the line of defence is one known to be unpopular with the judge in a case. A barrister may wish to avoid getting a reputation for 'throwing mud at the police' or of clashing too frequently with trial judges. It is also said among barristers that for those with an ambition to become a judge it is wise to do a balance of prosecution and defence work. It is axiomatic that those with a reputation for hostility towards the police are unlikely to be briefed by Crown Prosecution Service. All this may tend to inhibit the barrister and result in too great a deference to the smooth functioning of the system at the expense of the interests of the defendant. The collegiate atmosphere at the Bar, and its relatively small size, encourage conformity and the perpetuation of particular practices (Hazell, 1978 esp. ch.6).

Plea Bargaining

An Essential Component of the Administration of Justice?

Pressures on defendants to plead guilty do not disappear in the Crown Court. The criminal judicial statistics show that seven out of ten defendants in the Crown Court plead guilty. There is no doubt that the majority of these pleas are properly entered by defendants who have been carefully advised by their lawyers but have no defence to the charges made against them. But some of the pleas will have been entered with some reluctance, and in some cases the pressure to plead guilty will have been the result of what is known as plea bargaining. That some of these pleas are regretted is evidenced by the number of appeals to the Court of Appeal seeking to have the convictions based on them quashed on the basis that the plea was not voluntary. The defendant may have resisted considerable pressures in deciding to go to the Crown Court for trial, and yet as a result of this process finally joins the many who plead guilty. As we shall see, there are positive and negative aspects to the process. Pioneering, and controversial, research by Baldwin and McConville of the Institute of Judicial Administration at Birmingham University is the main source of information about plea bargaining in England and Wales (Baldwin and McConville, 1977; Baldwin and McConville, 1979a).

The process of plea bargaining seems to have developed in the United States, and a word about its use there will help to understand plea bargaining in England. In the United States bargains between prosecution and defence have become an integral part of the criminal process. But two aspects of the American criminal justice system, which do not have counterparts in the English system, have encouraged its development. The first is the existence in many states of very severe mandatory penalties for specific offences. The second is the ability of prosecution counsel to recommend particular sentences. So defendants have much to gain by being able to bargain for either a guilty plea to a lesser offence which does not carry the harsh mandatory penalty, or for a recommendation from the prosecutor of a lenient sentence. The United States Supreme Court has endorsed and encouraged the process. In a decision which has been cited with approval on many subsequent occasions, Chief Justice Burger described the process as 'an essential component of the administration of justice', and went on to outline its benefits as follows:

> Disposition of charges after plea discussions is not only an essential part of the process but a highly desirable part for many reasons. It leads to prompt and largely final disposition of most criminal cases; it avoids much of the corrosive impact of enforced idleness during pre-trial confinement for those

who are denied release pending trial; it protects the public from those accused persons who are prone to continue criminal conduct even while on pre-trial release; and by shortening the time between charge and disposition, it enhances whatever may be the rehabilitative prospects of the guilty when they are ultimately imprisoned. (*Santobello* v. *New York*, [1971] 404 US 257, p. 261)

In *Roberts* v. *US* ([1980] 445 US 552), the Supreme Court explained that the process was approved because there was a relative equality of bargaining power between the prosecutor and defendant which prevented the process from being 'fundamentally unfair'. In the United States the vast majority of guilty pleas follow some negotiation or deal between prosecution and defence. The commonly obtained benefits are: sentence concessions, concurrent charging of multiple charges, the charging of a lesser offence, and the dropping of one or more charges altogether. The essence of the bargain is a guilty plea in exchange for some lessening of the sentence.

No Place in the English Criminal Process

The comments of the Supreme Court stand in marked contrast to judicial comments in England. In *R* v. *Atkinson* ([1978] 1 WLR 425) Lord Scarman said:

Plea-bargaining has no place in the English criminal law. It is found in some systems of law in which the prosecution are entitled to make submissions as to the character or length of sentence. In such systems of law it is possible for a bargain to be driven between the defence and the prosecution, but never, so far as my researches have gone, with the court itself. In our law the prosecution is not heard on sentence. That is a matter for the court, after considering what has to be said on behalf of an accused man. Our law having no room for any bargain about sentence between court and defendant, if events arise which give the appearance of such a bargain, then one must be very careful to see that the appearance is corrected.

Again in *R* v. *Wise* ([1979] RTR 57) Lord Widgery CJ said:

If the facts were successfully established and the plea bargain thereby sustained, it would be regarded as a very serious matter, and it would be open to question whether anyone who so blatantly indulged in plea bargaining could sit on the criminal law bench.

It would seem that the judicial denunciations of plea bargaining relate principally to bargaining involving the judge, particularly where the obvious conclusion to draw from the judge's comments is that he has presumed the guilt of the defendant. But bargains are struck in the English criminal justice system. It is clear that the ability of the prosecution to offer no evidence on certain counts on the indictment and to accept a plea of guilty to the lesser of alternative charges enables discussions about plea to take place between prosecution and defence that are really bargains. This ability to bargain is somewhat more fettered than in the United States, but few would deny that such practices are common aspects of the English criminal process. There is also the tacit bargain offered to all defendants in the form of the widely accepted and judicially approved sentencing discount with which a guilty plea will be rewarded (*see*, for example, *R* v. *de Haan*, [1968] 2 QB 108 and *R* v. *Cain*, [1976] Crim LR 464). Counsel who does not draw the attention of a client with a weak defence to this aspect of the sentencing process is not acting in the best interests of the client. On the other hand, it is virtually impossible for prosecution and defence counsel to bargain over specific sentences, because sentence is at the discretion of the court in all cases except murder, which carries a mandatory sentence of life imprisonment. Nor is it considered proper, as Lord Scarman noted in the quotation cited above, for prosecuting counsel to make recommendations about sentence.

More contentious are discussions involving the judge immediately prior to, or during the course of, the trial in which the matter of sentence is raised. The Court of Appeal has laid down strict guidelines governing such exchanges. The leading case is *R* v. *Turner* ([1970] 2 QB 321). Turner, a defendant with previous convictions, was on trial on a charge of theft. He had pleaded not guilty and the basis of his defence was an attack on the credibility of a police witness. During the course of the trial, his counsel advised him in strong terms to change his plea to one of guilty, indicating his view that a guilty plea would probably result in a non-custodial sentence, whereas if he persisted in his defence, he was likely to be sent to prison. Turner refused to change his plea. A little later counsel had a discussion with the judge in private. On his return, counsel repeated his advice, which was accepted. Turner changed his plea and was fined. Turner subsequently regretted his change of plea and appealed against his conviction, claiming that the change of plea was not voluntary, because he believed that counsel was expressing the views of the judge. The Court of Appeal allowed the appeal, treating the guilty plea as a nullity. A proper trial was ordered, known as *venire de novo*, to replace the trial regarded as a nullity because of the nullity of the plea. The Court of Appeal felt that in the circumstances, though counsel had not behaved in any way improperly, Turner had reasonable grounds for his belief that counsel had been expressing the views of the judge.

The Court went on to lay down guidelines on judicial involvement in discussions about a defendant's plea. Five points were made, between some of which there is an inherent tension:

1 Counsel must be free to advise a guilty plea and to indicate that this is likely to affect sentence. Counsel should always ensure that the defendant does not plead guilty unless he has committed the acts constituting the offence charged with the requisite intent.
2 The defendant must retain at all times complete freedom as to choice of plea.
3 There must be free access between counsel and the judge. As far as possible discussions between counsel and the judge should take place in open court.

But occasionally the need will arise for discussions in private where matters can be raised that it would be inappropriate to raise in open court. In such cases the discussion should be in the presence of both counsel and of the defendant's solicitor if he so wishes. Examples given in the judgment are discussions concerning a defendant with a terminal illness of which he had been kept in ignorance, and concerning the acceptability of a guilty plea to a lesser offence.

4 The judge must never indicate the type or length of sentence he has in mind unless he is able to indicate the form of sentence regardless of the defendant's plea.

5 Where any discussion has taken place in private, counsel must disclose the essence of the discussion to the accused.

The obvious purpose of the guidelines is to limit as far as possible any hint of pressure by the judge on a defendant to plead guilty, while preserving the ability of counsel to advise a defendant in strong terms to plead guilty where such advice seems appropriate. Nevertheless, since *Turner* there are still said to be occasions where bargaining involving the judge takes place. But, despite the covert nature of the process which makes establishing what actually transpired particularly difficult, there has been a steady flow of cases in which defendants have appealed against conviction on the grounds that unreasonable pressure has been placed upon them.

The Opportunities for Bargaining

The opportunities for bargaining are not difficult to find. At the pre-trial review, the judge learns from counsel of intended plea, number of witnesses, evidence agreed and the probable length of the trial (Philips Commission, 1981, Appendix 27). It is an informal process which has been described as in the nature of a supervised conference between the parties. Though counsel are trained to avoid plea bargaining at such reviews, there may well be discussions hinting at a deal if there is a guilty plea, and the opportunity clearly exists for more open bargains. The hinted bargain or unspoken understanding may be far more widespread than is commonly supposed (Baldwin and McConville, 1977; Baldwin and McConville, 1979a).

The results of empirical research into 121 cases tried in the Birmingham Crown Court where there was a late change of plea to one of guilty showed that only 35 defendants (28.9 per cent) could clearly be categorized as not involved in any deal or subjected to any pressure. The pleas of 22 defendants (18.2 per cent) were the direct result of an offer made and accepted by the defendant who gained some benefit from the deal. Of these cases, 13 fell within the *Turner* guidelines and nine outside them. A further 16 defendants (13.2 per cent) assumed that a bargain had been made, though no explicit bargain had. A very worrying figure is that some 48 defendants (39.7 per cent) claimed to have changed their pleas as a result of pressure from their own barristers even though unaccompanied by any offer. The Birmingham research indicated that some barristers involved in cases in their sample behaved improperly in acting oppressively in their advice to defendants to change their pleas. The advice went beyond advising defendants to weigh up the risks in an informed way and amounted to such pressure that the defendant could no longer be said to have a free choice of plea.

To check the strength of the case against the defendants in the sample, Baldwin and McConville had the committal papers assessed independently by a retired chief constable and a retired clerk to the justices. This assessment resulted in a prediction of acquittal in one of five of the cases. In these cases the disposition of the case on a guilty plea may not have been in accordance with the evidence. At best these assessments show that there may have been serious errors of judgement by counsel in some of the cases in the sample.

Evaluation

In evaluating the process of plea bargaining it is worth noting some of the factors which persuaded the United States Supreme Court to endorse the process. Key factors are the relative openness of the deal and the equality of bargaining power between prosecution and defence. The latter presumably refers to the existence of public sector lawyers acting for both prosecution and defence in many cases: District Attorney for the prosecution and public defender for the defence. But in the English system both safeguards are missing. The deal is done very much behind the scenes, and the nature of the deal is nowhere recorded. The open adjudication of criminal cases is replaced by 'nod and wink' understandings. Administrative convenience replaces due process. The issue of equality of bargaining is also very different. In the English criminal justice system barristers may be called upon to prosecute or defend. There is nothing corresponding to District Attorney and public defender, though there is now the Crown Prosecutions Service, and there are firms of private practitioners specializing in criminal defence work. There are also some barristers whose work is predominantly criminal prosecution or defence, but they lack the coherence and organization of the American counterparts.

The arrangements in England have led Baldwin and McConville to suggest that it is arguable that 'counsel's primary interests inevitably lie with the court system and not with the defendant'. This results in counsel quietly conspiring to ensure a smooth flow of cases in the Crown Court. Counsel may not want to get a reputation for being 'difficult'. At the end of the day appointment to the bench may depend on this co-operative attitude. The lack of openness also presents prosecutors with the temptation to 'over-charge' so that there will be something to bargain away for the guilty plea. The Birmingham research into this practice happily showed that there is no evidence of systematic over-charging of defendants.

It will be clear from all that has been said so far about our criminal justice system that it relies heavily on the guilty pleaders to avoid a colossal backlog of trials. The negotiated or bargained guilty plea clearly contributes to court efficiency. Where the guilty plea is the result of a pragmatic approach to the realities of the situation by all participants in the process, it has a useful purpose to serve. Equally it is easy to understand the sentencing discount for those pleading guilty. Its removal would undoubtedly be likely to encourage many more 'no-hopers' to contest their guilt. This leaves the key issue the presence of some notion of due process in plea discussions, and equality of bargaining position. The former could be achieved relatively easily by having a note placed on the record of any discussions between prosecuting and defence lawyers covering charges preferred or dropped, and by having the shorthand writer make a verbatim note of any exchanges taking place in judges' chambers (see *R* v. *Cullen* [1985] 81 Cr App R 17). If any complaint were subsequently made, there would be a record for the Court of Appeal to examine. This is now required practice, though it is not always followed: *R* v. *Smith (Terence)* ([1990] 1 WLR 1311).

The issue of equality of bargaining power is much more problematic, since it requires a change of attitude, and possibly a change of structures, within the legal profession. But it may be that the regulation of the process rather than a denial of its existence would itself lead to better judgments and fewer mistakes by all involved. So long as sentence remains discretionary, and it remains improper for prosecuting counsel to make recommendations on sentence, there is no reason to suppose that official recognition and regulation of the process would lead to an explosion of plea bargaining. Finally, more openness about the sentencing discount, perhaps even the development of guidelines, would enable counsel to advise defendants with greater uniformity and certainty about the impact on sentence of a guilty plea.

Selection of the Jury

Who is Eligible to Serve?

The principle underlying the selection of the English jury is that of randomness. The theory is that a jury chosen at random will be representative of the community. Any prejudices held by particular members of the jury are likely to be counteracted by the good sense of the other members of the jury. No attempt is made to enquire about these prejudices. In marked contrast the principle underlying the selection of the jury in the United States is that of securing a 'neutral' jury which will try the case dispassionately according to the evidence. This desire to secure a jury of 12 persons free of prejudices which might possibly affect a juror's ability to be strictly neutral as between prosecution and defence has resulted in complex jury selection procedures, known as *voire dire*. Potential jurors are subjected to detailed questioning either by counsel or by the judge to reveal any prejudices and to confirm neutrality. The significance of the principle of random selection which is deeply rooted in the English system will soon become apparent.

The basic qualification for jury service in England and Wales is a simple age and residence qualification. Prima facie all persons aged between 18 and 70 registered as Parliamentary or local government electors who have been resident in the United Kingdom for at least five years since attaining the age of 13 are eligible for jury service (s.1, Juries Act 1974). The advent of computerized databases means that today jury panels are selected genuinely at random from electoral lists using random selection computer programmes.

Certain groups of individuals are removed from this pool of eligible jurors (Sched.1, Juries Act 1974). Some, like lawyers, judges and the police, are removed because they might have an undue influence on the jury, while others like the mentally ill are not deemed competent. The reasons for the ineligibility of the clergy are less obvious. The Report of the Departmental Committee on Jury Service (Morris Committee, 1965) noted that they might be in a pastoral relationship with the defendant. The Report also notes that clergymen may be too inclined to compassion and 'might find it difficult to consider the claims of justice alone'. Finally monks and nuns are considered to lack the necessary experience of the world to qualify as jurors. It might have been preferable to leave the clergy to determine these issues for themselves and to have included them in the groups of persons with a right to be excused.

Persons with certain criminal convictions are disqualified either for life or for ten years depending on the seriousness of the offence.

Excusal from Jury Service

There is a group in the population who have a right to be excused if summoned; for them, service as jurors is optional. These include those over 65, members and officers of Parliament, the military and the medical profession including veterinary practitioners. Surprisingly teachers are not included in this group.

There are two general grounds on which a juror has a right to claim to be excused jury service. These arise, first, where the juror has attended court for jury service within the previous two years or where the juror has been excused jury service for a longer period which has not expired. It is not uncommon for judges to grant lifetime exemptions from further jury service to those who have served in long and complex trials. Secondly, a juror who shows, or about whom it becomes apparent, that he or she cannot act effectively as a juror because of a physical disability or insufficient understanding of English, must be discharged.

There is also a general discretion to excuse persons from jury service where they can show good reason for being excused (s.9, Juries Act 1974). Practice varies widely on what amounts to a good reason. Some Crown Court centres are generous, others are demanding. The generosity may vary from time to time depending on the number of jurors summoned and the expected number of trials where juries will be needed. As an alternative to excusal, attendance for jury service may now be deferred to more convenient days (s.9A, Juries Act 1974).

Where a person seeks to be excused from jury service, the application is initially made to an officer of the Crown Court. The decision of that officer may be appealed to a Crown Court judge, who has the final say in the matter though the person appealing has a right to make oral representations to the judge (r.25, Crown Court Rules 1982, SI 1982 No. 1109, as amended). That right does not extend to a right to be legally represented on the appeal, though the judge has a discretion to permit this (*R* v. *Guildford Crown Court, ex parte Siderfin*, [1989] 3 All ER 73). Each case must be decided on it merits; excusal is a personal matter (*Practice Direction*, [1988] 1 WLR 1162).

It has occasionally been suggested that all these provisions result in some of those most competent to try criminal cases being excluded. Much of this must, of course, be pure supposition.

Jury Vetting: the Historical Background

In so far as it is possible to identify any trend in developments concerning the processes of selection of jurors discussed above, it is the restriction of the ability of parties in the process to alter the composition of the jury in any case. The restrictions are entirely consistent with the policy of random selection of jurors. But another development, wholly unregulated by statute and largely hidden from public scrutiny, has clearly undermined the principle. This is the practice of pre-trial checks on those summoned for jury service, which has come to be known as *jury vetting.* It avoids confusion with the processes of jury selection discussed above if the term jury vetting is reserved for these pre-trial checks.

In essence, jury vetting is a preliminary investigation, usually by the prosecution, of the jury panel in order to establish whether there is any reason why a particular person should not be a juror. Armed with information resulting from the process of vetting, prosecution counsel can exercise the right of stand by to exclude the juror without having to disclose any reasons. The right to stand by a juror is an ancient common law right; it does not remove the juror completely, because, if a panel of 12 cannot be secured without the use of jurors who have been stood by, they can only be removed if challenged for cause (see below).

Jury vetting came to public attention in October 1978 during the so-called *ABC trial* (from the initial letters of the last names of the defendants in the case). The case involved the trial of a soldier and two journalists for offences under the Official Secrets Act 1911. It came to light that the 82 member panel from which the jury had been chosen had been vetted for 'loyalty' as a result of an application made to the judge which had not been disclosed to the defence. Strenuous objections were made by the defence to trial by a jury so selected. The objections were made more pertinent when it was discovered that the prosecution had not acted on information known to them which might have produced bias in favour of the prosecution. Two members of the jury were found to have signed the Official Secrets Act and the foreman of the jury had at one time been a member of the Special Air Services regiment. Initially the trial judge refused to discharge the jury, but the public outcry which ensued may have influenced the judge who acceded to a second application. Before the second trial began, defence counsel sought an assurance that there would be no vetting of the jurors on the panel. The assurance was refused and the defence was told that it could not see the Attorney-General's guidelines, which were a 'restricted document'.

Continuing public concern led to the publication by the Attorney-General of the guidelines, which were amended in November 1978 (*Note* [1980] 1 All ER 457) and later in 1980 (*Note* [1980] 3 All ER 785). A revised version was issued in December 1988 ([1989] 88 Cr App R 123). In essence the early guidelines provided that in exceptional cases checks could be made with the Criminal Records Office, with special branch, and with local CID officers to ascertain whether any members of the panel from which the jury might be chosen were 'unsuitable' jurors to try the case. Consent of the DPP was required for such a check and the grant of an authorization had to be referred to the Attorney-General. Though there was no duty on prosecution counsel to disclose information arising from such a check, the guidelines stated that defence counsel should be given an intimation of information which 'renders any potential juror unsuitable from a defence point of view'.

When the Attorney-General made the guidelines public, he stated that he had been notified of 25 cases where vetting had been authorized since August 1975 when guidelines were first introduced. These consisted of 12 terrorist cases involving the IRA (Irish Republican Army), two official secrets cases and 11 serious gang cases.

The Case Law

In 1980 the legitimacy of jury vetting was twice considered by the Court of Appeal, once by the civil division and once by the criminal division. The issue arose first in *R v. Crown Court at Sheffield, ex parte Brownlow*, ([1980] QB 530). Two police officers were on trial for assault occasioning actual bodily harm on an ordinary member of the public. Lawyers for the defence were concerned that if any member of the jury had criminal convictions, this might prevent their clients from obtaining a fair trial. A successful application was made to the trial judge for an order that the chief constable run a Criminal Records Office check against the whole of the jury panel and supply a copy to both prosecution and defence. The chief constable doubted whether there was jurisdiction in the Crown Court judge to make the order and sought to have it quashed on application to the High Court for judicial review. The High Court considered that it had no supervisory jurisdiction over the Crown Court when acting as a superior court, namely when it was dealing with a trial on indictment.

The chief constable appealed to the Court of Appeal, civil division. The Court of Appeal by a majority of two to one agreed with the High Court that there was no jurisdiction to interfere with the Crown Court judge's decision, but the judges in the Court of Appeal went on to comment *obiter* on the legality of the jury vetting. All three judges doubted the propriety of the practice. Lord Denning MR and Shaw LJ considered it 'unconstitutional'. Lord Denning also pointed out that, even assuming the legitimacy of the guidelines, the vetting in the case before them clearly fell outside them.

Given the comments of the Court of Appeal in *Brownlow*, it was certain that it would not be long before a defendant appealed against conviction on the basis that the jury which tried him had been vetted. That case was *R v. Mason* ([1981] QB 881). Mason was tried and convicted on various counts of burglary and handling stolen goods. The grounds of appeal included the claim that there had been a material irregularity in the course of the trial because the jury had been vetted and the right of stand by had been exercised to exclude from the jury to try him two jurors with criminal convictions of insufficient seriousness to disqualify them under the provisions of the Juries Act 1974. The Court of Appeal accepted, having heard evidence from counsel and solicitors as to the impanelling of the jury at the trial, that at least one juror was stood by who was not disqualified. Arguing that it was no more than 'common sense', Lawton LJ, delivering the judgment of the Court, upheld the practice of routine Criminal Records Office checks on jury panels.

It must be made clear that this case did not fall within the Attorney-General's guidelines. Nor was the information obtained as a result of the check made known to the defence. The Court dismissed the opinion of the earlier Court of Appeal in *Brownlow* with the simple assertion, 'we have been able to examine the issues raised in greater depth than our brethren were able to do.' The case now stands as authority for the legitimacy of routine Criminal Records Office checks in any case where the prosecution considers it appropriate. None of the safeguards enumerated in the Attorney-General's guidelines applies to this type of vetting.

Is it possible to reconcile the views of the judges in the two cases? It is submitted that it is not, and Lawton LJ admits as much in casting doubt on the correctness of the earlier decision. It would be difficult to argue that Criminal Records Office checks merely to establish whether potential jurors were disqualified under the Juries Act 1974 are unlawful. But the objectionable aspect of *Mason* is its explicit statement that convictions falling well short of the seriousness necessary to disqualify may be used by counsel to remove a juror from the panel from which the jury is to be selected.

Jury Vetting: Authorized Checks

In December 1988, honouring a promise made in Parliament during the passage of the Criminal Justice Act 1988, the Attorney-General issued a revised set of guidelines on jury checks ([1988] 3 All ER 1086). These checks, known as *authorized* checks, require the personal authority of the Attorney-General acting on the recommendation of the DPP. The guidelines begin by affirming three principles. First, juries are selected at random. Secondly, the Juries Act 1974 alone identifies those who are ineligible to serve, or are disqualified from serving, as jurors. Thirdly, the correct way to seek to exclude a member of the panel from sitting as a juror is by the exercise in open court of the right to request a stand by or, if necessary, to challenge for cause.

Despite these provisions, the guidelines say there are 'certain exceptional types of case of public importance for which the provisions as to majority verdicts and the disqualification of jurors may not be sufficient to ensure the proper administration of justice'. In these cases, further safeguards against the possibility of bias 'may be necessary'. Only two classes of cases are now covered by the guidelines: cases in which national security is involved *and* part of the evidence is likely to be heard in camera; and terrorist cases. In national security cases, the justification for further safeguards is said to be the danger that a juror, either voluntarily or under pressure, may make improper use of evidence heard in the case. In both national security and terrorist cases, it is asserted that there is a danger that a juror's political beliefs may be so biased as to go 'beyond normally reflecting the broad spectrum of views and interest in the community' such as might lead the juror to 'exert improper pressure on his fellow jurors'.

In such cases a limited investigation of the background of the jurors on the panel may be justified. This will involve enquiries of the police Special Branches and of the security services (MI5 and MI6). The earliest guidelines permitted enquiries to be made of local CID officers; these are not now permitted, because of their unreliability. Such information is 'soft' information, that is, information based on rumour and anecdote, which has not been put to the individual concerned and so has not been properly investigated or verified.

The result of an authorized check is sent to the DPP, who decides what, if any, information should be brought to the attention of prosecution counsel in the case. The DPP may alone authorize counsel to exercise the right of stand by on the basis of information so obtained. Counsel is, however, given a discretion as to the information to be disclosed to defence counsel in the case. Upward reporting of the use made of any information disclosed to counsel is required so that the Attorney-General can monitor the operation of the guidelines.

Jury Vetting: Criminal Records Office Checks

The Attorney-General has annexed to the guidelines on authorized checks, the recommendations of the Association of Chief Police Officers on Criminal Records Office checks. The guidelines note that 'any search of criminal records for the purpose of ascertaining whether or not a jury panel includes any dis-qualified person is a matter for the police as the only authority able to carry out such a search and as part of their usual function of preventing the commission of offences.' The recommendations are broadly drafted and reserve considerable discretion to individual chief constables. In *any* case where the chief constable or the DPP considers that it would be 'in the interests of justice' to carry out a Criminal Records Office check of jurors on the panel, such a check may be carried out. The recommendations state that it will normally be in the interest of justice to make a check where:

   there is reason to believe that a particular juror is disqualified or that 'attempts are being made to circumvent the statutory provisions excluding dis-qualified persons from service on a jury';
   in a previous related abortive trial, an attempt was made to interfere with a juror;
   the DPP or chief constable thinks it is particularly important to ensure that no disqualified juror serves on the jury.

Checks on behalf of the defence will only be conducted on the authority of the DPP. Information resulting from such a check will be passed to prosecuting counsel who will decide what use to make of it.

Jury Vetting: an Evaluation

It is alarming to see the requirements of due process so obviously eroded. One consequence of vetting where selected information is passed initially only to prosecuting counsel is that the court's determination of the suitability of a juror is being subordinated to the discretion of counsel for one of the parties. But the major point is that practices labelled by senior judges as unconstitutional are now governed by administrative directions and recommendations of senior police officers. Adherence to the principles of due process demand that the practice should either be abandoned or regulated by statute. If it is not, it will be difficult to counter charges that the jury is being subverted (Harman and Griffith, 1979). It is certainly impossible to reconcile the practice of vetting with the principle of random selection of jurors, which has formed the basis of Parliamentary policy in the legislation on juries and of much judicial comment on the jury system (Duff and Findlay, 1983; East, 1985).

Affecting the Composition of the Jury in the Court Room

The procedures described above involve enquiries made outside the court room, the result of which is seen in the court room when counsel object to a juror as he or she comes forward to swear the juror's oath at the start of the trial. There are a number of procedures that can be used in the court room to affect the composition of a particular jury that is to try a case. The law in this area is a mixture of common law and statutory powers (Buxton, 1990).

It is possible for either prosecution or defence counsel to issue a *challenge to the array*. This is an objection to the whole panel of jurors summoned to attend at the Crown Court on the grounds of bias or other impropriety by the summoning officer (*R* v. *Danvers*, [1982] Crim LR 680). Though there may be some life yet left in the procedure, it is so rarely used that it need concern us no further here.

The prosecution has the ancient common law right to ask jurors to *stand by for the Crown* without showing cause. There is no limit to the number who may be stood by in this way, save that if the number of jurors available to complete the jury from the panel is exhausted, then those stood by may be called to serve and may then only be challenged for cause. Under the system of pre-trial checks discussed above, the prosecution has used this right of stand by on the basis of information obtained in the vetting process.

Though the defence has no right of stand by, it has been held that the judge may in exceptional circumstances allow the defence to stand by jurors (*R* v. *Chandler*, [1964] 2 QB 322; *see also* Dashwood, 1972).

In November 1988 the Attorney-General issued guidelines on the exercise by the Crown of the right of stand by ([1988] 3 All ER 1086). The guidelines reminded counsel that the right should not be used 'in order to influence the overall composition of a jury or with a view to tactical advantage'. The right is to be used very sparingly 'on the basis of clearly defined and restrictive criteria'. The guidelines set out the circumstances in which the exercise of the right will be appropriate:

> where an authorized check reveals information about a juror which results
> in the Attorney-General personally authorizing counsel to stand by a
> particular juror;
> where a person about to be sworn in as a juror is 'manifestly unsuitable' and
> defence counsel agrees that the exercise of the right of stand by is the most
> appropriate way to remove the juror from the panel.

Either side may challenge any number of jurors *for cause*, that is, some reason
why the particular juror should not sit in the case. Counsel will have very little
information about jurors on which to base the challenge. All that is generally
available is a list of names and addresses. It used to be the case that occupations
were included, but a directive from the Lord Chancellor in 1973 required these
to be excluded. Nor will counsel be able to ask questions to establish the existence of good cause. Following the so-called *Angry Brigade trial* in 1972
(Dashwood, 1974) in which the trial judge acceded to a request to put certain
questions to jurors so that they might be excluded for cause, Lord Widgery CJ
issued a *Practice Note* ([1973] 1 WLR 134) banning such questioning of jurors
and restating the basic principle of jury selection as follows:

> A jury consists of 12 individuals chosen at random for the appropriate
> panel. A juror should be excused if he is personally concerned in the facts
> of the particular case, or closely connected with a party to the proceedings
> or with a prospective witness. He may also be excused at the discretion of
> the judge on grounds of personal hardship or conscientious objection
> to jury service. It is contrary to established practice for jurors to be
> excused on more general grounds such as race, religion, or political beliefs
> or occupation.

In September 1988 the Lord Chief Justice issued a *Practice Direction* ([1988]
1 WLR 1162) revoking the 1973 *Practice Note*. The salient paragraphs read:

> There will . . . be circumstances where a juror should be excused, for
> instance where he or she is personally concerned in the facts of the case or
> is closely connected with a party or prospective witness.
>   He or she may also be excused on grounds of personal hardship or
> conscientious objection to jury service. Each such application should be
> dealt with sensitively and sympathetically.
>   Any person who appeals to the court against a refusal by the appropriate
> officer to excuse him or her from jury service must be given an opportunity
> to make representations in support of his or her appeal.

Though on the face of it primarily concerned with excusals, such directions
have always been seen as indicating the bases on which a challenge for cause
might be appropriate. It will usually only be where the defendant himself iden-

tifies a juror to counsel as known to him that a challenge for cause will arise. In other cases it will be the juror who takes the initiative if known to the defendant or a witness. The only other possibility is that counsel will have some information as a result of pre-trial checks. The limited basis for challenges is perfectly consistent with the underlying principle of random selection.

There used to be a right of *peremptory challenge* of up to three jurors, which belonged exclusively to the defence. No reason whatever needed to be given for the challenge and in cases where there was more than one defendant each could challenge up to three jurors. The peremptory challenge gave defendants a limited opportunity to secure a jury believed to be as sympathetic as possible to the defendant. Defendants, of course, had no real information to go on, but they could at least remove those whose demeanour they believed would make them hostile to their cause. Peremptory challenges were used most by counsel to influence the composition of the jury in accordance with supposed notions that certain types of juries are more lenient than others. Typical jury lore suggested that women are less likely to convict than men, except in cases involving sexual offences, and that younger juries are more sympathetic than older juries (Vennard and Riley, 1988). But the results of Baldwin and McConville's research into the correlation between jury composition and outcome showed that views popularly held among lawyers are no more than legal mythology. They concluded that:

> We can confidently state that no single social factor (nor, as far as we could detect, any group of factors operating in combination) produced any significant variation in the verdicts returned across the board. (Baldwin and McConville, 1979b, p. 104)

Peremptory challenges have also been used to secure representation by members of ethnic minorities on juries. They are abolished completely by section 118(1) of the Criminal Justice Act 1988.

Securing Ethnic Minority Representation on the Jury

The results of Baldwin and McConville's research in Birmingham revealed a serious underrepresentation of members of ethnic minorities on juries. There has been a steady stream of claims for representatives of ethnic minorities on juries trying defendants from these communities (Dashwood, 1972).

In cases involving members of ethnic minorities, there has been some small evidence of judicial sympathy for the proposition that the jury should contain a proportion of jurors from that ethnic minority (R v. *Binns*, [1982] Crim LR 522 and 823). It has long been accepted that there is a residual common law discretion in a trial judge to discharge a particular juror who ought not to be serving on the jury (R v. *Mansell* [1857] 8 E and B 37). This is part of the judge's duty to ensure that there is a fair trial. In *Binns* Judge Stocker was not prepared to go as far as authorizing the summoning of a new panel to achieve a racially balanced jury. It was not necessary in *Binns* because the jury sworn after the use of the peremptory challenge contained three jurors from ethnic minorities.

The example given above in *Binns* may be an example of exceptional circumstances justifying allowing the defence an opportunity to exercise a right of stand by, and certainly offers a convenient way to secure racial balance in a jury where this is appropriate. Such a suggestion was made in *R* v. *Chandler* (No 2) ([1964] 2 QB 322). In *R* v. *Bansal* ([1985] Crim LR 151) the trial judge gave directions that the jury panel should be selected from a geographic area known to contain members of the Asian community. More recently in *R* v. *Thomas* ([1989] 89 Cr App R 370) it was accepted that a discretion vested in the trial judge to use the power of discretionary discharge to alter the composition of the particular jury to try a case in order to achieve what was felt to be an appropriate racial representation.

But in *R* v. *Ford*, ([1989] 3 WLR 762) the Court of Appeal in a judgment handed down by the Lord Chief Justice held that the trial judge enjoyed no discretion to interfere with the composition of a jury to secure a multi-racial jury for particular trials. Earlier decisions suggesting otherwise were wrongly decided. In a statement which stands in marked contrast to the views taken by the judiciary on pre-trial jury checks, the Lord Chief Justice said:

> If it should ever become desirable that the principle of random selection should be altered, that would have to be done by way of statute. It could not be done by any judicial decision.

The Role of Judge and Jury

Questions of Law and Questions of Fact

The division of functions between the judge and jury is that the judge deals with questions of law and the jury deals with questions of fact. The distinction between questions of law and questions of fact is a subtle one. Most people would recognize that the issue of whether the defendant was at a particular place at a particular time is a question of fact. Indeed lawyers would call this a question of primary fact. But in a criminal trial where intention is relevant, that too is a question of fact, though it will require an evaluation of all the surrounding circumstances in coming to a conclusion about the defendant's state of mind. For example, in a case of shoplifting (the offence of theft) a jury might be called upon to determine whether the defendant took the goods while in a state of confusion resulting from the side-effects of medication and so had no intent to steal. In complex cases of fraud or deception, these issues are often more important than the primary facts. By contrast, defining the constituent elements of the offence of theft is a question of law for the judge.

The Judge is the Arbiter of the Law

The judge controls the trial and directs the jury. At all stages, the role of the jury is passive. The trial may last as little as a few hours to as long as a month or more; the average length of contested cases is just under nine hours, which is about two days of court time. The judge may exclude the jury while points of law, often involving the admissibility of evidence, are argued and decided, but otherwise the jury listen and form opinions about the veracity of witnesses. The judge may direct the jury to return a verdict of not guilty. Once the jury has been impanelled, the trial can normally only end following a decision of the jury on guilt or innocence. If during the course of the trial it becomes clear that a conviction cannot, as a matter of law, be sustained in the case, the judge is required to direct the jury to return a verdict of not guilty. This is a direction which the jury cannot ignore. The resulting verdict is called a *directed acquittal*. The importance of the directed acquittal is indicated by the fact that research studies have shown that an average of around 10 and 20 per cent of all acquittals result from such a direction to the jury, with a further 10 per cent of acquittals resulting from a judge's direction before a jury is impanelled. Apart from this power, the judge cannot instruct the jury as to the verdict they must return. He certainly cannot direct them to convict (*R v. Gent*, [1989] 89 Cr App R 247).

The judge has the last word before the jury retires to consider a verdict when he sums up the case for the jury. The summing up is very important. In it the judge, from an independent and impartial standpoint, summarizes the case, explains the legal issues in contention and may comment on factors which lend weight to, or cast doubt on, certain evidence. Verdicts are called perverse either when the jury must have ignored the judge's explanation of the law in coming to its decision or when the jury returns a verdict with which neutral observers would disagree on the basis that it goes against the weight of the evidence.

The Jury is the Arbiter of Fact

All issues of fact are for the jury. They must debate in their secret deliberations whom they believe and disbelieve. They must form a view collectively as to what happened many months before constructing a single reality from the evidence before them. They alone determine whether the defendant's actions constitute the offence charged. Once the jury has retired, all must await the outcome of their deliberations. None may interfere. The jury will be kept isolated from outside contacts, for days if need be, until a decision is reached. Sometimes juries cannot agree and if every effort at coming to a decision fails, they will be discharged and a retrial will be necessary. Such a jury is known as a 'hung' jury.

Majority Verdicts

Formerly juries were required to be unanimous. But to mitigate the burden on all concerned of retrials, the majority verdict was introduced by the Criminal Justice Act 1967. It is now possible to acquit or convict if ten jurors agree where the jury consists of 11 or 12 members, or if nine agree where the jury consists of ten jurors. Juries sometimes fall below 12 members if one or more dies, or falls ill, during the course of the trial. Provided that the number does not fall below ten, the trial will continue.

Before a majority verdict can be returned, the jury must have retired for at least two hours in an attempt to come to a unanimous decision. In practice, if after 2 hours and 20 minutes they have not done so, the judge will recall them and give them a direction permitting the return of a majority verdict (s.17, Juries Act 1974 and *Practice Direction*, [1967] 1 WLR 1198). Majority verdicts have occasionally been linked with the issues of vetting and of selection of jurors as evidence of subversion of the jury (Harman and Griffith, 1979), but the arguments are overstated. Given respect for the random selection of jurors, majority verdicts merely enable extreme views to be discounted by the jury in its deliberations. For example, in a trial on a charge of incitement to racial hatred, it would enable the racist views of a member of an extreme right wing political party to be discounted in the jury's decision making.

Where a judge suspects that one or more jurors is being unnecessarily difficult, there has been controversy over the extent to which the jury should be encouraged to work together to reach a conclusion. In *R v. Watson* ([1988] 1 All ER 897) a five judge Court of Appeal has stressed the need to ensure that a jury must be free to deliberate without any form of pressure being imposed upon them. But a model direction for use in such cases either in the principal summing up or when the majority direction is given was recommended in the following terms:

> Each of you has taken an oath to return a true verdict according to the evidence. No one must be false to that oath, but you have a duty not only as individuals but collectively. That is the strength of the jury system. Each of you takes into the jury box with you your individual experience and wisdom. Your task is to pool that experience and wisdom. You can do that by giving your views and listening to the views of others. There must necessarily be discussion, argument and give and take within the scope of your oath. That is the way in which agreement is reached. If unhappily, [ten of] you cannot reach agreement you must say so.

Control of Jury's Decisions

Acquittal by a jury is sacred; there is no appeal available to the prosecution against an acquittal. Even convictions carry some finality. The basic rule is that the Court of Appeal will not reopen or reconsider a jury's decision unless there has been an open and material defect of procedure taking place outside the confines of the jury room. Where this occurs, it is really a failure by the trial judge to conduct the trial properly. The Court of Appeal will certainly never enquire into the deliberations of the jury (*Ellis v. Deheer*, [1922] 2 KB 113).

An illustration of the application of this rule is *R v. Thompson*, ([1962] 1 All ER 65), in which it was discovered that the jury had been in favour of acquittal until the foreman of the jury had produced a list of the defendant's previous convictions. Such information is deliberately kept from juries to avoid the possibility of prejudice to the defendant. The Court of Appeal would not interfere with the conviction. They refused to enquire into the jury's deliberations.

By contrast an appeal was allowed in *R v. Dubarry* ([1976] 64 Cr App R 7).

In this case the jury had retired and were deliberating when the need arose to send a question to the judge. A member of the jury took a note to the door of the retiring room and handed it to the jury bailiff. The door of the jury room opened on to the courtroom and the juror saw the defendant obviously on trial for other offences. The jury bailiff advised the judge, who simply asked the short-hand writer to note the event. The Court of Appeal said that he should have considered the issue of prejudice to the defendant. Having failed to do so, the defendant must be given the benefit of the doubt that his trial had been prejudiced and the conviction was quashed. Modern courtroom design avoids having jury rooms opening directly on to the court.

Obviously the respective roles of judge and jury demand that the judge does not abuse his position by placing unreasonable pressure on the jury to come to a decision. This happened in *R v. McKenna* ([1960] 1 QB 411), where the judge's impatience with the jury overflowed into a demand for an instant verdict. The conviction based on it was quashed. In another case a conviction for murder was quashed when the judge sent private notes to the jury imposing a time limit for them to return a majority verdict failing which he would discharge them as a hung jury (*R v. Rose*, [1982] AC 822).

Jury Decision Making

Perhaps more ill-informed words have been written on the matters that influence juries and whether they acquit too readily than on any other aspect of the criminal justice system. The reason is clear: much of it is based on pure supposition. Even scholarly research presents great difficulties. Research has never been allowed into the deliberations of 'live' juries; most has involved the use of simulations using volunteers. It is not difficult to appreciate the caveats that must, and do, surround the results of such research. Even the research of Baldwin and McConville, generally acknowledged as the most authoritative yet produced, is based on post hoc analysis of real cases, and does not include discussions with the actual jurors.

For many years convention alone required jurors not to disclose their deliberations. But the increasing frequency of disclosure, culminating in the publication of the views of jurors in the Jeremy Thorpe trial in the New Statesman (see *Attorney-General* v. *New Statesman and Nation Publishing Co. Ltd*, [1980] QB 1), led to the passing of s.8 of the Contempt of Court Act 1981. It is now an offence to obtain, disclose or solicit any particulars of the deliberations of a jury except in the course of criminal proceedings. The section not only catches the objectionable aspects of cheque book journalism but also effectively closes the door firmly on research into jury decision making based on the experiences of actual jurors.

Work with simulated juries both at the London School of Economics (LSE) (Sealy and Cornish, 1973) and at the Oxford University Penal Research Unit (McCabe and Purves, 1974) suggests that jurors approach the task of determining guilt as a serious responsibility. They listen carefully to directions from the judge. The LSE Jury Project's findings suggest that the jury's knowledge of a defendant's previous convictions do increase the probability of a guilty verdict somewhat but, contrary to popular supposition, jurors generally complied with a direction by the judge to disregard these convictions. It also showed that the form of words used to describe to the jury the standard of proof laid on the prosecution had little impact on the outcome of cases, despite lawyers beliefs that this aspect of the summing up is crucial to outcome. The results of both research studies strongly suggested that jurors do indeed try cases according to the evidence and not on personal whims or hunches.

The Oxford University Penal Research Unit analysed the reasons for acquittals in 173 cases in their sample into six groups (McCabe and Purves, 1972). In only 15 cases (9 per cent) could the verdicts be described as wayward, in that interviews with other participants in the process described them as unjustified in the light of the evidence. But in a number of these it was possible to suggest that 'feelings of fair play' accounted for the verdict. Having regard to all the surrounding circumstances and in the face of evidence strong enough to convict, the jury nevertheless chose to acquit. This is sometimes labelled jury equity. The largest group of acquittals (34 per cent) were those directed by the judge where the prosecution case clearly failed at an early stage. Some of these failures were the result of technical flaws in the prosecution evidence or were identifiable as policy prosecutions with little hope of success. Indeed a number of acquittals by the jury (25 per cent) were considered to be attributable to policy prosecutions, particularly in a number of shoplifting cases in the sample. It was noted that the failed prosecution may nevertheless serve a purpose in gaining publicity for a police drive against particular types of offence. In 28 cases (16 per cent) it was the defendant's explanation which was considered to have accounted for the acquittal, while in eight cases (5 per cent) it was the failure of prosecution witnesses to 'come up to proof'. This phrase is lawyers' jargon for the situation where a witness provides a good written statement of evidence (called a 'proof' of evidence) prior to the trial, but when giving evidence and subjected to cross-examination fails to be as convincing as the written statement given earlier. The remaining 20 cases in the sample (11 per cent) were simply weak prosecution cases. In these cases the prosecution was just about strong enough to put to the jury but was not strong enough to secure a conviction.

Other research has concentrated on whether jurors acquit too many defendants. Such research became very topical following the assertions made by Sir Robert Mark, a former Metropolitan Police Commissioner, in the 1973 Dimbleby Lecture that 'the proportion of . . . acquittals relating to those whom experienced police officers believe to be guilty is too high to be acceptable . . .' and that there was a cadre of 'lawyers producing, off the peg, the same kind of defence, for different clients'. The defences were described as 'concocted far beyond the intellectual capacity of the accused' (Mark, 1973).

Following the Dimbleby Lecture, much attention was focused on the allegations made by Sir Robert Mark. It was noted that seven out of ten defendants plead guilty in the Crown Court to the charges against them and that a significant proportion of acquittals result from a judge's direction to acquit. A major plank in Sir Robert's case was the argument that 'professional' criminals were able to manipulate various features of the criminal process to their own advantage. Both Zander (1974a; 1974b) and Baldwin and McConville (1974; 1979b, ch. 7) concluded that there was no significant difference in the probability of acquittals of those who might be described as professional criminals when compared with all defendants. Only the research of Mack (1976) has shown any success at avoiding conviction by professional criminals when compared with others. The success cannot be described as more than marginal, and his results have not gone unchallenged (Sanders, 1977). Sir Robert also suggested that a significant number of acquittals resulted from concocted defences by crooked lawyers. These allegations have never been substantiated despite requests from the Law Society for details of cases known to Sir Robert Mark. Baldwin and McConville have also shown that there would appear to be no evidence to back up Sir Robert's assertions (Baldwin and McConville, 1978).

Baldwin and McConville's major research on jury trials (Baldwin and McConville, 1979b) focused on 370 defendants tried by juries out of a total of 2406 defendants passing through the Birmingham Crown Court in the study period. There is also some comparison with cases tried in London. The opinions of judges, of prosecution and defence lawyers, of defendants and of the police were sought on a wide range of aspects of the cases. The researchers examined the incidence of agreement and disagreement with the verdicts of the juries. There was a higher incidence of disagreements with both acquittals and convictions than had been indicated by earlier research studies. In all cases of acquittal, participants were generally agreed on the most important reason for the acquittal. The most commonly mentioned factors were the strength of the defence case, the weakness of the prosecution case, and the jury's being swayed by sympathy for the defendant or antipathy to the victim of the crime. This latter category was described as part of 'jury equity' in which juries are prepared to allow extra-legal considerations to influence their decision making. This factor was identified as the most important factor in about a quarter of the cases resulting in acquittal.

Baldwin and McConville went on to examine more closely the incidence both of questionable acquittals and of doubtful convictions. They preferred the label 'questionable' to wayward or perverse to indicate that this group reflected the questions and doubts raised by other participants in the process. An acquittal was regarded as questionable if the judge and one other respondent voiced doubts about it. This produced 41 cases of questionable acquittal out of 114 acquittals (36 per cent). Though one might have expected some correlation between these cases and those where respondents had mentioned factors involving jury equity, this was generally not the case. Indeed Baldwin and McConville could discern no common characteristics of the group of questionable acquittals. They concluded:

The number of defendants who seem to us to have been acquitted in questionable circumstances, without any apparent equitable justification save in a handful of cases, suggests that trial by jury is a relatively crude instrument for establishing the truth. (p. 67)

When they applied the same sort of analysis to convictions, there was no disagreement with the juries' verdicts in nearly nine out of every ten cases. But in the minority of cases where doubts were expressed, these amounted to serious concerns about the correctness of the conviction. In considering the possible reasons for doubtful convictions, Baldwin and McConville identified two factors as important: first, that the juries appeared to have been too easily satisfied of the guilt of the defendants and did not demand proof beyond reasonable doubt, and, secondly, that the juries seemed to have failed to comprehend the issues involved. There is also a hint that racial prejudice might be involved: blacks were over-represented in the group of doubtful convictions. This evidence must, of course, add weight to the arguments of those who claim that trial by jury is not an appropriate form of criminal trial in the twentieth century. This simplified summary of some of the findings of the research does little justice to the wealth of information and comment in the researchers' book, *Jury Trials*, which should be read by all those interested in the issues involved in consideration of the merits of trial by jury.

From time to time alternatives to the jury are suggested, such as lay assessors sitting with judges or trial by a bench of judges, and examples are given of such systems of criminal trial in other jurisdictions. But it is virtually inconceivable that trial by jury will disappear in the English criminal process; public opinion regards it as a vital part of the trial of serious criminal offences. Though the jury is far from perfect (Findlay and Duff, 1988), the alternatives seem even less attractive (Knittel and Seiler, 1972; Freeman, 1981).

Trial and Sentencing

The Guilty Plea

The order of events in a trial on indictment is not markedly different from that in a summary trial. Briefly the main stages of the trial are as follows. First comes the arraignment. The clerk of the court calls upon the defendant by name, reads out the indictment and asks him or her how he or she pleads. Ignoring the rare cases in which the defendant remains silent for which there are special procedures, the defendant will then plead either guilty or not guilty.

Following a plea of guilty, the proceedings are virtually identical to summary trial, though the prosecution will be represented by counsel. In most cases there will be a social enquiry report available to assist in the sentencing process. The prosecution will also indicate whether the defendant has asked for other offences, not on the indictment, to be taken into consideration in assessing sentence. If there are, a schedule of offences agreed by the defendant and his or her counsel is presented to the court. These offences are known colloquially by their initial letters as 'tic's'. Though technically not convicted of these offences, the defendant can 'wipe the slate clean' and will in practice never be prosecuted for them. Following presentation of this information, the defence may make a plea in mitigation before the court proceeds to sentence.

The Not Guilty Plea

The defendant is brought before the court and the substance of the indictment is put to him or her. If the plea is one of not guilty, then a jury must be impanelled. The clerk announces to the group of potential jurors who will usually be waiting at the back of the court:

> Members of the jury in waiting, please answer to your names and step into the jury box as you are called.

The 12 chosen are then named. The clerk then addresses the defendant:

> Prisoner at the bar, the names you are about to hear called are the names of the jurors who are to try you. If therefore you wish to object to them or to any of them, you must do so as they come to the book to be sworn, and your objections shall be heard.

Each juror is then required to swear, or affirm, in the following terms:

> I swear by Almighty God that I will faithfully try the defendant and give a true verdict according to the evidence.

The clerk will then read the indictment to the jury and tell them that the defendant has pleaded not guilty, for example:

> Members of the jury, are you all sworn? The prisoner stands indicted for that he on the third day of May 1990 did steal £500 in money, the property of Sterling Limited. To this indictment he has pleaded not guilty and it is your charge to say, having heard the evidence, whether he be guilty or not.

Battle can now commence. Prosecuting counsel then makes an opening speech outlining the case to be made against the defendant. The prosecution witnesses then give evidence and are cross-examined by defence counsel and, if necessary, re-examined by prosecuting counsel.

At the end of the prosecution case, defence counsel may make a submission that there is no case for the defendant to answer if he or she considers that the prosecution has not adduced sufficient evidence to prove its case or if cross-examination has cast such doubt on the evidence that it cannot be regarded as sufficient to ground a conviction and renders it unnecessary for a defence case to be put. Such a submission is made in the absence of the jury. Following the submission, the judge should direct the jury to return a verdict of not guilty if there is no evidence on which, if it were accepted, a reasonable jury, properly directed, could convict. But if the doubts relate to the weight of the evidence or the credibility of witnesses, the question should be left to the jury. The judge will direct the jury on this issue and the jury will retire to consider the issue (*R* v.

h, [1981] 1 WLR 1039). Of course, if the jury think there is a case to
, they will simply decline to return a verdict of not guilty at this stage.
case for the defence may then be put. Defence counsel is only permitted
ke an opening speech if the defendant and other witnesses are to be called
e evidence on the facts, as distinct from evidence as to the character of the
derendant. The defence case is then put. At the end of the defence case, prosecuting counsel and defence counsel, in that order, make their closing speeches
to the jury. These are followed by the judge's summing up. Immediately this is
ended, the jury must retire to consider their verdict. Following the return of a
verdict of guilty, the prosecution puts any previous convictions and the defendant's antecedents to the court and the defendant is permitted to make a plea in
mitigation before the court proceeds to sentence.

What was said in chapter 5 about the efficacy of the adversarial system as a
means of establishing the truth applies equally to trial on indictment. Equally the
comments on the sentencing process also have relevance here. There has, however, been little research on disparities in sentencing at the Crown Court level
(but see Moxon, 1988). This may be because the numbers so tried are much
smaller, or that the regular reporting of decisions of the Court of Appeal on
sentencing questions results in fewer obvious anomalies. There is even a set of
reports (Criminal Appeal Reports (Sentencing)) designed to aid practitioners and
judges in determining the appropriate sentence and a loose-leaf encyclopedia of
sentencing law and practice with similar objectives (Thomas, 1983). Though
these deal with sentencing in both magistrates' courts and the Crown Court,
these materials are most frequently used in Crown Court cases. The importance
of guidance handed down by the Court of Appeal should not be underestimated.
From time to time the opportunity is taken to give general guidance on
sentencing matters. But the guidance given by the Court of Appeal has built up
in a piecemeal way, and detailed guidelines apply only to a small range of cases
(Moxon, 1988). The new appeal against a too lenient sentence at the instance
of the Attorney-General clearly has as one of its main objectives the promotion
of greater consistency in Crown Court sentencing practice. The very first such
appeal gives detailed guidance on sentencing practice in incest cases (*Attorney-
General's Reference 1989/1*, [1989] 3 WLR 1117).

One example of the Court of Appeal's giving guidance is *R* v. *Bibi* ([1980] 1
WLR 1193) in which Lord Lane CJ with the concurrence of the Lord Chancellor
exhorted judges to make sentences for less serious types of offence as short as
possible. This was partly to ease overcrowding in prisons, but also no doubt
reflected the growing opinion that the main impact of sentences of imprisonment
comes in the first few months of the sentence. After the initial period, imprisonment may even become counter-productive, in that bitterness and despair set in
reducing the chances of any rehabilitative effect. Offences involving violence
were excluded and it was confirmed that for these offences medium or longer
sentences were appropriate.

Another factor accounting for the apparently greater uniformity of sentencing
in the Crown Court is the smaller number of judges. There are also conferences
organized by the Judicial Studies Board which include sentencing exercises which

judges are expected to attend and which contribute to a greater uniformity of approach. The absence of research into sentencing in the Crown Court attracted the interest of the Home Office in 1980. The Home Office funded a three year project starting in October 1980 to look at judicial attitudes and sentencing practice. The research was initially supported by the Lord Chief Justice, who approved a pilot project. A short report on the pilot project was submitted to the Lord Chief Justice in October 1981. This showed that judges jealously guarded their autonomy in the matter of sentence and dismissed disparities in sentencing by reference to the special facts of each case. Judges appeared not to see the value of sentencing principles and suggested that policy initiatives aimed at altering practice in particular cases could easily be side-stepped.

The results of the pilot project revealed a need for a thorough reassessment of sentencing in the Crown Court. A number of possibilities were suggested ranging from heightening the awareness of judges of principles of sentencing to greater control over the wide autonomy in sentencing enjoyed by individual judges. The pilot project's most controversial finding related to the listing practices of some Crown Court officers. Certain cases were directed towards judges labelled as 'strong' sentencers and away from those labelled as 'weak' sentencers. The overall message of the pilot project was that there was a considerable gap between the Lord Chief Justice's aim of securing a uniformity of approach in the sentencing of offenders and the practice of the judges sitting the Crown Courts up and down the country (Ashworth, 1984).

Unfortunately the pilot project is all that survives of this research project. In December 1981 the Lord Chief Justice withdrew co-operation, which meant the project could not continue. In the Lord Chief Justice's view, continued research would merely fuel ill-informed criticism of the judiciary. Sentencing is an art and not a science, and he could see no benefits accruing from the research. The Lord Chief Justice could not think of any aspects of judicial sentencing on which research might prove useful.

Concluding Comment

Consideration of trial on indictment has drawn attention to certain areas where, at the very least, there is some concern about the process. Two views are possible of the process in the Crown Court. The first is that it is indeed a model of due process, and that the defects that have been identified in this chapter occur in only a small number of cases. They are the result of aberrations which can be avoided by fine tuning of the process. The opposing view is that the defects are symptoms of fundamental faults in the system. There are design faults which will not be removed by tinkering. Any injustice which results is not merely an aberration, it is systemic. The system needs radical change (McBarnet, 1981). Because this distinction between aberrational injustice and systemic injustice is relevant to the whole of the criminal process, and not just to trial on indictment, it is an issue which is taken up in chapter 8.

7

Challenging the Decision of the Trial Court

The Reasons for Having an Appeal System

Just as summary trial and trial on indictment are two very distinct forms of criminal trial, so too the systems for challenging the decisions of the trial courts are very different. Both systems of appeal, however, have three main purposes: to ensure that the defendant's trial was fair and that there was no material irregularity in the proceedings; to allow for the development of rules of criminal procedure and of the substantive criminal law; and to ensure some degree of consistency in the administration of criminal justice and in the sentencing of convicted offenders. There is no overriding principle that the purpose of appeals is to avoid miscarriages of justice. One reason for this is the traditional reluctance to interfere with the jury's findings of fact, which has had some impact on criminal appeals following summary trial. The appeal is not regarded as a second trial, even where the procedure allows a complete rehearing of the evidence.

Appeals may be against conviction or against sentence, or against both. It is important to grasp the distinction between appeal against conviction and appeal against sentence. A defendant appealing against conviction is claiming that he has been improperly convicted. The reasons may be that the trial judge or magistrates misdirected themselves as to the applicable law, or that there was a prejudicial procedural error, or that the defendant maintains his innocence of the offence. By contrast an appeal against sentence is a disagreement only with the harshness of the penalty imposed by the trial court. It is, therefore, possible to appeal against sentence even after a plea of guilty before the trial court, whereas it is not possible to appeal against conviction after a properly entered plea of guilty. The defendant who has pleaded not guilty may, of course, appeal against both conviction and sentence. As a general rule only defendants may appeal, though there are important exceptions and qualifications to this general rule described later in this chapter.

The courts concerned with criminal appeals are the Court of Appeal, Criminal Division and the Crown Court, with the High Court enjoying a supervisory jurisdiction over magistrates' courts and over the Crown Court when exercising its appellate function. The Court of Appeal considers appeals following trial on indictment, whereas the Crown Court and the High Court consider appeals following summary trial. The significance of appeals from summary trial is generally regarded as less than that of the Court of Appeal. Indeed much less attention has been focused in the literature on criminal appeals following summary trial than on the role of the Court of Appeal.

Appeal following Summary Trial

Three Types of Challenge

A decision of a magistrates' court may be challenged in one of three ways: appeal on the merits to the Crown Court; appeal by way of case stated to the High Court; and application to the High Court for judicial review. Appeals on the merits against conviction or sentence lie to the Crown Court, but applications for judicial review and appeals by way of case stated lie to the Queen's Bench Division of the High Court.

Appeal to the Crown Court lies as of right and is concerned with the merits of the conviction or sentence. This appeal is available only to the defendant. Both prosecution and defence can appeal by way of case stated and the purpose of this special type of appeal is solely to correct an error of law or an act in excess of jurisdiction. Applications for judicial review are available to either prosecution or defence in order to cure some illegality in the trial proceedings or in appellate proceedings of the Crown Court. The primary purpose of the appeal and the party wishing to appeal will be the principal determinants of the procedure chosen.

Appeal to the Crown Court

Persons convicted in a magistrates' court may appeal as of right to the Crown Court against sentence if they pleaded guilty, or against conviction and/or sentence if they did not (s.108, Magistrates Courts Act 1980). These appeals will be heard without a jury by a Circuit judge or Recorder sitting with between two and four justices. There are a number of unusual features of these appeals, which are the result of historical accident and piecemeal reform of the appellate system following summary trial. Originally justices met in quarterly meetings to exercise their judicial functions, but as early as the seventeenth century, the justices were authorized to exercise their judicial functions 'out of sessions', that is, other than in the quarterly meetings. But a person aggrieved by a decision made out of sessions could have the case heard again in quarter sessions. In time the out of sessions or summary jurisdiction became the norm and the quarterly meetings or 'quarter sessions' increasingly dealt with more serious crime and with the re-hearing of cases heard in petty sessions. In the nineteenth century borough courts of quarter sessions consisting of a professional judge, known as a Recorder, sitting with lay justices began to become commonplace. Both petty sessions and quarter sessions were inferior courts. Even with the advent of the ability of quarter sessions to try certain cases on indictment, their status as inferior courts remained.

The reforms contained in the Courts Act 1971 did not affect the system of criminal appeals which had developed; the new Crown Court simply inherited the appellate jurisdiction of quarter sessions. The result is somewhat curious. The Crown Court is a hybrid. For certain purposes it is a superior court of record of equal status to the High Court, while for others it is an inferior court susceptible to the supervisory jurisdiction of the High Court. For all purposes connected with trial on indictment, the Crown Court is a superior court (s.45, Supreme Court Act 1981; *ex parte Brownlow* [1980] QB 530) but in the exercise of its appellate jurisdiction, it is deemed to be an inferior court (ss.28 and 29, Supreme Court Act 1981). Sometimes the Divisional Court, perhaps understandably, overlooks this distinction and exercises judicial review of the Crown Court in its indictable jurisdiction. This happened in *R v. Central Criminal Court, ex parte Crook* ([1984] *Law Society's Gazette* vol. 82, p. 1408). It is also arguable that the Divisional Court lacked jurisdiction to deal with the problem of conscientious objection to jury service which arose in *ex parte Siderfin* ([1989] 3 All ER 73).

Aggrieved defendants wishing to appeal to the Crown Court must file a notice of appeal within 21 days of the decision of the magistrates' court with which they take issue. It is not necessary to state the grounds of appeal, though it is sensible to indicate in general terms the nature of the defendant's grievance with the decision at first instance. Most appeals against conviction assert simply that the conviction was 'against the weight of the evidence', while appeals against sentence are usually against custodial sentences which are considered 'excessive or wrong in principle' (Scott, 1977).

The appeal adopts the unusual form of a complete rehearing. The historical development of the remedy described above, coupled with the absence of written records in the magistrates' courts, accounts for this. The practical effect of the appeal by way of rehearing is that the case must be re-created before the Crown Court. Proceedings on an appeal against conviction will look just like a trial in the magistrates' court, while an appeal against sentence will look just like proceedings on a guilty plea at first instance. But case law affirms the appellate nature of the proceedings (*Drover v. Rugman*, [1951] 1 KB 380) and, of course, the judge and justices hearing the appeal will know that there has been a conviction in the magistrates' court. Nevertheless the function of the proceedings is not to decide whether the magistrates decided correctly, but is to make a fresh decision on conviction or sentence in the light of the evidence adduced in the Crown Court. The result of an appeal against conviction will be expressed in terms of a confirmation or quashing of the conviction. The Crown Court has wide powers and may in addition vary the decision appealed, remit the matter back to the magistrates with their opinion, or make such other order as the court thinks just (s.48, Supreme Court Act 1981).

When considering sentence, another unusual feature is present. It is open to the Crown Court to impose any sentence available to the magistrates even if it is more severe than that actually imposed by the magistrates (s.48(4), Supreme Court Act 1981). This is one of only two occasions on which an appeal court can increase the sentence imposed by the court below. The Crown Court only rarely increases sentence.

Around 17,500 appeals against conviction and/or sentence are made to the Crown Court each year, making it the main focus of appeals against decisions of magistrates. There are about 6000 appeals against conviction, of which one in three succeeds, and about 11,500 appeals against sentence, of which about half are successful. This may seem a large number of appeals, but measured against the 2.5 million cases dealt with by magistrates each year, it represents an appeal in less than one in 100 cases. It seems that there are very few appeals in respect of offences triable only summarily and motoring offences. It also seems that there are very few appeals against sentence other than custodial sentences. Since less than two per cent of those defendants convicted on summary trial receive immediate custodial sentences, these figures are perhaps not so surprising (Scott, 1977). Nevertheless it appears that the appeal to the Crown Court is underutilized. The James Committee was wisely cautious about assuming that the reason for the paucity of appeals was general satisfaction with summary trial and noted that delay, expense, the avoidance of further anxiety, a wish for finality, and the possibility that the Crown Court might increase sentence were all disincentives to appealing (James Committee, 1975, paras. 38 and 251).

Expense is a major factor. If legal aid has been available for the proceedings in the magistrates' court, that will include the provision of advice as to any grounds of appeal (Legal Aid Act 1988, s.19(2)). But legal aid is not readily available in magistrates' courts, and it is unlikely that an unassisted litigant at first instance will obtain legal aid for an appeal. In all cases a separate consideration of the merits is required before the grant of legal aid for appellate proceedings.

The only subsequent appeals available after appeal to the Crown Court are the exercise of supervisory jurisdiction by the High Court. Either prosecution or defence may seek judicial review to cure some illegality or appeal by way of case stated, but no further appeals on the merits are available.

Appeal by Way of Case Stated

Either prosecution or defence may apply for a case to be stated by the magistrates' court, or Crown Court, where they believe that the decision of that court is wrong in law or in excess of its jurisdiction (Magistrates Courts Act 1980, s.111). Such appeals, when taken successfully by the prosecution, can operate to reverse an acquittal, and are an exception to the general rule that acquittals are final. There are few appeals by way of case stated each year, though they often include important points of law and practice. In 1988 there were only 189 such appeals, 171 from magistrates' courts and 18 from the Crown Court. One in three was successful (Lord Chancellor's Department, 1989).

The grounds of appeal are limited to complaints that the magistrates' court acted in excess of jurisdiction or in error of law. The reason for the former

ground is historical and today duplicates the remedy of *certiorari* available on
application for judicial review (see below). Most appeals by way of case stated
are for this reason based on errors of law, and most go to the correctness of the
conviction rather than to issues of sentence. The time limit for entering such an
appeal is again 21 days from the date of the decision. Procedure on application
for a case to be stated by a magistrates' court is as follows, though where the
application relates to a decision of the Crown Court, there are some differences.
The application for a case to be stated is sent to the clerk to the justices, who
is principally responsible for drafting the case to be sent to the High Court. The
case consists of a statement of the charge, the facts as found by the magistrates,
the arguments adduced on the law and the justices' decisions on the law, the
outcome of the case, and the question upon which the opinion of the High Court
is sought. The only circumstances in which the evidence before the court is summarized is where the ground of the appeal is that the justices erred in law by
making a finding of fact for which there was no evidence, or where the justices
made findings of fact which no reasonable justices could have made on the evidence before them. In drafting the case, the clerk will consult the justices and the
parties and will take account of representations made by them. In applications
relating to decisions of the Crown Court, the appellant's solicitors will be responsible for the initial drafting of the case for signature by the Circuit judge or
Recorder. The final version of the case is sent to the appellant's solicitors who
are responsible for lodging it in the Crown Office at the Royal Courts of Justice
within ten days of its receipt.

The appeal is heard by a Divisional Court of the Queen's Bench Division, that
is, by at least two judges of the High Court, and usually by three. It is common
practice for these appeals to be heard by the Lord Chief Justice and two puisne
judges. If a two judge court is evenly split, it seems that the decision of the court
below stands (*Flannagan* v. *Shaw*, [1920] 3 KB 96). The Divisional Court hears
only legal argument and no evidence. In disposing of the case, the Divisional
Court has wide powers similar to those of the Crown Court when exercising its
appellate function.

Application for Judicial Review

If there has been some illegality in the proceedings, either prosecution or defence
may seek to correct that illegality by way of application to the High Court for
judicial review (Rules of the Supreme Court, O.53). Leave to seek judicial review
is always required and forms part of the application. There are three orders
available. *Certiorari* quashes an unlawful decision in the course of proceedings
of an inferior court, for example, the imposition of a sentence in excess of that
allowed in magistrates' courts. Mandamus compels an inferior court to carry out
its functions, for example, to secure consideration of the appropriate legal
criteria for the grant of legal aid or bail. Finally, prohibition orders an inferior
court to cease acting unlawfully; for an example see the case of *R* v. *Hatfield
Justices, ex parte Castle* ([1981] 1 WLR 217).

Applications for judicial review of criminal proceedings are not numerous. In

1988 there were 120 applications determined by the High Court, of which 55 resulted in the grant of an order (Lord Chancellor's Department, 1989).

Interrelationships of the Appeal Procedures

Overlap exists between the three different types of challenge to decision of magistrates' courts. An application for a case to be stated on the grounds of an excess of jurisdiction overlaps with an application for an order of *certiorari*; and there is a choice of appeal to be made where a defendant believes the magistrates erred in their interpretation of the law, where appeal to the Crown Court and appeal by way of case stated on the grounds of error of law overlap. An appeal by way of case stated precludes appeal to the Crown Court, whereas there is always the possibility of an appeal by way of case stated following the rehearing of the case by the Crown Court, if the defendant believes there is still an error of law in the decision. Where application for judicial review and the appeal by way of case stated coincide, the Divisional Court has made it clear in *R v. Crown Court at Ipswich, ex parte Baldwin* ([1981] 1 All ER 596) that judicial review should only be used for straightforward applications. Where detailed information from the justices is likely to be an important part of the appeal, the case stated procedure is considered the only convenient and proper way to bring the case before the High Court.

The confusing overlap of procedures and the piecemeal development of appeals following summary trial result in a system of appeals that lacks coherence. There is clearly a case for removing the hybrid status of the Crown Court and for transferring to it the jurisdiction currently vested in the High Court to entertain appeals by way of case stated and applications for judicial review. Such cases ought to be listed before a High Court judge sitting in the Crown Court. All that would be lost would be the supervisory jurisdiction of the High Court over the Crown Court, which is exercised in very few cases each year. The Crown Court would then become the forum for all appeals from criminal proceedings in magistrates' courts. This could relieve the overburdened High Court of a small body of cases without swamping the Crown Court, whose status as the equal of the High Court would be recognized in its exercise of appellate jurisdiction.

Appeal following Trial on Indictment

A Heavily Circumscribed System

Compared with the generous, but under-used, provision for appeal following summary trial, appeals following trial on indictment are hedged about with conditions and the powers of the Court of Appeal, criminal division, are heavily circumscribed. The reason for this is the sanctity of the jury verdict, which has meant that it is extremely difficult to reopen the findings of fact upon which the jury will have based its decision to convict.

Once again an appreciation of the historical development of criminal appeals following trial on indictment helps to explain some of the anomalies of the present system. Until 1848 decisions resulting from trial on indictment were final. At best a trial judge could refer a question of law following a conviction informally to his fellow judges before delivering judgment or before the sentence was put into effect. If the judges considered that the conviction was mistaken, a recommendation would be made that a pardon be granted. This informal procedure was institutionalized in 1848 with the creation of the Court for Crown Cases Reserved, but the reserving of cases was at the absolute discretion of the judges (Holdsworth, 1956). This unsatisfactory state of affairs continued until the enactment of the Criminal Appeal Act 1907, which established the Court of Criminal Appeal. There had been 35 previous attempts to secure legislation on criminal appeals and it is generally accepted that it was the imprisonment for seven years of Adolf Beck on mistaken identification evidence which finally stirred consciences sufficiently to establish a formal system of appeals following trial on indictment. But the Court of Criminal Appeal was an odd hybrid court at the periphery of the court system; it built on the experience of the Court for Crown Cases Reserved more than it represented a radical innovation in the criminal justice system. The Court of Criminal Appeal was presided over by the Lord Chief Justice who usually sat with two High Court judges to hear appeals. It was therefore a court without its own judiciary, which consisted of trial judges sitting by rotation to review the work of their colleagues.

Criminal appeals did not take on their modern form until the reforms of the Criminal Appeal Act 1966, which followed the study of criminal appeals by the Interdepartmental Committee on the Court of Criminal Appeal known as the Donovan Committee (Donovan Committee, 1965). Under the Criminal Appeal Act 1966 the Court of Criminal Appeal was abolished and reconstituted as a division of the Court of Appeal. The new division is headed by the Lord Chief Justice and all the Lords Justices of Appeal are judges of the Court, though High Court judges retain their eligibility to sit in the criminal division of the Court of Appeal. It remains common for a court to be composed of a Lord Justice of Appeal and two High Court judges. Indeed courts consisting of two judges may now dispose of appeals against sentence (Supreme Court Act 1981, s.55). Most of the law relating to criminal appeals following trial on indictment has been consolidated in the Criminal Appeal Act 1968.

Getting Advice on Appealing

Virtually all defendants tried in the Crown Court have the benefit of representation under a criminal legal aid order. It has long been the case that legal aid for such purposes includes the giving of advice on any grounds for appealing against either conviction or sentence, or both, and, if such grounds exist, to meet the cost of preparing and filing the application for leave to appeal (Legal Aid Act 1988, s.19(2)). But a survey in 1970 based on interviews with prisoners showed a significant failure to provide such advice with the result that the Court of Appeal was inundated with hopeless handwritten applications for leave to appeal

(Zander, 1972b). The response was a *Practice Note* ([1974] 1 WLR 774) and an accompanying pamphlet, which required solicitors and counsel to ensure that defendants convicted at the Crown Court were automatically advised whether there were any grounds of appeal, and that provisional oral advice should be confirmed by letter. The procedure was amended in 1976, and a new edition of the pamphlet, approved by the Lord Chief Justice, was produced in 1983 (Thompson, 1983; Zander, 1975b). There is some evidence that the new procedures did not operate as intended (Baldwin and McConville, 1979b; Benson Commission, 1979). The Benson Commission considered that the rules governing advice on appeal should be made more formal.

Lord Widgery CJ expressed his frustration by announcing in 1980 that time spent awaiting appeal would not normally count as part of the sentence if the recommended procedures had not been followed (*Practice Direction*, [1980] 1 All ER 555). The current Guide requires solicitors to instruct counsel to give advice and assistance on appeal following conviction and sentence in the Crown Court. Solicitors and counsel should see defendants immediately following conviction and sentence, and counsel should express a provisional view on the existence of any grounds of appeal. Within 14 days counsel must send written advice on appeal to the solicitors accompanied, where appropriate, by signed grounds of appeal. These documents are then sent to defendants to reach them within 21 days of conviction and sentence. If counsel has advised an appeal, the solicitors should forthwith complete and lodge application for leave to appeal to reach the Registrar of Criminal Appeals within 28 days of conviction and sentence. Some, though little, sympathy may be expressed for the profession. No doubt it is difficult to explain to defendants who believe that they have just been victims of miscarriages of justice that the grounds of appeal against conviction and sentence are narrow and technical, and that appeal against conviction is not a general means of obtaining a review of the correctness of the conviction. But that is no excuse for what appears to be a widespread failure to comply with mandatory guidelines, albeit guidelines for breach of which there are few effective sanctions.

Appeals against Conviction: the Need for Leave

The Registrar of Criminal Appeals has stated that the Court of Appeal is essentially concerned with two questions in considering appeals against conviction:

was the result right?
was the trial conducted in an acceptable manner? (Meador, 1973, p. 97)

Few would argue with these purposes. The two questions relate to different aspects of the trial process. The first considers whether there has been a miscarriage of justice, despite all the safeguards built into the system, which has resulted in the conviction of an innocent defendant. The second goes to issues of due process; regardless of the outcome of the case: did the trial meet the required standards of fairness and impartiality?

An aggrieved defendant may appeal *as of right* against a conviction on the ground that a question solely of law is involved, or where the trial judge has granted a certificate that the case is fit for appeal on a ground involving a question of mixed fact and law, or of fact alone. Appeals as of right are rarities and account for only about one in 60 appeals against conviction. This is because most issues are regarded as involving a question of mixed fact and law simply because the question of law arises in the factual context of the case. This narrow construction makes it difficult to envisage cases involving questions of law alone; such questions need to be completely severable from the evidence in the case. An example might be a serious misdirection by the judge in summing up as to the standard of proof required in criminal cases. Where the appeal appears to be wholly without merit, the Registrar of Criminal Appeals may refer it to the court for summary determination, that is, for dismissal without a full hearing on the basis that the appeal is wholly without merit. This power exists in all appeals, but is of greatest significance where a person claims to appeal as of right.

Appeals based on mixed fact and law, or fact alone, are only available where leave has been obtained from the Court of Appeal. Within 28 days of the conviction and sentence, notice of application for leave to appeal and the grounds of appeal must be lodged with the Registrar of Criminal Appeals. These may be accompanied by a transcript of the judge's summing up or of part of the evidence if that is relevant to the appeal. These are then considered by one of the judges eligible to sit in the Court of Appeal, criminal division, known as 'the single judge'. There is an element of discrimination in favour of privately represented applicants at this stage in that it seems that it is common practice for applications by such persons to be referred directly to a full court of three judges (Meador, 1973). Cases of special importance or particular difficulty, which are not so represented, may also be referred to a full court, in which case the Registrar will normally grant legal aid for this purpose and will also arrange for the Crown to be represented.

Consideration of the application by the single judge is on the papers alone. Refusal of leave at this stage is not final, but there are risks for a defendant in pursuing the matter further. A defendant refused leave by the single judge may give notice within 14 days that he wishes to renew his application before the full court. At this stage no legal aid is made available to the applicant and the full court will consider the application on the papers alone. This is again in marked contrast to privately financed applications and applications referred by the Registrar, where representation is common. The decision on the renewed application is given in open court, at which time the court may, if the application is refused, make directions that time spent in custody since the filing of the application is not to count as part of any custodial sentence imposed on the defendant (*Practice Direction*, [1980] 1 All ER 555). This loss of time, which may also be ordered by the single judge in cases deemed to be unarguable, operates as a powerful disincentive to the pursuit of appeals. Nearly three-quarters of all applications for leave to appeal against conviction fall by the wayside at this stage.

If leave is granted, legal aid will normally be granted for the arguing of the appeal, but unless the collection of new evidence is needed, this will be limited to counsel only. To obtain an extension to include legal aid for a solicitor, counsel must apply in writing to the Registrar showing that there is work to be done which can only be done by solicitors (Thompson, 1983). This rule operates in practice to isolate defendants from their legal advisers; counsel will normally argue the case on the basis of the papers prepared in connection with the advice on appeal and the filing of the notice for leave, plus perhaps a brief conference with the defendant on the day of the appeal.

Appeal against Conviction: the Grounds of Appeal

An appeal against conviction must be based on one or more of the three grounds set out in s.2(1) of the Criminal Appeal Act 1968:

> the conviction is, in all the circumstances of the case, unsafe or unsatisfactory;
> or the trial judge made a wrong decision on a question of law;
> or there was a material irregularity in the course of the trial.

The first ground of appeal is the only one which can readily be used as the basis for an appeal where the defendant's essential grievance is that the conviction was against the weight of the evidence. Prior to the amendments made by the Criminal Appeal Act 1966, the test had been more strict; to be quashed the verdict had to be one which was 'unreasonable or could not be supported having regard to the evidence'. The Court of Criminal Appeal had construed the provision very narrowly refusing to intervene except in cases where there was literally no evidence against the defendant to support to conviction. The new test is subjective. Lord Justice Widgery (as he then was) expressed it thus in *R v. Cooper* ([1969] 1 QB 267):

> In cases of this kind the court must in the end ask itself a subjective question, whether we are content to let the matter stand as it is, or whether there is not some lurking doubt in our minds which makes us wonder whether an injustice has been done. This is a reaction which may not be based strictly on the evidence as such; it is a reaction which can be produced by the general feel of the case as the court experiences it. (p. 271)

This broad interpretation of the power was prefaced by a reminder of the sanctity of jury decision making, and represents a considerable qualification of the test:

> It has been said over and over again throughout the years that this court must recognise the advantage which a jury has in seeing and hearing the witnesses, and if all the material was before the jury and the summing up was impeccable, this court should not lightly interfere. (p. 271)

Despite the more generous wording of the current legislation, criticism has been expressed that the Court of Appeal is reluctant to quash convictions on the ground that they are unsafe or unsatisfactory. An analysis of the case law since 1966 suggests that of those cases where leave to appeal is granted which are argued on this ground, about four in ten succeed. However, it is the presence of a procedural irregularity or a series of small problems in the conduct of the trial which appear to provide the basis for many of these decisions. There are very few cases which can be said to be a review of the merits of the conviction. It does not seem that appeals often succeed on this ground where no fault can be found with the trial. In a recent report, JUSTICE could identify only six cases since 1968 where convictions were quashed because of doubts about the correctness of the jury's verdict (JUSTICE, 1989). The 'lurking doubt' test laid down in *Cooper* will usually only be satisfied by pointing to some defect in the trial. Because of this the Court of Appeal is still able effectively to wash its hands of the issue of guilt, and to restrict its determinations to whether there was sufficient evidence upon which a reasonable jury could convict or whether there was some error of law or procedure made by the trial judge. The search for error is clear from the other two grounds of appeal, which are largely self-explanatory.

If one of the grounds set out in s.2(1) of the Criminal Appeal Act 1968 is made out, the Court of Appeal is required to allow the appeal unless they consider that no miscarriage of justice has actually occurred. This is known as *applying the proviso* and is a means of avoiding quashing convictions where a harmless error has occurred. By its very nature it might seem to have little application to cases based on the argument that the conviction is unsafe or unsatisfactory, but because many such appeals do point to some fault or error in the course of the trial, this is not necessarily true. The Court of Appeal has shown itself reluctant to apply the proviso. This again reflects a reluctance by the Court of Appeal to put itself in the shoes of the jury. The test applied by the Court of Appeal is whether, despite the establishment of the ground of appeal, there is sufficient evidence and a sufficient direction for a reasonable jury definitely and fairly to convict (*R* v. *Whybrow*, [1951] 35 Cr App R 141).

Analysis of the case law suggests the following conclusions (Knight, 1973). Once speculation arises about the effect the error might have had on the jury or about the impact of the evidence apart from the error, the court will not apply the proviso. But even serious errors may be overlooked, though some errors are regarded as so serious that, despite a clear intimation by the Court of Appeal that they believe that the defendant has been rightly convicted, the interests of justice are seen to demand the quashing of the conviction (see *Maxwell* v. *DPP*, [1935] AC 309). It also seems that the court is reluctant to apply the proviso in cases where there has been a majority verdict. Within the constraints of a system which allows a conviction to stand even after a relatively unfair trial, it seems that the proviso is applied fairly. But in some cases a conviction is quashed where it is against the justice of the case. It has unfortunately become easier to have a conviction quashed because of some error of law or procedure at the trial than to redress a miscarriage of justice.

There are around 1200 appeals against conviction each year, of which one in ten results in the quashing of the conviction.

Appeal against Conviction: the Powers of the Court of Appeal

The Court of Appeal has powers to quash a conviction, to admit fresh evidence, to order a retrial and to convict in the alternative.

The hearing of appeals normally involves only legal argument and not any rehearing of evidence. Where evidence given at the trial is relevant to the appeal reliance will be placed on a transcript of the trial proceedings. But it may be that an appellant wishes to adduce evidence not put at the trial in support of the appeal. The Court of Appeal always has a discretion to receive evidence, but is only required to receive evidence in limited circumstances (s.23, Criminal Appeal Act 1968). Fresh evidence, which the court does not regard as so marginal that it would not afford a ground for allowing the appeal, must be received if:

it appears likely to be credible; and
it would have been admissible at the trial; and
there is a reasonable explanation for the failure to adduce it at the trial.

The court has construed these requirements very strictly and has shown a marked reluctance to admit fresh evidence. It has also adopted a restrictive view of its function in evaluating the effect of fresh evidence. The court must ask itself whether in the light of the fresh evidence and all the circumstances of the case, the conviction is unsafe or unsatisfactory (*Stafford* v. *DPP*, [1974] AC 878). The test laid down in *Stafford* v. *DPP* replaced the old rule that, if the evidence was considered relevant and capable of belief, the court should ask itself whether, notwithstanding the fresh evidence, a reasonable jury would inevitably have convicted. The differences between the two tests are significant as was made clear in *Stafford* v. *DPP*. Lord Devlin has criticized the new rule as one which usurps the function of the jury and undermines the complimentary power of the Court of Appeal to order a retrial (Devlin, 1979).

It is interesting to note that the Court of Appeal is exhorted to abandon its reluctance to stand in the shoes of the jury when otherwise the result would be more retrials. The provisions of the Criminal Appeal Act 1968 relating to retrials permit the Court of Appeal at its discretion to order a retrial where the court allows an appeal by reason of fresh evidence. The Act would appear to be contemplating a situation in which the fresh evidence seems credible and relevant, but it is impossible to know how this would have influenced the jury at trial when taken with all the other evidence. There are only a handful of retrials each year, and this lends weight to Lord Devlin's arguments that the decision of the House of Lords in *Stafford* v *DPP* has eroded the statutory scheme in this area.

Whether the incidence of miscarriages of justice could and would be reduced by giving the Court of Appeal a general power to order retrials has been a highly contentious issue. The Tucker Committee, whose report prefaced the introduction of the power to order a retrial in fresh evidence cases, were divided on this issue. A majority of five to three rejected the idea (Tucker, 1954). The JUSTICE Committee which considered the issue was also divided but by a majority of nine to four came down in favour of granting the court such a power (JUSTICE, 1964). Those opposed to a general power see basic values embedded in the criminal justice system as being at stake. It is argued that to allow retrials would be to erode not only the finality of jury verdicts but also the finality of the trial process itself. There was also concern expressed that the floodgates would be opened and that there would be too many retrials at huge public expense. Finally it was considered that defendants tried for a second time might be prejudiced since the jury would almost certainly learn that it was a second trial and might infer that the Court of Appeal had ordered a retrial because they felt that the defendant was guilty.

The arguments in favour of a general power maintain that the power is needed to provide a further safeguard against miscarriages of justice. Ordering a retrial would avoid the conviction of the innocent and, given the difficulty the Court of Appeal has over the application of the proviso, would avoid the quashing of convictions in favour of unmeritorious appellants on technicalities. Such defendants could be retried in conformity with the rules of due process (*see also* Spencer, 1982). Finally, it is argued that the experience of other jurisdictions does not bear out the fears expressed by those opposed to the court's having such a power. A new factor not considered in the above deliberations is the empirical evidence which suggests that the number of doubtful convictions and questionable acquittals is considerably larger than previously thought (Baldwin and McConville, 1979b).

The arguments in favour of such a power certainly seem more compelling than those against. Parliament has at long last agreed; s.43 of the Criminal Justice Act 1988 has swept away the restriction on the Court of Appeal's power to order a retrial only in fresh evidence cases. The effect is to allow the Court of Appeal a discretion to order a retrial whenever it allows an appeal against conviction if it appears in the interests of justice to do so. The new power is likely to be used to avoid those unsatisfactory appeals where a conviction is quashed on a technicality. In such cases the defendant can be sent back for a trial at which the rules of due process are followed. Quite how the Court of Appeal will exercise its discretion remains to be seen. But given the arguments for and against the power outlined above, it would not be surprising to see the Court of Appeal reserving the exercise of the discretion for those cases where the offence charged was very serious and where the Crown Court had imposed a substantial custodial sentence.

Amendments to the procedural rules governing retrials are designed to mitigate the disadvantages of delay and a lack of finality introduced by the wider power. Where a retrial is ordered, the defendant must be brought to trial within two months, unless leave of the Court of Appeal has been obtained. The defendant is entitled to make representations on any application for an extension of the time limit. Provision is made for limiting extensions to cases where the prosecution has acted 'with all due expedition' and there remains 'good and sufficient cause for a retrial in spite of the lapse of time' (s.43, Criminal Justice Act 1988).

Finally, the Court of Appeal has the power to substitute an alternative verdict provided that:

it was open to the jury to have convicted on an alternative charge, and the jury did not expressly acquit on that charge; and

the court is satisfied that the jury could on the evidence before it have convicted on that charge.

An example makes this easier to understand. A defendant is tried on a two count indictment charging theft and handling, and is convicted of theft, but expressly acquitted of the handling charge. In this case, the Court of Appeal has no power to substitute a verdict of guilty of handling for that of theft, even if it thinks that it is the correct verdict, since the jury acquitted on the handling charge. But if in such a case the trial judge on receiving the verdict of guilty on the theft charge had discharged the jury in respect of the handling charge, the Court of Appeal could substitute a verdict of guilty on the handling count for the theft conviction.

Venire de Novo

The Court of Appeal's power to order a retrial is often confused with the power to order a new trial by issuing the old common law writ of *venire de novo*. This is the power to order a fresh trial where the first trial was a nullity because of some fundamental defect. A good example is a trial before a judge not qualified to sit as a judge (*R v. Cronin*, [1940] 1 All ER 618). Another is a conviction based on a wrongful plea of guilty induced by oppression. In *R v. Rose*, ([1982] AC 822) the House of Lords confirmed that *venire de novo* is only appropriate where the defect renders the proceedings a nullity from beginning to end and is not available to secure a retrial where a serious irregularity will necessitate quashing a conviction on a technicality. These cases are now accommodated because a retrial can now be ordered; this may be the sort of case for which the wider power to order a retrial was designed.

Appeals against Sentence

Appeals against sentence are separate appeals from those against conviction. If a defendant appeals against conviction, but not against sentence, and is unsuccessful, the Court of Appeal has no power to vary the sentence imposed by the Crown Court. There is no right of appeal against sentence following trial on indictment unless the trial judge grants a certificate that the case is suitable for appeal. This is very rare. For the offence of murder there is no appeal against sentence at all, since the penalty of life imprisonment is required by statute. In all other cases leave of the Court of Appeal is required.

Leave to appeal against sentence is obtained in exactly the same way as leave to appeal against conviction. Appeals against sentence are far more numerous than those against conviction. About one in three appellants succeeds in

obtaining leave. The risk of losing time applies equally to appeals against
sentence.

Section 11 of the Criminal Appeal Act 1968 which governs appeals against
sentence does not spell out the grounds upon which such appeals are based. The
basic ground will, of course, be that the defendant regards the sentence as too
severe having regard to all the circumstances of the case. The abundant case law
of the Court of Appeal, which is now sufficient to justify its own set of law
reports (Criminal Appeal Reports (Cr App R) (Sentencing)) makes clear that the
grounds of complaint must be that the sentence imposed by the Crown Court
was clearly excessive or wrong in principle. The traditional view is that the Court
of Appeal does not put itself in the shoes of the trial judge and replace the sentence of that judge with the sentence it would itself have imposed. The court
starts by accepting the sentence and then determines whether it is a sentence that
it was clearly improper for the trial judge to have imposed. The result is that a
margin of appreciation is allowed to the trial judge, who, like the jury, will have
seen the defendant and heard all the evidence in the case. Thus the Court of
Appeal will not interfere merely with harsh sentences, but only with sentences
so harsh that they can be regarded as clearly excessive. The phrase 'wrong in
principle' can apply to the severity of a sentence of imprisonment, but is also
applicable when the form of the sentence is inappropriate. An example would be
the inappropriate imposition of an immediate custodial sentence rather than
some non-custodial sentence. There is some evidence that the traditional view is
changing, much to the chagrin of trial judges (Ashworth, 1984). The Court of
Appeal appears to have adopted a practice of tinkering with sentences. Trial
judges complained that the Court of Appeal had started making small reductions
in terms of imprisonment, so interfering with the trial judges' sentencing autonomy.

If the Court of Appeal allows an appeal against sentence, it may vary the sentence by substituting any sentence which was available to the Crown Court, but
it may not, taking the case as a whole, deal with the defendant more severely
than the Crown Court. The proviso that allows the court to take the case as a
whole means that where there is an appeal against conviction and sentence on
two counts and the conviction on one of them is quashed, the court can increase
sentence on the other provided that the substituted sentence is no more severe
than the total sentence of the Crown Court.

There are about 6000 appeals against sentence each year, of which about one
in five results in some reduction of the sentence imposed by the Crown Court.

Home Secretary's References

Aggrieved defendants have 28 days in which to apply for leave to appeal against
conviction. If there was no other possibility of seeking a judicial review of the
conviction other than within this time, considerable injustice could be caused
where fresh evidence comes to light only at a later date. It would be possible to
leave all such matters to be dealt with by the prerogative powers discussed later
in this chapter, but s.17 of the Criminal Appeal Act 1968 allows any person con-

victed on indictment to make application at any time to the Home Secretary, who may refer the whole or part of the case to the Court of Appeal. The Home Secretary may make such a reference even though there has already been an appeal to the Court of Appeal and even though the Home Secretary has previously referred the same case to the Court of Appeal. When the Home Secretary refers the whole of a case to the Court of Appeal, it is treated in effect as an appeal against conviction by the defendant who may bring up and argue matters additional to those which have led the Home Secretary to make the reference (*R v. Chard*, [1984] AC 279). Though petitions to the Home Secretary are numerous, averaging around 2650 each year (Home Affairs Committee, 1982), many are unsubstantiated complaints and grievances.

References are only likely to be made if there are extensive efforts at fact-finding at the instance of friends or relatives of the convicted person which attract the support of a public figure. Since petitions to the Home Secretary are also made with a view to securing the recommendation of a pardon, there is a subtle line to be drawn between situations in which it will be appropriate to grant a pardon or remission of sentence and those in which reference to the Court of Appeal is appropriate. The former is concerned principally with mercy, while the latter is part of the administration of justice. It seems that a very heavy burden lies on a petitioner to establish a case for a pardon, while a lesser burden will be required for a reference to the Court of Appeal. In the latter case the test appears to be whether the information in the petition casts real doubt on the correctness of the conviction (Home Affairs Committee, 1982). It is still a hurdle few clear. Each year there are only a handful of references.

The Attorney-General's Reference: following an Acquittal

There is one situation in which a point of law arising on an acquittal can be referred to the Court of Appeal, but the sanctity of the jury's acquittal is preserved because the proceedings in no way affect the decision to acquit. Section 36 of the Criminal Justice Act 1972 allows the Attorney-General to refer a point of law arising in a trial in which the defendant was acquitted to the Court of Appeal for its opinion. The power is used sparingly and there have seldom been more than a handful of references in any one year. Even though the procedure does not prejudice acquitted defendants, they are entitled to have counsel present argument on their behalf at the public expense.

The Attorney-General's Reference: on Sentence

Sections 35 and 36 of the Criminal Justice Act 1988 introduce an Attorney-General's reference on sentence. It is in effect a limited prosecution appeal against an unduly lenient sentence. Only the Attorney-General can refer a sentence to the Court of Appeal for review of a sentence imposed in the Crown Court. The power is only available where the offence is triable only on indictment, or is an either way offence specified in an order made by the Home Secretary. No such order has yet been made. Where such a reference is made the Court of Appeal may quash the sentence imposed by the Crown Court and replace it with any sentence they consider appropriate up to the maximum available to the Crown Court.

The first reference under the section has been made in a case involving the offence of incest, for which there were previously no sentencing guidelines. The result of the appeal was the increase of the three year sentence imposed in the Crown Court to six years imprisonment. The bulk of the Court's judgment contains detailed guidelines for Crown Court judges on the sentencing of those convicted of incest (*Attorney-General's Reference 1989/1*, [1989] 1 WLR 1117).

Following the review by the Court of Appeal, either party may, subject to obtaining a certificate from the Court of Appeal, and with leave of either the Court of Appeal or House of Lords, further refer the case to the House of Lords for their opinion on any point of law of general public importance.

The first attempt to introduce a power of review was made during the passage of the Prosecution of Offences Act 1985, but attracted so much hostility that it was dropped from the Act. The scheme proposed then was rather milder than that implemented in the Criminal Justice Act 1988. Under the 1985 proposals, the reference on sentence would have worked much like the reference following an acquittal. It would not have prejudiced the defendant. There has clearly been a remarkable change of opinion in just three years, because the new scheme permits sentence to be increased. Under the new scheme, it is not yet clear what range of offences will be covered. The intention is clearly that some either way offences will be included, yet there remains no power of review of sentencing in magistrates' courts. Magistrates' courts sentence those offenders charged with either way offences whose offence is of insufficient gravity to warrant trial on indictment. Yet, presumably magistrates' courts are no less likely than Crown Court judges to pass 'rogue' sentences. The decision to seek a referral lies with the Crown Prosecution Service, which introduces the spectre of prosecution concerning itself, at least after sentence has been imposed, with its propriety. This may be more of an imaginary than real problem, since the types of sentence referred will be those where something has obviously gone wrong with the sentencing in the Crown Court. If this is the case, then the requirement of obtaining leave is unlikely to be a contentious issue. But the wider the range of cases, the more difficult this issue will be. No guidance is given in the statutory provisions as to the test to be applied by the Court of Appeal in permitting a reference to proceed.

The Royal Prerogative of Mercy

This quaint title refers to the Crown's prerogative powers to grant pardons and remissions of sentence (Smith, 1983). There is a clear theoretical distinction between the exercise of mercy and the operation of justice. Justice is achieved through the judicial process, but there may be a variety of reasons why justice should be tempered with mercy. Grounds of compassion may demand that a convicted prisoner be granted a pardon or remission of sentence. It is also clear that the criminal justice system is not infallible and produces miscarriages of justice. A succession of *causes célèbres* have shown that miscarriages of justice have occurred with a frequency many regard as unacceptable (JUSTICE, 1968; JUSTICE, 1989). For these cases the prerogative of mercy provides the last safety net. It is with such cases that we are concerned here.

In discussing the power of the Home Secretary to refer cases to the Court of Appeal, reference was made to the large number of petitions submitted to the Home Secretary. If a petition suggests that there are substantial grounds for believing that a miscarriage of justice has occurred, then the Home Office will cause further investigations to be made by the police. The propriety of leaving these investigations, many of which allege police misconduct, in the hands of the police has been questioned. The process of inquiry is also conducted with a lack of openness that is a source of complaint. The notion that some of these difficulties could be overcome by introducing an independent element in the review of petitions has been suggested by JUSTICE (JUSTICE, 1968; JUSTICE, 1989), and by the Devlin Committee (Devlin Committee, 1976) and has been taken up by the Home Affairs Committee in its report on miscarriages of justice (Home Affairs Committee, 1982). The recommendations of the Home Affairs Committee are that the Home Office should continue to be responsible for the initial reviewing of petitions, but if it appeared that there was evidence which was not considered at the trial, the matter would be referred to an independent review body. The chairperson would charge one of the members with the task of investigating further. If necessary evidence and argument could be adduced before the independent body whose deliberations would culminate in a reasoned opinion containing advice to the Home Secretary as to whether it was an appropriate case for intervention. Consideration by the independent review body would also replace references to the Court of Appeal by the Home Secretary except perhaps where a point of law was involved.

Unanswered questions relate to personnel and the resources for the investigative function of the independent review body. Not even tentative costings were produced for such a scheme. The Government response stressed the role of the Court of Appeal as the primary reviewer of convictions, and made lame noises about the readiness of the Court of Appeal to exercise its existing powers generously, which are not borne out by its practice. This was followed by a rejection of the proposal for an independent review body. (Government Reply to Miscarriages of Justice, 1983).

JUSTICE has recently published a further report on miscarriages of justice (JUSTICE, 1989) which estimates that there are at least 15 people a year wrongly convicted after trial by jury. Five common themes are identified in such cases: incorrect identification; false confessions; perjury by a co-defendant or witness; police misconduct; and poor tactics by defence lawyers. The Court of Appeal is criticized for its restrictive attitude to quashing convictions on the basis that they are unsafe or unsatisfactory. Only six cases since 1968 could be identified where convictions had been quashed because the Court was in doubt as to the correctness of the jury's verdict. The charge is made that the establishment is too concerned with maintaining the correctness of convictions. A renewed call is made for an Independent Review Body to deal with miscarriages of justice, whose members would be appointed by the Lord Chancellor.

In appropriate cases the Home Secretary can recommend the grant of a free pardon or the remission of the whole or part of a sentence. The use of free pardons has been criticized as inappropriate where its purpose is to provide redress for a miscarriage of justice. The notion of a pardon suggests that there is some wrongdoing to be forgiven. The Home Affairs Committee recommended some change of nomenclature and in its reply the Government did accept the point and will consider an amendment to legislation to introduce a new label for the process when the opportunity arises. The opportunity to do this has not been taken in the Criminal Justice Act 1988.

The award of a pardon does not carry with it any right to compensation, although the Home Secretary as a matter of course offers *ex gratia* payments to those pardoned as a result of a miscarriage of justice. The compensation is said to be based on ordinary civil law principles of damages and the Home Secretary takes the advice of the chairman of the Criminal Injuries Compensation Board, but there have been reports of ludicrously low offers (Smith, A., 1983). The reported range of awards is enormous: from a low figure of £180 to a high of £77,000 (Home Affairs Committee, 1982; Smith, A., 1983), but there is little systematic information relating figures to particular cases and so these figures are not very informative. Dissatisfaction with the right to, and assessment of, compensation has led JUSTICE to call for a statutory right to compensation, which would be fixed by an independent tribunal, the Imprisonment Compensation Tribunal, which would be modelled on the Criminal Injuries Compensation Board (JUSTICE, 1982).

Section 133 of the Criminal Justice Act 1988 introduces a statutory right to compensation where a person has been convicted and sentenced for a crime he or she did not commit. The circumstances in which compensation will be paid are drafted extraordinarily narrowly. The aggrieved person must apply for compensation; it is not automatic. That person must:

> have been pardoned on the ground that a new or newly discovered fact shows
>   beyond reasonable doubt that there has been a miscarriage of justice; or
> have had a conviction quashed on an appeal made out of time; or
> have had a conviction quashed following a Home Secretary's reference under
>   section 17 of the Criminal Appeal Act 1968; *and*
> was not wholly or partly responsible for the non-disclosure of the unknown
>   fact which now establishes innocence.

The Home Secretary determines entitlement to compensation and there is no appeal on this, though the decision may be challenged by judicial review. Straightforward cases where a conviction is quashed on initial appeal to the Court of Appeal are excluded, even though such persons may have spent considerable periods in custody awaiting trial and the outcome of their appeal. The number of cases meeting these very strict criteria will be very few indeed.

The number of pardons granted each year is around 75, of which around ten will involve those wrongfully imprisoned.

Appeal to the House of Lords

From the Divisional Court

There is no appeal following a decision of the Crown Court in the exercise of its appellate jurisdiction other than to the Divisional Court. But appeal direct to the House of Lords in a criminal cause or matter lies from a decision of the Divisional Court (Administration of Justice Act 1960, s.1). Following summary trial, the Court of Appeal, criminal division, has no role whatsoever to play in the appellate process.

Before an appeal from the Divisional Court to the House of Lords is possible, two conditions must be satisfied. First, the Divisional Court must grant a certificate that a point of law of general public importance is involved. If no certificate is granted, no appeal is possible; there is no appeal against a refusal of a certificate. Secondly, either the Divisional Court or the House of Lords must grant leave to appeal. It is sometimes seen as curious that a court refuses leave to appeal in the face of a certificate that a point of law of general public importance is involved in the case. The reason for this curiosity is once again to be found by delving into history. But the issue is so closely bound up with the creation of a system of appeals following trial on indictment, where an identical rule governs appeal from the Court of Appeal, criminal division, to the House of Lords, that it is best to offer the explanation in that context.

From the Court of Appeal

Following a decision of the Court of Appeal, either party may appeal to the House of Lords. The pattern is similar to that for appeals following summary trial from the Divisional Court. There are two preconditions for such an appeal. First, the Court of Appeal must grant a certificate that a point of law of general public importance is involved and, secondly, the Court of Appeal or House of Lords must grant leave on the basis that the appeal is one which the court ought to hear.

History tells us the reasons for these twin tests and provides the explanation for the seemingly curious situation in which it is accepted that a point of law of general public importance is involved but no leave is granted by either court. Appeal to the House of Lords in criminal cases grew out of the unsatisfactory procedure of the writ of error on the fiat of the Attorney-General. The procedure was replaced by the Criminal Appeal Act 1907 which allowed the Attorney-General, on the application of either the defendant or the DPP, to grant a certificate that the decision of the Court of Criminal Appeal involved a point of law of *exceptional* public importance and that it was desirable that a further appeal should be brought. This would allow the House of Lords to consider an appeal. It seems to have been accepted that cases referred to the House should raise questions of general importance involving either statutory interpretation or the solution of particularly difficult problems of the common law. Such considerations were the basis of the grant of certificates by the Attorney-General. It has been suggested that the requirement that the point be of public importance indicates that wider considerations than the justice of the case in which the point arises are relevant (Anon., 1957). Doubts have also been expressed at the propriety of leaving the grant of such certificates in the hands of the senior law officer of the Crown (Prevezer, 1962).

The system was changed to its present form in 1960 (Administration of Justice Act 1960, s.1). The test to be applied by the Court of Criminal Appeal, and subsequently by the Court of Appeal (or Divisional Court following summary trial), was made more generous; the requirement is that a point of law of *general* public importance is involved. In the course of the Parliamentary debates on the two limbs of the leave requirements, it was contemplated that, in the face of a certificate, leave of the lower court or the House of Lords might nevertheless be refused for one of three reasons: that the point is obscure and unlikely to arise again; that the point is so clear as to require no further argument; or that the point is so long established that it ought not to be disturbed. These reasons do not seem very convincing (Downey, 1961), and it is difficult not to conclude that the real reason is simply to keep the conditions for a second appeal as restrictive as possible in order to avoid cases reaching the House of Lords while retaining some flexibility about the cases that are actually heard.

Since case law seldom discusses the criteria for the grant or refusal of a certificate or leave, any suggestions as to these criteria must be speculative. It seems that it is proper for the Court of Appeal or Divisional Court to grant a certificate but to refuse leave where they accept that a point of law of general public importance is involved, but where the Court of Appeal believes that there is only one possible answer to that point, which is to be found in its judgment (see *R* v. *Henn and Darby*, [1980] 2 WLR 597). In such cases it will always be open to the aggrieved party to seek leave from the House itself. The Divisional Court and Court of Appeal often appear to take the view that it is for the House of Lords itself to exercise the gatekeeping function. Under the modern system it has been suggested that the case law indicates that the following criteria are relevant in considering whether the House ought to hear the appeal (Smith, A., 1984):

> are there likely to be other cases whose outcome may be affected by the resolution of the point of law?
>
> does the point have considerable social implications, as in the consideration of intoxication as a defence in *DPP* v. *Majewski*, ([1977] AC 443)?
>
> is the law in the area unclear either because of conflicting cases or because of a dearth of cases?
>
> does the point offer an opportunity to modify a decision of the House which has worked injustice?

It was stressed in the analysis that the House does not seem to be concerned with the notion of doing justice to the individual appellant; that is seen as the role of the first appeal.

The procedure for appeal against a determination on an Attorney-General's reference following an acquittal is different: no certificate is required. The Court of Appeal merely states that the point is one which ought to be considered by the House. If it does not, the matter may be referred to the appeals committee of the House of Lords. The Court of Appeal may also of its own motion refer the point to the House of Lords. Appeals following Attorney-General's sentencing references follow the normal rules.

It has been said that the purpose of criminal appeals to the House of Lords is the attainment of certainty in the criminal law (Cross, 1962; Paterson, 1982). The system has been criticized as not being appropriate to this purpose:

> The House of Lords does not introduce certainty into the law, and it does not treat its task of deciding questions of general importance as being part of the law reform exercise (Smith, A., 1984, p. 147).

In a modest proposal for reform, Smith goes on to suggest that appeals from the Divisional Court should go to the Court of Appeal, but no further, and that the ability of the Crown to appeal to the House of Lords should be replaced by an extension of the Attorney-General's reference to decisions of the Court of Appeal with which the prosecution took issue. Because the Attorney-General would be extracting a point of principle, the House should receive *amicus curiae* ('a friend of the court') argument from others concerned in the development of the law, such as the Law Commission, so that a better contribution could be made to the development of the criminal law (Smith, A., 1984).

Concluding Comment

This chapter has covered such a diverse range of procedures that the drawing of coherent conclusions on criminal appeals is very difficult. The most striking features of the system are the great difference between the procedures following summary trial, where the appeal by way of rehearing has been accepted and causes few problems, and those following trial on indictment, which are narrow and technical. At present the procedures are least satisfactory where they need to be most satisfactory, that is, where the offences are more serious and consequently the penalties are more severe. The Court of Appeal does not achieve success either in producing certainty in the criminal law, nor does it ensure that convictions are based on accepted principles of due process and that doubtful convictions are properly reviewed. There is a pressing need for further development of the appellate process in criminal cases, not only to produce a more coherent system, but also to ensure that the objectives of justice, due process and consistency of decision making are better achieved.

8

Understanding the Criminal Justice System

The Rarity of the Contested Trial

The preceding chapters have guided the reader through the pre-trial, trial and appellate processes in criminal cases. Where the system appears to operate unfairly or unsatisfactorily, the tone has been critical. The reader will by now see that few defendants are subjected to the process of trial and so proof of guilt by contested trial before magistrates or judge and jury is the exception rather than the rule. The initial interaction between the suspect and the police is a principal determinant of later processes. The private interactions of the suspect or defendant with the police, friends, lawyers and even judges seem more important for most defendants than the public process of adjudication seen by the public in the courtroom. With this basic appreciation of the interdependence of the various phases of the criminal justice system, we are equipped to consider the operation of the system as a whole. One of the most fruitful ways of looking at the system as a whole is to compare its performance against theoretical models. If a particular model appeals, then adherence to the philosophy behind that model may well justify acceptance of action which, when seen in isolation, would be unlikely to be acceptable.

The notion of central ideals in a criminal justice system is not just the creation of academic comment on the operation of the system. Even though concerned only with the criminal justice system up to the point of trial, the recommendations in the Report of the Royal Commission on Criminal Procedure are based upon the notion of a fundamental balance between the interests of the community in bringing offenders to justice and the rights and liberties of persons suspected of having committed criminal offences (Philips Commission, 1981). Much of the Report is concerned with constructing a package where new powers for the police in the investigation of offences are carefully balanced by safeguards against their abuse. The Report concludes:

> Ultimately however society faces and will always have to face an ineluctable problem. The nature of the criminal justice process is such that there will continue to be areas in which pressures meet, where interests conflict,

where checks and safeguards may have been provided but prov
to deal with a particular situation. The tensions that these
cannot always be relieved by the application of good sense
tion or by *ad hoc* and informal adjustments. The role of
society and their relationship with the public are, in our view
tant for that. If the fundamental balance in pre-trial procedures i̇̄
firmly and steadily within the limits of public understanding and ẗ
and if the best use is to be made of scarce resources, a critical respon.
falls on Parliament. Our proposal for regulating in a comprehe
statutory framework arrangements for the investigation of offences and
prosecution of offenders affirms that Parliament has the duty of striking th.
fundamental balance and of keeping it under regular review. (Philips
Commission, 1981, at para.10.16)

This long quotation quite clearly indicates that there is a political choice as to
where the fundamental balance lies, which in turn requires a clear understanding
of the objectives of the criminal justice system. Indeed much criticism of the
Police and Criminal Evidence Bill at the first attempt in 1983 to produce an Act
(essentially the same as the 1984 Act) was based on the argument that the variations from the Royal Commission's recommendations altered the fundamental
balance so much that the carefully sewn package was unstitched (LAG Bull.,
1983a; 1983b; Hansen, 1983a; 1983b). The notion of the fundamental balance
can also be applied to the trial and appellate stages of the criminal process.
   Modelling the criminal justice system in order to develop improved systems for
handling the business of the system is also a concern of the Home Office. The
passage of defendants through the police, magistrates' courts, Crown Court and
prison systems can then be simulated through a series of stages over a number
of years. This enables estimates of future resource needs to be made. More significantly, alternatives can be modelled to see whether the flow of defendants can
be speeded up or resources used more efficiently (Morgan, 1985; Pullinger,
1986). Two areas of particular concern in recent years have been the effect of
committal proceedings on the throughput of defendants and the use of custody
on the remand population. The current proposals for alternatives to mode of
trial proceedings and committal proceedings owe something to the use of such
models.
   Research and writing in the United Kingdom on theoretical models of criminal
justice is comparatively new, but is already leading to new perspectives on the
operation of the criminal process. This chapter is an introduction based on the
ideas contained in this new literature.

Models of Criminal Justice

The Work of Herbert Packer

Any discussion of models of criminal justice must begin with the work of the
American scholar, Herbert Packer, who argued that systems of criminal justice

could usefully be examined to see to what extent they corresponded with two theoretical models: the *due process model* and the *crime control model* (Packer, 1968).

The due process model is immediately recognizable to most readers as that which corresponds to the rhetoric of the English criminal justice system. The hallmarks of this model are the presumption of innocence and the requirement of proof of guilt beyond all reasonable doubt. At all stages of the process suspects and defendants enjoy safeguards against self-incrimination. There are obstacles in the face of the police and prosecutors which operate as a form of quality control ensuring that the criminal process constantly weeds out all those who appear to be innocent. At the centre of the due process model is the trial stage, which is again marked by restrictions on the introduction of prejudicial material not directly relevant to the offence or of doubtful probative value. Ultimately the due process model accepts that the price paid for the certainty that no innocent person is convicted will be the occasional acquittal of the guilty.

The contrasting crime control model replaces the judicial procedures with administrative procedures and formal processes with informal processes. Great trust is placed on informal fact-finding, that is, what the police know rather than what is admissible in a process of formal adjudication. The conclusions of the police as fact-finders are the principal determinants of guilt. Repression of criminal conduct is seen as the most important function of the criminal process. Criminal procedure becomes geared to the speedy processing of suspects and defendants. The obstacles of the due process model disappear to be replaced by low visibility administrative processing. Packer comments that:

> If there is confidence in the reliability of informal fact-finding activities that take place in the early stages of the criminal process, the remaining stages can be relatively perfunctory. (Packer, 1968, pp. 160–1)

The presumption of innocence in the due process model is replaced by an implicit presumption of guilt, so that the police are relied upon by courts to weed out the innocent at the investigation stage.

The crime control model is usually rejected as inapplicable to the English criminal justice system. But the rejection seems premature when the evidence of routine violation of the rules governing the police powers of arrest, search and seizure, and interrogation are considered. Add to this evidence showing how rarely suspects rely on the right of silence and the overwhelming number of guilty pleas, where no proof of guilt is required, where there is currently no independent assessment of the evidence and where there are no adversarial procedures, and the crime control model begins to look remarkably apposite. Perhaps the operation of the system does not correspond to the rhetoric of due process regarded as the proud heritage of every citizen.

Other Models

Packer's models have not gone unchallenged, and other writers have added further models to the two posited by Packer. In his study of the guilty plea in the magistrates' court, that most common phenomenon of the English criminal justice system, Michael King has trawled the literature and identified a further four process models (King, 1981). When taken with the due process and crime control models, King argues that these will provide a multi-theoretical approach which will 'avoid the errors and distortions that may result from total subjectivity or from the use of one ideological viewpoint to the exclusion of all others' (King, 1981, p. 11). The various models need not be viewed as mutually exclusive; indeed there may be considerable overlap.

The third model identified by King is the *medical model*. This is based on the social function of rehabilitation. The committing of crimes is a symptom requiring social intervention. Rehabilitation will result in the offender refraining from conduct labelled as criminal. The processes seen in this model are the traditional medical processes of diagnosis, prognosis, treatment and cure. The role of the police and of the courts is to collect appropriate information for evaluation by decision makers who act in an informed way on the basis of that information to determine the right treatment for the offender. Where custodial sentences are meted out by the courts, these are seen as having a rehabilitative function. This model along with the due process and crime control models is most likely to be seen as reflecting the attitudes of regular participants in the criminal process. As such, they are labelled 'participant approaches'. Probation officers and social workers are most likely to subscribe to the medical model. Any who favour this model to the exclusion of others will need to explain why major decisions are left to non-specialist decision makers: lay justices in the magistrates' courts and juries in the Crown Court.

While the first three models reflect the general attitudes of regular participants in the process, the remaining three models reflect the different views of the process as perceived in the literature of sociology and may be labelled 'social models'. The fourth model is the *bureaucratic model*, which stresses management considerations. The hallmarks of such a model are the processing of suspects and defendants according to standard procedures by actors independent of political control by the government of the day. Because bureaucratic institutions tend to standardize and streamline procedures to encourage speed and efficiency, rewards are given for co-operation with the system and sanctions are imposed for time-wasting and unnecessary prolonging of procedures. Recording of decisions is seen as important. The role of the various actors – police, lawyers, court staff, probation officers, judges – are seen as complimentary with little overlap of function.

The *status passage model*, the fifth model, relies upon the process of stigmatization both to indicate the antisocial nature of the behaviour of a suspect or defendant and to strengthen 'cohesiveness among law-abiding members of society'. In such a system the ritual aspects of the process involving degradation and isolation of the suspect or defendant have an important role to play. The stigmatization is usually temporary and acts as a deterrent both to the offender and to others. It is not insignificant in this context that public appearance in court on a criminal charge with the possibility of a report of criminal conduct in a local newspaper is viewed by many defendants as the worst part of the brush with the law (King, 1981, pp. 92–5).

The final model is the *power model* whose function is seen as the maintenance of class domination. King describes this model as follows:

> This perspective sees the courts and the agents of criminal justice very much as part of the state machinery, a machinery which is dominated by the interests of the ruling class. This does not mean that policemen, lawyers, magistrates, clerks and probation officers are all conspirators in a plot to maintain and perpetuate the dominance of the ruling class, but rather that the state creates the conditions by which through the pursuit of their apparent self-interests each of these groups helps to advance the interests of the state and thus the dominant power elite. (King, 1981, p. 27)

This process is cloaked in some legal rationality. This model is the hardest to visualize, but one feature which can be identified is the narrow range of individuals represented among the judiciary and an official version of the operation of the system which denies its capacity systematically to disadvantage any group or interests.

Michael King's approach is multi-theoretical because he advocates measuring the ideals contained in the three participant approaches against the operation of the criminal justice system to identify 'the gap between aspiration and performance'. The social models may then be deployed because their application may explain why certain ideals are chosen for the system and why there is a gap between aspiration and performance in a given case, particularly where the system appears to be pursuing multiple objectives.

Models as an Aid to Policy Making

The thumbnail sketches offered above of six process models show just how complex the criminal process is. It is also possible to find evidence in the current system which fits each model, though no single model seems alone adequate to encapsulate the whole system. This is hardly surprising for the system itself changes gear or mode depending upon such matters as the seriousness of the offence or the intended plea of the defendant. The same data is also subject to differential interpretations. Let us take for example the role of representation of defendants. Under the due process model, the function of representation is seen as a safeguard of the rights of defendants; the lawyer will probe and test the evidence adduced by the prosecution against the defendant. Under the crime control model representation may be interpreted as a device for ensuring public confidence in the fairness of the system or in smoothing the way for a guilty plea. Under the medical model representation is part of the exercise of information gathering prior to the determination of the appropriate treatment for the defendant. The lawyer's role in the bureaucratic model is to contribute to the efficient functioning of the system by providing independent advice to defendants which will result in the minimum court time in the processing of defendants. The lawyer knows the rules of the process and can secure client compliance with them, thus contributing to the smooth running of the institution. In the status passage model, the defence lawyer may be called upon to join in the denunciation of the defendant in the kind of statements traditionally offered by way of plea in mitigation. The physical distance placed between defendant and lawyer, even where the defendant is not required to be in the dock, also contribute to the degradation of the defendant. The role of the law can also be fitted into the power model; it is clear that the lawyer has power over the defendant and can tell the defendant what action should be taken in certain situations in the defendant's own best interests. The oppressive conduct by some counsel in their advice to defendants discussed in the material on plea bargaining in chapter 6 provides a good example of the exercise of power. The irresistibility of the power of expertise is summed up by one defendant in Baldwin and McConville's research:

> I never made any decisions, they were all taken for me. I felt I wasn't controlling things with the solicitor and barrister; I was just being dragged along on the tide of what they said. I had to follow a set route all the way through. I couldn't say 'No, I don't want to go down that way', the way it was put there was only one route to follow. It's just like a blind-folded man being guided through a maze; I had to go but I wasn't sure where I was going. (Baldwin and McConville, 1979b, pp. 85–6)

In the above examples the role of representation has been interpreted differently in fitting it into each model. Is one interpretation correct or are there elements of truth in each of the interpretations? What is certain is that interpretations at variance with the official rhetoric of a due process model are easy to sustain. Comparing the operation of the system against theoretical models broadens the conceptual framework for evaluation of the system and invites a broader analysis of the many interactions that go to make up the criminal justice system.

For the policy maker who is contemplating some reform or change, the device of process models allows a more ready identification of personal value preferences for the system. Thus, if the ideals of the due process models are preferred, the type of reform likely to be seen would be further barriers to the prosecution such as the mandatory exclusion of improperly obtained evidence. The obstacles to the proof of guilt become tougher to protect the liberties of the individual. The ideals of the crime control model would reduce these obstacles and be likely to admit any material indicative of guilt however obtained. Obviously a system like that obtaining in England and Wales where broad discretions repose with the judges allowing the acceptance or rejection of improperly obtained evidence are ambivalent on this point.

An Alternative Analysis

The use of process models has provided an aid for measuring the gap between aspiration and performance. This suggests that once the ideals are chosen and the fundamental balance struck, the gap can be measured and changes made to bring aspiration and performance into congruence. This assumes that the gap is caused by aberrations which careful monitoring and tuning of the system can avoid. Doreen McBarnet has argued that this is a false dichotomy. There is a gap, but it is between the rhetoric of the law and its actual operation. In other words the system officially operates in one way while proclaiming that it operates in another way. The defects are therefore no longer aberrational, but become systemic (McBarnet, 1981). Under this analysis, it is not the operation of the law which is problematic; it is the law itself. Dr McBarnet concludes:

> Focusing . . . on the gap between the law in the books and the law in action, in effect whitewashes the law itself and those who make it. . . . Shifting the focus to the substance of the law places responsibility for the operation of criminal justice . . . squarely on the judicial and political elites who make it. (McBarnet, 1981, p. 156)

Let us take a closer look at the arguments used to back up such claims. Even towards the more serious end of the trivial/serious spectrum of crimes, the overwhelming majority of prosecutions result in guilty pleas. Few cases are contested and even fewer are resolved using jury trial. The principal feature of guilty pleas is that the formal protection of due process is almost totally absent. There is no formal consideration or testing of the evidence; the mouthing of the word 'guilty' removes evidential obstacles and virtually forecloses the possibility of appeal. The processes which have resulted in conviction have taken place in the police station where all the evidence shows routine violations of the rules designed to protect the interests of suspects. The response is that the incidence of guilty pleas is justified and represents no more than the accommodation of the criminal justice system to a massive workload. Though there is little research in this area in the United Kingdom, there has been research in the United States on the incidence of plea bargaining by reference to the severity of workloads of courts. This showed that even where court resources were under utilized, bargains were still struck with the same frequency as in heavily pressed courts (Nardulli, 1979).

Does not all this suggest that all the actors in the criminal process – especially the police, lawyers and judges – develop working relationships which emphasize co-operation rather than confrontation, and that all work to eliminate the uncertainties and conflict inherent in the trial process. Due process becomes a matter of last resort rather than of first resort. Interaction with the police in the form of admissions and informal advice on plea are greater determinants of a guilty plea than the adversarial process. The police control information exclusively at the early stages of the criminal process and lawyers do not effectively challenge that monopoly on information which in the case of the guilty plea is never broken.

Apologists for the defects in the English criminal justice system will continue to assert that problems arise only as a result of aberrations from the ideal standards of due process, and that where the courts are faced with these aberrations, they are recognized as unlawful actions. The question is raised as to how this condemnation of unlawful action can be seen as consistent with systemic injustice. Adherents to the systemic theory would respond that judges are adept at dealing with such issues. Judges manage the ideological gap between official practice and rhetoric by the process of individualizing cases and issues. When faced with a complaint based on a failure to meet the standards required by the rhetoric of the law, they are frequently able to find particular aspects of individual cases allowing the claim to be rejected while at the same time making general statements reinforcing the rhetoric of the law.

McConville and Baldwin have also taken up the theme of systemic injustice in their examination of the prosecution process (McConville and Baldwin, 1981). They see the need to change some central features of the system if its defects are to be remedied. The major change seen as necessary is the reduction in the numbers of guilty pleas, which in turn requires changes in the ability of the police 'to decide the fate of the suspect in conditions that they alone control' (p. 210). The protections demanded by due process must be entrenched so that judges cannot 'strip formal protections of any meaning'. Their conclusions are pessimistic and, of course, there must be real cause for concern if the defects of the criminal justice system are design faults rather than merely bugs in the system.

Concluding Comment

This short chapter has tried to encapsulate the arguments of a number of books. The material is important because it sets an agenda for reform depending upon the theory which is accepted and utilized.

The aberrational theory is optimistic because as the failings of the law in action are recognized, steps can be taken to avoid them for the future. The criminal justice system is seen as essentially healthy and can improve by a process of evolutionary change. The depressing feature of systemic injustice is its official tolerance and acceptance of a system without due process. To cure systemic injustice revolutionary change is needed.

The use of models and theories highlights the central role of the police in our criminal justice system, a centrality found only in few other systems. To note this centrality is not to attack the police. Criticisms of their dominance is as much a criticism of the system as of the police. Indeed the proposals for the now implemented independent prosecution service were designed to remove one source of conflict in their role. Whether it will have been enough to secure fundamental change remains to be seen. The use of models and theories can also help to evaluate the impact of change. In terms of structures and models, we can ask whether new statutory provisions like those of the Bail Act 1976, or the right to have a person reasonably named notified of detention at a police station under s.62 of the Criminal Law Act 1977 (now s.54 of the Police and Criminal Evidence Act 1984) secured real improvements in the operation of the system or merely added to the rhetoric of criminal justice.

Ultimately the main question is: are the defects of the English criminal justice system aberrational or systemic? If aberrational, they can be corrected by adjustments to the system; if systemic, the system itself needs to be designed afresh.

Part III
The Civil Process

9

Dealing with Small Claims

The Context

In 1986 the Office of Fair Trading, a statutory agency, conducted a large-scale survey into consumer dissatisfaction with goods and services (Office of Fair Trading, 1986). This revealed that 18 million people have about 30 million consumer complaints a year. Around 12 million complaints related to six categories where the average purchase price of the goods or services exceeded £100: furniture, household appliances, cars, car servicing, building and holidays. In these areas four out of five consumers took some action to redress their grievances. The most common action was to complain to the supplier. Persistence pays off, because those who refused to take no for an answer frequently achieved some success with their complaints. The survey, however, quantified the residual group of unresolved complaints at 4.5 million.

For many, going to court appeared not to be an option. Less than one in 50 complainants threatened court action. Ignorance of the role of the county courts in providing a forum for the resolution of consumer complaints was one factor accounting for this (National Consumer Council, 1979). Even where the existence of this forum was known, many consumers were reluctant to use the county courts for fear of cost, publicity, formality and the worry generated by going to court.

The Challenge

Access to the courts for persons wronged is a fundamental aspect of the English legal system. This proposition is as applicable to the machinery for processing minor disputes as it is for that determining liability in serious accident cases and contractual disputes. But litigation is an expensive business and the cost of taking action even in a small case can soon exceed several hundred pounds. The process costs (meaning not only lawyer's fees and court costs but also loss of earnings in attending court and placing a money figure on stress and the risks of litigation) involved in pursuing a small claim can easily exceed the amount in dispute. This makes it uneconomic to pursue the claim which may consequently be abandoned. If the claim was justified in the first place, then justice will not have been done. This chapter is concerned with the accommodations the English legal system has made to try to avoid such denials of justice.

Defining small claims is not easy. It is possible to define such claims either by monetary limits or by type of dispute. Since much of the focus of the debate in this area is on consumer complaints, then one approach would be to define a small claim as any complaint concerning the quality of goods or services regardless of the cost of the goods or services. After all the essential factual and legal questions involved in a dispute concerning the quality of a hi-fi system costing £200 or £2000 will be the same. Though such an approach might be fruitful, it has not been adopted. It is now generally accepted that a small claim is any dispute involving damages or loss not exceeding £500, though there is considerable pressure to revise this figure upwards. The Lord Chancellor's Civil Justice Review, which reported in June 1988, recommended an increase to £1000 (Civil Justice Review, 1988). This recommendation has now been implemented.

The discussion of small claims invariably centres on the role of the locally based county courts. The present system of county courts was set up in 1846 in what was then a radically new model for dispensing civil justice on a local basis. The establishment of the new courts was opposed by barristers who feared that their livelihoods would be lost to solicitors who were given rights of audience before county courts (Cocks, 1983). The main purpose of county courts in 1846 was to provide for the speedy and easy recovery of small debts, but the courts were so successful that they soon became courts enjoying a wide civil jurisdiction (Holdsworth, 1956, vol. I). Today practice and procedure in the county courts and in the High Court are being increasingly brought together with monetary limits on claims determining the distribution of business between them, though the jurisdiction of the county courts remains local and wholly regulated by statute.

Justice Out of Reach

The current wave of concern about the processing of small claims can be traced back to the 1970 report *Justice Out of Reach* in which the Consumer Council showed that the county courts were then an inadequate forum for the processing of consumer complaints. Far from being the court for the ordinary person, it was the court in which the ordinary person was sued for debt. The county courts had become part of the machinery of debt collection (Consumer Council, 1970; *see also* National Consumer Council, 1989). The Consumer Council recommended changes in county court practice and procedure in order to make the courts a more attractive forum in which consumers could pursue their claims. The official response to the report was that more use was made of the provision in the county courts legislation allowing arbitration of disputes. Small claims were to be diverted away from the formal adversarial system of dispute settlement by means of trial in open court to a less formal private resolution of the dispute before a registrar or judge. Amendments and refinements over the years have led to this procedure coming to be known as the 'small claims procedure' in the county courts. It currently operates automatically in all cases involving £1000 or less, though with the agreement of the parties, it can be used for disputes involving larger sums.

County courts deal with over 2.5 million cases each year. In 1988, 53,551 cases were referred to arbitration and set down for an arbitration hearing. 49,524 cases were actually heard; some 6500 of these involved sums in excess of £500. All but 332 were heard by registrars. These numbers should be set in the context of only 21,000 trials taking place in the county courts (Lord Chancellor's Department, 1989).

Despite these developments in the county courts, other independent initiatives have been tried. Some have failed; others continue. Their contribution to providing the means of settling small claims will also be considered in this chapter.

Practice and Procedure in the County Courts

Discouraging the Use of Lawyers

The procedure described in this section applies to all money claims in the county courts where the damages or loss are £1000 or less. For these claims the system is designed to be accessible to the litigant without the need to have representation in court by lawyers. Indeed the use of lawyers for this purpose is discouraged by two rules: the costs of representation are not normally recoverable by a successful party; and, civil legal aid will not normally be granted where the money claim does not exceed the small claims limit. Of course, advice and assistance under the Green Form scheme will be available, but this does not cover representation in court. To encourage use of the county courts without solicitors, the Lord Chancellor's Department has issued a booklet entitled *Small Claims in the County Court – How to sue and defend actions without a solicitor* (Birks, 1984). This is given free of charge to all parties to money claims involving less than £1000 and explains the likely steps involved in taking or defending a small claim. The booklet runs to 72 pages and requires a fair degree of literacy to be used effectively. Research for the Civil Justice Review found that two-thirds of plaintiffs had seen the booklet and four of five of this group found it useful (Touche Ross Management Consultants, 1986a) and the National Consumer Council describes it as 'very useful in telling people how to go about suing' (National Consumer Council, 1989). For those determined to press their claims, the booklet gives comprehensive guidance, which is necessary because the system remains adversarial. Court staff will assist with the completion of forms but will not advise on the merits of the claim or on the likelihood of success.

Starting the Action

The plaintiff is expected to have sent a letter before action threatening proceedings if the grievance is not settled forthwith. The booklet provides a precedent. In beginning proceedings destined ultimately for arbitration, a plaintiff uses the ordinary means of beginning any action in the county court. The plaintiff must choose which of the two types of summons to request: a fixed date summons or a default summons. Default summonses are used for all money claims, whether debt or damages, to be assessed by the court, and fixed date summonses for seeking a remedy other than money. Virtually all small claims will be begun by default summons.

The form of request for a summons is a straightforward document, but it may well seek information the plaintiff does not have. The plaintiff is required to provide the name and address of the defendant. This may sound straightforward, but there may be hidden difficulties. If the plaintiff is suing a limited company, the registered office address must be given and a company search may be needed to establish this. For a lawyer this is a simple task and could easily be done over the telephone in a few minutes within the scope of advice and assistance. But for litigants in person it may seem an unnecessary difficulty placed by the system in their path. If the defendant is a person trading in partnership under a partnership name, then it will be necessary to find the name and address of at least one partner. This may be problematic; it is not uncommon for disreputable traders deliberately to disguise their identities by failing to comply with the requirements that notepaper shows the names of partners in a business and that these names are displayed at business premises. It is always the plaintiff's responsibility to provide the correct name and address of any defendant.

The plaintiff must also ensure that the action is begun in an appropriate county court; there must be some connection between the dispute and the county court in which proceedings are taken. Since most small claims begun by individuals are consumer claims based on contract, this usually presents no problem since the rules on jurisdiction are couched reasonably generously. The plaintiff's local county court will usually have jurisdiction.

Having completed the request for a default summons, the plaintiff must also prepare particulars of claim. The county court will provide appropriate blank forms. The general standard of particulars of claim in the county courts is poor. For example, it is common practice for businesses simply to use a copy of their invoices to customers as particulars in their debt claims. But the better drafted the particulars, the better the chance of early settlement of the claim. Again the booklet contains useful precedents, but even first year law students often find the task of preparing particulars daunting and so it would be wrong to assume that this is never problematic for litigants in person. It is a pity that more use is not made of advice and assistance for drafting particulars.

The request for summons and enough copies of the particulars of claim for each defendant plus one for the court and one for the plaintiff's own file should be presented at court together with the fee for filing a claim; this is 10p in the pound with a minimum of £7 and a maximum of £43 for claims up to £1000.

Once issued the summons must be served on the defendant. It is best to pay the extra fee to have the county court's own bailiffs serve the summons, since this avoids possible difficulties of proving good service later in the proceedings. The plaintiff will be given a plaint note which acts as a receipt for the plaint fee and states the plaint number, a unique number used by the court to identify the case in its own records. Once the summons and particulars have been served on the defendant, a note to that effect is sent to the plaintiff.

Responding to the Claim

With the summons and particulars, the defendant will have received a Form of Admission, Defence and Counterclaim. Defendants who wish to avoid having judgment entered against them in default must complete and return this form within 14 days of service. If the defendant does nothing, the plaintiff can enter judgment against the defendant without the need for any hearing and can then proceed to enforce the judgment (see below). The Form of Admission, Defence and Counterclaim is set out in questionnaire form and enables the defendant to respond to the claim as follows:

to admit the claim in full and to make proposals as to payment, either in full by a set date or by instalments, in which case details of means must be provided; or

to admit part of the claim and dispute the rest, and to make proposals as to payment of the admitted amount; or

to deny the whole of the claim and file a defence to it; and, if appropriate, to add a counterclaim against the plaintiff to any of the above.

A copy of any response by the defendant will be sent to the plaintiff. If the defendant has admitted the whole claim and made proposals on payment, the only matter in issue will be the manner of payment of the debt. Unless the plaintiff considers the defendant's proposals inappropriate, judgment will be entered in the terms of the offer. Otherwise there must be a hearing to fix the manner of payment; such hearings are called 'disposals'. If the defendant has admitted part of the claim and contested part, the plaintiff may abandon the contested amount and settle on the terms of the offer. But if the plaintiff takes issue with the partial defence, or if the defendant has filed a defence to the whole claim, then at this stage the proceedings are automatically referred to arbitration by the registrar, renamed the district judge by s.74 of the Courts and Legal Services Act 1990, and a date for a preliminary consideration of the case will normally be fixed.

The Reference to Arbitration

Arbitration is much less formal than trial in open court. The Lord Chancellor's booklet describes it as follows:

The purpose of arbitration is to enable people to have small disputes resolved in an informal atmosphere, avoiding so far as possible the strict rules of procedure usually associated with court proceedings. This does not mean that rules are not observed because the object of all court procedure is to protect the interests of each party to an action and to ensure that the case is tried fairly. Nevertheless the formalities are kept to a minimum and you should have no difficulty handling your own case. (Birks, 1984, p. 3)

At this stage either party may make application to vary the reference to arbitration by the district judge. Either party may apply to have the dispute referred to arbitration by the judge or by an outside arbitrator rather than the district judge. Such applications are very rare. More importantly either party may apply to the district judge to have the reference to arbitration rescinded, which will have the effect of bringing into play the normal trial rules in the county court. Order 19, r.4 of the County Court Rules 1981 (CCR) specifies four grounds on which the district judge may rescind the reference:

a difficult question of law or a question of fact of exceptional complexity is involved; or
a charge of fraud is in issue; or
the parties are agreed that the dispute should be tried in court; or
it would be unreasonable for the claim to proceed to arbitration having regard to its subject matter, the circumstances of the parties or the interests of any other person likely to be affected by the award.

No figures are available for the number of cases in which the reference is rescinded, and so the practical significance of the rule is unknown. In *Pepper* v. *Healey* ([1982] RTR 411) the Court of Appeal upheld the decision of a registrar, affirmed on appeal by the judge, that inequality in the positions of the parties justified rescission under CCR O.19 r.4(d). In the case, the defendant had representation in court and was contesting liability in a motor accident case relying in part on expert evidence, but the plaintiff was a litigant in person. The reference was rescinded in order to enable the plaintiff to obtain representation and, if successful, to recover the costs of instructing the solicitor.

The Preliminary Consideration

The first stage of arbitration is the preliminary consideration. The district judge will fix a date for such a consideration unless the dispute appears so simple that it would be best to proceed immediately to the arbitration itself. It is important that both parties either attend or make written representations to the district judge, because if either simply ignores the preliminary consideration, judgment may be given in favour of the party appearing after hearing what they have to say about the case. Though such a decision may be set aside on application by the other party, this cannot be guaranteed. The purpose of the preliminary consideration is for the district judge and the parties to discuss the dispute and to consider how the action can best be dealt with. The district judge will seek to secure agreement on as many facts as possible, and may advise the parties what steps need to be taken in order best to prepare for the arbitration. An attempt may be made to secure settlement of the case on agreed terms there and then. The role of district judges is crucial and their attitude to the parties will always affect the accessibility of the small claims procedure for the unrepresented litigant. District judges may at this stage themselves call for an expert report or invite an expert to attend the hearing as assessor. But this power is only rarely used. Because the proceedings remain rooted in the adversarial tradition of litigation, it is far more likely that the district judge will advise a party whose case turns on expert evidence to obtain an expert's report in good time for the arbitration. Many consumer claims turn on expert evidence as to the cause of the defect about which the plaintiff is complaining.

Arbitration

If the preliminary consideration does not result in a decision in favour of one of the parties, the district judge will set the case down for arbitration. Unless any special directions are needed, such as orders for the production of particular documents, the reference will be in the standard terms laid down in CCR O.19. The arbitration may proceed on the basis of documents and written submissions presented by the parties, but it is advisable to attend. The hearing should be as informal as is consistent with making a fair decision and the formal rules of evidence do not apply. Again the role of the district judge in putting the parties at ease and enabling them to feel comfortable about putting their case effectively is an essential ingredient to the success of the process. Unfortunately the one ingredient necessary to ensure this is in short supply: time. Both preliminary considerations and arbitrations are frequently listed at 15-minute intervals. Some leeway is provided by parties who fail to attend, but there is inevitably considerable pressure on time. In one survey it was found that a quarter of cases in the sample lasted less than 15 minutes and a further quarter less than 30 minutes (National Consumer Council, 1979). Figures from the Lord Chancellor's Department based on 6328 arbitrations by registrars in 1975 showed that 60 per cent lasted 30 minutes or less while only 16 per cent lasted longer than one hour (Applebey, 1979). Having heard the parties or considered their representations, the district judge will give judgment.

The adversarial nature of the proceedings is illustrated by the case of *Chilton v. Saga Holidays plc* ([1986] 1 All ER 841) which was a small claim for £184 arising out of a holiday provided by Saga Holidays plc for the plaintiffs, Mr and Mrs Chilton. The plaintiffs were unrepresented, while Saga Holidays plc was represented by a solicitor. The defendant's solicitor wished to cross-examine Mr Chilton on certain evidence he had put to the registrar who was sitting as arbitrator. The registrar refused to allow this and insisted that any questions for Mr Chilton be directed through him. The plaintiffs secured judgment against the defendant company, who then applied to have the award set aside. The judge refused and Saga Holidays plc appealed to the Court of Appeal, where they were successful. In the course of his judgment, Sir John Donaldson MR said:

> Both courts and arbitrators in this country operate on an adversarial system
> of achieving justice. It is a system which can be modified by rules of court;
> it is a system which can be modified by contract between the parties; but
> in the absence of one or the other, it is basically an adversarial system, and
> it is fundamental to that that the other party shall be entitled to ask ques-
> tions designed to probe the accuracy or otherwise, or the completeness or
> otherwise, of the evidence which has been given.

The decision has been criticized (Smith, P. 1986) as being out of sympathy
with the objectives of small claims arbitration and as failing to tackle the issue
of how rules of natural justice should operate in the context of the inequality of
the positions of the parties where one is represented and the other is not.

Section 6 of the Courts and Legal Services Act 1990 amends the County
Courts Act 1984 to enable rules to be made concerning the procedure and rules
of evidence to be followed in small claims cases, including, in particular, provision concerning the manner of taking and questioning evidence. It is certain that
there will be a statutory overruling of the decision in *Chilton* v. *Saga Holidays
plc*, when amendments are next made to CCR O.19.

As part of the judgment successful plaintiffs will be able to recover most of
their out-of-pocket expenses. It has already been stated that the costs rules which
apply to small claims are designed to encourage direct access by litigants to the
county courts and to discourage representation by solicitors in small claims. But
it is only solicitor's taxed costs which are not recoverable; the successful plaintiff
who has used a solicitor will be able to recover in respect of the solicitor's charges
the fixed sum for such costs entered on the summons. This is a small sum which
varies according to the money sum claimed and bears no relationship to solicitor's costs actually incurred. All successful plaintiffs will be able to recover as
part of the judgment their reasonable out-of-pocket expenses in pursuing the
claim and this will include the cost of obtaining an expert report. If a party has
acted unreasonably in the proceedings and the arbitrator so certifies, solicitor's
taxed costs will be allowed as an exception to the normal rule. It is clear that
attempts to manipulate the arbitration procedure to gain a costs advantage will
be unreasonable conduct (*Newland* v. *Boardwell*; *MacDonald* v. *Platt*, [1983]
3 All ER 179). The Civil Justice Review found that the practice of registrars in
the award of expenses varied so much that like cases were not treated alike. The
award of expenses appears to be based on individual discretion of registrars
rather than on any uniform principles.

Challenging the Decision

The party who loses has only very limited rights to challenge the decision of the
district judge. There is no right of appeal against the decision. There are only
very limited grounds on which the decision of the arbitrator can be set aside on
application to a judge. In *Meyer* v. *Leanse* ([1958] 2 QB 37) it was held that

the power to set aside the decision of an arbitrator under the county court legislation was no wider than the power of the High Court to interfere with arbitrations. Thus there must be an error of law on the face of the record or evidence of misconduct by the arbitrator. So in *Caro* v. *Taylor* (Judgment of 8 December 1981, Lexis transcript) the Court of Appeal refused to allow an appeal against the refusal of a judge to interfere with a county court arbitration decision where oral evidence showed that the arbitrator had made a serious mistake in the law applied to the dispute, but where the record of the decision did not show that mistake. There was no error on the face of the record. The record in arbitrations in the county court will always be very brief and will not usually state reasons. In *Caro* v. *Taylor* Ormrod LJ said:

> So it will be virtually impossible to show an error on the face of the award in these cases, and thus it will be almost impossible for a dissatisfied party to take the matter to the judge, if he wishes. But. . . it may well be that it was the intention of Parliament, in dealing with these small claims in the County Court, that there should be finality; and if justice tends to be rough justice in certain cases, the overall effect will be beneficial in that it will cut out all these appeals.

In two other cases in 1980 and 1981 (*Rogers* v. *Owen*, Judgment of 28 April 1980 and *King* v. *Car Commercial Exports*, Judgment of 12 March 1981, Lexis transcripts) the Court of Appeal cited *Meyer* v. *Leanse* with approval. In a third case in 1980 the case was impliedly approved (*Leung* v. *Garbett*, [1980] 1 WLR 1189). In all three cases the Court appears to have overlooked the replacement by s.1 of the Arbitration Act 1979 of the jurisdiction of the High Court to review arbitrations with a new, wider jurisdiction allowing judicial review of an arbitration on any question of law arising out of the award. It must at least be arguable that all three cases were decided *per incuriam*, that is, in ignorance of a relevant statutory provision. The law governing challenge to arbitrations must now be regarded as far from clear. In 1988, there were 1524 applications to set aside an award of an arbitrator; about half succeeded.

Enforcing the Judgment

If the award of the arbitrator is for the payment of a sum of money, this has the same effect as a county court judgment and there remains the need to enforce the judgment if payment is not forthcoming. This is a separate exercise. To assist the Lord Chancellor's Department has produced another booklet entitled *Enforcing Money Judgments in the County Court – How to obtain payment without a solicitor*, explaining the various methods of enforcing money judgments in the county courts (Birks, 1980). The Civil Justice Review found that two-thirds of successful plaintiffs were paid the award in full, but only one-third reported prompt payment. One in four fails to obtain payment of the award at all.

How Effective is the County Court's Small Claims Procedure?

The statistics show that plaintiffs overwhelmingly succeed with their claims. The annual judicial statistics show that over 90 per cent of plaintiffs are successful. But there is some evidence to suggest that there is an increasing use of the procedure for debt collection by businesses (Applebey, 1978). The Touche Ross study for the Civil Justice Review (Touche Ross Management Consultants, 1986a) suggested that three-quarters of litigants using the small claims procedure were 'small litigants' and one-quarter were 'large litigants'. Small litigants were defined as small businesses, local professional firms and private citizens, while large litigants were defined as large companies, banks, credit institutions and public utilities. These figures may be unreliable as an indicator of the overall use of the procedure (Whelan, C. 1987), since the consultants were asked to ensure that at least three-quarters of the sample were cases brought by individuals and small businesses! But even on the Touche Ross figures only 38 per cent of plaintiffs were private citizens, whereas 58 per cent of defendants were private citizens. Only one in ten claims involved faulty goods or services. In the Touche Ross survey 67 per cent of cases were decided in favour of the plaintiff, 19 per cent in favour of the defendant. In the remaining 14 per cent of cases no judgment was recorded; these cases were settled or withdrawn at a late stage.

The National Consumer Council survey showed some confusion in the minds of consumers about the procedures and recommended the creation of an entirely separate small claims division in each county court with its own self-contained code of procedure and the abandonment of the current principle of diversion to arbitration when a defence is filed. A model code of procedure has also been produced (National Consumer Council, 1980; Thomas, 1982). The Civil Justice Review recommended that greater emphasis should be placed on giving the small claims procedure a separate identity from ordinary county court work. Though there is no recommendation to establish a separate division of the county courts for small claims, it is recommended that greater use should be made of the terms 'small claims' and 'small claims court' in descriptions of the procedure.

The National Consumer Council survey uncovered different approaches among courts to litigants in person; some were models of helpfulness, others regarded such litigants as nuisances (National Consumer Council, 1979). There also appear to be wide variations of approach by registrars to the task of acting as arbitrator. It is argued that it is difficult for registrars trained in and working for much of their time with adversarial procedures to adopt a sympathetic inquisitorial or investigative approach in arbitrations. There is also the problem that the small claims procedure is not genuinely inquisitorial; it still leaves the conduct of the case to the parties. It is important to remember that the ordinary civil burden of proof applies and it is therefore seen as improper for registrars to descend too willingly into the arena, particularly if one party is represented (Applebey, 1978; National Consumer Council, 1979; Applebey, 1979).

The findings of the Civil Justice Review underlines this variation of practice among registrars sitting as arbitrators. Some adopt an overtly investigative approach to the determination of small claims, whereas others operate arbitration as mini-courts relying on rules of evidence, requiring evidence to be given on oath, and remaining largely passive while the plaintiff attempts to establish the claim with little assistance from the arbitrator. Of those unrepresented parties surveyed in the Touche Ross study, 45 per cent thought that the registrar did not help them to put their case. The Civil Justice Review recommended:

At the hearing, the registrar should:
(a) conduct the hearing according to the circumstances of each case and adopt an interventionist role, dispensing with the formal rules of evidence and procedure, and assuming control of the questioning of the parties and their witnesses;
(b) give short reasons for his decision;
(c) explain the legal terms he finds it necessary to use.

The rules should be clarified so as to make it plain that the district judge may require questions to be directed through him. (Civil Justice Review, 1988, Recommendation 68 p. 100). Section 6 of the Courts and Legal Services Act 1990 enables rules of court to be made to reverse the ruling of the Court of Appeal in *Chilton* v. *Saga Holidays plc*, ([1986] 1 All ER 841).
Other significant recommendations of the Civil Justice Review are:

the avoidance of legal jargon in documents used in small claims cases;
district judges should of their own motion be able to rescind the reference to arbitration, acting on the current grounds;
the preliminary consideration should be abolished and small claims be disposed of at a single hearing which should be fixed by the court on receipt of a defence;
litigants should be able to be represented by any representative of their choice;
specific guidance should be given to courts on the award of expenses recoverable in small claims cases;
carefully monitored experiments should be conducted in early evening arbitrations and in the determination of claims on a documents only basis.

The county court procedures are really an attempt to combine processes of conciliation, arbitration and adjudication in one system. There is a policy of seeking to achieve a settlement acceptable to the parties at the stage of the preliminary consideration, coupled with a process of adjudicating between competing claims in an informal atmosphere. But the requirement of party presentation of claims and the level of formality required in particular in starting the proceedings is too great to be universally attractive. If the do-it-yourself approach is to work for everyone, and not just for the articulate person of above average intelligence, then the processes need further simplification by transferring some of the responsibilities away from the parties and onto the decision maker. A research study into 15 American small claims courts supports this view. It revealed the substantial need for court-provided assistance to litigants, if they were to develop their cases to their full potential (Weller et al., 1984).

It was some of these problems and issues which led to two important experiments in alternative methods of dispute resolution for small claims: the voluntary small claims arbitration schemes in London and Manchester.

The Voluntary Small Claims Schemes

Two major independent voluntary schemes have been established outside the official court structure to offer alternative methods for settling small claims. Both have ceased to operate through shortage of funds. The first was the Manchester Arbitration Scheme which operated between 1971 and 1980 (Foster, 1973a; National Consumer Council, 1979; Applebey, 1979). The second operated in London; between 1973 and 1977 it was known as the Westminster Small Claims Court and between 1977 and 1979 as the London Small Claims Court (Sherwin, 1975; National Consumer Council, 1979; Applebey, 1979; Conway, 1980). A third scheme in Lewisham closed after one year having heard only one case. Though there were detailed differences in the ways in which the Manchester and London schemes operated, there were sufficient similarities to justify a conflation of the two schemes for the purposes of our consideration of their contribution to our knowledge of processes for settling small claims.

The schemes were genuinely inquisitorial. The claimant indicated the nature of the dispute and the onus was then on the scheme to elicit all the relevant information from the parties and, if necessary, to obtain an expert report. Representation was banned. Use of the two schemes was restricted to claims in contract or tort by private individuals not in business, though small businesses could use the schemes other than for the recovery of business debts. In Manchester the financial limit on claims was £500, and in London £350; at the time these figures were well in excess of the small claims limit in the county court. Proceedings were begun by contacting the scheme and by completing a simple form which outlined the complaint and contained the agreement to arbitration. Very low registration fees were payable: £1 in Manchester, and in London a £2 registration fee plus a court fee of £3 for claims under £100 and £8 for claims in excess of £100. The next step was for the staff of the schemes to try to secure the consent of the defendant to arbitration under the scheme. If that consent was not forthcoming the scheme could not be used. This was because the schemes were arbitrations within the meaning of the Arbitration Acts 1950 to 1979 and in order to displace the jurisdiction of the county courts there must be a valid agreement to arbitrate concluded by the parties to the dispute. Despite broad support for the schemes from local trade and business organizations, it seems that refusals of consent were significant. Complete figures for all the years of operation are not available, but reported figures show refusal rates varying from 20 per cent to 51 per cent of claims registered (Applebey, 1979; National Consumer Council, 1979).

At the time that the agreement of the defendant was sought, the defendant's views on the complaint were also sought. All the facts and documents needed to consider the claim were collected in a file, following which a hearing was fixed, which could be 'on site' if that would be useful. Arbitrators under both schemes were appointed by the presidents of the local Law Societies from a list of volunteers. A fair number of arbitrators in Manchester were not lawyers; expert adjudicators included engineers, architects and surveyors. In London most arbitrators were lawyers. In London arbitrators were unpaid, but in Manchester a nominal fee of £25 for a session of three or more arbitrations, or £10 for a session of less than three arbitrations, was paid. A documents only arbitration was possible, as were hearings outside normal office hours. Though legal or other professional representation was disallowed, both schemes allowed a friend to accompany the parties to the dispute. The arbitrator was not bound by the rules on evidence and would consult an expert of his or her own motion. The gradual building up of a case file without the single culminating equivalent of a trial is very reminiscent of civil law inquisitorial procedures. The administrator of the London Small Claims Court commented:

> The Court attempted to create, by the method it used to conduct hearings, an atmosphere which was friendly and unintimidating and where the parties involved fully understood what was going on. I believe the Court was successful in this respect. (Conway, 1980, p. 231)

The costs rules operating under the schemes were simple. In Manchester the £1 registration fee was never recoverable, whereas under the London scheme the arbitrator had a discretion to order reimbursement of the claimant's court fee. Under both schemes the arbitrator could as part of the award order one party to pay a sum towards the schemes' expenses, such as experts' fees, up to a maximum of £10, though in London advance agreement on meeting the expert's fees was often sought between the parties.

The awards of the arbitrators were usually met without difficulty, and this is unsurprising since both parties had agreed to the process of settlement. In any event as a valid arbitration, the enforcement procedures of the county court were available on registration of the award with the county court. In order to do this a plaint fee would of course have to be paid to the county court.

The schemes themselves argued that they were speedier, cheaper, simpler and more 'user-friendly' than the county court schemes. The claims to simplicity and a sympathetic approach to litigants in person can certainly be sustained. Empirical research in Manchester where the independent scheme operated in competition with the small claims procedures in the county courts showed the preference of litigants for the informal procedure. A survey was conducted to see what further steps were taken by persons who had begun proceedings under the Manchester Arbitration Scheme, but where the defendant had not agreed to submit the case to arbitration. Some 65 per cent decided not to proceed. Within this sample, 25 per cent abandoned the claim because they felt they could not cope with the county court procedures, 12.5 per cent because they thought it would be too expensive or that an expert report would be needed, and eight per cent because they considered it would be too time consuming. Though a small sample, and though county court procedures have been somewhat simplified by subsequent rule changes, the survey does suggest some misunderstandings and fear of the procedures available in the county courts among a group which had been sufficiently motivated to try to get a claim off the ground under the Manchester Arbitration Scheme (Applebey, 1979).

More doubt surrounds the claims to speed and cheapness. Given the small scale of the two schemes, comparisons of the time lags between filing a claim and decision between these schemes and the county courts are meaningless. Costs are disguised; there is clearly a transfer of some process costs from claimant to the scheme. But again problems of comparing like with like make comparisons with the county courts of doubtful validity. What the schemes did show was that it was possible to set up genuinely inquisitorial procedures for small claims which were readily accessible to claimants and, even on a voluntary basis, largely acceptable to defendants.

Trade Association Arbitration Schemes under OFT Codes

Under the provisions of the Fair Trading Act 1973, the Director General of Fair Trading has a duty to promote codes of practice among trade associations laying down standards of conduct designed to remove abuse, promote higher standards and provide machinery for the proper handling of complaints. Over 20 codes have now been approved, many of which contain procedures for arbitration of disputes. Adherence to the codes is usually voluntary. There are also a number of schemes operated by trade associations where there is as yet no code of practice approved by the Office of Fair Trading (OFT). Obviously since each code is tailor made to a particular trade or product, there are significant variations in the schemes set up under them. But it is common to find an initial conciliation procedure whereby consumer and retailer or contractor seek to agree a friendly settlement of the dispute. If this fails independent arbitration may follow (Thomas, R. 1988; National Consumer Council, 1991).

A good example is to be found in the Association of British Travel Agents (ABTA) Tour Operators' Code of Conduct which provides that in the event of a dispute between a tour operator and a consumer, ABTA is prepared to offer help and impartial guidance with a view to the conciliation of the dispute. If this fails, the dispute may be referred to arbitration under the special scheme devised for the travel industry by the Institute of Arbitrators by arrangement with ABTA. Under the arbitration scheme an independent arbitrator is appointed by the President of the Institute of Arbitrators. The scheme offers a documents only procedure, but a deposit must be paid on a reference to arbitration which is calculated by reference to the number of people in the group on holiday. A deposit of £23.00 is paid by the claimant plus £7.45 for each additional member of the claimant's immediate family aged 12 or more and £9.45 for other members of the party aged 12 or more. This deposit is returnable at the discretion of the arbitrator if the claimant wins. If the claimant loses, liability for costs is limited to twice the amount of the deposit. There is a provision for requesting an attended hearing, but if the claimant loses, the liability for costs is unlimited. Before agreeing to an attended hearing, the arbitrator may request security for costs. The upper limit for claims fixed at £7500 is not only in excess of the small claims limit, but is also in excess of the county court's jurisdictional limits at the time of writing. But many claims are for far more modest sums. About half succeed, though many for considerably less than the amount claimed.

An interesting and useful provision of independent expert testing is to be found in the Voluntary Code of Practice for Footwear. It is also of some importance because complaints about footwear are estimated to account for some 14 per cent of consumer complaints. It is made clear in the code that retailers are responsible for providing redress, but if there is a disagreement about the cause of a fault, then an expert opinion may be sought from the independent Footwear Testing Centre in Kettering. The parties file a Test Application Form outlining the dispute. The test fee is £14.50; the retailer pays £10.00 and the consumer £4.50, which will be refunded by the retailer if the report is favourable to the consumer. All documents and the test report are seen by both retailer and consumer. The system seems to work well for those who use it; it seems to be cheap, quick and involves little paperwork. Not all codes have such satisfactory procedures.

The main drawback of the schemes in the codes is their diversity and a general ignorance about their existence. Use of the schemes varies dramatically (Thomas, R. 1988). There are few, other than consumer advisers who could claim to be certain about how many products and services are covered by codes. The lack of consumer awareness of the codes means that the advantage to the retailer of being a member of the code is lost if consumers do not choose where they shop on the basis of adherence to a code. The ignorance of the codes exists not only among consumers, but also among lawyers and even at shops which are parties to the codes. Among those who are aware of the schemes under the codes, there is some concern about the impartiality with which complaints are considered. Some are very slow (National Consumer Council, 1979). In 1981 the OFT reviewed the redress procedures under codes of practice. The review concluded that the arbitration schemes were useful alternatives to the county court procedures, but that improvements were needed. All arbitrations should be on a documents only basis and the speed of decision making should be improved. Arbitrators should always give a reasoned decision (OFT, 1981). Unfortunately none of the proposals do anything to improve the lack of awareness of the provisions of the codes. They will normally only be used if a complaint is initially made to a Consumer Advice Centre or Trading Standards Department, who are among the few agencies likely to link a complaint to the availability of a remedy under a code of practice. Finally, given the strength of the substantive law protecting the consumer, there is an argument that the proliferation of codes with individual systems for redressing grievances tends to superimpose a veneer of 'pseudo-law' and to detract from the enforcement of legal rights and duties using the small claims procedure in the county courts.

Strategies for Reform of Small Claims

The trends and experimentation in the processing of small claims have highlighted the need to achieve a delicate balance. That balance is between the need for individuals to be able to enforce by process of law, rights given to them by the common law and statute as consumers and the requirement that disputes are judged fully and impartially by decision makers (Whelan, 1990). To put it another way: can we afford to meet the cost of providing justice for small claims? These themes have over the last decade been played against a backcloth of a general movement away from formality and procedural complexity and towards informal, simple and accessible procedures in the administration of justice (Economides, 1980). But it is only possible to have a simple informal system of processing disputes if there is a simple informal body of legal rules governing those disputes. One charge levelled at arbitration schemes under trade associations' codes of practice, and indeed at the voluntary schemes, is that they substitute for the relevant legal rules some general concept of fairness between the parties (National Consumer Council, 1979; Economides, 1980).

Reactions based on concerns that some of the simpler and cheaper alternatives do not pay sufficient regard to the framework of applicable legal rules have caused many to see the long-term solution as lying with changes in the official court system. This is certainly the position adopted by the National Consumer Council in proposing a separate small claims division in each county court. The difficulty here is that the major contribution of the Manchester and London schemes has been to show that inquisitorial procedures are appropriate for these claims and can work effectively. The National Consumer Council was right to call for a new national system of small claims divisions in county courts. Implementation of the recommendations of the Civil Justice Review will, in effect, establish such a system. Though evolutionary in nature, the recommendations of the Civil Justice Review will significantly improve the small claims procedure in county courts.

The issue of representation in any small claims procedure is a difficult one. The independent schemes were able to dispense with representation because they adopted a full inquisitorial model, placing a duty upon the arbitrator to find the facts needed to determine the claim. Though there is an important role for lawyers in inquisitorial procedures, their banning in small claims can be justified on economic grounds and in order to ensure some equality between the positions of the parties.

The National Consumer Council has changed its view on the banning of representation in county court procedure. In 1970 the Consumer Council in *Justice Out of Reach* argued strongly for a ban on legal representation, even though only a minority of jurisdictions operate such a ban in small claims cases. In 1979 the National Consumer Council took the view that legal representation should not be necessary in small claims proceedings and that it should not be permitted. Despite features designed to discourage representation, one party was legally represented in 48 per cent of cases in the Touche Ross study, though this appears to have little impact on outcome. One in ten cases involved legal representation of both parties. The dilemma over the issue of whether or not to ban legal representation is that a ban restricts individual freedom without necessarily securing the objective of improving the informal conduct of the proceedings so that the need for representation disappears. The National Consumer Council has recently modified its position:

> We concluded that although the procedure should aim to make representation unnecessary, litigants should have the right to be accompanied or represented by the person of their choice. Legal costs should not be allowed. (National Consumer Council, 1989, p. 294)

This is in line with the recommendations of the Civil Justice Review. It acknowledges the difficulty of providing a do-it-yourself litigation scheme capable of being used effectively by all members of the public.

The arguments concerning the banning of representation are often clouded by pointing out that there might still be inequality between the parties. This is undoubtedly true. Companies or businesses sued under a system which did not permit representation would undoubtedly send along to any hearing a competent articulate representative. It is also possible that companies and businesses might be sued more than once and so their representatives would become experienced in small claims procedures. As 'repeat-players' they would have considerable advantages over 'one-shotters'; this has been shown to be a general problem in the use of litigation (Galanter, 1974). This relative advantage for 'repeat-players' is accentuated in an adversarial system, but within an inquisitorial procedure the decision maker can ensure that it does not operate to the disadvantage of the 'one-shotter'.

The use of full inquisitorial procedures in all cases involving £1000 or less in the county courts would present a problem: that of numbers. A feature of inquisitorial procedures is early court intervention. At present about 1.5 million default summonses resulting in judgments for less than £500 are issued each year in the county courts. Something in the order of 14 out of every 15 such cases resolve themselves. Either judgment is obtained by default or the exchange of particulars and the Form of Admission, Defence and Counterclaim results in settlement of the dispute. Obviously, there would be considerable resistance to any procedure which required examination of these cases. There is a case to suggest that they should be examined, because many are debt claims settled in favour of the plaintiff even where the defendant has a full or partial defence (Payne, 1969; Ison, 1972). However, it is perfectly possible to have an inquisitorial system whose intervention takes effect after the initial stage of processing. If no settlement is reached, then the arbitrator must enquire fully into the case. Such a system might encourage the raising of defences at an early stage.

In examining the issue of small claims there is a tendency to consider that the choice is between formal procedures involving adversarial trial processes with detailed rules of evidence, representation and full rehearsal by each side of the legal arguments in the case, and informal processes involving much simpler, more

general inquiries in friendly surroundings where the facts are laid by the parties
before an arbitrator who applies a compromise judgment based on his own
enquiries and knowledge of the law. The loss of the safeguards of the formal
process is seen as the price to be paid for general accessibility without lawyers
to a system of redress. Economides has suggested that there is a third route,
which he labels 'post-formal' justice, which represents a synthesis of both formal
and informal justice (Economides, 1980). The National Consumer Council's
model code of procedure is a good basis for such a system, though it fails to
address fully the issue of a move from adversarial to genuinely inquisitorial procedures. In commenting on the rules, Thomas stresses the need for a consumer
orientation in the services offered by the courts, for the role of the court to
change fundamentally so that it does not remain 'aloof from the arena of battle',
for judicial activism and for a style of judicial decision making appropriate to the
nature of the dispute (Thomas, 1982). But the model code does not introduce
dramatic new procedures and new duties on the court likely to secure these
objectives.

A belief that evolutionary change will never succeed has led Ison to argue that
radical changes are needed (Ison, 1972). Writing in 1972, before the major
developments in county court procedure to accommodate litigants in person with
small claims, Ison described the handling of small claims as 'probably the most
deplorable feature of the administration of civil justice'. But Ison's proposals
have not been overtaken by the new small claims procedure because he maintains
that improvements in procedure have only a marginal impact. Arguing that the
county courts have become merely collecting agencies for business in their handling of debt claims with enquiry into the merits of claims being almost wholly
absent, Ison proposes the abolition of the debt action. This would result in
greater care being taken by credit-granters in their predictions of the capacity of
the credit-receiver to repay the loan. The ease with which debts can currently be
collected through the county courts is, Ison argues, inconsistent with government
policy to increase protection of the consumer, particularly where consumer credit
transactions are involved. To encourage consumers to pursue claims, Ison proposes a system of well-paid, young (under 33 on appointment with compulsory
retirement at 45) highly mobile judges fearlessly and vigorously investigating
complaints by consumers. Ison comments:

> It may be hard to imagine a judge moving around the community, resolving
> disputes on the spot, and keeping in touch with his office by two-way radio;
> but why not?

The proposals are as imaginative as they are unrealistic, but they are backed
by considerable argument and represent one of the few more radical proposals
to resolve what is generally acknowledged as a problem for the legal system. As
such they deserve consideration.

Most proposals for reform have argued that the small claim is the context in
which most members of the community are likely to come into contact with the
civil justice system and that the absence of a fair, accessible system for resolving

such disputes is likely to bring the whole of the civil justice system rapidly into disrepute. Such proposals often go on to suggest two key objectives in designing a small claims system: reducing the costs of litigation and making procedures simpler. The tension between these two objectives is not always fully explored. Reducing the cost to the litigant and making the procedures simple for the litigant probably increase the costs of operating the system. Costs are transferred from the parties to the dispute to the system. In a climate of expenditure cuts and a general reduction of public spending, such proposals are likely to be unattractive to government.

Reform of the effective legal protection of the consumer is likely to proceed on three fronts, seeking to provide both new substantive rights and new procedural machinery for the settlement of disputes (Applebey, 1987). The first approach is to seek new and better substantive rights for consumers, like a general direct liability of manufacturers to consumers for defective goods. Certainly one commentator has suggested that the focus on procedural reform is misplaced (Foster, 1975). The second approach is to improve public enforcement of consumer rights by extending the role of the OFT and local Trading Standards Departments (Thomas, R. 1988). This technique is known as surrogate advocacy. Its effectiveness depends upon the aggressiveness of the agency charged with the protection of the public interest. There is a danger of tokenism or purely symbolic protection (Cappelletti, 1978, vol. III). The third approach is pressing for procedural reform. This can take the form of simplification or structural changes in court procedures as discussed in this chapter or the development of new remedies, like the class action allowing the collective obtaining of remedies against manufacturers or suppliers by all consumers of particular products (Van Bueren, 1983).

Ultimately optimists will argue that evolutionary change on a broad front will in time produce a fair, balanced system, while pessimists will argue that only revolutionary change can succeed in providing effective access to adjudication for litigants with small claims. What is a little depressing is that nearly one and a half centuries after their creation, county courts are still predominantly used for the collection of debts by business.

10

Dealing with Personal Injuries Claims

The Context of Litigation

Access to the courts for persons wronged is a fundamental aspect of the English legal system. The object of civil proceedings will usually be the determination of the rights and duties of individuals or companies as between each other. Examples are the determination of rights arising under contracts, of obligations to pay damages for torts, of rights of property and succession and of questions of status, such as divorce, adoption and custody of children. Most of these rights are of a private nature, but there is also a body of civil law of a public nature, such as, for example, questions concerning taxation, immigration and compulsory purchase orders. In most civil proceedings the person instituting the proceedings will be the *plaintiff* who sues, or brings an action against, a *defendant*. The plaintiff will usually be seeking *damages* (monetary compensation) but may also ask for an *injunction* (an order prohibiting the defendant from committing or continuing to commit some wrongful act). The plaintiff usually has the burden of proof which is said to be on the balance of probabilities; this means that the plaintiff must show that it is more probable than not that what is alleged is true. The civil claims with which this chapter is concerned are claims in tort for compensation for personal injury as a result of negligence or breach of statutory duty.

The focus of much of the material written in the area of civil procedure conceals an important aspect of the resolution of civil claims: most are settled even before the start of proceedings. This aspect of the negotiation of settlements by the parties either without recourse to the courts at all or without the resolution of the dispute by the trial process means that the various steps in civil procedure need to be assessed not only to determine their effectiveness in ensuring a full and fair trial, but also to determine whether they give one party an unfair advantage in the process of negotiation that so frequently leads to a pre-trial settlement.

One factor which accounts for the settlement of so many personal injuries claims is the presence of insurance. It is now a requirement of law that insurance for potential liability to accident victims is carried by motorists and employers. Accidents on the road and at work are, of course, common phenomena. While the legal system resolutely ignores the taking over of a claim against an insured party by the insurers, requiring everything to be done in the name of the insured, the actuality is that the efficient routines of insurance companies in processing accident claims swing into action as soon as an accident is reported. Where the injuries sustained are not too serious and the question of liability is reasonably arguable, many insurers seek to settle, since, in the long term, this is far cheaper than fighting every claim. Whether all these settlements are fair to victims is another question and will often depend on whether victims receive legal advice as to the amount of damages (called *quantum* by lawyers) appropriate to their injuries and loss. It is probably true to say that most insurance companies do not behave unscrupulously, but all try to settle claims for the lowest sum possible, thus maximizing profits and keeping premiums down.

Accidents and Claims

It is estimated that there are over three million accidents involving personal injuries each year. Of these about 215,000 occur on the road, 350,000 at work and the remainder elsewhere, mainly in the home. Almost 750,000 of those suffering accidents believe some other person was wholly or partly to blame for the accident. Accidents causing personal injuries result in about 300,000 compensation claims each year. Because liability is fault based, these must be based on the principle that the person causing the injury was in some way at fault. In nine out of every ten claims insurance covers liability. Settlements are reached in 86 per cent of cases without the need to begin court proceedings. A further 13 per cent are settled after issue of proceedings but before trial. Only about one per cent actually result in a contested trial (Pearson, 1978). About 55,000 personal injuries cases are brought each year; around 31,000 in the High Court and 24,000 in the county courts; though the division between the High Court and the county courts will change as a result of the reforms introduced by the Civil Justice Review.

One of the most alarming statistics is that two-thirds of those suffering injuries, which they feel to have been caused by the act or omission of another person, take no steps towards making a claim for compensation in tort. Among reasons given are absence of serious injury, ignorance of how to go about making a claim, fear of costs, too many practical difficulties and a feeling of inability to prove the claim (Pearson, 1978 and Harris et al., 1984). One survey showed that only 12 per cent of all seriously injured accident victims claimed damages through the tort system (Harris et al., 1984).

Despite the significant number of cases which settle, court decisions have a considerable impact on the operation of the system of processing accident claims. Case law lays down the criteria for determining the fault upon which liability is based. One decision of the Court of Appeal may lead to the settling of many thousands of cases by insurance companies. Case law also gives important guidance on the matter of quantum of compensation for particular injuries (Atiyah, 1987).

No consideration of accident compensation claims would be complete without noting that there is an elaborate mosaic of state benefits which may provide some compensation for accident victims regardless of any determination of fault. These include free medical treatment within the National Health Service, industrial injuries benefits, sickness benefit and, as a matter of last resort, income support and other means-tested benefits which are not conditional upon contributions to the National Insurance scheme. Broadly speaking the state benefits are based upon *need* whereas compensation in tort is based upon *actual loss* and will almost always give rise to higher levels of compensation. This system of mixed and overlapping state benefits must inevitably account for a fair number of those cases where accident victims do not pursue tort claims. The welfare state always provides some financial provision to cushion the losses arising following an accident.

Relevant Tort Principles

Liability

Most personal injuries actions will be pleaded in negligence. Basically, the plaintiff will have to show, on the balance of probabilities, the existence of a duty of care by the defendant to the plaintiff and a breach of that duty causing the plaintiff damage which is not too remote. The system is based on fault. Sometimes the law will presume a breach of duty by the application of the latin maxim *res ipsa loquitur* (the matter speaks for itself) if the accident was caused by something under the defendant's control which would not normally happen without a lack of care: for example, a car being driven into a tree. In some cases, notably accidents at work, the plaintiff may also plead breach of statutory duty alleging that the employer has failed to provide a safe system of work.

Road accidents produce the greatest number of claims as a proportion of claims to accidents. One in three victims of road accidents brings a personal injuries claim. Fault is often a major issue in such cases with arguments from each side that the other driver failed to take proper care. If there has been a conviction for a relevant driving offence, the burden of proof is effectively reversed, because s.11 of the Civil Evidence Act 1968 renders the conviction admissible in civil proceedings as proof of fault. The defendant can only avoid this where it is possible to show that the conviction was wrong or irrelevant.

The occurrence of claims in road traffic accident cases is a consequence of the system of compulsory insurance required of drivers covering their liability to third parties. Claims can even be made against uninsured drivers because the Motor Insurers' Bureau operates an Uninsured Drivers Agreement under which it accepts responsibility for the liabilities of uninsured drivers, from whom the Bureau in turn seeks to recover any damages paid to victims of road accidents caused by such drivers.

Accidents at work raise issues of breach of statutory duty as well as negligence and other common law principles. The most important will be the rules governing vicarious liability, where the employer can be held liable for the negligence of employees acting in the course of their employment. The employer is the favoured defendant since there is a statutory requirement that employers carry insurance against liability to injured employees. One in four of those injured at work claims against the employer.

The Law Reform (Miscellaneous Provisions) Act 1934 provides that existing causes of action survive against or for the benefit of the estate of the deceased party. The claim does not die when one of the parties does. An action brought by the estate of a deceased plaintiff is dealt with on the same basis as if the plaintiff were alive and the measure of damages is generally the same. The Fatal Accidents Act 1976 gives the dependants of a deceased accident victim a cause of action for the loss of their dependency if the deceased would have had an action if he or she had lived. The action is usually brought by the personal representatives of the deceased in conjunction with a 1934 Act claim, but if no action is started within six months of the deceased's death, any dependant can sue on behalf of all the dependants.

One of the big growth areas in accident compensation claims is actions by victims of medical negligence. Such cases can be very complex, raising novel issues concerning the standard of care required and of causation. They can also involve very large sums in damages, especially where plaintiffs are young and will need high levels of care for the rest of their lives.

Apart from a defence based on a denial of any lack of care, the main defence that is met is that the plaintiff was also negligent and such negligence was a contributory cause of the injuries suffered. Such a plea is known as a *plea of contributory negligence*. Where contributory negligence is pleaded, the courts have power to apportion the blame for the accident by reducing the damages payable. The reduction can be 100 per cent in extreme cases. The defence most often arises where the cause of action pleaded is negligence, but it is not limited to such cases and may be pleaded in other cases, such as, for example, cases of breach of statutory duty.

Another defence that may be pleaded is consent to the risk, known by the latin phrase *volenti non fit injuria*. In such pleas, the defendant must show that the plaintiff agreed to take the risk of injury resulting from the lack of reasonable care involved, knowing the nature and extent of the risk. The standard of consent to the risk is high and the plea is not often successful.

Damages

The objective of personal injuries claims is compensation, which goes some way to placing the plaintiff in the same financial position after the accident as before it. The law of damages is a complex topic, but the broad division is into *general damages* and *special damages*. General damages cover compensation for a number of heads: past, present and future physical and mental pain and suffering resulting from the injuries and the treatment for them; loss of amenity, which refers to the extent to which the injuries prevent the plaintiff from taking part in pre-accident activities; future loss of earnings; and loss of earning capacity. Damages for pain and suffering for particular types of injury are calculated by reference to a sort of tariff established by the case law. Special damages are the actual financial losses flowing from the accident, covering past loss of earnings and expenses incurred as a result of the accident.

Interest must now be awarded on all damages in excess of £200. The purpose of interest is the obvious need to compensate the plaintiff for the delay in receiving the compensation for the accident. Where large damages are expected, but there is dispute as to the amount, *interim damages* may be appropriate. Such damages are payments on account of damages usually by insurance companies, which put the plaintiff in receipt of some funds and avoid the lengthy wait for the final amount of damages to be fixed by the court.

Formerly, only one award of damages could be made. If subsequent events showed that the damages were too generous or too niggardly, nothing could be done. The accident compensation system simply accepted that there are plaintiffs who are under-compensated and others who are over-compensated. Cases in which the plaintiff's injuries were such that there was a chance of the plaintiff developing some serious disease or serious deterioration in his or her physical or mental condition presented very great problems, since the calculation of damages in such cases requires a figure to be placed on the risk of the onset of the further condition. The device of *provisional damages* has now been introduced to cope with such cases. The effect of asking the court to consider provisional damages is that the court is given the opportunity to make two awards of damages. The first award is of damages at the appropriate level for the injuries ignoring the possibility that the serious disease or deterioration of health will occur. If within a period specified by the court (which may be for life) the serious disease or deterioration occurs, the plaintiff can return to the court for a second award of damages for the condition which has occurred. Provisional damages have not been used often; it seems that plaintiffs and insurers like to close the files with a once and for all settlement. The cases in which provisional damages have been pleaded to date have generally involved head injuries carrying the risk of the onset of epilepsy, spinal injuries which carry the risk of future paralysis, and respiratory disorders resulting from exposure to substances such as asbestos, which can result in lung cancer. Provisional damages are an option for the plaintiff and will only be considered where the plaintiff asks for consideration of them.

Where very large sums in damages (in excess of £250,000) are involved, consideration is often given to what are known as *structured settlements* under which a regular income linked to the retail price index is awarded for a fixed term, which may be the remainder of the plaintiff's life.

The Civil Justice Review

In its official response to the Report of the Royal Commission on Legal Services, the Government indicated that the Lord Chancellor would undertake 'a complete and systematic review of civil procedure' in order to identify causes of delay and inconvenience and to restructure the system so as 'to achieve the most expeditious and convenient disposal of business'. (Government Response to Benson, 1983). Lord Chancellor Hailsham set up the Review Body on Civil Justice in February 1985 with the objective of improving the machinery of civil justice in England and Wales by means of reforms in jurisdiction, procedure and court administration and, in particular, to reduce delay, cost and complexity. The Civil Justice Review focused on five main areas of business, as well as considering general issues: small claims, personal injuries, debt, housing and commercial cases. As with small claims, which were considered in the previous chapter, factual studies based on specification documents prepared by the Review were commissioned to inform the recommendations of the Civil Justice Review. Inbucon Management Consultants investigated personal injuries litigation. The factual study resulting from this enquiry then formed the basis of a consultation document and the Report of the Review Body on Civil Justice (Cm 394) followed in June 1988. Primary legislation was needed to implement some of its recommendations and this is contained in Part I of the Courts and Legal Services Act 1990.

The Inbucon Management Consultants factual study examined a sample of 433 cases, started in 1980–2 (234 in the High Court and 199 in the county courts), 251 cases tried in 1984, 92 cases set down for trial in District Registries (High Court centres in the provinces) and 20 cases drawn from insurers' files. In 721 cases the nature of the accident could be identified: 320 concerned injuries suffered on the road and 304 at work. The conclusion drawn from detailed consideration of the cases was that the accident compensation system is inefficient, dilatory and disproportionately expensive. It can take between three and six years for cases to be resolved. Three important points of delay are highlighted. First, it can take three years after the accident to get a case started. The limitation period in most cases before the claim is time-barred by statute is three years. Secondly, it can take two years from the start of a case in the High Court for a defendant to be given full details of the plaintiff's case. Finally, even when both sides are ready for trial, they will often have to wait up to a year for a date to be set in the High Court for a trial.

The expense of the system is also a matter of great concern. In county courts, for every £100 paid in damages, £125 or £175 (depending on the method of calculation) is spent on costs. Because awards of damages are higher in the High Court, the ratio is better: for every £100 in damages, £50 or £70 (depending on the method of calculation) is spent on costs.

Delay means injustice in the form of unnecessary stress and anxiety to plaintiffs and their families as well as financial hardship resulting from the absence of early payment of much needed compensation. It is not in the public interest to have so slow and cumbersome a system of dispute resolution.

A central feature of the new scheme for the handling of civil cases is that all civil cases should be dealt with at the lowest level appropriate to the case and this will entail a dramatic shift for most cases from the High Court to the county courts. Whereas the county courts have traditionally been seen as a local forum resolution of smaller disputes, they will now become the focal point for tigation. The High Court is to be reserved for judicial review cases, for st cases, and for other cases of unusual complexity or importance. The move will be achieved in stages, since county courts lack the resources to absorb the significant increase in their work. Initially, the old upper limit of £5000 in anticipated damages on their jurisdiction in cases in contract and tort is to disappear. County courts will have no formal upper limit on their jurisdiction. The amount of damages expected will, however, be a factor in determining whether the case is more suitable for trial in the county court or the High Court. Cases which are not expected to involve damages in excess of £25,000 will normally be tried in the county courts. This will result in 90 per cent of personal injuries cases being triable in the county courts. There will then be a band of cases potentially involving damages of between £25,000 and £50,000 which may be tried either in the county courts or in the High Court depending upon their complexity. Cases involving more than £50,000 in damages will usually be tried in the High Court. For personal injuries litigation, all cases will be started in the county courts and those cases justifying consideration by the High Court will be transferred there once the likely amount of damages or the complexity of the case has been established.

The Civil Justice Review also made a number of recommendations concerning the progress of cases through the courts designed to secure greater openness and court control in the processing of personal injuries claims.

Rules of Civil Procedure

The English system of civil procedure is based upon the adversary principle: a series of statements of fact are put forward by one party to be attacked by the opposing party. The judge acts principally as umpire or referee and leaves it to the parties to put the case before him. The rules of civil procedure which govern the handling of cases are technical, complex and detailed. They are designed to regulate the conduct of the parties and their advocates in an adversary trial. They can be found in the large volumes entitled The Supreme Court Practice (known among lawyers as 'the White Book') and The County Court Practice (known among lawyers as 'the Green Book'). This mass of rules really has three objectives. The first objective is to ensure that the facts on which a claim is based are accurately found and appropriately arranged so that the issues between the parties can be identified. The second is to ensure that the correct and appropriate rule of law is found and applied, and the third objective is to ensure that the remedy or remedies prescribed by that rule of law can be adequately enforced. It is not necessary to dwell on the detail of the rules of procedure, since a broad outline of the process in actions in contract and tort will serve for our enquiry. Whether the rules actually achieve their objectives remains to be assessed, but there has been a succession of calls over the last 30 years for the redrafting of the rules in order to make High Court practice and procedure quicker, simpler and cheaper (Evershed, 1953; Winn, 1968; JUSTICE, 1974; Pearson, 1978 and

Cantley, 1979). Few of their recommendations have been implemented. The recommendations of the Civil Justice Review pick up some of these recommendations and their implementation will mark the start of a new era in the processing of civil disputes. Some commentators suggest that their significance is equal to the great procedural reforms of the nineteenth century.

Claims Consciousness

If accident victims are to benefit from the tort system, they must become aware of the possibility of claiming compensation. Many do not take any action. Legal advice will usually be needed. Research surveys have shown a marked failure by accident victims to seek out legal advice (Abel-Smith et al., 1973; Adamsdown, 1978; Harris et al., 1984; and Genn, 1987). Significant factors accounting for failure to take legal advice are fear of cost and ignorance of the legal aid scheme. This is unfortunate because the legal aid scheme and related schemes can provide speedy and cheap advice.

Between 1976 and 1977 the Oxford Centre for Socio-Legal Research carried out a large scale study of accident victims, which has come to be known as the National Compensation Survey (Harris et al., 1984). The study involved interviewing just over 1000 people who had suffered injuries which had stopped them from carrying out their normal activities for over two weeks at some time in the preceding five years. The study sought to identify reasons why claims were not made as well as the outcomes of those that were made. Almost three out of every four accident victims did not even consider making a claim. Of the quarter who did, only about half actually took any further steps. The six main reasons for not making a claim were:

    ignorance of the procedure for claiming
    problems in collecting evidence
    fear of cost
    accident was their own fault
    ignorance or confusion
    injuries not regarded as sufficiently serious to warrant claiming.

Some respondents did not know they had to make a claim. A man knocked down by a bus said, 'The police came to see me and I thought I would hear from the company, but never did.' Another said, 'I felt so poorly after the accident, I couldn't face doing anything.' A man injured at work said, 'I was grateful that the firm employed me at my age of 62 and I didn't want to cause any bother.' Among those who said someone else was to blame for the accident, four in ten did not make a claim. Paradoxically, two in ten of those who did claim said they did not blame anyone else for the accident. It seems that the factor most likely to lead people to claim is advice to claim by a third party. Three in four of those claiming said the idea of claiming had been suggested by someone else. The researchers conclude:

The accident victims who do succeed in obtaining damages for their
injuries are a strange group. They are not necessarily the most seriously
injured, nor those who have suffered the most prevalent types of accident,
nor are they necessarily those who blamed some third party for the accident. They are not the people with most wealth and influence. But they do
appear to have an important advantage in that they have access to advice
about claiming and often receive this advice without soliciting it. (Harris,
1984, p. 76)

Once the threshold of actually making the claim is overcome, the chances of
obtaining some compensation are good, though the survey showed that the
longer a claimant delays in instructing a lawyer the less the chance of recovering
damages. Four out of every five claimants received something, though many of
the amounts paid were very modest.

A scheme run by the Greater Manchester Legal Services Committee to raise
claims consciousness proved very successful. A leaflet giving simple information
about personal injuries claims and explaining how and where legal advice might
be obtained was made readily available in hospitals and advice agencies. A free
diagnostic interview was offered by participating solicitors. It uncovered some
serious cases where individuals would not otherwise have taken any action
(Genn, 1982).

The success of the Manchester scheme persuaded The Law Society that the
idea was a good one. The scheme has been introduced nationally as the Accident
Legal Advice Service (ALAS) and is administered by local law societies. As a
result coverage is patchy since not all local law societies are willing to act as coor-
dinators for such a scheme. Levels of efficiency are also variable. The underlying
concept of the scheme is to provide the free diagnostic interview in order to
'capture' clients by offering the initial service without charge. Strong cases will
proceed on the usual fee-paying basis or under the legal aid scheme.

Financing the Claim

Paying the Lawyer

Becoming claims conscious, finding a lawyer and financing the claim are crucial
stages on the route to accident compensation. Personal injuries claims are one of
the main areas of litigation where some solicitors have considerable expertise.
Getting good legal advice is crucial to success and is vital in obtaining a good
settlement. Once claimants have found a lawyer, they are almost wholly dependent on the lawyer's knowledge and expertise. Finding the right lawyer is very
important, but accident victims are in a poor position to measure the expertise
of their lawyers. All solicitors tend to hold themselves out as doing accident compensation work, but many do only a very small amount of the work and even
fewer will have followed a contested case through to judgment in court.

Finding the right lawyer is something of a lottery because claimants have very little information on which to base their choice. Hazel Genn, in her study of negotiated settlements (Genn, 1987) catalogues the dangers of having an inexperienced lawyer handling your accident compensation claim:

it is difficult for non-specialists to keep up to date with court procedure;
they may be reluctant to go to court to fight the case and so will settle at any price;
they tend to delay the issue of court proceedings and so build unnecessary delays into the process;
the delay leads to problems in the collection of evidence which may have gone stale;
defendants' insurance companies will take advantage of the inexperienced plaintiff's solicitor;
if negotiations break down, it may be too late to prepare the case adequately for a trial;
they might advise the plaintiff to accept a low settlement in the knowledge that this advice is unlikely to be challenged.

Michael Joseph in his book *Lawyers Can Seriously Damage Your Health* (Joseph, 1984) makes similar points, though based on anecdotal evidence and polemic rather than the skilled research methods used by Hazel Genn. Some of the issues of competence are being addressed in the consideration being given by The Law Society to the circumstances in which solicitors can hold themselves out as specialists in particular areas of work. Some favour the creation of panels of specialists who would have to establish their competence or experience in the work in order to be admitted to a panel of designated specialists.

Legal aid under the Legal Aid Act 1988 offers considerable assistance for plaintiffs in accident compensation claims. For those within the Green Form financial limits, the solicitor can begin to collect evidence, write preliminary letters and make an application for a civil legal aid certificate. After matrimonial proceedings, legal aid certificates are most frequently granted in personal injuries claims. The applicant must satisfy both a means test and a merits test. The applicant's means are considered by the Department of Social Security (DSS) and, depending on income and capital, a contribution may be required towards the cost of the legal services. While the DSS is assessing the financial position, an official of the Legal Aid Board will be determining the merits test. This is in two parts. First, the applicant must show that there are 'reasonable grounds for taking' the proceedings. This requires an applicant to show that there is an issue of fact or law which it is reasonable to submit to the court for decision. The second part permits the Legal Aid Board to refuse legal aid where it appears to the Board that in the particular circumstances of the case it is 'unreasonable' that the applicant should receive legal aid. This is sometimes called the 'paying client test' and would justify refusal if a paying client would not consider the cost of the proceedings justified in the particular case. The notes for guidance indicate that care should be taken in the application of the 'paying client test'. The reasonableness test might also justify refusal where the applicant has other means of financing the claim, for example, if the applicant could rely on some help under a legal expenses insurance policy. In personal injuries cases it is not generally difficult to satisfy the merits test.

Once a legal aid certificate has been granted, the assisted person (as he or she is then known) will have the services of a solicitor, and if necessary of a barrister, at no greater cost than the amount of any contribution required. But there is one snag. If the assisted person wins, then the compensation and any costs awarded must be paid into the Legal Aid Fund, which must then take the first slice of that money to recover for the Fund the amount paid out for the assisted person's legal services less any contribution paid by the assisted person. This is the operation of the 'statutory charge' which the Legal Aid Board is required under s.16(6) of the Legal Aid Act 1988 to apply in all cases. Thus, at the end of the day, the assisted person has received no money from the Legal Aid Board. What assisted persons gain is a guarantee against greater liability for legal costs than the amount of the contribution if they lose, and an interest free loan to meet the legal costs if they win. Where assisted persons lose the case, the court can in exceptional cases order them to pay a contribution to the winning party's costs in addition to any contribution already paid, but this is limited to an amount the assisted person is deemed able to afford.

For many accidents at work trades union support will be available to meet any legal costs. Contingent fee arrangements, whereby a solicitor agrees to take no fee if the claim fails but will take a percentage of any compensation gained if the plaintiff wins, have also been suggested as a way of helping those outside the legal aid financial limits (Zander, 1968, 1978; White, Robin, 1978), but these have not found favour with the legal profession. The Lord Chancellor's Green Paper on Contingent Fees (Cm 571) in January 1989 resurrected interest in such schemes, but the outcome has been only a modest change in the current basis for funding litigation. The Courts and Legal Services Act 1990 empowers the Lord Chancellor to make regulations permitting lawyers to be instructed on a conditional fee basis, that is, that the lawyer will receive a fee only in the event of the action proving successful. The need for an uplift in the normal fee levels to compensate the lawyer for the risk of receiving nothing is accepted, but the maximum amount of the uplift will be controlled by the Lord Chancellor. The scheme is modelled on the speculative fee of the Scottish legal system. A serious defect is the lack of protection against having to meet the other side's costs if the case is unsuccessful and this will be a major inhibition to its use. Those put off taking a case because they cannot meet their own costs are unlikely to be willing to risk having to pay a like sum to the other side's lawyers.

For those outside the legal aid limits, legal expenses insurance, which has in recent years been marketed with some vigour and with the support of The Law Society but with little market penetration, invariably provides cover for this type of litigation (Levin, 1982; White, Robin, 1984).

As indicated above most defendants will be protected by insurance and the insurance company will pay the legal costs arising in the defence of any claim.

The System of Costs

Anyone embarking on litigation needs to know the rules on costs; this refers to the fees paid to the lawyers involved in the case and the reimbursement of out-of-pocket expenses in connection with the case. An award of costs is a matter for the discretion of the court, but the court usually exercises its discretion in favour of the winning party. The loser will be ordered to pay most of the winner's costs. This is said to be the application of the principle that 'costs follow the event'. The award of costs in litigation is said to be on the 'standard basis', under which there is allowed a reasonable amount in respect of all costs reasonably incurred in the conduct of the litigation. Where an item is disputed, any benefit of the doubt on the question of reasonableness is given to the paying party.

A second basis of costs is the 'indemnity basis' which is similarly the allowing of all costs reasonably incurred, except in so far as they are of an unreasonable amount or have been unreasonably incurred. In this case the benefit of any doubt is given to the receiving party. This standard replaces the 'solicitor and own client' basis, which was the contractual basis of costs, under which a reasonable amount was allowed in respect of all costs incurred on the client's instructions.

Collecting Evidence

The next hurdle faced by the plaintiff will be the collection of evidence in support of the claim. Here the plaintiff will often be at a disadvantage. Usually the accident will have been reported to the insurance company by the insured party. The insurance company will commonly, and very wisely, advise that no statements be made without the insurers' knowledge. The insurers will collect statements and conduct a general enquiry for their own use in determining whether to settle any claim, but these statements will not be made available to the plaintiff. In many cases plaintiffs, or their lawyers, will only consult witnesses after the insurers have seen them and may well find them uncooperative. Plaintiffs suffer the twin disadvantages of not being in a position immediately after the accident to collect evidence and of being dependent on their solicitors for the early collection of evidence. In addition to the inevitable disadvantage which arises for plaintiffs of instructing lawyers later than defendants, plaintiffs suffer the further disadvantage that lawyers often seek no evidence apart from the plaintiff's own statement (Genn, 1987). Solicitors, it seems, take an office-bound approach to the collection of evidence; they rarely make site visits, take photographs or instruct engineers to make investigations on behalf of the plaintiff. It is not even universal practice to obtain a copy of the police report of a road traffic accident. Hazel Genn's study of settlement (Genn, 1987) concludes that the failure of solicitors to obtain information at an early stage of the case will trail an effect across the whole case, since the absence of detailed information affects not only the solicitor's ability to make a sound judgment on the claim, but also counsel's ability to give advice. It is clear that the collection of good, relevant evidence is crucial to the plaintiff's claim.

If there has been a motoring accident upon which a police report has been made, that report, including any witness statements, will be made available to the plaintiff on payment of the prescribed fee, though where criminal proceedings are pending some police forces will not disclose the report until the criminal proceedings are concluded. The Civil Justice Review recommended a change of this practice so that such reports could be made available to accident victims at the earliest opportunity. In cases of accidents at work, the most that can be expected from HM Inspector of Factories, who may have investigated the accident, is a factual account, which will not include any comments by the inspector, nor statements given, nor even the names and addresses of witnesses. Despite recommendations that the Factory Inspectorate should follow the same practice as the police (Winn, 1968), practice has not changed.

Normally the courts will not intervene to assist a party to obtain information in order to bring a claim. Sections 33 and 35 of the Supreme Court Act 1981 are of assistance to a plaintiff seeking to establish whether there are grounds for beginning proceedings by allowing certain orders to be made *before* proceedings are started. Both the High Court and county courts can in personal injuries and fatal accident claims order the production of relevant documents from a party who might become a defendant. This provision covers such things as hospital notes or engineer's reports, but will not extend to witness statements. Secondly, under s.33(1) of the Supreme Court Act 1981, the High Court or a county court can in any action make orders for:

(a) the inspection, photographing, preservation, custody and detention of property which appears to the court to be property which may become the subject matter of subsequent proceedings . . ., or as to which any question may arise in any such proceedings, and
(b) the taking of samples of any such property as is mentioned in paragraph (a) and the carrying out of any experiment on or with any such property.

The section could cover inspection of such things as a machine in a factory or a car involved in a motoring accident.

Basic Practice and Procedure

'Without Prejudice' Negotiations and the Letter before Action

At this stage the plaintiff will be in a position to begin serious negotiations with the insurance company. The first step, if it has not already been taken, will be the sending of a letter making a formal claim for compensation. It is at this stage, where there is a dispute which might result in litigation, that privilege can attach to correspondence between the parties. Such correspondence will be headed 'without prejudice' and all communications properly so headed cannot be used in evidence in any subsequent proceedings. What this means is that as part of the negotiating process, each party can make admissions and compromise suggestions which will not be held against them if the case proceeds to trial. Lord Griffiths confirmed the purpose of the rule in *Rush & Tompkins Ltd* v. *GLC* ([1989] AC 1280):

> The 'without prejudice rule' is a rule governing the admissibility of evidence and is founded on the public policy of encouraging litigants to settle their differences rather than litigate to the finish. (p. 1299)

Lord Griffiths cited with approval Oliver LJ in *Cutts* v. *Head* ([1984] Ch 290, pp. 306–7) who had stated that parties should not be discouraged from entering into negotiations for settlement by any fear that what was said or not said in correspondence or other communications would be used to their prejudice in the course of the proceedings.

The privilege seems to work well in practice because such negotiations usually take place between lawyers and insurers. It provides a useful and effective incentive to early settlement since admissions can be made and the strengths and weaknesses of cases aired without prejudice to what might later be argued in court. Its effectiveness probably depends upon the parties negotiating being familiar with the process and skills of negotiation; litigants in person may well lack these skills. A typical subject of without prejudice exchanges would be discussion as to the amount by which damages might be reduced because the victim was partly to blame for the accident. A privileged admission that there was a degree of contributory negligence would not preclude a complete denial of contributory negligence in any trial of the action.

If no settlement is achieved, it will be necessary to send a formal 'letter before action' threatening the issue of proceedings within seven or fourteen days if the claim is not admitted. The purpose of such a letter is to make clear the plaintiff's intention to pursue the claim before the courts; it will preclude any claim by the defendant to have been taken by surprise by the litigation. It has already been noted that some 86 per cent of claims are settled at or before this stage.

For those cases that do not settle, proceedings will need to be issued. This must usually be done within three years of the date of the accident failing which the Limitation Acts may bar the action. What follows is a description of the main procedural steps in a typical High Court action. The procedural steps in county courts are becoming increasingly similar. Practice and procedure in the county courts takes on much greater significance now that the county courts are the single point of entry into the courts for personal injuries cases.

Writ and Acknowledgment

The plaintiff's solicitor will prepare three copies of the writ by filling in the blanks on a standard form obtained from a law stationers. The writ must contain the names and addresses of both plaintiff and defendant and must contain a brief statement of the nature of the claim. It will not state the amount of damages claimed since in personal injuries cases these are for the court to assess, if there is no agreement between the parties. Such claims are said to be unliquidated. The writ must be 'issued' by taking it to the Central Office of the High Court in London, or to a District Registry in one of the main provincial cities. A fee (at the time of writing £60) is paid and each copy of the writ is stamped with the court seal. One copy is lodged with the court. The writ is now issued and must be served on the defendant within four months. The significance of issue is simply that it formally places the dispute within the jurisdiction of the High Court. The writ is usually served on the defendant's solicitors, but if they have not agreed to accept service, then the writ must be served personally on the defendant. This will usually be done by employing professional process servers. One copy is handed to the defendant and the final copy is endorsed to show how and when service was achieved. A form called 'Acknowledgment of Service of the Writ of Summons' will be served with the writ. Within 14 days of service of the writ, the defendant must file the Acknowledgment form with the court. It is not a complex form. It simply acknowledges receipt of the writ and indicates intent to contest the case. The defendant's solicitors literally tick a 'yes/no' box in answer to the direction, 'State whether the defendant intends to contest the proceedings'. On receipt of the form, the court places the court seal on it, enters the details in the court's records and sends a photocopy to each party. Return of the form does not preclude defendants from claiming either that they are the wrong party to sue or that there is an irregularity affecting the validity of the writ. But failure to return the form at all has serious consequences. The plaintiff can enter judgment by filing an *affidavit* (sworn written statement) of service. The plaintiff may also enter judgment immediately if the form is returned with an indication that there is no intent to defend. Such judgments are called 'interlocutory judgments', since the amount of damages remains to be fixed by the court in the absence of agreement between the parties. All proceedings prior to trial itself are labelled interlocutory.

The issue and service of the writ will trigger a further round of negotiated settlements. Nothing concentrates the minds of insurers who feel that a claim might wither on the vine more than receipt of a writ which shows that the plaintiff means to persist with the claim. At this stage no detailed statement of the allegations made by the plaintiff against the defendant will have been presented to the defendant. The clarification of the matters in dispute and notification of the allegations made by each party is the principal objective of the next stage of the proceedings, called 'pleadings'.

Pleadings

Whereas a failure to comply with the time limits for issuing the writ, or for filing the acknowledgment of the writ, have serious consequences, the time limits expressed in the Rules of the Supreme Court, usually 14 days from receipt of last pleadings, are widely ignored with impunity. Solicitors commonly allow each other significant extensions of the formal time limits. Clients are seldom consulted over these informal extensions. Even where one party objects and applies to the court for an order that particular pleadings be filed within 14 days, the court normally grants one or more extensions provided there is some plausible reason for the delay (JUSTICE, 1974).

Pleadings are opened by the preparation on behalf of the plaintiff of the statement, or particulars, of claim. This document is in practice drafted by counsel instructed by the plaintiff's solicitor. The statement is a brief account of the material facts upon which the plaintiff relies for the claim. It does not set out the evidence to be adduced in support of the allegations and it contains no argument on the law. Again in practice the statement will be drafted by reference to a standard form precedent for such claims; counsel will seek to leave open every avenue of attack against the defendant. Typical personal injuries statements are in four parts:

a statement of the date, time and place of the accident and of the persons involved;

an allegation of negligence against the defendant following a ritual formula;

details of the injuries suffered by the plaintiff and of any damage to the property of the plaintiff and of his actual loss of earnings; and

a formal claim for damages.

Plaintiffs claiming personal injuries must also provide a medical report setting out the nature of the injuries together with a schedule of special damages to date and an estimate of any future expenses and losses including earnings and pension rights, unless the court has given leave for these to be filed at a later date. If there is any change in the plaintiff's medical condition requiring an additional medical report, a copy of that report must be served on the defendant together with an up-dated schedule of special damages.

Statements in pleadings tend to give very little away because part of the skill of drafting statements of claim is in keeping open as many issues as possible to permit later room for manoeuvre. This is really only possible because the plaintiff is not required to give any indication of the evidence available to support the allegations made. Given that so few cases come to trial, the only point at which evidence is considered in detail, allegations may be made in pleadings for which there is little or no evidence available. Recent amendments to rules of court are designed to ensure that pleadings are more informative than in the past.

On receiving the statement the defendant must formulate a strategy for response. If some part of the statement of claim is unclear, further and better particulars of the claim can be requested. Indeed if a defendant wishes to be obstructive, this is quite a good ploy, because it increases the other side's costs (as well, of course, as the defendant's own) and may throw the other side into disarray. But the usual response is the filing of a defence.

The Rules of the Supreme Court provide that any allegation of fact is deemed to be admitted unless it is specifically denied. This means that defendants cannot file blanket defences to the effect, 'I didn't do it'. They must where they deny facts alleged, put forward their own allegations of the true position. What happens in practice is that the defendant will admit the fact of the accident's having occurred and the persons involved. This means that there is no need for the plaintiff to adduce evidence as to these facts. But the defendant will go on to deny the allegation of negligence. Often there will be an allegation that the accident was caused wholly or partly by the negligence of the plaintiff and there will be detailed allegations of how the plaintiff was negligent. The details of the injuries and loss will be not admitted; this is different from a denial and means that the plaintiff must adduce evidence to prove the injuries and loss. The defendant is not denying that the plaintiff was injured, but is simply requiring the plaintiff to prove the injuries and loss. This is known as 'putting the plaintiff to proof'. Finally, the defendant will usually put in a blanket denial of all other matters. If the defendant does not file a defence then the plaintiff can obtain judgment by default.

In motor accident claims, defendants will often counterclaim from plaintiffs for their own injuries and loss. Though often genuine, there is scope here for obstructionist tactics. The ball is now back in the plaintiff's court. The plaintiff may, if there is a need, seek further and better particulars of matters raised by the defendant, but, sooner or later, must file a defence to any counterclaim. Normally, pleadings are closed 14 days after delivery of the defence or defence to the counterclaim. Even practitioner commentators acknowledge the limited scope of particulars and draw attention to the duty of the draftsman of pleadings to leave open as much room for manoeuvre as possible (Barnard, 1985). The JUSTICE Report *Going to Law* (JUSTICE, 1974) uses a colourful analogy:

> Pleading therefore resembles nothing so much as naval warfare before the advent of radar, when each side made blind forays into the sea area of the other, while giving away as little as possible about the disposition of his own forces. (para.50)

Pleadings are exchanged between the parties and it will not be until a later stage of the proceedings that copies are lodged with the court. At this stage all the court has is the writ and the Acknowledgment of Service.

Preparation for Trial

After close of pleadings comes the stage of directions for trial. In personal injuries cases (except medical negligence claims) a system of automatic directions applies. There is no need for formal application to be made. The following directions apply automatically:

> discovery of documents must take place within 14 days of close of pleadings with inspection seven days later;
> where a party wants to call expert evidence at the trial, the substance of that evidence must be disclosed within ten weeks and agreed with the other side if possible;

photographs, sketch plans and any police report are receivable without calling
the person who made them and should be agreed if possible;

the place of trial will be the trial centre for the place where the action is
proceeding;

the mode of trial will be by judge alone;

setting down for trial should take place within six months and the court
notified on setting down of the expected length of the trial.

Another group of cases will settle at this stage of the pre-trial proceedings,
because the next step is a tedious labour intensive exercise. It is known as
discovery. Each side must compile a list of all documents relevant to the dispute
and exchange it with the other side. This may sound a simple task, but it is not.
Often there will have been no attempt prior to this stage of the proceedings to
collect together all possible documentation; only the most relevant will have been
used. Once all the documents have been collected they must be separated into
three categories:

those the party has and is prepared to disclose;

those the party has but is not prepared to disclose because privilege attaches
to them; and

those the party has had but no longer has, stating the reason the party no
longer has them.

Examples in the last category would be originals of copy letters listed in the
first category or an accident report book sent to the Factory Inspectorate.
Documents to which privilege attaches are principally 'without prejudice' letters,
solicitor/client communications, witness statements and documents prepared for
the purposes of litigation. The reason for privilege attaching to solicitor/client
communications is obvious; there must be no inhibition to free and frank disclosure even of prejudicial matters between solicitor and client. Arguments may and
often do arise over whether privilege attaches to a particular document,
especially where the claim to privilege is based on a claim that it is a document
prepared for the purposes of litigation. Under the rule in *Waugh* v. *British
Railways Board* ([1980] AC 521) the test is whether the dominant purpose of
the author in preparing the document was the submission of advice or assistance
to a legal adviser in the conduct of contemplated litigation. The above rules on
discovery apply unless the claim is one in which liability is admitted or is a motor
accident claim. In these cases the plaintiff need only disclose documents relating
to special damages claims.

Obviously the lists exchanged on discovery tell the other side very little. The
process of inspection follows, whereby each party arranges for the other side to
see all documents, other than those to which privilege attaches, and to photocopy such as the other party selects. It is an important step because it is the only
opportunity before trial to make any assessment of the true strength of a part of
the other side's case. If there is some specific document one side believes the other
side has but is not disclosing, application can be made to the court for an order
of specific discovery requiring the production of the document.

The final preparations for trial are again time-consuming and labour intensive. Since a trial now seems likely, counsel will be asked for detailed advice on evidence. This may involve further interviews with witnesses. There will also be the work of preparation of bundles of documents and of service of notices requiring the other side to produce specific documents at the trial. As with discovery and inspection, this labour intensive, and hence expensive, exercise induces a further round of settlements. Another factor inducing settlement will be the knowledge that trial itself is the most expensive part of the whole process. It seems that costs are virtually doubled where the case goes to trial (Zander, 1975a).

Trial

Up to six years after the date of the accident, that rare case which 'goes all the way' will be tried. This is the moment where evidence is produced and tested by the procedures of examination and cross-examination of witnesses. It is a dramatic ritual event. The judge will know very little about the case; at best he or she will have read the pleadings, while at worst nothing will have been read. The trial proceeds on the basis of orality; almost every document and every piece of evidence, even though agreed by the parties, is read out. Every word spoken is recorded either by mechanical means or by a shorthand writer and may be used later if there is an appeal. In the county courts, which are not courts where verbatim records are kept, the same principle of orality applies but the only formal record of the proceedings will be the judge's notes. By and large the judge plays very little role in the proceedings, leaving it to counsel to call witnesses and pursue lines of enquiry in their questioning of their own choice. Much of what was said about the unreliability both of human testimony and of the adversary process as a means of eliciting the truth in the criminal trial applies equally to the civil trial. At the end of the presentation of the case for the plaintiff and for the defendant, and much of the dispute is likely to be about facts and not about the law that applies, the judge gives a reasoned judgment in which the judge will determine both liability and quantum either immediately or at some later time. The latter is called a *reserved judgment*. In some cases there will have been no dispute about liability and the sole issue will be that of quantum.

One result of the recommendations made by the Civil Justice Review will be the increased use of split trials, that is, the separate trial of separate issues. The usual split will be between the issue of liability to pay compensation and the determination of the amount of compensation to be paid. Both the High Court and county courts are given wider power to order split trials. In personal injuries litigation, courts should consider whether a split trial should be ordered even where neither side makes application for this to happen.

Defence Strategies

The discussion of the system of costs made clear that the prospect of perhaps losing after an expensive trial, in which case losing defendants will have to pay not only damages but also their own and the plaintiffs' costs, is in itself a powerful incentive to settle early before costs have begun to pile up dramatically. Equally a party for whom costs do not represent any inhibition to litigation can seek to escalate costs at every opportunity and to 'scare off' the opposing party. The Rules of the Supreme Court (and in county court cases the corresponding County Court Rules) themselves use costs as an incentive both to early settlement and to the proper conduct of the case.

The device of *payment into court* places considerable pressure on a plaintiff to settle. At any point after service of the writ, the defendant can pay a sum into court. This frequently occurs where there is an allegation of contributory negligence, which reduces damages payable to the plaintiff. The plaintiff is notified of the sum paid into court, and must either accept or reject it. If he or she accepts it, that effectively ends the proceedings, though the plaintiff will be entitled to costs up to settlement. If the plaintiff rejects the sum paid in, serious costs consequences ensue. At trial the judge is not told of the payment into court. Provided the plaintiff wins damages at trial in excess of the amount paid into court, the usual costs rules apply. But if the plaintiff wins less, the judge will usually award the plaintiff costs up to the date of the payment into court and the defendant costs from that point onwards. Since we have seen that costs escalate the further the case progresses, costs awarded against the plaintiff will be far more than those awarded in the plaintiff's favour. Plaintiffs who reject payments into court are effectively gambling to 'beat' the payment into court. If the defendant assesses the damages skilfully, and assessment of damages is not an exact science, the plaintiff has a real dilemma in deciding how to respond. More than one payment into court may be made. Defendants' lawyers often advise that the best strategy is to make a reasonable but not too generous payment into court at the earliest opportunity after issue of the writ. If the plaintiff does not accept this, a higher payment into court should be made at a later date. But more than two payments into court may be counter-productive because it may be seen as a sign of weakness.

Negotiated Settlements

The civil justice system encourages settlement and provides incentives for this to occur. The principal encouragement is the protection against the use in court of 'without prejudice' communications in which each party can bargain freely without fear that admissions or concessions will be used against them if negotiations break down. The high incidence of settlement in personal injuries litigation may be seen to be a credit to the system. However, those settlements must be fair to the parties and not be the result of an unequal bargain. The National Compensation Survey concluded:

> . . . in practice, the damages system produces relatively low sums of money, which can seldom achieve the goal of the system, viz. to put the plaintiff, so far as money can do so, back into the position he would have been in

had the accident not occurred. . . . the precision of the rules on assessing damages which aim to give the plaintiff 'full recompense' for his injuries and losses, gives way in out-of-court settlements to many practical pressures towards lower amounts. The full amount which a court would be likely to award if 'full' liability were established against the defendant, is heavily discounted in an out-of-court settlement in order to take account of all the uncertainties facing the plaintiff . . . . (Harris et al., 1984 pp. 88–9)

The major study of negotiated settlements is Hazel Genn's book *Hard Bargaining* (Genn, 1987), which shows that the process is not one of equal bargaining, but of a one-sided exercise disguised as a co-operative process for assisting victims of accidents. An American commentator, Owen Fiss, has argued that negotiated settlements are not desirable (Fiss, 1984). He argues that processes of settlement out of court assumes an equality of bargaining position between the parties. Settlement in such circumstances is the anticipation of the outcome of a trial and assumes that the terms of the settlement are the product of the parties' predictions of that outcome. Since the rough equality needed for a fair settlement is seldom present, Fiss does not approve the process, regarding it as a highly problematic technique for reducing the number of cases which come to trial and as the 'civil analogue of plea bargaining'. Justice may not be done. He concludes:

There is, moreover, a critical difference between a process of settlement, which is based on bargaining and accepts inequalities of wealth as an integral and legitimate component of the process, and a process like judgment, which knowingly struggles against those inequalities. Judgment aspires to an autonomy from distributional inequalities and it gathers much of its appeal from this aspiration. (Fiss, 1984, p. 1078).

Hazel Genn carried out in-depth interviews with 30 solicitors, 20 barristers and 12 insurance companies involved in the bargaining process, and analysed the results of 131 questionnaires sent to solicitors' offices. The results show that claiming compensation is a highly adversarial activity. Insurance companies owe their primary obligation to their policy-holders and strive to keep costs to a minimum. They do not offer a 'fair' amount but the least that they believe the plaintiff will accept. Even where the plaintiff is legally represented, insurance companies feel that it is legitimate to take advantage of any weaknesses in the way the case has been prepared. Many plaintiffs' solicitors believe they are acting in the best interests of their clients in seeking settlements, but proceed on the basis that nearly all cases will settle. Defendants' insurers take advantage of the generally half-hearted pursuit of the claim by plaintiff's solicitors by making low offers. Once negotiations break down, they know that the plaintiff's solicitors will be in a very weak position with little evidence to take to trial and little chance of constructing a convincing case at this stage. Waiting until the eleventh hour can still result in a low settlement, which the plaintiff's solicitor recommends the plaintiff to accept secure in the knowledge that the advice is unlikely to be challenged.

Hazel Genn's overall conclusion is that there are both structural and situational inequalities between the parties in personal injuries litigation which have a profound impact on the processes of negotiation and settlement. She notes that the specialist plaintiffs' solicitors do not talk of a co-operative approach, but recognize the adversarial nature of the process and adopt a confrontational approach to negotiating settlements, which seizes the advantage from the insurers' solicitors. By contrast the non-specialists speak of the importance of keeping on good terms with insurers in the interests of reaching speedy settlements. Hazel Genn concludes:

> If there is, indeed, a public interest in seeing that injured plaintiffs obtain 'fair' compensation for their injuries, then the analysis of out of court settlement processes contained in this study suggests that there is a strong argument for attempting to reduce some of the imbalance between the parties by improving the access of unknowledgeable plaintiffs to solicitors who genuinely specialize in personal injury litigation; for speeding-up personal injury litigation procedure, particularly the low-value claims; for providing incentives to defendants to settle claims quickly; and for providing a means by which out of court settlements become more visible or subject to scrutiny. (Genn, 1987, p. 169)

No-fault Schemes

Respondents to the Civil Justice Review argued strongly that for some claims a system of no-fault compensation was the solution to the difficulties encountered by the system of adjudicating such claims. A number of these issues have been considered before. The Royal Commission on Civil Liability and Compensation for Injury (the Pearson Commission) (Cmnd 7054) reported in 1978 on a number of issues related to accident compensation and its interaction with the social security system (Bourn, 1979). Among its many recommendations was the introduction of a no-fault scheme for road accident victims. The scheme would cover all accidents involving motor vehicles in places to which the public has access. The recommendation proposed that the scheme should be funded by a levy on petrol, since this would relate the costs approximately to the degree of risk created by each motorist in terms of mileage driven. The report calculated that a levy of one penny per gallon would raise £64 million after five years. The proposals did not attract much support and were quietly shelved. Yet the idea of a no-fault scheme will not go away.

Recommendation 62 of the Civil Justice Review is that the Lord Chancellor consider, in consultation with the insurance industry, the feasibility of a no-fault scheme restricted to less serious road accidents and financed by private insurance. The advantages of reduction in uncertainty for claimants, the avoidance of delay and costs associated with litigation and the saving in court time would have to be off-set against the inevitable increase in motor insurance premiums. There has also been a private members' bill seeking to introduce a no-fault system for victims of medical accidents.

11

Dealing with Debt Cases

Introduction

Nearly nine out of every ten cases started in the Queen's Bench Division of the High Court and in the county courts concerns debt. That is over two million cases. In virtually all these cases the plaintiff is a business or institution suing a private individual for unpaid debts arising from the supply of goods, services or credit. Many will relate to rent or to fuel debt owed to a gas or electricity board. A phenomenon of recent decades has been the growth in the availability of credit. This has led to an increase in debt cases, though the availability of credit has increased at a much faster rate than the incidence of debt claims. One explanation why so many cases involve institutional plaintiffs and individual defendants is that litigation among those likely to have a continuing business relationship is seen as inconsistent with the maintenance of goodwill between the parties. Where disputes arise, negotiation is seen as a far more satisfactory solution. Bad debts tend to be litigated because the likelihood of a continuing relationship in the face of serious bad debt is negligible (Macaulay, 1963; Beale and Dugdale, 1975).

Very few debt cases are contested. The Payne Committee in 1969 (Payne, 1969) reported:

> Actions for the recovery of debts engage the legal machinery at its least point of strain. The recovery of debts is very largely an administrative process and the handling of uncontested claims forms such a large part of the work of the courts that one cannot over-emphasise the need to make machinery for obtaining judgments in the High Court and in the county courts as simple as possible (para.64)

The Civil Justice Review recognized the importance of the debt enforcement work as the largest component of the work of the civil courts, accounting for a substantial proportion of their resources, but also drew attention to the two long-standing concerns about the system of debt enforcement:

From the point of view of the debtor there are complaints that the system allowed creditors to proceed to enforcement without obtaining adequate information about the debtor's ability to pay; while from the point of view of the creditor there are complaints about the ineffectiveness of the enforcement procedures. . . . (para.534)

The Causes of Debt

Research studies into the causes of debt have been consistent in concluding that the overwhelming majority of debtors fall into the 'can't pay' category rather than the 'won't pay' group. The Consumer Councils all agree that there are three broad categories of debt (National Consumer Council and Welsh Consumer Council, 1983; Scottish Consumer Council, 1988):

People who have suffered an unexpected drop in income, perhaps brought about by unemployment, sickness or marriage breakdown. Simply meeting normal household bills to maintain lifestyles becomes difficult and often money is borrowed at high interest rates.

People in long-term poverty, who typically generate housing and fuel debts, but may also get into difficulties repaying loans to buy essential household goods, such as a cooker or a washing machine.

Relatively affluent people seduced by easily available credit facilities who commit their income very fully. Any fluctuation in income or outgoings, as when mortgage interest rates rise, results in an inability to service the loans obtained.

Despite the high profile given in the media to the third group, it remains a minority of total debt problems, though in some cases the scale of debt accrued in a short time is impressive.

The Touche Ross Management Consultants factual study for the Civil Justice Review (Touche Ross Management Consultants, 1986b) tends to confirm these earlier findings. Most defendants in the sample were male, over 30 and married with dependants. Their average income was only £105 per week. Over a third were unemployed at the start of the proceedings.

The Amount Claimed

The most recent figures on the amounts claimed in debt actions are those in the Touche Ross study. In the county courts, three quarters of claims were for less than £500 and one in three was for less than £100. Such claims would, of course, be dealt with as small claims. Only one in nine was for more than £1000. The average claim in the county courts was for £230. By contrast the average amount claimed in the High Court was £5000, though just over half of all claims were for less than £5000. Two-thirds of debtors sued in the High Court were businesses, compared with only three in every ten defendants in the county courts. It is therefore fair to note that the character of High Court and county court debt work is different. The High Court tends to deal with business debt, while the county courts deal with personal debt.

Some 23 enterprises were identified by the Touche Ross study as 'bulk creditors', that is, those, broadly speaking, issuing 1000 or more summonses a year. These included mail order businesses, the utility companies (gas, electricity and water boards) and banks. Five of these indicated that they had a definite policy of pursuing smaller debts in the High Court because the chances of success were improved. But the thresholds varied. One set the threshold at over £2000, three at over £600 and one at over £300. Bulk creditors account for about 60 per cent of the two million debts cases begun each year. One study has suggested that bulk creditors can be divided into two groups: those who had information suggesting that the debtor could pay and those which did not. The Inland Revenue and the banks tended only to sue if they had reason to believe that the debtor had the resources to pay the debt. Other bulk creditors, however, brought cases to court as a matter of routine. If enough debts were processed, then the debt recovery department would show an overall profit. Such creditors would typically send a series of demands before taking court action, but would not visit the debtor and seldom had any information as to the reasons for non-payment of the debt (Cain, 1986). The Touche Ross study seems to suggest that the majority of creditors use the courts in this way.

Basic Practice and Procedure

Default Actions

Debt claims, which are claims in contract, may be started either in the High Court or the county courts. Only one in ten such claims is filed in the High Court. For this reason, and because actions in the High Court are often concerned with business debt, what follows focuses mainly on practice and procedure in the county courts.

Debt actions in the county courts are begun by using the default summons procedure. The plaintiff files a request for summons together with the particulars of claim at the appropriate county court. On payment of the court fee, which is determined by reference to the amount claimed, the court will prepare the summons to the plaintiff. Two copies of the particulars of claim must be filed: one for the court to keep and one for service on the defendant. The request for summons is a simple form giving the addresses of the plaintiff and defendant and providing the information which establishes the geographic link necessary to establish the jurisdiction of the county court to which the request is made. The particulars of claim used in county courts are very different from the formal pleadings used in the High Court, or even in personal injuries actions in the county courts. Often the particulars of claim in debt actions are no more than a copy of the unpaid bill or invoice which has been sent to the defendant. Bulk creditors normally use standardized pre-printed forms of request for summons which also incorporate the particulars of claim. If the request and particulars are in order, the county court will, on receipt of the court fee, issue a plaint note giving the court's unique number for the case and will prepare a default summons for service on the defendant. Some bulk creditors prepare their own summonses, which simply require sealing by the court before service.

Service of the summons on the defendant in debt actions is usually achieved by first class post. If the summons is returned undelivered, the court will tell the plaintiff who has the opportunity to provide a new address. The court will then try to serve the summons again.

Default actions require defendants to deliver an admission with an offer of payment, or a defence, within 14 days after service of the summons. Failure to take such action entitles plaintiffs to enter judgment by default, usually on terms that the full amount is payable forthwith. This is done by administrative action. There is no judicial consideration of the merits of the claim, nor any requirement to prove the facts upon which the claim is based. Two-thirds of all debt actions result in judgment by default. The case only proceeds to trial if the defendant lodges a defence to the claim. Very few defendants obtain legal advice in debt actions and very few actions are defended. Only 74 of the 1002 cases in the sample used by the Touche Ross study were defended. The study does not indicate the nature of the defence nor whether those cases resulted in contested trials. The role of legal aid is minimal; no more than around 3000 defendants receive legal aid each year to defend debt actions. Three-quarters of individual debtors in the Touche Ross study had received no advice at all about the case against them.

If the plaintiff admits all or part of the claim coupled with an offer to pay by instalments, the defendant may accept this or request a hearing, known as a 'disposal' at which the district judge will hear the parties' views and decide upon the instalments the defendant must pay. The district judge may require the sum to be paid in a single instalment.

In some cases defendants write back admitting part of the claim but denying liability for the higher sum claimed. Plaintiffs can, in such cases, choose to accept the lesser amount in full satisfaction of the whole claim or elect to have the case treated as a defended claim. The first hearing of defended cases will be the pre-trial review before the district judge. This has two purposes. The first is to determine whether there is a reasonable case in law to be tried. If there is not, then judgment for either plaintiff or defendant, as appropriate, can be entered there and then. In the case of judgment for the plaintiff, this will only occur if the plaintiff is present and ready to prove the claim. The second purpose is to give directions for the proper preparation of the case for trial. The pre-trial review, therefore, differs significantly from the summons for directions in the High Court. The district judge has a discretion to enter judgment for either party at the pre-trial review, whereas judgment is never given on a summons for directions in the High Court.

Summary Judgment

In some cases, the defendant will file a defence which has little or no merit merely to put off the day of reckoning when judgment will be entered against him or her. The summary judgment procedure, which is little used in the county courts, is designed to enable the plaintiff to obtain judgment at the earliest opportunity.

In any case where the plaintiff has claimed more than £500 and where the defendant files a defence, the plaintiff can apply for summary judgment on the ground that, notwithstanding the filing of a defence, the defendant has no real defence to the claim. The plaintiff must serve on the defendant, not less than seven days before the date fixed for the hearing of the application, a notice of the application together with a copy of the affidavit verifying the claim and asserting a belief that there is no defence to the claim. The hearing will usually also be the pre-trial review, at which the spurious nature of any defence can, in any event, be raised. It is probably for this reason that the procedure is little used in the county courts, though it does serve to give formal notice of the plaintiff's intention to seek judgment at the pre-trial review. The corresponding procedure in the High Court under RSC O.14 is much more potent; money sums are higher, the debt is often a business debt, and a process is needed to accelerate the time scale within which judgment can be entered for the plaintiff in the face of a defence which has no merit.

The Enforcement Process

Obtaining judgment in debt cases is merely the tip of the iceberg, because obtaining judgment and enforcing it are entirely separate processes. Many litigants breathe a huge sigh of relief when they obtain judgment in their favour, believing the long battle is over. Judgment is, however, merely a declaration of their success and enforcing a money judgment is a separate and sometimes lengthy and complex process. It is for the plaintiff to make strategic decisions about which of a range of enforcement measures will be sought. There are a host of these, but the four main methods of enforcing a judgment are execution against the debtor's goods, attachment of earnings, charging orders, and garnishee orders.

There are different systems of enforcement in the High Court and in the county courts. In the High Court, sheriff's officers working for private companies do the work of enforcement. These companies are accountable to Under Sheriffs who are usually solicitors in private practice appointed by the High Sheriff of each county. The area for which each Under Sheriff is responsible is known as the 'bailiwick'. The private companies make their money from the fees paid on the valuation of goods in connection with the process of execution. The Under Sheriffs make their money from a percentage of the debt recovered, a sort of performance related pay. In contrast to this privatized system, county court enforcement is carried out by bailiffs who are employees of the court service answerable to a supervizing bailiff. Plaintiffs pay fixed fees for enforcement measures in the county courts.

Where plaintiffs know little about the financial position of defendants, they can request an oral examination of the defendant. This procedure compels debtors to attend court in order to be questioned about their financial position. Most of these inquisitions, which occur only in a small number of cases, take place before executive rather than judicial staff of the court. Around 80,000 oral examinations take place each year. Only one in five will be before the district judge. Where a debtor persistently fails to attend for an oral examination, a warrant for his or her arrest may be issued. Imprisonment following such arrest can be avoided by the completion on the spot of a questionnaire about his or her means. The following section describes the four main enforcement measures in the county courts with some comment on the corresponding High Court measure.

Warrants of Execution

The fearsomely titled warrant of execution is a direction to the bailiff to seize and sell goods belonging to the defendant to the value of the warrant. The only goods which are exempt from seizure are clothes and bedding belonging to debtors and their families up to a value of £100 and the tools of the debtor's trade up to a value of £150. All other goods, including cookers and heating appliances, may be seized provided that they belong to the debtor. Goods on hire purchase do not become the property of the hirer until all instalments under the agreement are paid. The High Court counterpart to the warrant of execution is the writ of *fieri facias*, commonly known as the 'writ of *fi. fa.*'. Over one million warrants and writs are issued each year, of which 95 per cent are county court warrants. Creditors may seek warrants for the full amount of the debt or for a lesser sum, and may seek as many warrants as are needed to recover the full judgment debt. One advantage of seeking a part warrant is that the fee is lower and the exercise can be used to discover whether the debtor has goods of sufficient value to make further warrants cost effective.

In practice very few warrants actually result in the sale of the debtor's property. Only one in two hundred warrants actually results in seizure and sale. Debtors are often keen to retain their possessions. Sometimes they pay the amount of the warrant to the bailiff. Sometimes the bailiff will allow a reasonable time to find the money to meet the warrant. In such cases the debtor is required to acknowledge that the bailiff has taken notional possession of goods belonging to the debtor and agrees not to dispose of the goods. This is called agreement to 'walking possession'. Where such an agreement is signed, the bailiff is entitled to break into the home if the debtor subsequently refuses to open the door when the bailiff calls. Many debtors borrow money in order to keep the bailiff away, often compounding their financial difficulties.

Attachment of Earnings

An attachment of earnings order is an order directed to the debtor's employer authorizing deductions from the debtor's wages which are sent to the court in settlement of the judgment debt. Attachment of earnings orders are only available against debtors in employment; income from self-employment cannot be attached. Once an application is made and details of the debtor's earnings have been established, the court will fix the 'protected earnings level' and the 'normal deduction rate'. The protected earnings level is the amount below which the court thinks that the debtor's income should not be reduced; it is calculated by reference to income support rates under the Government's scheme of means-tested social security benefits. The normal deduction rate is the amount the court considers it reasonable for the debtor to have deducted from wages each week or month in satisfaction of the judgment debt. The procedure for obtaining an order can be quite lengthy, but for a debtor in stable employment, the order is an effective method of enforcement. Around 70,000 orders are made each year and about a quarter of a million orders are in force at any one time.

Charging Orders

Charging orders provide a means of treating land and securities as security for the judgment debt by imposing a charge on the asset for the amount of the judgment debt. The charge has the same effect as a mortgage on a house. This means that the land or securities cannot be sold without part of the proceeds being used to meet the judgment debt. Once a charging order has been obtained, the creditor may apply to the court for an order compelling its sale and for the discharge from the proceeds of sale of the judgment debt. The court has a discretion as to whether it is appropriate to order sale.

The creditor initially obtains the order *nisi* (the latin word for 'unless') which becomes an order absolute unless the debtor shows cause why the order should not be granted, for example, by paying the judgment debt. The order *nisi* operates to freeze the debtor's assets. The use of charging orders is a comparative rarity. There are about 35,000 orders a year.

Garnishee Orders

The garnishee order is another quaintly named remedy. The order requires a bank, building society, or other person who owes money to the debtor to pay that money direct to the creditor in satisfaction of the outstanding judgment. The order is first granted on a *nisi* basis, which freezes the assets in the hands of the bank, building society, or other party owing money to the debtor. Many orders are not made absolute because the debtor pays the amount being sought. There are around 7,000 orders made each year.

Administration Orders

Generally there is no system of priority applicable to judgment debts. The plaintiff who is the first to seek an enforcement order will be the first to get paid. The administration order may, however, be sought by debtors and offers some protection against enforcement measures from a variety of creditors. The order is available to a debtor with multiple debts, of which at least one is a judgment debt. The applicant asks the court for an order that allows the debtor to discharge all the debts by making regular payments under the order which are then distributed among the creditors on a pro rata basis. Where an administration order is in force, all other enforcement measures are barred. Such orders are only available in the county courts, but the judgment on which the order is based may have been obtained in the High Court. The Touche Ross study found that one third of the 98 administration orders they examined were scheduled to last for five years, one third for between five and ten years, and one third for more than ten years. The longest order would take 70 years before the debts were fully paid!

The Dominance of Warrants of Execution

The statistics show that the use of warrants of execution – in reality, a threat to seize and sell the debtor's goods – overshadows all other forms of enforcement. The Touche Ross study is confirmed by the findings of the Queen Mary College project on the enforcement of county court judgments for debt, cited in this chapter as the QMC study (Phipps, 1990). Warrants of execution are issued in two-thirds of judgments and in one-third of all cases two or more warrants are issued. Since 1984 the minimum figure for a warrant seeking to enforce part of a judgment has been £50 plus costs. Both the Touche Ross study and the QMC study report that between eight and nine full or part warrants out of every 20 issued will be paid in full. The main cause of warrants failing to produce payment is that the debtor has no goods worth seizing for sale. One in three warrants fails on this count. One in five fails because the debtor cannot be traced; either the address given is incorrect or the debtor has left that address. Most warrants are finalized on two visits and within three months. The conclusion drawn by the QMC study is that where the debtor has goods worth seizing and where the correct address is supplied to the court, most warrants will be successful.

The QMC study notes that there are a number of bulk creditors who use the county courts as part of their own debt enforcement machinery. Cost effectiveness and the need to streamline procedures become the principal determinants of action. A quarter of judgments for debt will not require any enforcement action; the debtor will pay, or make satisfactory arrangements to pay by instalments, on receipt of the judgment. In around half the warrants issued, full payment of the debt will ultimately be achieved, often without any further information being obtained about the debtor. Oral examinations are unpopular because the procedure is time-consuming and so expensive. Any action which requires a court hearing is expensive and unpopular among creditors. Equally other enforcement action requires information and cannot so readily be built into streamlined office procedures. Even if successful they will not necessarily provide a quick and substantial payment.

The QMC study points out that each enforcement measure carries a qualifying condition (Phipps, 1990). For the warrant of execution, it is the ownership of goods worth seizing; for the attachment of earnings order, it is the receipt of sufficient wages from employment; for the charging order, it is property to which the charge can attach; and for the garnishee order, it is the existence of a debt owed to the debtor. In all cases except the warrant of execution, it is for the judgment creditor to establish the qualifying condition as part of the process of obtaining the remedy. But for the warrant of execution, it is the bailiff who establishes the qualifying condition *after* the order has been granted. The QMC study concludes:

> The most cost-effective way to use the existing system when the defendant goes into default is to set judgment terms according to a formula, and instruct the bailiff to collect the payments by way of part-warrants. This strategy provides an experience on which perceptions are based that most debtors are able but unwilling to pay, and, therefore, when warrants fail, it is perceived to be because either the bailiff is not acting correctly or the procedure is ineffective. (Phipps, 1990, p. 251)

The Northern Ireland Enforcement of Judgments Office

The *laissez-faire* first come first served approach to the enforcement of judgment debts adopted in England and Wales is sometimes contrasted with the different system which operates in Northern Ireland. There the Enforcement of Judgments Office (EJO) was established in 1969 (Anderson Committee, 1965; Hunter Committee, 1988), though it does not change the first come first served basis of enforcement. The Hunter Committee has, however, recommended a change to an asset sharing basis of enforcement, like that operating under an administration order.

In Northern Ireland, if a judgment is not satisfied within seven days, the plaintiff may apply to the EJO for enforcement. The EJO then interview the debtor either at home or at the EJO premises. A creditor's report is then prepared, often following a number of interviews with the debtor and verification of the information given. The EJO's enquiries determine which measures of enforcement are appropriate. If it seems that the debtor has no realizable assets or income, a certificate of unenforceability is issued. No measures of enforcement can be taken while such a certificate is in force.

Criticisms of the EJO are that the process is slower and more expensive than its creditor-driven counterpart in England and Wales. Defenders of the EJO argue that the EJO is considering the whole case of the debtor rather than merely the enforcement of the particular judgment debt. After examining the record of the EJO, the National Consumer Council concluded:

> We are wary about setting up a new bureaucracy that may prove slow and unwieldy. We do not suggest a completely new administrative structure. There are elements of the enforcement office idea, however, which could usefully be incorporated within the existing system. These include the emphasis on collecting information about debtors and dealing with all debts together. We wish to see the courts have the power to issue

certificates of unenforceability where enforcement procedures would serve no useful function. (National Consumer Council, 1989, p. 368)

The Payne Committee

In 1969 the Payne Committee presented the *Report of the Committee on the Enforcement of Judgment Debts* (Cmnd 3909). The most important result of the Committee's deliberations was the Government's acceptance of the recommendation of the minority that imprisonment as a method of enforcing ordinary civil debt should be abolished. The remaining exceptions to this exemption from committal to prison for non-payment of debts are maintenance debts and statutory debts in respect of fuel consumption (gas and electricity), water consumption, tax and non-payment of rates (now community charge or poll tax). The recommendations of the Committee also resulted in the introduction in 1971 of attachment of earnings orders.

Many other recommendations of the Payne Committee have not been implemented. A major criticism in the Report was the overlapping jurisdictions of the courts in debt cases, which presented the lay person with a 'bewildering multiplicity and choice of courts and procedures' (para.290). Enforcement was described as 'unduly cumbersome, inefficient and expensive'. The Committee continues:

> One would have thought it self-evident that there was every possible objection to proceeding with the enforcement of a money judgment against a debtor without first ascertaining what property, assets, earnings and means he has at his disposal and what are his financial commitments and his circumstances; the size of his family, the nature of his business, the ownership or tenancy of his dwelling-house and so forth. And yet steps in enforcement are frequently taken before this information has been obtained and often as a means of obtaining the information itself. (para.296)

The Payne Committee recommended the creation of a new enforcement office in the county courts which would collect information about debtors and select the appropriate means of enforcement. In short, the Payne Committee recommended for England and Wales what the Anderson Committee had recommended for Northern Ireland in the form of the EJO. The Payne Committee's enforcement office would also coordinate all enforcement activity, overriding the first come first served basis of enforcement. The Payne Committee also recommended that there should be a single system of enforcement operated through the county courts, but The Law Society fought a successful campaign to prevent implementation of the recommendation. Cynics accuse The Law Society of merely protecting the interests of those solicitors holding office as Under Sheriffs; others have commented that High Court enforcement is far more effective, though more expensive. The latter reason would seem to be supported by the number of cases brought in the High Court each year which are within the jurisdictional limits of the county courts, though it is not supported by the findings of the Touche Ross and QMC studies.

The Civil Justice Review Proposals

Reference has already been made to the factual study carried out by Touche Ross Management Consultants for the Civil Justice Review. Touche Ross established as their criteria for judging debt enforcement procedures the creditors' interest in getting the debt paid reasonably quickly at reasonable cost and using a fair procedure coupled with the debtors' interest in being treated fairly and sympathetically. Overall Touche Ross did not believe that root and branch reform was needed, preferring the strategy of making improvements to the current system.

In addition to the findings reported earlier in this chapter, the Touche Ross study showed that, contrary to popular wisdom, there was little difference between the recovery rate of county court bailiffs and High Court bailiffs. Within 15 to 18 months of the start of proceedings, over half the judgment debts remained unsatisfied in whole or in part. The majority of creditors who had used enforcement procedures considered that enforcement had not helped them to recover payment. But three-quarters of all creditors had taken no steps to obtain information about the debtor's circumstances. Indeed, two-thirds of business creditors in the county courts had made no credit checks at the time of the original transaction which had given rise to the debt claim. One in three defendants in the county courts said they had not filed a defence, but nevertheless disputed the claim.

The recommendations in the Report of the Civil Justice Review accept that fine tuning is what is needed rather than radical reform. Six objectives are set for debt recovery through the courts:

1 The system should aim to recover as much as possible of the debt quickly, cheaply and simply.
2 Creditors should be able to obtain adequate information about debtor's circumstances.
3 Maximum information should be available about debtors on public files.
4 There should be machinery for bringing together multiple debts.
5 The period for repayment should not last indefinitely and a debtor should be restored to full economic status as soon as possible.
6 Debtors and their families should not be subjected to unwarranted hardship, fear or humiliation.

The Civil Justice Review's recommendations focus on six areas: terminology, the distribution of business and representation, responsibility for enforcement, the functions of bailiffs and Sheriffs, administration orders, and extending the goods exempt from seizure under a warrant. There is welcome recognition that the terminology used in describing enforcement measures is quaint and old-fashioned and will mean little to debtors, though no suggestions are offered for the new generation of names for enforcement measures.

The recommendations on the distribution of business presented the Civil Justice Review with a dilemma. There is a general acceptance that there is merit in having a single point of entry into the court system for the most common actions and that this should be the county court. Opposition to this for debt cases in the responses to the consultation paper drew attention to the different nature of the debts the subject of actions in the county courts and the High Court. County court debt is mostly consumer debt, while High Court debt is mostly business debt. There remained the conviction (which we have seen is not supported by the empirical evidence) that High Court enforcement is more effective. Finally, the transfer of business to the county courts might overwhelm them. These arguments won the day and the Report recommends no change for the time being in the distribution of debt business between the High Court and the county courts. The Review recognizes the valuable work done by lay advice and assistance and accept that it is appropriate to permit lay representatives to appear in debt cases in the county courts. The formal recommendation on this appears in the chapter of the Review on access to justice and proposes a statutory right for a litigant in a debt case in the county court to be assisted or represented by a lay representative of their choice, subject to the discretion of the court 'to restrict the involvement of corrupt or unruly representatives, and, where necessary, to exclude them entirely' (Civil Justice Review 1988, para.254 and R.48). Section 11 of the Courts and Legal Services Act 1990 implements this recommendation.

The debate over the machinery for enforcement is one of long standing. Despite the findings of the factual study that there is comparatively little difference between the success rates of county court bailiffs and Sheriffs, the recommendation is again largely for no change. The different character of the nature and value of the business conducted by the two systems is seen to justify the maintenance of two systems. The recommendation of the Civil Justice Review seeks to reserve business debt for the High Court enforcement system and consumer debt for the county court bailiffs, but does not wholly erode the principal that the place where the action takes place determines the enforcement machinery available. The recommendation is that all judgments below £5000 and all judgments arising out of the various credit arrangements regulated by the Consumer Credit Act 1974 will be enforced by county court bailiffs, whereas judgments above £5000 should automatically be transferred, and county court judgments above £2000 and of a commercial nature may be transferred, to Sheriffs for enforcement.

The criticisms of the bailiff service in the county court are noted and recommendations are made for improving the management structure within the county court service to integrate the bailiff service more fully into the court service. The conduct of bailiffs should be more controlled and there should be greater recognition of their role as information gatherers. Local variations in practice demand the production of a complete, and publicly available, manual setting out the bailiff's duties. The recommendation relating to the High Court enforcement machinery is feeble, simply stating that the law governing the execution by Under Sheriffs and Sheriff's Officers should be the subject of detailed reform, though there is an agenda of largely technical matters for consideration by whichever body is to be charged with this task.

The Civil Justice Review again rather feebly recommends that the administration order should be the subject of detailed reforms. The recommendation for reform follows the recommendation made in 1982 that the procedure should operate as a 'poor man's bankruptcy' (Cork Committee, 1982). This is the one enforcement remedy available to either debtor or creditor which looks at the overall debt position of the debtor and seeks to satisfy the interests of all creditors. It is described as a sort of 'mini-bankruptcy'. Specific proposals are that the current £5000 limit should be removed, that the qualifying condition of the existence of a judgment debt should be dropped, and that a time limit of three years should be placed on the duration of the order. If the debtor cannot reasonably be expected to meet all his or her liabilities in that period, then a composition order should be made reducing the overall indebtedness to a level which can reasonably be met and paying creditors rateably. The same recommendation also proposes the introduction of a certificate of unenforceability similar to that operating in Northern Ireland. These proposals have been implemented in Part I of the Courts and Legal Services Act 1990.

The Civil Justice Review recommends that the goods exempt from seizure under a warrant should be extended so that the protection afforded by s.283 of the Insolvency Act 1986 applies to warrants of execution. Section 283 excludes two groups of possessions: tools of a trade and essential household equipment. The former are such tools, books, vehicles and other items of equipment as are necessary for the debtor for use personally in employment, trade or business. The latter are such clothing, bedding, furniture, and household equipment as are necessary for satisfying the basic domestic needs of the debtor and his or her family. The need for guidance on what is 'necessary' is noted. Section 15 of the Courts and Legal Services Act 1990 makes these changes.

The most significant omission from the recommendations of the Civil Justice Review is the summary rejection of the idea of an enforcement office, which had been canvassed in the consultation paper:

> The concept of an enforcement office has been rejected, mainly because of the extra cost and delay which this would introduce. (para.645)

The key function of the enforcement office is to investigate the means of the debtor and to select and process appropriate enforcement action. It is therefore unfair to suggest that the fees charged by an enforcement office should properly be compared with fees for execution against goods. The enforcement office is doing rather more. The fees only look expensive because at present creditors, and bulk creditors in particular, can get away without investigating the circumstances of the debtor. Little weight is given to the stark contrast between the position in England and Wales, and Northern Ireland. In England and Wales four out of five judgments necessitate some enforcement activity, whereas in Northern Ireland three-quarters of applications to the EJO for enforcement were settled without the need for an enforcement order. The Hunter Committee which reviewed the work of the EJO concluded:

> Most debtors who can pay will do so when they are confronted with enforcement proceedings and . . . it is only in the minority of cases that actual enforcement measures have to be taken. (Hunter Committee, 1988, para.3.35)

The Civil Justice Review did not examine the debt recovery jurisdictions that vest in the magistrates' courts concerning tax, the community charge (formerly rates), 'distress' for rent, and disconnection for unpaid fuel debts. There is evidence of regional variations by magistrates' courts in their approach to debt similar to those found in the exercise of their criminal jurisdiction.

Ultimately the complaint that can be levied at the Civil Justice Review is that, though one of its aims appears to be to focus more on debtors than individual debt, the recommendations it makes will make few inroads into the practice of most creditors of focusing on individual debt rather than the overall circumstances of the debtor.

The National Consumer Council Proposals

The National Consumer Council's response to the issues raised by the Report of the Civil Justice Review (National Consumer Council, 1989) felt that it was important that the system of debt recovery sought to distinguish between those who cannot pay their debts and those who will not pay them. The focus of the system on debts rather than debtors is highlighted. Many debtors have two or three other debts in addition to the judgment debt and there may be judgments in respect of the other debts. Yet the present filing arrangements within the county courts do not allow courts to discover if debtors are being pursued for other debts. This results in a situation where, unless the debtor makes use of the administration order, debt enforcement becomes 'a case of every creditor for himself'. The National Consumer Council's response is to propose the following plan for reform of debt recovery systems in the county courts:

> all consumer debts should be dealt with in the county courts;
> debtors should be protected against harassment and should have access to advice in negotiating informal settlements;
> defendants should be encouraged to put defences before the court by the use of well-designed forms, information and advice;
> court staff should review all documents carefully to ensure that all valid defences are referred for adjudication;
> courts should keep information about debtors, rather than individual debts, and this information should be used to inform decisions about enforcement orders to be used;

the threat to seize goods and sell them should be used as a last rather than
the first choice of enforcement activity;

the administration order should be reformed and expanded, and it should be
made more readily available through the provision of money advice;

debtors who show the courts that they have made their best efforts to pay and
also show that they were not fraudulent or reckless in incurring debt should
be given relief from liabilities after three years;

creditors who are individuals rather than institutions should be given greater
help and advice by court staff. (National Consumer Council, 1989,
pp. 369–70)

The National Consumer Council believes that the best forum for debt enforcement actions against individuals is the county court. The Council wishes to see
all debt jurisdiction concentrated there. This would transfer the civil jurisdiction
of magistrates' courts to the county court. All individual debts not exceeding
£25,000 should start in the county court. There would be a procedure whereby
the plaintiff could show that a debt for a lesser sum was incurred in the course
of a business and seek transfer to the High Court.

The National Consumer Council welcomes the recommendations on the functions of bailiffs, but hopes that there will be a separation of the investigative role
from that of the threat to seize goods. The authority to seize goods for sale
should not be available until the existence of goods worth selling is established
and an exploration has taken place of alternative methods of settlement of the
debt.

The reform of administration orders is also welcomed by the National Consumer Council, but expresses the view that 'specialist debt counselling is crucial
to the success of administration orders.' A study in Birmingham showed that
administration orders are much more likely to be used where the debtor has
access to debt counselling. The Birmingham Money Advice Centre was involved
in 19 out of the 31 administration orders made by the Birmingham County Court
in 1978. By 1982, two-thirds of the orders handled by the Money Advice Centre
were up to date, whereas only one-third of orders handled elsewhere met this
target. The success of the Money Advice Centre approach is attributed to their
dealing with the whole financial situation of the debtor, a willingness to deal
with debtors within and outside the order and the provision of continuing
encouragement and support (Davies, 1986).

The centrality of advice and assistance is stressed time and again in the
National Consumer Council's response. One experiment which seems to have
been a great success is the provision of a welfare officer at the Birmingham
County Court to assist debtors. The National Consumer Council reports:

The welfare officer is able to take referrals directly from the registrar during
the course of the hearing and can negotiate directly with creditors and put
the defendant's side for the case before the court. She approaches people
coming out of court where they appear to be confused about the order
made. She also ensures good liaison with other advice agencies in the city.

One registrar commented 'the present system is worth to me up to half a Registrar in the saving of judicial time'. (National Consumer Council, 1989, p. 377)

With exemplary regard for fairness, the National Consumer Council also call for court-provided advice and assistance for the individual creditor for whom the county court debt enforcement machinery will be as much unknown territory as for the debtor. This should extend to advice on enforcement of any judgment obtained.

Recent and Prospective Changes

Suitors' Cash

County courts have since their establishment in 1846 handled the cash payments resulting from judgments made by the court. This is known as 'suitors' cash', another term within the county court system which now has a quaint archaic ring to it. The requirement that all payments under a judgment must be paid into court by the debtor for payment out to the creditor has outlived its usefulness. Money is moved around by other means and the system merely duplicated administrative effort. It is, of course, particularly inappropriate for bulk creditors; many have been receiving payments direct under a system known as 'pass throughs' for some time. In such cases the creditor simply advised the court of money received direct from the debtor. From 1 April 1990, the county courts have only handled those cash payments that are necessary for the coherent and effective operation of the system or where to do otherwise would impose a burden on a third party not directly connected with the proceedings. The main payments that still pass through the court are payments under warrants and attachment of earnings orders, and payments into court in part satisfaction before judgment. All other payments pass directly between the parties who are responsible for keeping their own records. In practice, this probably means the creditor's records will be accepted in the case of dispute, since they are likely to be viewed as 'more official'. It would be remarkable if a debtor whose financial management has been called into question by the existence of the judgment debt suddenly developed the skills of setting up and maintaining a scrupulously accurate recording system for payments made to a creditor. A leaflet written in plain English advising debtors on such things as payment and record-keeping is available to them.

The new system applies both to existing cases and to new cases, though there are some transitional provisions. Most of the changes of procedure relate to amendment of forms, both to provide information and to obtain the address of the creditor for payment.

One means of finding whether there are other judgments against a debtor is the use of the Register of Judgments. Before the change in the handling of debtors' money, where at least £10 was outstanding on a county court judgment debt one month after judgment, the debt was recorded in a public register. Outstanding judgments remain on the register for six years, at which time they are automatically deleted. The register has been privatized, though responsibility for the register remains with the Lord Chancellor, and is operated by Registry Trust Limited, a non-profit-making organization set up by the credit industry.

From 1 April 1990 the system of registration has changed. All judgments for more than £1 are registered at the time judgment is entered in the action. The exception is defended cases which proceed to a hearing and where the losing party does not ask to pay by instalments. The presumption is that such cases will result in payment forthwith. It is open to a judgment creditor in such cases to obtain registration on application. A debtor who pays within one month may apply for a certificate of cancellation which removes the entry. Debtors who keep up instalment payments and duly pay off their debts may apply for a certificate of satisfaction which entitles them to have the entry in the register marked as satisfied.

The Court and Legal Services Act 1990

A number of changes enacted by Part I of the Courts and Legal Services Act 1990 implement recommendations of the Civil Justice Review, and will come into force on a day to be appointed. Section 11 paves the way for extending rights of audience in the county courts to permit lay assistance and representation in debt cases. It also enables the court to refuse to hear a lay representative 'who is behaving in an unruly manner in any proceedings'.

Section 13 makes changes to the law on administration orders, extending the range of parties who can make application for such orders, including a power for the court itself to make the order as an alternative to some other method of enforcement being sought by the judgment creditor. The duration of administration orders is limited to a maximum of three years. The order may also take the form of a composition order where the debtor's means are such that full settlement of the debts cannot be achieved within the three year period.

New powers are added permitting the court to make orders restricting enforcement where the debtor has no means of meeting the judgment. Section 15 amends the law on goods exempt from execution to bring the law into line with the provisions of s.283 of the Insolvency Act 1986 as outlined above.

Computerization: bulk processing of claims

In July 1987 the Lord Chancellor's Department issued a consultation paper outlining its proposal to establish a central Claims Registry for the processing of summonses by computer (Lord Chancellor's Department, 1987). The Claims Registry would send out all default summonses rather than individual county courts and would also be the forum for receipt of responses to such summonses. Defended cases only would be transferred to a county court near the defendant's home or place of business. Requests for judgment in default of any response and applications for warrants of enforcement would also be sent to the Claims Registry, who would notify local bailiffs within 24 hours of the request. Other enforcement action would be determined by a local court. All county courts would enjoy the benefits of a computer link to the Claims Registry. The new system will be particularly beneficial to bulk creditors whose procedures can become even more streamlined. It will be possible to pre-state the instalment offer that would be acceptable and if the defendant's response included an offer within those terms, judgment could be entered automatically in response to that offer. There are no immediate plans to implement the proposal.

The proposed new system has advantages and disadvantages. The main disadvantage is that the defendant will come to view the county courts as just another part of the overall bureaucracy, remote and faceless. Documentation may be misunderstood and queries may be met with the now classic response that 'the computer must be right'. Form design will be crucial. A serious criticism of many forms introduced with the computerization of administration is that they are designed to make data entry easy rather than to communicate with the applicant or person to whom they are addressed. A system which discourages a response from debtors would be a retrograde step, since it would increase the proportion of default judgments. The Touche Ross study reported that one third of those who did not contest the debt claim maintained that they had some defence to the claim. There is also the risk that responses will not be scrutinized to see whether they raise a defence, but will merely be scanned for the information needed for computer data entry.

The potential advantages of computerization are the release of staff from routine administration for retraining to provide assistance to members of the public using the courts. Computers can also allow information not currently available to be readily available. System design could meet the objective of providing a complete picture of the circumstances of the debtor enabling enforcement methods to be matched to the debtor's circumstances. Judgment creditors will be able to obtain information about debtors in order to inform their decisions on what enforcement action to take, though bulk creditors will have even less incentive to select methods other than execution, since this will be the only method for which computer application can be made.

Conclusion

Debt claims, more than any other claims, are handled as administrative matters, both at the merits stage and at the enforcement stage. The county courts, which were designed in 1846 to be the local forum for the ordinary person as plaintiff, have become the forum in which the ordinary person is sued and part of the machinery of debt collection (Consumer Council, 1970). Many procedures in this area are designed with the interests of bulk creditors in mind rather than the interests of the individual debtor. On balance, the changes resulting from the Civil Justice Review give more to creditors than to debtors. For the second time in 20 years, the opportunity has been missed to substitute a system based on informed choices about debtor's circumstances for a system of routinized justice which fails to be fair to debtors and is often perceived by creditors as being inefficient in securing payment of debts.

12

Dealing with Social Security Benefit Claims

Introduction

Many disputes are dealt with by bodies other than courts. These include tribunals, which are now a formal part of the system of adjudication. In 1957, they were recognized as such (Franks Committee, 1957), and in 1968 they were described as a 'more modern form of court' (Abel-Smith and Stevens, 1968). Three factors have tended to make classification of tribunals difficult. The first has been the link between the work of some tribunals and the development of a fully-fledged system of administrative law in England and Wales. The second has been the sheer number of institutions calling themselves tribunals. The third was the unfortunate linking of the work of tribunals and enquiries in the Report of the Franks Committee, which has led many writers to feel obliged to discuss tribunals and enquiries together.

There are three principal functions of tribunals and enquiries: adjudication, regulation and advice. The function of adjudication is the determination of the rights and duties of the parties presenting their dispute to the tribunal. The claimant takes issue with a decision made by a decision maker, for example, with an adjudication officer concerning entitlement to a social security benefit, or with an employer concerning a dismissal. The issue is then referred to an independent tribunal for a binding decision as to whether the claimant is entitled to the benefit or has been unfairly dismissed.

The second function of tribunals is regulation. Here the tribunal is the decision-making instrument chosen by government for the implementation of some scheme of government regulation. A good example is the Civil Aviation Authority determining entitlement to an air transport licence in accordance with the general objectives laid down in the legislation. The distinction between adjudicatory and regulatory tribunals is that the former are making a binding decision following a reference by a person aggrieved by a decision which has already been made, whereas the latter are directly applying a system of government regulation rather than supervising or reviewing the proper application of the system of government regulation. It is a characteristic of both adjudicatory and regulatory bodies that they produce a binding determination of the issue before them. Binding does not necessarily mean final, because the determination may be subject to reconsideration by an appellate body. But, unless and until the determination is successfully challenged, it will be binding.

The third function, which belongs principally to ministerial and public enquiries, is advice. One example from a multitude of possible examples is the compulsory purchase order enquiry. Local authorities have for many years enjoyed a power to purchase land compulsorily in order to carry out their statutory functions relating to highways or general development. If agreement to purchase land needed for particular projects cannot be secured and a compulsory purchase order is made, persons affected may object. If those objections are substantial, the relevant minister will order an enquiry into the proposals and the objections to them. This will be conducted locally by an inspector appointed by the minister who will hear evidence and argument both from the local authority and the objectors. The inspector will also visit the site. Following the hearing and site visit, the inspector will prepare a report for the minister, who will then decide whether to affirm the compulsory purchase order which he may do with or without variations, or whether to decline to make the order. The inspector's report is not binding on the minister; it is merely advisory. The report will be sent to the parties together with the minister's letter of decision, which will set out the factors which have influenced the minister. The exercise is principally an informational one: it ensures not only that the minister is informed of local views for and against a proposal but also that those views are tested in the inspector's enquiry, and fully considered in the subsequent report by the inspector to the minister.

Other types of enquiry are also advisory, but are more investigative in nature. An example would be an *ad hoc* public enquiry into a serious railway accident. The functions of such an enquiry would be to appraise ministers of the full facts surrounding the accident following an investigation of the causes of the accident. Whereas the compulsory purchase order enquiry is fairly passive, relying on party initiative to inform the minister, the investigative enquiry is more active in that it seeks out information. The characteristic of both informational and investigative enquiries is that the results are advisory and may be accepted or rejected by the minister, though they will be used as part of the process of ministerial decision making. This and the following chapter describe the work of two of the main court-substitute or adjudicatory tribunals: the social security appeal tribunals and the industrial tribunals.

The Franks Committee

No discussion of tribunals can ignore the impact of the Report of the Franks Committee, which is still viewed as laying down the ground rules for the operation of tribunals. Tribunals might well have continued to develop without any critical analysis of their impact on the administration of justice, had it not been for one of those incidents of poor administration whose wider implications cannot be ignored. The catalyst was the Crichel Down Enquiry in 1954 by the Minister of Agriculture into the sale and subsequent choosing of a tenant for Crichel Down in Dorset which had been purchased during the war as a bombing range (Griffith, 1955). This incident, despite having nothing to do with the operation of tribunals led to the establishment in 1955 of the Committee on Administrative Tribunals and Enquiries under the chairmanship of Sir Oliver Franks (as he then was). The Committee came to be known as the Franks Committee, and reported in 1957 (Franks Committee, 1957). The Franks Report has had a major impact on critical analysis of tribunals. The terms of reference were:

To consider and make recommendations on:

(a) The constitution and working of tribunals other than the ordinary courts of law, constituted under any Act of Parliament by a minister of the Crown or for the purposes of a minister's functions.
(b) The working of such administrative procedures as include the holding of an inquiry or hearing by or on behalf of a minister on an appeal or as a result of objections or representations, and in particular the procedure for the compulsory purchase of land.

The coupling of tribunals with ministerial enquiries has dominated the treatment of tribunals since the report of the Franks Committee. The report also began the dangerous process of generalization about tribunals and enquiries by identifying 'general and closely linked characteristics which should mark these special procedures'. This general approach rather clouded the other important conclusion that tribunals are a new method for the independent adjudication of disputes. The Committee distinguished tribunals from 'ordinary courts' but went on to say:

We consider that tribunals should properly be regarded as machinery provided by Parliament for adjudication rather than as part of the machinery for administration. (Franks Committee, 1957, para.40)

Key recommendations made by the Franks Committee concern the impartiality of tribunals and their supervision. Membership of tribunals should not be within the patronage of the Minister, the decisions of whose officials are under review. The Committee suggested that the Lord Chancellor should appoint chairmen and clearly favoured an increase in the use of lawyer chairmen principally because lawyers were considered to have a good grasp of principles of procedural fairness. As a general principle it was recommended that hearings should be in public and that reasons should be given for decisions. Legal representation was not viewed as necessary, but rules prohibiting legal representation were considered undesirable. A proper system of appeals from decisions of tribunals should also be introduced.

Finally the Committee proposed the creation of two Councils on Tribunals (one for England and Wales, and one for Scotland) to exercise general supervisory powers over the operation of tribunals. Most of the Committee's recommendations were speedily implemented in the Tribunals and Inquiries Act

1958, which was amended by the Tribunals and Inquiries Act 1966. The legislation has been consolidated and the law can now be found in the Tribunals and Inquiries Act 1971.

The declared characteristics of tribunals specified in the Franks Report were 'cheapness, accessibility and freedom from technicality, expedition and expert knowledge of the particular subject' and stated that the objectives of tribunal procedure are 'openness, fairness and impartiality'. Little need be said of the declared hallmarks of the proper procedures of tribunals of 'openness, fairness and impartiality'. These are the hallmarks of any system of decision making under any scheme of government regulation in a democratic society. The qualities have even been described as 'so vague as to be virtually meaningless, at least without being transposed into much more explicit features' (Farmer, 1974, p. 185). How far can the characteristics suggested for tribunals be said to be true of tribunals to the exclusion of other forms of dispute resolution? The answer is that they cannot. Tribunals are only cheap in the sense that no fees are payable on filing claims and that allowances are generally paid for out of pocket expenses in attending the tribunal. This is simply a transfer of spending from litigant to the State. Indeed effective use of tribunals may be more expensive to a claimant. There is little possibility of any recovery of the costs of using a lawyer from the losing party and legal aid will not finance representation.

Accessibility and freedom from technicality may be taken together. In this respect post-Franks developments of tribunals have overtaken the Franks Report. Tribunals tend to be geographically accessible, because they sit locally, like both magistrates' courts and the county courts. On the other hand, the problems of direct access without assistance or representation are currently the subject of consideration within the Lord Chancellor's Department. The problem of accessibility is linked to the technical nature of the legal rules applied by many tribunals. The substantive law applied in many tribunals has become more complex since 1957, while procedural rules have developed which need to be fully understood and carefully observed to make the most effective use of the tribunal decision-making process. By contrast, rules operating in some courts, particularly in the small claims jurisdiction of the county courts, have become less complex. Even with the remaining difficulties, arbitration in the county court is certainly as accessible and free from technicality as pursuing an unfair dismissal claim before an industrial tribunal. It has become clear over the years that a level of formality is required for fair and impartial decision making, though it is equally clear that proper decision making does not always require ritual conduct or observance of the formal rules of evidence.

The issue of delay depends upon a comparison of like with like. The speed of decision making of some tribunals is broadly comparable with that of magistrates' courts and the county courts. If compulsory purchase order enquiries were contrasted with inferior courts, the courts would be speedier. Looking at the time lag between the filing of a claim and final disposition is in any event a crude measure. What is more important is to discover the causes of delay, without which general conclusions are likely to be unhelpful.

To suggest that tribunals have greater expert knowledge of the subject matter of disputes before them, than judges, is rather insulting to the judges. It is sitting as chairman or lay member of a tribunal which gives tribunals expertise, just as the senior barrister appointed to the Bench will soon acquire expertise in those areas of law which did not form part of his or her practice before appointment. The general qualities of those appointed as judges, chairmen or lay members of tribunals, are considered more important than a detailed knowledge of the law relating to the particular types of dispute likely to be considered by those persons. The increasing incidence of the full-time lawyer chairman has narrowed the gap between judicial appointment as a judge and as a tribunal chairman. It is probably fair to say that full-time tribunal chairmen are considered of roughly equal status to circuit judges, with Presidents, regional chairmen and lawyer members of appellate tribunals roughly equal to High Court judges.

The thrust of this argument is that tribunals which resolve disputes have matured beyond the framework envisaged by the Franks Report. The aims of the modern tribunal are:

to reach the right decision in law;
to give the parties an impartial, fair and sufficient hearing;
to use the advantages of tribunal procedure to enable claimants to have greater participation in the resolution of their dispute.

Essential History

Early Days

Though it is possible to trace a system of remedies outside the court structure back a thousand years (Wraith and Hutchesson, 1973), it is unnecessary to go back beyond the National Insurance Act 1911 for an historical background to modern tribunals. Following the scheme set up in Germany, Lloyd George introduced a new system for the settlement of disputes arising out of claims to the new unemployment benefit provided by the Act and administered by the Board of Trade. Initial decisions on entitlement were made by employees of the Board of Trade known as insurance officers. A claimant dissatisfied with the decision of the insurance officer could have the decision reviewed by a local Court of Referees consisting of a chairman appointed by the Minister of Trade, one member chosen from an employers' panel and one member chosen from a workmen's panel. There was a further final appeal to a national appellate authority known as the Umpire, a lawyer appointed by the Crown. The adoption of this system of dispute resolution was in part a borrowing of the German experience, but was also a reaction to the unsatisfactory operation of the resolution of disputes in the county courts concerning workmen's compensation for injuries suffered at work. This had not been intended to be legalistic, but in practice the claimant had been put in the position of an ordinary plaintiff in a civil case arguing a case against a powerful insurance company or mutual insurance society (Potter and Stansfield, 1950). The new idea introduced by local Courts of Referees was the free local non-legal forum for the settlement of particular disputes. They were very successful and provided a model for review procedures connected with a variety of benefits under the burgeoning national insurance scheme.

Not everyone welcomed this new development. Some judges and lawyers saw in the development a serious threat to the independent impartial adjudication of disputes by the courts. The concern culminated in the publication in 1929 by the Lord Chief Justice, Lord Hewart, of his book *The New Despotism* in which these arguments and the theme that arbitrary power was being concentrated in the hands of the bureaucracy were elaborated. By way of response the Government established the Committee on Ministers' Powers which reported in 1932 and has come to be known as the Donoughmore Committee (Donoughmore, 1932). The terms of reference were narrowly drawn and the Committee's report did not include any grand plan for the future development of a tribunal system. Nor did it agree with the fear expressed by Lord Hewart. Effectively the seal of approval was given to the type of tribunal established under the National Insurance Act 1911.

The system set up by the National Insurance Act 1911 was continued under the subsequent amending legislation, but the benefits dealt with were insurance benefits and provided no help for the uninsured. The Unemployment Act 1934 introduced a national assistance scheme for the unemployed to be managed by the Unemployment Assistance Board under the direction of the Minister of Labour under which allowances became payable to assist unemployed persons. This replaced the system of public assistance, a locally administered means-tested benefit. Under the scheme of public assistance, a person refused a payment had the right to make representations to a local Public Assistance Committee (PAC). Because of the existence of PACs and of the Court of Referees for benefits under the insurance schemes, the new national scheme included an appeals system. PACs were replaced by unemployment assistance tribunals to which a person aggrieved by a decision not to make a payment, or as to the amount of a payment, could appeal with leave of the chairman. The tribunals consisted of a chairman appointed by the Minister of Labour, a workpeople's representative appointed by the Unemployment Assistance Board from a panel drawn up by the Minister and a third member representing the Unemployment Assistance Board (Lynes, 1976). Not surprisingly these tribunals have been criticized as not being independent of the Ministry of Labour or of the Unemployment Assistance Board. Their importance lies in the fact that they were the grandparents of supplementary benefit appeal tribunals, just as the Courts of Referees, (from 1936 known as unemployment insurance appeal tribunals) were the ancestors of the national insurance local tribunals. The pattern of welfare benefits which had become established was that of social insurance covering the major causes of loss of income and paying flat-rate benefits at no more than survival level with a residual public assistance scheme for those in desperate need who were not covered by social insurance.

The Beveridge Plan

This coupling of social insurance with a safety net of means-tested benefits was taken up in the Beveridge Plan which settled the framework of the welfare state after the Second World War (Beveridge, 1942). Having received official blessing from the Donoughmore Committee, tribunals mushroomed, particularly in connection with the social security legislation introduced after the Second World War (Wraith and Hutchesson, 1973). The Beveridge Plan was to raise the level of insurance benefits from survival level to subsistence level and to protect adults against loss of income through a comprehensive system of social insurance benefits to which legal entitlement would arise on payment of the requisite contributions. This system of social insurance was coupled with a proposal for a system of non-contributory family allowances to meet the needs of families. But the Beveridge Plan accepted the need for a safety net of means-tested benefits for those outside insurance, which it was envisaged would play very much a minor role in the new welfare state. The Beveridge Plan inspired the post-war burst of legislation establishing the welfare state. Under the National Insurance Act 1946 provision was made for tribunals to be established to consider questions of entitlement to, and amount of, contributory benefits, thus establishing the national insurance local tribunals. Under the National Assistance Act 1948, a National Assistance Board and national assistance tribunals replaced the Unemployment Assistance Board and the unemployment appeal tribunals, and became the parents of supplementary benefits appeal tribunals.

Despite the grand hopes of the Beveridge Plan, it has not succeeded. Following the introduction of the reforming legislation, successive governments have failed to keep the level of benefits payable under the system of social insurance in line with rising costs. Payments soon fell below subsistence level. Family allowances were never introduced at the level recommended by the Beveridge Plan, and the level of child benefit, which has replaced family allowances, remains less than is necessary to meet family needs. The very small sums allowed for children under social insurance benefits have been kept deliberately low because of the presence of a separate system of payments for children. Other groups were not covered by the Beveridge Plan, notably the disabled. The result has been that the system of social insurance does not dominate the system of welfare benefits organized by the state. The dominant benefit is the means-tested income support replacing supplementary benefit (formerly national assistance) in April 1988, whereas under the Beveridge Plan this was to be a minor benefit providing a safety net for those not otherwise covered.

With the replacement of national assistance by supplementary benefit in 1966, a major change took place in relation to the means-tested benefits. Section 4 of the Ministry of Social Security Act 1966 gave entitled persons, that is those whose resources were not sufficient to meet their requirements, a legal right to supplementary benefit. Prior to the 1966 Act there had been a duty imposed on the National Assistance Board to give assistance to those in need by the payment of national assistance, but no corresponding right for individuals to receive assistance. The legacy of establishing need in order to trigger the duty to make payments still haunts the administration of means-tested benefits and has flavoured supplementary benefits appeal tribunals with Victorian notions of identifying those who are 'the deserving poor'. By contrast the insurance principle behind contributory benefits has always resulted in there being a more ready appreciation of a legal right to benefit as a result of the insurance contract, albeit a compulsory one. This is one factor which explains the very different approaches taken historically by supplementary benefit appeal tribunals and national insurance local tribunals to their respective tasks. A major change was made in 1980 when the policy of the Department of Health and Social Security in administering supplementary benefit was reduced to detailed secondary legislation, so that the supplementary benefit scheme is now as rooted in statutory provisions as the national insurance benefits. In April 1988 supplementary benefit was replaced by income support and social fund payments.

National Insurance Local Tribunals (NILTs)

As we have seen, National Insurance Local Tribunals (NILTs) took over the administration of the insurance based benefits in 1948. NILTs were composed of a chairman and two members. The chairman was invariably a lawyer, though there was no formal requirement to this effect, appointed by the Secretary of State from a panel drawn up by the Lord Chancellor. The other members were appointed by the Secretary of State, one from a panel of persons representing employers and the self-employed and one from a panel of persons representing employed earners. The chairman was charged by regulations with the supervision of the overall conduct of cases before NILTs. The two members were required to be impartial; they were not representatives of the interests of employers and employees. The high incidence of unanimous decisions suggests one of two things. Either the members were impartial in their approach or the chairman so dominated the proceedings that dissent was difficult. Indeed the highest incidence of minority opinions was dissent by the chairman which could be said to lend weight to the second view, though a more probable explanation is that the lay members took a view on the merits which the chairman regarded as untenable in law.

Research published in 1962 showed that the lay members were likely to be active trades unionists and managerial workers (McCorquodale, 1962). Later research showed that most chairmen and members were aged between 45 and 65, whereas most claimants were aged less than 45. There was a serious underrepresentation of women. All chairmen were social class I, the majority of employers' representatives were social class II and over 80 per cent of employees' representatives fell within social classes II and III (Bell et al., 1974). The research concluded:

> Our data on chairmen and members suggest that the people who serve on tribunals may come from a 'local squirearchy' involved in a wide range of community activities, including welfare, church, education and training organizations, local politics, trade unions and professional associations. (Bell et al., 1974, p. 315)

A further interesting finding was that one in three chairmen, one in nine employers' representatives and one in seven employees' representatives were also justices of the peace or held similar 'judicial or semi-judicial office' such as that of coroner. These findings are also supported by other research (Frost and Howard, 1977).

The administrative arrangements for NILTs were made by a clerk to the tribunals, who was a civil servant in the employment of the DHSS (as it then was). Every effort was made to ensure that tribunals normally sat in buildings other than the premises of the DHSS in order to emphasize their independence from the Department. But a separation from government departments generally was not often secured. It was common for sittings to take place in rooms contained in buildings whose primary purpose was to house other government departments. Other common venues were local Town Halls. The accommodation provided was often fairly spartan.

NILTs have always been regarded as representing the acceptable face of tribunals. The influential Bell study gave them largely a clean bill of health as a model for determining disputes concerning entitlement to benefit. But three key findings have set the scene for subsequent debate on the system. First, there was a need for a broadly based and accessible advisory facility so that claimants could receive independent and impartial advice on their entitlement to state benefits. Secondly, there was recognition that direct access to the tribunals by claimants was not apt to produce a fair result in every case. There was overwhelming evidence of a different standard of treatment of represented and unrepresented claims, as well as marked differences between attended and non-attended appeals. To combat some of these problems, there should, argued Bell, be increased opportunities for representation before the tribunal. Thirdly, there was a need to upgrade the standard of adjudication with tribunals playing a 'more positive enabling role in relation to appellants' (Bell et al., 1974).

Supplementary Benefit Appeal Tribunals (SBATs)

The Ministry of Social Security Act 1966 created the Supplementary Benefits Commission (SBC) to administer the supplementary benefit scheme and for the first time those whose resources did not meet their requirements had a legal entitlement to the payment of benefit. But there was no change in the system of adjudication; national assistance tribunals simply became SBATs. The implications for the tribunal system of the change to a system of benefit based on entitlement seems to have been overlooked. Unlike national insurance benefits, the award of supplementary benefit depended in the bulk of cases on the exercise of discretionary powers, which have been described as 'wide, problematic and in some cases ambiguous'. (Bell, 1975). The legal entitlement to benefit came to be governed by secret codes circulated within the Ministry and designed to ensure uniformity of decision making by benefit officers, who like their counterparts under the national insurance scheme, made decisions on claims to benefit. All that was available to claimants was the Supplementary Benefits Handbook which set out the broad basis upon which the SBC exercised its discretion. Over the ensuing years a battle was waged between those who saw the discretion present in supplementary benefit decision making as a necessary part of a flexible response to human need (Titmuss, 1971) and the burgeoning welfare rights movement, which demanded genuine legal rights to income maintenance with equality of access to decision-making guides and judicial appellate procedures.

Prior to the changes made in 1980, SBATs were generally regarded as the slums of the tribunal system. Research studies showed that the original SBATs were travesties of due process (Bell, 1975; Adler and Bradley, 1975). They were composed of three members: a chairman and two members, one a representative of workers, the other drawn from a panel of persons appearing 'to have knowledge or experience of conditions in the area to which the panel relates and of the problems of people living on low incomes'. The chairman historically was a person who had served on the tribunal as an ordinary member for some time. In 1973 it seems that only 6 per cent of SBAT chairmen were lawyers. Research conclusions were that SBATs suffered a serious problem of non-attendance of claimants, that it 'required telepathic powers to understand' the reasoning in written decisions, that the informality with which proceedings were conducted led to inadequate enquiry into appeals and an imbalance between claimants and the SBC's presenting officers, which rendered SBATs partial in their decision making. Presenting officers, far from being scrupulously fair to claimants took advantage of the informal procedure to introduce improperly, material prejudicial to claimants. The tribunals tended to be ineffective in sifting and weighing evidence and all too often accepted the presenting officer's arguments on SBC policy as the law on entitlement. There was also evidence that clerks took part in the tribunal's decision making (Lister, 1975). Other studies confirmed this amateurish and ineffective system of appeal (Bell, 1975).

The Bell study proposed a three stage rescue programme. Stages I and II were to be directed to the improvement of tribunals by the strengthening of their personnel, and in particular by appointing lawyer chairmen, with a senior chairman appointed for each region. The system of adjudication was to be improved by setting out clearly the roles of presenting officer and tribunal clerk. A guide to procedure should be produced so that everyone would have an outline of a desirable order of events and to ensure proper standards of fairness and impartiality. Moves should be made to develop assistance for claimants to enable them to present their claims more effectively. Better facilities for representation were also needed. Stage III contained longer-term proposals that a second tier appellate tribunal should be created to provide rules of precedent value for the SBC and SBATs.

The response to the Bell proposals was positive. From a figure of six per cent in 1973, the proportion of lawyer chairmen had increased to 36.4 per cent by October 1982. Training programmes for both chairmen and members had been introduced. The role of clerks became separated from the decision making of tribunals and presenting officers became much less adversarial in approach, both developments being the result of special training. A guide to SBAT procedure was produced by the DHSS. In 1978 an appeal to the High Court on a point of law was introduced, which was replaced by the appeal to the National Insurance Commissioners, renamed the Social Security Commissioners, in November 1980. The 1980 changes, which had been canvassed by the DHSS discussion document *Social Assistance* (DHSS, 1978), included the abolition of the SBC and the transfer of its functions to the DHSS. The SBC's secret codes were replaced with detailed regulations spelling out entitlement to benefit. The function of SBATs changed from review of the application of discretion by the SBC to interpretation of rules of law. This paved the way for the merging of NILTs and SBATs as social security appeal tribunals (Harris, 1983).

Figures on representation for 1982 show that of 55,893 claims heard by SBATs, the claimant attended in 58 per cent of cases (DHSS, 1983). Their success rate was about one in four cases. For the 42 per cent who did not attend, the success rate was about one in thirteen. Representation was most frequently by a friend or relative, or by a social worker, though there was a large unhelpful category labelled 'other', which might well include welfare rights advisers. Solicitors represented less than two per cent of those represented. Overall, representation increased the chances of success to about one in three, but if representation by a friend or relative is excluded, then the success rate for those with 'expert' representation rose to about two in five cases. The situation was very similar to that obtaining in NILTs. Representation increased the chances of success dramatically. No amount of procedural fairness could compensate for lack of knowledge of the complexities of the law. Unattended and unrepresented claimants' appeals did not appear to be tested as carefully as those of attended and represented claimants. Yet there was no legal aid and the provision of a representative was the product of a chance linking of claimant with an agency providing representation.

Social Security Appeal Tribunals (SSATs)

On 23 April 1984, the Health and Social Services and Social Security Adjudication Act 1983 amalgamated NILTs and SBATs to form social security appeal tribunals (SSATs). The Department of Health and Social Security handed over all its responsibilities for the new tribunals to a newly created statutory authority known as the Office of the President of Social Security Appeal Tribunals (OPSSAT). The new central authority is headed by a Circuit judge assisted by seven regional chairmen, who are in turn assisted by a full-time chairman. All are appointed by the Lord Chancellor. OPSSAT still receives its funding resources from the Department of Social Security with whom it negotiates a finance budget and a staff allocation. Staff of OPSSAT act to the instructions and priorities set by the President of SSATs. There are 268 social security appeal tribunals throughout England and Wales, and Scotland, which hear appeals most days of the week. At their busiest, the annual case load of tribunals exceeded 300,000 cases, though this has now stabilized at around 150,000 cases a year as a result of limitations placed on the rights of appeal under the income support and social fund scheme introduced in April 1988.

SSATs consist of a lawyer chairman sitting with two lay members. Most cases are heard by part-time chairmen who must be solicitors, barristers or advocates of five years standing. They are appointed by the Lord Chancellor for renewable three year terms of office. Members are appointed by the President from those considered to 'have knowledge or experience of conditions in the area and to be representative of persons living or working in the area' (Social Security Act 1975, Sched. 10, para.(2)). The President has the responsibility of supervising the overall operation of SSATs, as well as of organizing meetings, training courses and of preparing material for the guidance of SSATs. The system of adjudication of social security benefits is now integrated, but the price has been the judicialization of the tribunal system without sweeping reforms in the provision of assistance and representation for persons wishing to claim. The main arguments which have led to the creation of the new tribunals with their own appellate tribunal have centred around the complexity of social security law, and yet there is no increased provision of funding for assistance through legal aid, law centres or welfare rights services.

The Modern Social Security System

The present social security system is laid down mainly in the Social Security Acts 1975 to 1990. Social security benefits can be divided into three groups. First there are contributory benefits, which used to be called national insurance benefits. They provide flat-rate payments for insured workers against loss of income resulting from sickness, unemployment for up to one year, maternity, becoming widowed, or from retirement. Eligibility is conditioned upon satisfaction of the relevant contribution tests: basically, claimants must have made sufficient payments into the national insurance fund to entitle them to claim the benefit. The contribution tests vary with the type of benefit claimed. Secondly, there are non-contributory social security benefits payable without any means-test. These are child benefits, industrial injuries and death benefits, certain invalidity benefits, and attendance and mobility allowances. Thirdly, there are the means-tested benefits, which are non-contributory. These are income support and family credit, housing benefits, help with the costs of educating children (for example, free school meals and transport) and help with health and welfare needs (for example, free prescriptions).

The Contribution System

Since the Beveridge Plan was predicated on a system of insurance, it is not surprising to find the concept of premiums reflected in the requirement that potential beneficiaries of the various social insurances should pay contributions. There are four classes of contributions. Class 1 contributions are paid by workers in employment and are deducted from their pay at the statutory rates. Class 2 and Class 4 contributions are paid by self-employed persons who are entitled to all contributory benefits except unemployment benefits. Class 2 contributions are payable at a flat rate while Class 4 contributions are payable as a percentage of profits. Class 3 contributions are voluntary contributions paid by non-employed persons; the usual reason they are paid is to bring the number of contributions up to a level to entitle the person to a benefit. It will be clear that contributions are usually paid out of income and that entitlement to benefits is dependent upon contributions having been paid. The system of credited contributions covers the situation where individuals are precluded through no fault of their own from making payments, because there is no income from which they can be paid. A good example is the credit allowed to a person who is unemployed. The system is complicated and credited contributions are for some purposes not as good as paid contributions.

Adjudication

Initial adjudication of claims to social security benefits will generally take place in a local office of the Department of Social Security or Department of Employment depending on the benefit claimed. Claims to some benefits are, however, dealt with by centrally-located benefit offices. All claims will require investigation of entitlement. Decision making is split between adjudication officers and officers known as Secretary of State's representatives. Adjudication officers are employees in the relevant Department but exercise independent judgment on claims in making decisions within their province. They alone have authority to award benefit. Certain decisions are taken by officers designated as Secretary of State's representatives. Such decisions relate primarily to satisfaction of the contribution conditions, but the legislation gives them competence on specific questions at many points. Where medical questions are involved, specific decision-making powers are given to medical adjudicating authorities. SSATs only have jurisdiction to consider an appeal against a decision of an adjudication officer. The proper remedy for dissatisfaction with a Secretary of State's decision is appeal on the question of law to the High Court. The scale of decision making within the Department of Social Security and Department of Employment is vast; adjudication officers make decisions in more than 25 million claims each year. They are expected so far as practicable to make decisions on benefit entitlement within 14 days, but this time limit is frequently exceeded. In *R* v. *Secretary of State for Social Services, ex parte CPAG*, ([1989] 1 All ER 1047) the Court of Appeal affirmed a decision of the High Court in which the trial judge had said that the practicability of such speedy decision making was not such that the Secretary of State was required to appoint sufficient adjudication officers to enable claims to be decided within 14 days, and recognized that workloads may lead to delays beyond the time limit expressed in the Social Security Act 1975.

Once a decision is made it must be communicated in writing to the claimant, who then has three months in which to appeal against it to the SSAT. The document communicating the decision advises the claimant of the right of appeal. Fewer than one in five hundred decisions are appealed.

Practice and Procedure in SSATs

The Nature of Tribunal Adjudication

The three members of the tribunal share the responsibility for decision making on appeals; the lawyer and the lay members have an equal say on all issues whether of law or fact. The main role is the adjudication of the dispute between the claimant and the relevant department on entitlement to benefit. The process of judging in SSATs involves five tasks:

reading the case papers;
identifying the legal test relevant to the appeal;
considering the evidence and making findings of fact relevant to the legal test;
applying the legal test to the facts as decided by the tribunal and making a fair
    decision on the law;
properly recording the evidence heard and considered, the facts found, the
    decision of the tribunal and the reasons for it.

The foreword by the first President of the SSATs to *The Guide to Procedure* stresses the enabling functions of the tribunals:

Most claimants at the time of their appeal will be too troubled and hassled by the more practical day to day problems of their plight ever to have the emotional energy to study the nuts and bolts of the machinery by which their appeal will be processed. For them, any meaningful guide of one hundred pages is one hundred pages too long, no matter the style in which it is written. For people in this category my message is short: 'Comply with the instructions set out in the forms which bring your case before the tribunal. Once there, let others whose job it is to look after procedure do so. Don't worry about it yourself.' (p. vii)

Tribunals should adopt a flexible procedure which facilitates the presentation of evidence and argument by claimants and representatives with a range of communication skills, some outstanding, some very limited. Within the requirements laid down by the Franks Report of the need for openness, fairness and impartiality, the objective is to achieve a formal procedure with an informal atmosphere. The Social Security Commissioners too have stressed the investigative or inquisitorial role of the tribunals. In *R(S)1/87*, Commissioner Hallett said:

The jurisdiction of . . . the social security appeal tribunal . . . is investigative or inquisitorial. A social security appeal tribunal is exercising quasi-judicial functions and forms part of the statutory machinery for investigating claims in order to ascertain whether the claimant satisfies the statutory requirements which entitle him to be paid benefit. It is not restricted, as in ordinary litigation which are proceedings between parties, to accepting or rejecting the respective contentions of the claimant on the one hand and the adjudication . . . officer on the other. . . . Its investigatory function has as its object the ascertainment of the facts and the determination of the truth. (para. 14(3))

A Tribunal of Commissioners echoes these sentiments in *R(S)4/82*, where they described the judicial process in tribunals as 'fair play in action'.
A recent study, which included observation of tribunals, showed that tribunal

chairmen in the tribunals believed in the investigative approach to the determination of appeals:

> During observations of social security appeal tribunal hearings the vast majority of chairs were found to be courteous, sensitive and at pains to be helpful to appellants, reflecting, presumably, the 'enabling' role that has been stressed under the new regime and the belief expressed by all chairs that hearings were fundamentally 'inquisitorial'. In this context, the term inquisitorial seems to mean that chairs feel they have the freedom to investigate cases and elicit the information they think they need in order to get to the truth of the situation, rather than to choose between competing arguments. (Genn and Genn, 1989, p. 159)

Making the Appeal

Making an appeal to an SSAT is a very simple task. The appeal may be made by completing the form provided for this purpose by the Department or by writing a letter of appeal. No fee is payable on filing an appeal. The time limit of three months from notification of the adjudication officer's decision is important. Appeals can only be accepted outside the time limit if there are 'special reasons' for the delay and the case law on these is not particularly generous to claimants. Though the appeal should set out the grounds on which the appeal is based, appeals which fail to do so will not be regarded as inadmissible. The grounds of appeal are not viewed formally and may be enlarged at a later stage. But there are two reasons why it is advisable to set out in full the reasons and facts upon which the appeal is based. The first is that, as we shall see, the letter of appeal will be included in documents made available to the tribunal in advance of the hearing and a good clear account will ensure that the chairman and members are clear about the claimant's grievance.

The second reason is that an appeal triggers a reconsideration of the case by an adjudication officer, who may revise the decision in the claimant's favour forthwith. The more information the adjudication officer has, the more likely will be a revision in the claimant's favour. In order to make the best of a case at this stage most claimants will need advice and assistance because preparing a case for appeal involves three tasks: establishing the facts of the case, understanding the applicable legal rules and integrating facts and law in a well-constructed argument which includes meeting the reasons put forward by the adjudication officer for denying the claim. This issue of getting help is considered in more detail below. But the claimant who has received no help should not despair, because there is a significant element of inquisitorial procedure in the tribunal's decision-making process.

The Adjudication Officer's Written Submission

The adjudication officer must in all cases prepare a documentary case for submission to the tribunal in advance of the hearing. This is also sent to the claimant. It will contain details of the claim and of the adjudication officer's decision, together with a note of the statutory provisions and decisions of the Commissioners upon which the adjudication officer is relying. The claimant's letter of appeal will be included and there will be a full written submission by the adjudication officer setting out the facts and law as they have been determined and applied to the claimant's case. For the unrepresented claimant, these papers are undoubtedly daunting. They will be accompanied by informational literature about the tribunal, but success at the hearing will be determined in part by the use made of the information provided in the written submission. It seems that a curtain of gloom falls over some claimants at this stage who abandon their fate to their own written statement of appeal. Bell's research on NILTs concluded that a major cause of non-attendance at the hearing results from 'a combination of pessimism about the outcome and practical difficulties' (Bell et al., 1974).

The Hearing

The tribunal hearing itself is in an informal setting. All participants sit around a large table. Typically the tribunal members will sit along one side of the table, the clerk at one end and the adjudication officer and claimant opposite the tribunal members. Normally six cases will be listed for a half day, which would allow about 30 minutes per case if all the claimants attended, but a significant number do not. This allows more time for attended cases, since non-attended cases tend to be dealt with very speedily. The tribunal clerk will have some idea of the numbers likely to attend and to be represented from the replies to the short questionnaire sent to claimants with the adjudication officer's submission. It seems that most chairmen do offer a brief explanation of the tribunal's procedures, though these may be rather perfunctory.

The hearing is technically in public, though it is very rare for anyone other than those immediately involved to be present. The claimant can request a private hearing. The procedure is for the chairman to decide. It is usual for the claimant to be asked to outline the reasons for the appeal following which the adjudication officer may ask questions of the claimant and of any witnesses brought along by the claimant. The tribunal chairman and members will also ask questions as the case proceeds. Witnesses do not give evidence on oath. The formal rules of evidence that apply in courts do not apply in tribunals. Any material which is relevant and helpful may be considered, though the weight to be attached to different types of evidence will vary. Tribunals will generally regard first hand evidence as more likely to be correct than second-hand evidence, but there is no general requirement that what the claimant says must be corroborated by another person's evidence. Nor is there any requirement that evidence must be in writing to be persuasive.

The adjudication officer, who will not normally be the one who made the initial decision, will then put forward any submissions he or she may wish. It is clear that the role of the adjudication officer at the tribunal is not to be an adversary of the claimant defending the Department's original decision. On more than one occasion the courts have stated that the procedure is investigatory and that the role of the adjudication officer is to act as *amicus curiae* (friend of the court) assisting the tribunal in its investigation of the claim (*R* v. *Deputy Industrial Injuries Commissioner, ex parte Moore*, [1956] 1 QB 456; *R* v. *National Insurance Commissioner, ex parte Viscusi*, [1974] 1 WLR 646). Though the onus of proving entitlement to the benefit claimed is normally on the claimant, in a number of cases the burden of proof is placed on the adjudication officer to satisfy the tribunal on the balance of probabilities of particular facts. One example is disqualification from receiving unemployment benefit following the termination of employment as a result of misconduct (Commissioner's Decision *R(U)2/60*).

Attendance at the tribunal need not result in a claimant being out of pocket because the cost of transport to the tribunal and of any loss of earnings is reimbursed by the tribunal. Similar costs incurred by witnesses reasonably called to support the claimant's case will also be met out of public funds.

The Decision

Once the tribunal has heard the submissions of the parties, everyone except the tribunal members leaves the room while the tribunal deliberates. It is presidential policy that, wherever practicable, claimants should be told the outcome of their appeals on the day, but in all cases the claimant and adjudication officer must be sent a written record of the decision which includes a note of the evidence and submissions of the parties, a statement of the tribunals findings of fact and of the reasons for the decision. The grounds for any dissenting opinion must also be stated. The written decision is usually relatively brief, though it must be sufficiently full and complete that the claimant can tell what facts have been accepted and rejected, the reasons for the rejection of any evidence and how the law has been applied to the facts as found. Commissioner Watson said in *R(SB)5/81*:

> Findings and reasons need not be lengthy; indeed brevity clearly indicating them is often to be preferred to a lengthy and possibly ambiguous record. It is not possible to lay down a general rule for recording findings and reasons since that depends on the nature of the evidence and of the case. (para.10)

If the decision is so brief as to be inadequate, this may provide grounds for an appeal to the Commissioners, since it will amount to an error of law. Where the decision is adverse to the claimant, information about the right of appeal to the Commissioners must be given.

In deciding appeals before them, SSATs are bound by decisions of the Commissioners. Their decisions form a self-contained body of rules of precedent value both for adjudication officers and for tribunals. It follows that it is important for relevant decisions to be considered in deciding cases.

Setting Aside, Reviews and Appeals

There are three ways in which the decision of the tribunal can be changed. The first is where it is set aside, in which case it is treated as if it had never existed. There are three gateways to the setting aside of a decision:

> a document connected with the appeal was not received in time by one of the parties or their representative;
> a party to the appeal of their representative was not present;
> there has been a procedural mishap.

Once one of these grounds has been established, the party seeking the setting aside, which can be the adjudication officer or the claimant, must show that it is just to set the decision aside. The tribunal which decided the case considers the application, but, if it is allowed, the case must be listed for a tribunal composed of different people to be heard afresh.

Review is only available to adjudication officers, who can revise the decision where it is shown that it was given in ignorance of, or mistake as to, a material fact, or there has been a relevant change of circumstances. Again, once the ground for review has been established, the adjudication officer must consider whether it is right to revise the decision in the light of the circumstances now revealed. Any decision given on review attracts a further right of appeal just like the original decision.

The final way in which the decision might be varied is on appeal. Decisions of tribunals may be appealed to the Social Security Commissioners on a point of law. Leave must be obtained from the chairman of the tribunal which decided the case, but if it is refused, then leave can be sought from the Commissioners. The time limit for appeals is three months.

The Social Security Commissioners

Appeals from decisions of SSATs lie, with leave, to the Social Security Commissioners, who are all lawyers. They normally deal with appeals individually, but the Chief Commissioner may decide to convene a Tribunal of three Commissioners to hear appeals involving questions of law of particular difficulty. The main procedure is a written one. Legal aid is not available for representation, though advice and assistance under the Green Form scheme will provide assistance. A former Chief National Insurance Commissioner has described the procedure on appeal as a good example of a procedure which is informal and yet under which an appellant's case is considered fully and fairly. He suggested that, in the vast majority of cases, the procedure was accessible to unrepresented appellants (though he did concede that they should receive assistance) and that it would be undesirable to extend legal aid generally to cover such appeals (Micklethwait, 1976). It is difficult to see how unrepresented claimants who fare so badly in tribunals of first instance could expect to fare better at the appellate level; indeed representation has increased considerably over the past few years. The claimant sets out the grounds of appeal, though these need not be detailed. But the clearer the grounds of appeal, the better the chances of success. The adjudication officer is then asked to respond and the claimant is given an opportunity to comment on those responses. The construction of a written case demands perhaps even greater skills than the preparation of oral argument. It is vital to cover all the ground and to be clear and accurate since there is no immediate opportunity to clarify matters by the process of question and answer. At this stage the parties can request an oral hearing which will be granted unless the appeal is an obvious winner or loser. Many appeals are decided on the papers alone. The Commissioners take considerable trouble to ensure that all relevant arguments are canvassed in the written case, and will invite observations on issues which appear to be relevant and which have not been raised in the written case. Following the decision of the Commissioners, a full written record of the decision is sent to the claimant and to the adjudication officer.

Decisions of the Commissioners are binding on adjudication officers and on tribunals, but not all decisions of the Commissioners are reported. It is the task of the Chief Commissioner to decide which decisions are to be reported and he or she is assisted by the Commissioners starring decisions they consider worthy of reporting. Parties and their legal advisers, as well as welfare organizations, may also make representations that a decision should be reported. The criteria for selection for reporting are that the case involves an issue of legal principle and contributes to the orderly development of the law. The Chief Commissioner seeks to ensure that all reported decisions have the assent of a majority of Commissioners. It remains open to claimants and the adjudication officer to cite unreported cases, but advance notice of their intention to do so is required. Adjudication officers are expected to rely on reported decisions as far as possible. The existence of this body of appellate decisions in social security matters has the obvious effect of contributing to consistency of decision making not only by adjudication officers in their initial decisions on claims, but also by SSATs. About one in four appeals is successful.

Though appeals are available from the Commissioners to the Court of Appeal, these are rare. One reason for this has been the deference shown by the Court of Appeal to the expertise of the Commissioners, a deference which appears to be justified by the thoroughness of the re-examination of the cases by the Commissioners. The effective bypassing of the High Court (judicial review remains theoretically available) also reflects an increasing recognition of the Commissioners as being of the same judicial standing as High Court judges (Ogus et al., 1988). Attempts have been made to use judicial review to challenge a refusal of leave, but these have found little favour with the High Court (*R v. Social Security Commissioners, ex parte Morris*, reported as an appendix to Commissioner's Decision *R(A) 5/83*). Overall little criticism can be levelled at the Commissioners' decision making, though there is a problem over help for appellants to the Commissioners.

ndance and Representation

search in 1970 on NILTs showed that about half of claimants do not attend
e hearing and that representation was present only in one in five cases (Bell et
al., 1974). In so far as later information is available, no dramatic improvement
of these figures is indicated (Frost and Howard, 1977; White, Robin, 1982;
Genn and Genn, 1989). One study showed that trades union representation was
the major type of representation followed by relatives and friends with lawyers
representing only three per cent of those represented, about the same number as
social workers (Bell et al., 1974). But this is a fairly old study. Though the
overall level of representation does not appear to have improved dramatically,
it seems that the numbers represented by specialist lay advisers have increased so
that now the most common representative is the trades union representative or
the specialist lay adviser.

There is a significant variation in success rates depending on representation.
The overall success rate has remained fairly constant over the years at about one
in five cases. But if the claimant is not represented and does not attend, the
success rate falls to one in twelve, while unrepresented attenders win in about
one in six cases. Represented claimants are successful in two out of every five
cases (Bell et al., 1974). A similar sort of pattern emerged in SBATs, as noted
earlier in this chapter. These marked differences between represented and
unrepresented cases must place some question marks after the claim that the
tribunals are genuinely inquisitorial and that their processes are accessible to
claimants appearing in person.

Concern over the reported variations in success rates of represented and unrepresented applicants to tribunals led the Lord Chancellor in 1987 to commission
a two-year research project to investigate the effectiveness of representation at
tribunals (Genn and Genn, 1989). The research would inform planning and
decision making over the use of legal aid in tribunals. The project was designed
to establish whether representation affected the outcome of tribunal hearings,
and to analyse the contribution of representation both to pre-hearing processes
and to the hearings themselves.

This research showed that the level of advice and representation in SSATs is
lower than in the other tribunals investigated. One in five appellants had made
some attempt to obtain advice prior to the hearing, but only one in eight appellants is represented by an expert, as distinct from being accompanied by another
member of the family or a friend without expert knowledge. About a third
of the help came from advisers in Citizens Advice Bureaux. The presence of
specialist representation increases the chances of success from one in three to one
in two. Specialist lay representation tended to be more successful than representation by solicitors and barristers. The research also showed that attending the
hearing, especially if a witness was brought along, also significantly improved the
chances of success. Even the identity of the chairman could affect the likelihood
of success. The study reported that one by-product of representation is that the
tribunal tends to scrutinize other cases more carefully. So success rates in urban

areas, where representation is more likely to be present, were higher than in outlying areas.

In commenting on the enabling function of the tribunal, the research study speaks of the heavy burden placed on the tribunal of eliciting all the relevant information about the case and applying the law to the facts in an impartial and objective manner. Compensating for the absence of representation could be time consuming and difficult when appellants are confused or inarticulate.

Social security appeal tribunals are categorized as the least formal of the tribunals investigated, but it is reported that appellants nevertheless found attendance before them a nerve-wracking ordeal. Many appellants reported extreme anxiety and bewilderment and confessed to having had difficulty expressing themselves.

The study concludes:

It has been persistently asserted by policy-makers, some administrative law scholars, and those concerned with the administration of tribunals, that the informality of tribunals, their simplicity, and their accessibility, have rendered representation both unnecessary and undesirable. The evidence of this study indicates that while simplicity in initiating proceedings, informality in surroundings, and procedural flexibility are valuable qualities worthy of preservation, they should not be used as a justification for denying the contribution that representation makes to tribunal decision-making processes, nor the need of appellants to have cases advocated on their behalf. (Genn and Genn, 1989, p. 248)

Conclusion

Social security appeal tribunals are generally regarded as the least formal system of adjudication. Social security legislation by contrast is a complex web of primary and secondary legislation. It is a tribute to the tribunals that the technicality at the heart of the appellate process in these tribunals can and does coexist with the relative informality in atmosphere and with procedural flexibility. These are qualities which the Genn study argued should be preserved. Yet the Genn study in particular shows that no amount of enabling by the tribunal can compensate for the difficulties claimants face in attending the tribunal and arguing their cases. It is unknown territory leading to confusion and bewilderment.

The challenge to the Lord Chancellor's Department is to preserve the best features of the tribunal system while providing the necessary advice and support needed by claimants to ensure that all of them put their cases at their best. When these tribunals operate at their best, they offer a consumer orientation sadly absent from other areas of adjudication.

13

Dealing with Unfair Dismissal Cases

Introduction

Many tribunals are concerned with disputes between the citizen and authority in some form. The social security appeal tribunals are a typical example. They are concerned with grievances held by individuals against the two Government Departments who administer social security benefits. By contrast, industrial tribunals in the exercise of the unfair dismissal jurisdiction are concerned with disputes between employee and employer. Such disputes are often disputes between citizen and citizen, though the employer will often be a partnership or company. Much of the jurisdiction of industrial tribunals is concerned with rights given to individuals to be exercised against their employers. The unfair dismissal jurisdiction accounts for about three-quarters of the business of the tribunals. This represents around 30,000 cases a year.

The major study, the Dickens study, of the operation of the unfair dismissal jurisdiction of the industrial tribunals is that conducted by a team of researchers from the University of Warwick (Dickens et al., 1985) which involved large-scale interviewing of those involved in the tribunal processes in three regions of England and Wales. The interviews sought information on 'the nature of the parties; what happened to them; their expectations, experience, perceptions and assessments of the industrial tribunal system'.

Industrial Tribunals

Industrial tribunals were established under s.12 of the Industrial Training Act 1964 with a narrow jurisdiction to consider appeals against the levy on employers to finance the industrial training boards set up under that Act. In the following year they were given a new jurisdiction concerning redundancy payments, and concerning statutory rights to information about particulars of contracts of employment. Even with this fairly technical jurisdiction, some commentators saw the tribunals as providing the nucleus of a system of 'labour courts' (Whitesides and Hawker, 1975). The boost to their growing jurisdiction came when the Royal Commission on Trades Unions and Employers' Associations (Donovan Commission) of 1968 approved the extension of tribunal jurisdiction (Donovan, 1968). The Donovan Commission had approved tribunals as 'an easily accessible, speedy, informal and inexpensive procedure' for the settlement of disputes between employers and employees. The unfair dismissal procedures first introduced in the ill-fated Industrial Relations Act 1971 survived the repeal of that Act by the Trades Union and Labour Relations Act 1974.

The structure of industrial tribunals has long been settled. Tribunals consist of a lawyer chairman, many of whom are full-time appointments, sitting with two lay members, one representing employers and one employees. The lay members are intended to bring industrial experience and practical knowledge to bear on the issues coming before the tribunal. They are of equal standing to the chairman. One commentator says of lay members:

> Lay members, experienced in industrial relations, know what an employer should or should not put up with, equally they know what an employee can expect. They know the unwritten custom and practice which form such an important part of industrial relations. Thus they have a most valuable part to play in reaching a just decision. (Jukes, 1978, p. 5)

A presidential system has been adopted. A President is appointed who is responsible for the overall operation of the system. He is assisted by a network of regional chairmen. The system is organized around a central office in Bury St Edmunds, with regional offices in large cities in the regions and local offices in other cities. Each tribunal has a clerk who deals with the administration of the tribunal. Clerks are also expected to assist unrepresented parties with advice on the procedure adopted in the tribunals. Today the industrial tribunals enjoy a wide jurisdiction over statutory employment rights. The most important, at least numerically, of these jurisdictions has been the unfair dismissal jurisdiction, but other employment disputes within their jurisdiction include discrimination and equal pay claims, redundancy payments claims and claims concerning particulars of contracts of employment. The jurisdiction upon which attention will be focused in this chapter is unfair dismissal claims. The current law is to be found in Part V of the Employment Protection (Consolidation) Act 1978, as amended by subsequent employment legislation. Proposals are currently under consideration to transfer contractual disputes arising out of the employment relationship from the civil courts to the industrial tribunals, but no enabling legislation has yet been implemented to secure this.

A former President of the industrial tribunals has said that:

> The tribunals are meant to provide simple informal justice in an atmosphere in which the ordinary man feels he is at home . . . an atmosphere which does not shut out the ordinary man so that he is prepared to conduct his own case before them with a reasonable prospect of success. (Conroy, 1971, p. 4–5)

As this chapter will show, this goal has not been achieved because the tribunals have adopted an accusatorial or adversarial model of hearings. The procedure is very like that operating in the county courts despite the provisions of the rules of procedure which state that tribunals 'shall so far as appears . . . appropriate seek to avoid formality in its proceedings' and the absence of formal rules relating to the admissibility of evidence.

Protection against Unfair Dismissal

Before examining the practice and procedure of industrial tribunals, an outline of the law relating to unfair dismissal will be offered. This is, of necessity, an incomplete and oversimplified account which reflects a typical claim before the tribunals. The employment protection legislation has created for certain employees a proprietary right in their jobs. Before this proprietary right was granted, the relationship between employer and employee was regulated solely by the contractual terms agreed between employer and employee and embodied in the contract of employment. Thus, provided that an employer gave the notice required by the contract, the employer was free to terminate an employee's contract. The employment protection legislation operates to restrict the grounds on which an employer can terminate the contract of employment with impunity. The protection is acquired once an employee has been in a particular employment for two years, though there are special rules concerning part-time employees and for calculating the date up to which the continuous employment is measured. No protection exists for men over 65 or women over 60 or for persons over normal retiring age in a particular employment whether that age is more or less than the ages given above. Once the protection is acquired, the employee can make a claim that he or she has been unfairly dismissed. The employer must then establish before a tribunal the reason, or if there is more than one, the principal reason, for the dismissal, and must show that it was one of the following reasons:

> a reason relating to the capability or qualifications of the employee for the particular employment; or
> a reason relating to the conduct of the employee; or
> that the employee was redundant; or
> that some legislation precluded the continuance of the employment; or
> some other substantial reason justifying dismissal.

These general grounds have been elaborated by decisions of the Employment Appeal Tribunal on appeal from decisions of industrial tribunals. Establishing the existence of a reason for dismissal falling within the legislation is only the first hurdle upon which the employer has the burden of proof. But there is also a reasonableness test, where there is no burden of proof placed on either party. The reasonableness test is for the tribunal to consider, though both parties will normally make representations to the tribunal on this issue. The tribunal is required to determine whether the employer acted reasonably or unreasonably in treating the established reason for dismissal as sufficient reason for dismissing the employee, having regard to equity and the substantial merits of the case and to the size and administrative resources of the employer's undertaking.

Three remedies are available for persons found to have been unfairly dismissed: reinstatement, re-engagement or compensation. Reinstatement involves treating employees as if they had never been dismissed. So they must be paid all arrears of wages, granted full pension rights accruing through continuity of employment, and given any pay increases that would have been their due if they had not been dismissed. Re-engagement involves offering the employee a fresh contract of employment. Significantly, the employee will have to serve in that employment for two years before again gaining the protection of the unfair dismissal legislation. Compensation is calculated to a complex formula which includes a basic award related to gross earnings and length of service and a compensatory award which seeks to meet the employee's actual and future losses arising as a consequence of the dismissal. Interest is payable on all sums due to applicants following industrial tribunal awards. The most common remedy is compensation.

Practice and Procedure in Unfair Dismissal Claims

Pre-action Procedures

In the consideration of the plight of litigants in the civil courts, reference was made to the difficulty of collecting evidence to support a claim. In some cases, notably personal injuries cases, rules of court have provided special machinery to assist a plaintiff. In employment law three rules provide substantial assistance to an employee. The first is the requirement that not later than 13 weeks after the beginning of the employment, an employee is entitled to a written statement containing particulars of the terms of the employment, which must include details of disciplinary and grievance procedures available to the employee, unless the employer employs fewer than 20 people. An employee denied such a statement may refer the matter to a tribunal which will determine the particulars which should have been included and referred to in such a statement. In this way, all employees are able to ascertain the main terms of their employment. Many employees do not worry about such matters until a dispute arises, but the provisions do enable employees and their advisers to obtain details of the main terms of the contract of employment without too much difficulty.

The second rule assisting employees is the provision contained in the legislation entitling any employee of at least two years' standing to a written statement of reasons for dismissal. Not only is this statement admissible in tribunal proceedings, but unreasonable refusal to provide such a statement renders the employer, on the application of the employee to a tribunal, liable to a penalty payable to the employee of a sum equal to two weeks' gross pay. This is an extremely useful provision which requires early disclosure by the employer of the case against the employee.

The third rule is that an application to a tribunal claiming unfair dismissal casts the burden of proving a reason for the dismissal falling within the Act on the employer. This is in marked contrast to the position of most other applicants or plaintiffs who will have the burden of proving the facts on which their claim is based. The justification for the reversal of the burden of proof in unfair dismissal cases is that employers will be in the best position to explain what reasons they had for terminating the employment.

The Originating Application

Armed with the written statement of reasons for the dismissal, an employee is in a position to begin proceedings before the industrial tribunal. Commentators still tend to remark on the informality of industrial tribunal procedure (Farmer, 1974; Walker, 1985), but the industrial tribunal's rules of procedure are no longer informal, and it has become an adversarial forum (Dickens et al., 1985; Genn and Genn, 1989). There are detailed rules contained in regulations, which can be used strategically by representatives, and the documents used to outline the grounds of claims are increasingly being regarded as pleadings, so that inconsistencies or changes of tack revealed later may prejudice the parties. Great care therefore needs to be taken over the completion of documents.

The employee opens the proceedings by completing an Originating Application (also known as Form IT1); this is accompanied by some notes for guidance, and the employee will usually have the Department of Employment booklet on unfair dismissal claims. The Originating Application requests the names of the parties, details of the employment and remuneration, of the date of dismissal, a statement of the grounds of the claim and a non-binding intimation of the remedy sought. The form also, quite inappropriately, requests the employee to proffer an opinion as to the reason for dismissal. This is inappropriate because the burden of showing the reason for dismissal rests with the employer. Experienced advisers never respond to this question, but the unrepresented applicant often responds to the question with bizarre unsupportable allegations of bias and corruption by the employer which are sometimes seized on by the tribunal to the prejudice of the applicant. The completed form is sent to the Central Office of the Industrial Tribunals in London (COIT). It must arrive within three months of the 'effective date of termination' of the employment, basically the date of dismissal or some later date deemed by statute to be the date the employment ended. No fee is payable on filing a claim.

The Notice of Appearance

On receipt of the originating application, the COIT copy the application and send it to the employer with a Notice of Appearance (Form IT3), which the employer must complete and return within 14 days, showing whether the claim will be resisted and, if so, on what grounds. Failure to respond has draconian consequences. The employer ceases to be entitled to take any part in the proceedings. Since the employer has the burden of proof, this will usually be fatal to the employer's case. For this reason failure to respond is rare and late responses are deemed to include an application for an extension of time, which is invariably allowed. On receipt of the Notice of Appearance, the COIT send a copy to the applicant and send the papers to the most convenient Regional Office, who in turn allocate the case to the most convenient local office. Either party, or the tribunal of its own motion, may request further and better particulars of the grounds on which the claim or reply is based.

The Dickens study tells us that not every dismissed employee eligible to claim unfair dismissal does so. Only about one in ten of those eligible to claim actually does so. Among those who apply there is a greater tendency to bring unfair dismissal proceedings where the employer is a small single establishment employer with below average unionization. Nearly half of all applications are against employers with fewer than 20 employees. The larger the employer, the less likely it is that there will be an unfair dismissal claim. There are a number of possible explanations for this pattern of application. Larger employers are likely to have internal appeals procedures and failure there, where union representation may have been provided, is the point at which the employee draws the line. Employees may feel a sense of powerlessness in taking on a large organization or it may be that advisers are more reluctant to take on large organizations.

The typical applicant to the tribunal is a male, middle-aged, non-union manual worker dismissed after a relatively short period of service. The study found that access to advice was an important factor, tending to be haphazard. Even where applicants had some access to advice and representation, that service itself adopted procedures for selecting the cases in which representation before the tribunal would be provided. The Genn study confirms this profile of applicants (Genn and Genn, 1989).

Seven out of ten applicants sought advice and half of these approached solicitors (Genn and Genn, 1989). A real difficulty here is that legal aid does not extend to representation in the tribunal. The Green Form scheme is the only relevant part of the legal aid scheme and will provide advice only. Respondent employers also sought advice frequently, almost always from solicitors or in-house employment law experts.

Conciliation

While the parties are sorting out any issues over the grounds of the claim, a formal statutory process of conciliation is brought into play. Conciliation officers from the Advisory Conciliation and Arbitration Service (ACAS) will have been sent copies of the Originating Application and Notice of Appearance. They will intervene to try to secure a settlement of the claim without its being determined by an industrial tribunal, and in doing so they are required to seek to promote the reinstatement or re-engagement of the employee. In practice conciliation officers tend to view the achievement of a settlement as their principal function, with the actual remedy a secondary consideration. Most settlements are for compensation.

Typically the conciliation officer will contact each party or their representatives to discuss the case. It is important for the parties to realize that the conciliation officer will tell the other side what each has said about the claim. Conciliation officers are often reluctant to express an opinion about the likelihood of success before the tribunal, but will make clear an opinion whether the case appears to them one which is strong or weak and so ought to settle. In particularly weak cases the conciliation officer will go so far as to advise the applicant to withdraw the claim. About one in three claims which do not go to a hearing are dropped by applicants. The process can be a useful one to get the other side talking about settling. Conciliation officers are very useful for advising employers of the tasks before them at a tribunal hearing. Even 20 years after the introduction of employment protection, there are still many small employers who do not appreciate its impact on managerial decision making. The negotiations are conducted on a 'without prejudice' basis and information communicated through conciliation officers is by statute not admissible at tribunal hearings unless the person who gave the information to the conciliation officer consents. The success of conciliation can be measured by the volume of withdrawals or conciliated settlements. Around two-thirds of all cases result in withdrawals or conciliated settlements. Agreements resulting from conciliation are normally registered with the tribunal as a form of consent decision.

Though a formal part of the processes which operate when an unfair dismissal application is made, conciliation is a separate process from adjudication by the tribunal. This is emphasized by conciliation being the province of ACAS and by the confidentiality which surrounds the process. Conciliation and adjudication are alternative methods of dispute settlement. There is a long history of the use of conciliation in employment relations, justified because one objective is to secure the continuance of the relationship between the parties in dispute. The process of conciliation in unfair dismissal cases serves two purposes. The first is to facilitate agreement between the parties on the settlement of the dispute on terms selected and agreed between them. The second is to act as a filter to ensure that only those cases which for some reason need to proceed to a formal process of adjudication do so. The conciliation process is very effective as a filter disposing of two out of every three applications without the need for adjudication.

The Dickens study showed that the parties generally viewed the involvement of ACAS favourably, though opportunities for complaint about their involvement were limited in the interviews conducted by the researchers. Other writers have complained, particularly in discrimination cases, that conciliation officers are too willing to encourage settlement at any price and fail to provide the support an unrepresented applicant may need against the relatively advantaged position of the employer (Gregory, 1987).

Four out of every five settlements achieved by conciliation officers are for compensation and only one in ten for reinstatement or re-employment. The Dickens study concludes:

> Very few offers of settlement conveyed by the conciliation officer are refused by applicants. The inequality in the employer–employee relation-

ship and the relative disadvantage of an unfair dismissal applicant within the industrial tribunal system is perpetuated, not ameliorated, by the neutral stance required of ACAS in conciliation. In the context of a tribunal system used by unaided and unrepresented applicants the description of conciliated settlements as voluntary agreed outcomes of an assisted bargaining process, qualitatively superior to tribunal imposed awards, is inappropriate. The description might have more applicability if there were rights enforcement officers to aid unrepresented applicants. Inherent in some of the criticism made of ACAS conciliators . . . is the assumption that they should take a more positive, rights-enforcing, stance. (Dickens, 1985, p. 180)

Interlocutory Applications

The process of conciliation runs alongside other pre-hearing procedures. These include power to strike out an application because the applicant is not taking the proper steps to further the claim, or because it is 'scandalous, frivolous or vexatious'. Because the formal rules of evidence do not apply, there is no automatic procedure equivalent to discovery and inspection, but documentary evidence is often important in unfair dismissal claims and there are powers to order the production of key documents on the application of one of the parties. There are also powers to compel the attendance of witnesses by obtaining a witness order.

Pre-hearing Assessments

At this stage either party can invoke a procedure introduced in 1980, which can place pressure on the other side to withdraw or settle at an early stage. This is the pre-hearing assessment. The tribunal may also direct of its own motion that there be a pre-hearing assessment. Though available to either party it is in reality a procedure designed to enable employers faced with weak cases to apply a potential costs sanction to encourage the early demise of weak cases. The purpose of the pre-hearing assessment is to sift out those applications which are unlikely to succeed.

Application for a pre-hearing assessment can be made by letter, and the obvious time for an employer to request such a hearing is when returning the Notice of Appearance. The chairman will consider the paper claims and decide whether to allow the application. If it is allowed, both parties are invited to make written submissions and to attend a hearing before a full tribunal of three members. At this hearing no evidence is called, but the tribunal does like to have a full account of the claims of each party and of the evidence to be called to support them. The tribunal then decides whether to issue an 'unlikely to succeed' warning to either party, the result of which is that if that party persists with the claim or a contention as part of a claim at the hearing, and loses, then costs may be awarded against that party. The full hearing of the claim must be before a differently constituted tribunal who will not know until the end of the case of the warning. In 1982 pre-hearing assessments were requested in six per cent of cases filed, about half by the tribunal of its own motion. The procedure is an effective means of scaring off applicants. In 1982, 78 per cent of cases in which pre-hearing assessments had been requested did not proceed to a full hearing. Of course, what is not revealed by these bald figures is anything qualitative about the claims. Without research into the merits of the claims, it is impossible to say with authority whether most claims terminated in this way had no hope of success or whether applicants are forced to withdraw by the fear of costs.

The procedure has, however, not worked as well as expected and its use has declined. In 1987 it was used only in one case in 400 (DoE, 1988). It also seems that applications to the tribunal selected for a pre-hearing assessment are more likely to proceed to a hearing than other cases, while at the same time the success rate for those who proceed in the face of an 'unlikely to succeed' warning is not very different from other cases (DoE, 1988). In order to tackle the perceived problem of unfounded applications, the Government had proposed in 1986 in its White Paper *Building Businesses . . . Not Barriers* that there should be a £25 fee payable on making an application to an industrial tribunal. This proved an unpopular suggestion against which the charge of taxing justice was made. The Department of Employment therefore proposed an alternative of giving industrial tribunal chairmen, acting alone, discretion at the pre-hearing stage, on the application of one of the parties or of its own motion, to require a deposit of up to £150 from the other party as a condition of proceeding further, if the chairman considered that the case had no reasonable prospect of success. Deposits would be returned to the payee unless the case went to a full hearing and the party which had paid the deposit lost and had an order for costs made against them, in which case the deposit would be forfeit as part of the costs payable.

The consultation paper also proposes the abolition of pre-hearing assessments and the substitution of a pre-hearing review by a chairman acting alone which would have three objectives:

	to ascertain and clarify the issues in dispute, and record admissions and
		agreements;
	to give directions;
	to determine any jurisdictional issues not reserved for a tribunal, as distinct
		from a chairman acting alone.

At a pre-hearing review the chairman would have power to give a costs warning and to order the payment of a deposit. The necessary rule-making power to accommodate the new system has been included in the Employment Act 1989.

The Hearing

If the applicant has survived this far and avoided a pre-hearing assessment, the case will be listed for hearing. Most industrial tribunal buildings are purpose built and are reasonably comfortably equipped. The physical distance between the parties and the tribunal members is minimized. The tribunals sit in public and, for this reason, the members may sit on a slightly raised dais. Otherwise there is little of the ritual of the courts, though everyone is expected to stand when the tribunal members enter or leave. When questioning witnesses and addressing the tribunal, parties and their representatives do not stand. It is for the parties, and not for the tribunal, to see that all relevant evidence and legal argument is adduced. The procedure at the hearing is determined by the tribunal within the framework of the statutory rules which provide that the tribunal shall 'so far as appears to it appropriate seek to avoid formality'. The formal rules of evidence do not apply.

The usual order of events is for the employer to open the proceedings by making a short opening address. Then witnesses are called. Evidence is given on oath and witnesses are subject to cross-examination. If the parties are not represented, it is usual for the chairman and members to ask many questions. Where the parties are represented, interventions from the tribunal are less frequent. The employee then puts his or her case in a similar manner. Once all the evidence has been given, each side may address the tribunal by way of summary and legal argument. One chairman has commented that tribunals operate a sliding scale of formality. Where representation is present and the 'stakes are high', the proceedings will be very formal, but where there is no representation, the proceedings are much less formal (Macmillan, 1983). In practice the procedure is one which is best coped with by those with appropriate forensic skills in the questioning and cross-examination of witnesses, and the marshalling of evidence and argument, coupled with a sound knowledge of the legal framework within which such cases are determined.

The tribunal members retire and deliberate once both sides have presented their cases. The lay members have the same say as the chairman. Majority decisions are rare. The tribunal returns and the chairman announces their decision. This may be a brief summary of reasons or a full decision dictated by the chairman. In coming to a decision the tribunal is bound by decisions of the Employment Appeal Tribunal and must ensure that its decisions take full account of the cases presented to them and any others that are relevant. In general, tribunal chairmen are well-informed and familiar with most authorities. Having said that, most cases turn on their facts and not on points of legal principle. The parties are later sent by post either a summary decision or a full written decision as soon as it has been typed up and signed by the chairman, which is accompanied by information about applying for a review of the decision and of appealing to the Employment Appeal Tribunal. Since March 1985 a full written decision has only been provided at the request of either party. The purpose of the change was to save time and money, but the change is not wholly welcome, because in practice it will draw an even sharper distinction between represented and unrepresented parties. Representatives ask for a full written decision as a matter of course, whereas unrepresented parties are less likely to exercise the right to a full written decision.

Contested cases where there is representation can easily last a full day, or even longer if the facts are at all complicated, and the written decisions are lengthy, often running to six or seven pages of single-spaced typescript. Employees are successful in about one in three cases.

Representation at the Hearing

It appears that around one half of applicants are represented at industrial tribunals. About 33 per cent of applicants are legally represented, as compared with 63 per cent of respondents (Macmillan, 1983). The Dickens study reported that 55 per cent of applicants and 67 per cent of respondents were represented, though in the remaining cases the companies' representatives' status could not be readily identified (Dickens et al., 1985). The Genn study reported that 38 per cent of applicants were represented either at a hearing or during settlement negotiations, though 70 per cent had sought advice about their application. Employers had expert representation at hearings in 74 per cent of the cases in the sample, compared with 57 per cent of applicants. Both parties were represented in 48 per cent of cases and neither party in only 17 per cent of hearings. In 12 per cent of cases an unrepresented applicant faced an employer represented by a lawyer, while an unrepresented employer faced an employee represented by a lawyer in only five per cent of the cases; when non-lawyer experts are included, this figure increases to nine per cent (Genn and Genn, 1989). The overall picture is represented in figure 6.

In response to a question in Parliament in 1984, figures based on a 10 per cent sample were given of the comparative success rates of different types of representation. The success rate of lawyers was consistently better than that of trades union representatives and of individuals representing themselves over the four years from 1979 to 1982 covered (DoE, 1984). The success rate of lawyers in 1982 was 36.9 per cent whereas that for trades union representatives and for individuals representing themselves was 25.1 per cent. The Department of

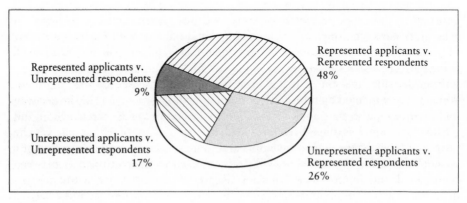

Figure 6   Representation   in   Industrial   Tribunals   (including   only   expert representation)
Source: *Genn, 1989*

Employment review of representation (DoE, 1981) concludes that the initial views that industrial tribunals should be bodies where representation was not necessary must now be re-evaluated in the light of an increasing trend not just towards representation, but towards legal representation.

The Genn study is the most recent on the effect of representation and concluded:

> As far as representation is concerned, applicants can only improve their chances of success through representation when the respondent is not represented. Where the applicant is legally represented and the respondent is not represented, the probability of the applicant succeeding is increased from 30% to 48%. Where the applicant has no representation and the respondent is legally represented the applicant's probability of success is reduced to 10%. Where the applicant is represented by a non-lawyer, and the respondent is represented by a lawyer the probability of the applicant succeeding is 18%. (Genn and Genn, 1989, p. 99)

The Royal Commission on Legal Services' treatment of tribunals was lamentably weak (Benson, 1979). The only issue discussed in any detail was that of representation. The Commission expressed concern at the figures showing that the unassisted lay person was at a disadvantage:

> Whatever the tribunal and however informal its procedure, representation, whether by lawyer or a skilled layman, in the majority of cases confers an advantage on the represented party. (Benson, 1979, para.2.17)

The Commission's task in tackling this problem was complicated by the generous provisions of the rules of procedure of adjudicatory tribunals as to rights of audience. Whereas representation before the civil and criminal courts is normally limited to solicitors and barristers, adjudicatory tribunals allow anyone to act as representative. As we have seen, representation other than by lawyers has become an important form of representation before tribunals. A major factor accounting for this development is the absence of legal aid for representation before tribunals. It is important to have a clear understanding of the impact of legal aid on tribunal representation. Save for the exceptional case of Mental Health Review Tribunals, legal aid does not cover representation before tribunals of first instance. The Green Form scheme will provide two hours' work by a solicitor on a case (more with an extension), but the solicitor cannot recover the cost of appearing before a tribunal to argue a case under this component of legal aid. Unless the solicitor is prepared to act without charge, at the point at which the client most needs a lawyer, the lawyer apparently abandons the case. At best a written submission for presentation to the tribunal will be prepared, but this is not normally an adequate substitute for the interactive process of actual appearance before the tribunal. Few parties before tribunals have the resources to fund the use of a lawyer. It will therefore come as no surprise that empirical research confirms the low level of activity in welfare benefits and tribunal work among solicitors (Lawrence, 1980a). Finally, it should be noted that legal aid only remunerates lawyers and not other representatives.

The Royal Commission made three recommendations to tackle the problem of representation: the simplification of tribunal procedures, the development of lay advice and representation, and the extension of legal aid. On the first limb of the response, the Royal Commission rather lamely noted that the procedures of some tribunals have become 'legalistic', mainly because the law governing their work has become more complex, and recommended that procedures be reviewed 'to ensure that applicants in person are able to conduct their own cases wherever possible'. The work of advice agencies was praised and it was recommended that public funds should be available for their development. Parties to tribunal proceedings should be sent a list of agencies in the area offering advice and representation. No effort was made to quantify the need or to address a major issue with public sector legal services generally. At present, there are not enough specialist lay advisers to meet the demand for their services. As a consequence, such agencies are selective in the cases they will represent. In some cases all that is offered is advice; in the busiest agencies even the amount of advice and assistance offered may be rationed.

The third limb of the Royal Commission's policy was the recommendation that legal aid be extended. It was accepted that there are some cases before all tribunals where legal representation is needed. This being so, it was necessary to establish an appropriate merits test. The traditional requirement that there be reasonable grounds for taking the proceedings was accepted, and to this was added the subsidiary test that it must be reasonable to employ a legal representative. In applying the second limb of the merits test, the Royal Commission felt that the relevant criteria should be:

> Does a significant point of law arise?
> Is the evidence so complex or specialized that the average lay person could reasonably wish for expert help in assembling and evaluating the evidence and in testing or interpreting it?
> Is it a test case?
> Is deprivation of liberty or the person's occupation at stake?
> Is the amount at stake, though small, significant in relation to the financial circumstances of the applicant?
> Is suitable lay representation available?
> Are there any special circumstances making legal representation desirable or would hardship follow if it was withheld?

The Government response has been to accept these recommendations in principle 'subject to further consideration being given to timing and the availability of resources' (Government Response to Benson, 1983). Unanswered questions relate to how the complementarity of roles of lay and legal advisers will operate, and when, in the current climate of Lord Chancellor's concern about legal aid expenditure, resources for an extension of legal aid to tribunals is likely to be available. No attempt has been made to establish criteria for distinguishing those cases where applicants might reasonably be expected to represent themselves from those where representation either by specialist lay adviser or by lawyer is appropriate. The Government response to the Genn study for the Lord Chancellor's Department may answer some of these questions.

Outcomes

The most common remedy granted is compensation. Awards after a hearing are significantly higher than those agreed by conciliation (Dickens et al., 1985; Genn and Genn, 1989). Most awards are for less than £1000. Research is needed to establish whether the level of conciliated settlements is fair to applicants or whether applicants simply prefer the bird in the hand to that in the bush. There are suggestions that conciliated settlements are finalized without conciliation officers taking a view on the equity of the monetary settlement they conciliate. The Dickens study concluded that the prime reason for the relatively low amounts awarded by way of compensation is the statutory rules for determination of compensation and the exercise of the tribunal's discretion in areas where this is open to them, such as in the consideration of future loss of earnings. The study also found tribunals frequently willing to attribute some contribution to the dismissal to the employee, which operates like a finding of contributory negligence to reduce the compensation payable. Overall the study considers that a low price is set on unfair deprivation of a job and that unfair dismissal compensation has little deterrent value for most employers wishing to dispense with the services of employees.

The industrial tribunal has no enforcement powers of its own. If an employer defaults on an award of compensation, then the employee must register the tribunal's decision with the county court and use the enforcement powers available in the county court to recover the award. If the applicant (or respondent) has avoided an 'unlikely to succeed' warning in a pre-hearing assessment, there is little risk of costs being awarded. The only basis on which costs can be awarded is that a party has acted 'frivolously, vexatiously or otherwise unreasonably'. Parties and witnesses are entitled to allowances for loss of earnings, subsistence and travel to and from the tribunal.

An Assessment of Industrial Tribunals

Both the law and procedure for unfair dismissal claims are complex. The money figures at stake can be high. The industrial tribunals have become arenas in which there is inequality between applicant and respondent. At present many more employers than employees are legally represented, and it is not uncommon for counsel to appear for employers. Furthermore non-legal representatives of employers, including in-house representatives, may well be highly trained personnel with considerable experience of employment law (Macmillan, 1983; Dickens, 1985).

No legal aid is available to provide representation for employees. The law is far too complex to justify a policy of allowing only advice and assistance. The understanding of the interaction of statute and case law required in this area is no different from that required in many cases pursued in the county courts and High Court. Nor is the law as self-contained as social security law; many employment cases require a command of principles of contract law. When this difficulty is coupled with the inequality of unrepresented applicant facing represented respondent, the case for the extension of legal aid is overwhelming. No procedural devices can accommodate such an imbalance of skills within what is a procedure requiring party presentation of the issues and the testing of evidence by process of cross-examination. This is not a criticism of the tribunals themselves, which contain some valuable devices to assist employees, but of the failure to provide the required assistance to employees to enable them to pursue their claims effectively.

Entrusting the decision in unfair dismissal cases to tribunals was a conscious decision designed to include as part of the decision-making process the industrial experience of employers and employees. There was some mistrust of mainstream court-based methods of determining these types of dispute. The presence of lay members would also, it was believed, contribute to informality. The Dickens study reports that the contribution of lay members on matters of industrial and practical knowledge are tempered by the carefully constructed legal framework within which unfair dismissal applications must be considered. In general lay members did not see their role as an enabling one and do not play a particularly active role in hearings. The research identified an 'underlying accusatorial model of hearings and a tendency towards legalism' (Dickens et al., 1985, p. 84). The JUSTICE Report defines legalism in two ways. The first refers to the manner in which the tribunals interpret and apply employment legislation, though the Report recognizes that the complex language and structure of the controlling legislation contributes to the potential for legalism. The second refers to the degree of formality in the physical arrangements and court room atmosphere; the major obstacle here is seen as the adversarial system of examining and cross-examining witnesses (JUSTICE, 1987). The Genn study is even more forthright:

> Industrial tribunals are totally adversarial. They are courts of first instance and their purpose is to adjudicate disputes between employers and employees, arising under employment protection legislation. (Genn and Genn, 1989, p. 198)

Review of Tribunal Decisions

Industrial tribunals enjoy a power to review their own decisions on application of either party within 14 days of notification of the tribunal's decision. The grounds for such a review are circumscribed by the tribunal's rules of procedure. Five grounds are listed:

the decision was wrongly made as a result of an error on the part of the
tribunal staff; or

a party did not receive notice of the proceedings; or

the decision was made in the absence of a party entitled to be heard; or

new evidence has become available which could not have been reasonably
known of or foreseen; or

the interests of justice require a review.

The procedure seems to work well providing a balance between finality of
decision making and the interests of justice in allowing the re-opening of certain
decisions. It is a simple and relatively cheap procedure for remedying mistakes
or obvious injustices, which complements the work of the Employment Appeal
Tribunal which can only deal with questions of law (McMullen, 1984).

Appeal to the Employment Appeal Tribunal (EAT)

The EAT is the indirect successor to the National Industrial Relations Court,
which was so unloved by trades unions that it could not survive in its original
form the repeal of the Industrial Relations Act 1971. After a short interregnum
in which appeals went to the Divisional Court of the Queen's Bench Division,
the EAT was established to hear appeals on points of law from industrial tribunals. The EAT is staffed by High Court judges who normally sit with two
additional members representative of employers and employees. The procedure
lacks the ritual formality of the High Court, but there can be no doubt that
serious legal issues are being considered. Legal representation is common and
legal aid is available to meet the cost of this. A party aggrieved by a decision of
an industrial tribunal has 42 days in which to file an appeal. The Employment
Appeal Tribunal Rules 1980 (SI 1980: No. 2035) set out standard forms for
appealing. Even at this stage conciliation is encouraged and the EAT is enabled
to take such steps as it thinks fit to enable the parties to avail themselves of the
opportunity for conciliation. The EAT has proved to be of major importance in
clarifying and elaborating the rules contained in the statutory material. Their
decisions are binding on industrial tribunals and have had a significant impact
on managerial practices by major employers. The sensitivity of employment law
issues may perhaps be gauged by the frequency with which employment cases go
to the Court of Appeal and House of Lords, though this may also have something to do with the looseness of the statutory language used in the legislation.

Alternative Proposals

The Dickens study offered as an alternative to the current system an arbitral
system as a way of overcoming the perceived disadvantages of the industrial
tribunal system (Dickens et al., 1985, ch. 9). The focus would move from the
determination of who is legally right and from consideration of the

reasonableness of the employer's action in the circumstances of the individual dismissal to the location of the dispute firmly in the realms of industrial relations, rather than employment law, where the search would be for a workable and acceptable solution which took account of the wider context. It was argued that such a system would generally be more favourable to employees and would be more likely to curb 'the exercise of managerial prerogative in the interests of individual job retention as well as avoiding the tendency to legalism'.

The JUSTICE Report takes a different tack. It recommends the introduction of two different procedures for determining unfair dismissal disputes: the investigative model and the adversarial model (JUSTICE, 1987). For nine out of every ten cases, the investigative model would be sufficient. The tenth case would require an adversarial approach backed by equality of representation and access to resources to enable the dispute to be presented effectively and efficiently. Such cases would go to a higher body, described as an upper-tier Industrial Court staffed by senior chairmen and members. The criteria for transferring cases to the Industrial Court would be:

> where a significant point of law arises;
> where the case has important implications beyond the interests of the individual parties;
> where the evidence is highly complex or specialized and raises difficult questions of evaluation.

For such cases the Report argues that legal aid should be available as in the lower courts.

For those cases dealt with by the investigative procedure, a chairman would direct, after reading the Originating Application and Notice of Appearance, preliminary investigations by an officer of the tribunal. It is envisaged that the investigation officer would be a legal officer in the Civil Service with special training, who would take full statements from parties to the dispute and any key witnesses and inspect all the documentation relevant to the case. The investigation officer would then prepare a full dossier to be sent to both sides prior to the hearing. The investigative role would not supplant the conciliation stage, which would remain with ACAS.

The tribunal members would read the dossier in preparation for the hearing and would take the initiative at the hearing by indicating the issues of fact and law on which evidence and submission remained necessary. The tribunal would itself take the lead in questioning, reducing the reliance of parties on representatives with the forensic skills of questioning and cross-questioning. The parties would have a secondary opportunity to ask questions of any witnesses and to make submissions on the law.

Conclusion

The industrial tribunals represent the tribunals whose practice and procedure is most like that of the courts. There can be little doubt that they have now become the forum for the expert. The evidence is overwhelming that the unrepresented party suffers serious disadvantage in this forum. The issue now facing policy makers is whether the tribunals are equated with the county courts and legal aid extended to them or whether structural changes are made which enable unrepresented litigants to have a fair chance to present their cases in a manner which gives them a fair chance of success.

14

Review and Supervision

Introduction

The parties to litigation, whether before a court or a tribunal, which results in trial and judgment have resisted many encouragements to settle the claim along the road to trial. Both parties will have been convinced of the correctness of their arguments on the facts and law. The party who loses will inevitably be disappointed. Sometimes the loser will not only be disappointed but also aggrieved because the trial judge or tribunal has taken some view of the facts and the law, which are believed to be wrong. Alternatively one party may be arguing for a significant change or development in the law, and might actually be expecting to lose at first instance. That party knows that only a higher court is likely to push forward the boundaries of some legal rule. For these cases the appellate process provides the remedy. In civil cases the rights of appeal are not ungenerous, though the overall system of civil appeals has been described as a 'hotchpotch' needing rationalization (Woolf, 1988). It is usual to be able to take one appeal as of right with a second appeal being possible with leave. Appeals are not retrials, but considerations of whether the trial judge erred in some way. This chapter is concerned, with the practice and procedure of appeals from courts and the appellate tribunals, and, with an introduction to the general objectives of appeals in civil cases.

From what follows it will be clear that the Court of Appeal, civil division, is at the heart of the civil appeal process. The House of Lords may be the highest court in the land, but it hears comparatively few appeals each year. Its contribution is particular rather than general, and some have questioned whether there is a need for two levels of appeal court.

The Processes of Review and Supervision

Two separate functions of appeals have been identified, which have been labelled review and supervision (Blom-Cooper and Drewry, 1972; Drewry, 1973). Review is the process by which defects in the trial process are corrected. These may typically be errors of practice and procedure, incorrect conclusions on the facts and inferences to be drawn from them, improper exercises of judicial discretion or an incorrect application of established legal principles. Supervision is the process of the laying down by the courts of guidelines for the development of legal principles. The process may involve a critical reconsideration of an area of law in the light of changing social conditions or an authoritative interpretation of a statutory provision. There is one type of appeal which falls in the grey area between review and supervision. This is the appeal which involves a review of an existing line of authority without any reconsideration of it. The Court of Appeal exercises the functions both of review and of supervision.

Gavin Drewry's analysis of the grant and refusal of leave to appeal to the House of Lords in 1971 demonstrated that leave was routinely refused in cases where the second appeal raised issues of review, that leave was granted in cases involving issues of supervision, and that there was a mixture of refusals and grants in cases falling in the grey area of reconsideration of authority without critical re-appraisal of the cases (Drewry, 1973). It also seems that the work of the Court of Appeal is predominantly the determination of appeals involving review. The grounds of appeal to the Court of Appeal most frequently relate to issues of fact or practice and procedure. The Court of Appeal is a very busy court which has to ration its time and manage its business carefully to avoid unacceptably long delays in the determination of appeals.

By contrast the House of Lords, though not short of cases, has a small workload of key cases. Time and the most careful deliberation of the issues raised are available in the House of Lords. It is the system of requiring leave to appeal which rations the case load of the House of Lords and filters out cases for attention which involve issues of supervision. Once the distinction between review and supervision is understood, the reasoning behind the conditions required for leap-frog appeals becomes more readily understandable. The conditions are designed to distinguish cases involving issues of supervision from those involving issues of review.

Judicial Control and Supervision of Tribunals

Some tribunals, like SSATs and the industrial tribunals, are part of a two-tier system with separate tribunals enjoying appellate jurisdiction. The constituent legislation of other tribunals contains provisions allowing access to the High Court, whereas some tribunals have to fall back on the appeals contained in s.13 of the Tribunals and Inquiries Act 1971. Indeed the decisions of some tribunals are not subject to any appeal. An example is the Vaccine Damage Tribunals established under s.4 of the Vaccine Damage Payments Act 1979 to review questions of the extent and cause of disablement by persons claiming to be entitled to payments under the Act as a result of disabilities arising from vaccination damage. The provision of appeals through separate tribunals enjoying appellate jurisdiction is generally more satisfactory than where reliance must be placed on the High Court. Making an appeal to a specialist appellate tribunal is cheaper, quicker and easier than using the High Court. Examples of appellate tribunals are the Social Security Commissioners and the Employment Appeal Tribunal, which were considered in the chapters 12 and 13. But review by the High Court of decisions of tribunals is a common feature of many other tribunals.

Section 13 of the Tribunals and Inquiries Act 1971 provides two forms of appeal to the High Court from specified tribunals. It is important to realize that this is not a general power in respect of all tribunals. To enjoy these types of appeal there must be specific statutory authority. Section 13 provides that a person dissatisfied with a decision of a specified tribunal on a point of law may either appeal against that decision to the High Court, or require the tribunal to state a case for the opinion of the High Court. The section further provides that rules of court may regulate and restrict the appeal in particular cases to one or other form of appeal (*see* RSC O.56, rr.7–12 and O.94, rr.8–11). In addition to the tribunals to which s.13 applies, there are a number of tribunals whose constituent legislation provides that a person aggrieved by a decision of the tribunal may require the tribunal to state a case for the opinion of the High Court. This is the same process as the stating of a case under s.13. The distinction between an appeal on a point of law and the requiring of a tribunal to state a case is important. The appeal operates like any other appeal; it will be for the appellant to formulate the grounds of appeal and to present the arguments in favour of the appellant's view to the High Court. The respondent may also adduce argument. The tribunal itself need do nothing to further the appeal, other than making available the notes of evidence and the chairman's record of the hearing. The appeal will be restricted to the point or points of law raised in the notice of appeal. By contrast requiring a case to be stated, just like the appeal by way of case stated from a decision of a magistrates' court or the Crown Court described in chapter 7, obliges the tribunal to set out its decision and the reasons for it together with a formulation of the questions to be considered by the High Court. The parties will, of course, have the opportunity to address argument to the Court on these questions. Unlike the position in criminal proceedings, the procedure may be used to enable a tribunal to obtain a preliminary ruling on a point of law which arises during the hearing of the case. The hearing will be adjourned pending the delivery of the High Court's opinion, at which time it will be relisted and a decision given on the merits in the light of the High Court's opinion on the law. This procedure is rarely used. Indeed appeals to the High Court from tribunals number about 100 a year, most of which are tax appeals. Once 'plugged' in to the High Court, the possibility arises of using the ordinary system of civil appeals to challenge the decision of the High Court. Thus ordinarily appeals will be available with leave to the Court of Appeal and thereafter to the House of Lords. Those tribunals with their own appellate tribunal do not enjoy the appeal to the High Court, but appeals on points of law lie with leave to the Court of Appeal from the EAT, Social Security Commissioners, and thereafter to the House of Lords.

Judicial Review

In addition to the statutory procedures described above, the Queen's Bench Division (QBD) of the High Court enjoys a common law power to control the operation of inferior courts and tribunals in certain circumstances by way of judicial review. The QBD may grant one of the three prerogative orders: *certiorari*, prohibition or mandamus. *Certiorari* quashes a decision which is found to be invalid because it is outside the powers granted to the court or tribunal (*ultra vires*), or has been given in proceedings in which the principles of natural justice were not observed, or where there has been an error of law on the face of the record. Prohibition lies to prevent some unlawful action by a tribunal on the same grounds as the granting of an order of *certiorari*. Whereas *certiorari* quashes past unlawful conduct, prohibition prevents future or continued unlawful conduct. Mandamus is a royal command to secure the proper performance of a tribunal's functions. It is usually sought in addition to an order of *certiorari* and is designed to ensure the performance of a public duty. For example, mandamus would lie to compel a tribunal to hear a case which it had mistakenly decided was not within its jurisdiction. The details of the availability, scope and grounds for such orders need not detain us here because they form part of substantive administrative law.

All these remedies are now sought by a single application for judicial review (Supreme Court Act 1981, s.31; RSC O.53; *O'Reilly* v. *Mackman*, [1983] 2 AC 237). Because the granting of a prerogative order is discretionary in nature, leave of the High Court must be obtained to make application for them. The distinction between appeal and judicial review is an important one to grasp. Appeal is concerned with the merits of the decision being appealed, while judicial review is concerned with the legality of the process by which that decision was reached. In the latter case the jurisdiction is described as being supervisory. If a bad decision on the law was made or the court or tribunal took a view of the evidence that no reasonable tribunal could take, which does not appear as an error of law on the face of the record, that is a matter for appeal rather than judicial review. Equally a perfectly proper decision on the law and facts taken in proceedings which did not meet the required standards of procedural regularity (for example, a decision of an SSAT where no reasons for the decision were given) could be quashed by means of judicial review. With the development of rights of appeal against tribunal decisions, the significance of judicial review is diminishing in relation to such tribunals. This is particularly so where tribunals have their own appellate tribunal. Very often the appeal to the appellate tribunal can cover matters that might be raised on judicial review. For example, the Social Security Commissioners will regard a failure to have regard to the principles of natural justice as an error of law which can form the basis of an appeal to them. Such a deficiency in the first instance tribunal's deliberations would also, of course, ground an application for judicial review. It is noticeable that, where the decisions of the appellate tribunal are not appealable to the Court of Appeal, as is the case with the Immigration Appeal Tribunals, more frequent use is made of judicial review. Nevertheless judicial review remains an important process for curing illegality.

In 1988 there were 1087 applications for leave to seek judicial review in all civil cases of which 618 were allowed to proceed to consideration of their merits (Judicial Statistics, 1988). Finally, it should be noted that s.14 of the Tribunals and Inquiries Act 1971, restating a rule first contained in the 1958 Act, provides that no provision in legislation prior to 1958 should be taken as ousting the supervisory jurisdiction of the High Court, thus making clear the Government's intention that all statutory tribunals should be subject to this jurisdiction regardless of whether other remedies are provided.

The overall importance of judicial review is reflected in the words of Sir Jack Jacob:

> The introduction in 1977 of the remedy of judicial review was a milestone in the history of English civil justice. It constituted one of the most benefi- cent, significant and effective innovations and improvements in the fabric of English civil justice. It restored credence in the creativity of the system of English justice; it provided a virile and vigorous procedure for remedies in the public law area to replace those that were in a weary and withering state. (Jacob, 1987, p. 180)

Rights of Appeal

Getting Advice on Appealing

Parties to litigation in the High Court or a county court do not receive a full written judgment containing the trial judge's reasoning. The official court docu- mentation will simply deal with the disposition of the case. Initially the parties will rely on the notes made by solicitors and counsel when the trial judge gave the reasons for his decision when delivering judgment in open court. In the High Court, if the case justifies the expense, a transcript of the judgment may be ordered from the shorthand writer who has kept the verbatim record of the pro- ceedings. Of course, in the High Court, a case of particular significance may be reported, but the law report will almost certainly not appear before the time allowed for appealing has passed. In the county court, apart from the judge's own note, there will only be the lawyer's notes of the decision, and there will also be a written decision from the first instance tribunal. By contrast, litigants before the Social Security Commissioners or the EAT will receive a full written decision. Losers may be aggrieved for a number of reasons: they may disagree with the findings of fact, statements of the law, award of damages, or even the way the case was conducted. In considering an appeal all these avenues will need to be explored.

Though not expressly so stated as in the case of criminal appeals where there is a criminal legal aid order, it seems that a civil legal aid certificate will also cover advice on appeal. If an appeal is merited, application can be made for an extension of the legal aid certificate to cover the appellate proceedings. This can be done expeditiously, though initially the extension will probably only cover the obtaining of any necessary transcripts and a formal opinion of counsel on the likelihood of a successful appeal. Once these papers are to hand there can be a proper consideration of whether or not there are good grounds for extending legal aid to cover the arguing of an appeal. If the litigant was not assisted at first instance, or before one of the appellate tribunals, a full application for a legal aid certificate must be made. In either case it is unlikely that all the legal formalities will have been completed in the time allowed for filing an appeal. The Court of Appeal has intimated that such cases are appropriate cases for the grant of extensions of the time allowed for appealing (Legal Aid Handbook, 1990).

From the County Courts

There is a right of appeal to the Court of Appeal, civil division, from decisions of the county courts in contract and tort where the claim is for £2500 or more. If the claim is for less, then leave of either the county court judge or of the Court of Appeal is required, unless the decision includes or preserves an injunction (County Courts Act 1984, s.77; County Courts Appeal Order 1981, SI 1981: No. 1749). The notice of appeal, or application for leave to appeal, must be filed within four weeks of the date the judgment was entered, unless an extension of time has been allowed either by the county court or the Court of Appeal. The correct procedure is to apply first to the county court judge for leave, but if leave is refused, the application may be renewed before the Court of Appeal. A single judge of the Court of Appeal may dispose of the application and there is no appeal against such a decision (Supreme Court Act 1981, s.54(6)). If the point raised is particularly complex, the single judge may decide to refer the matter to a court of two or more judges.

From the High Court

In actions in contract and tort, there is a general right of appeal to the Court of Appeal (Supreme Court Act 1981, s.16), which is excluded in relation to particular matters of which the only significant one for our purposes is the exclusion of a right of appeal against a decision of the High Court allowing an extension of time for appealing. The Court of Appeal may also allow an extension of time for appealing. The notice of appeal must be filed within four weeks of the date on which the judgment was entered. Changes made to rule-making powers in Part I of the Courts and Legal Services Act 1990 will result in changes to the general right of appeal. Leave will be required in specified circumstances (Donaldson, 1990a).

From the Social Security Commissioners

There is no general right of appeal, since this will be the second appeal following the decision of the SSAT. The appeal lies only where a point of law is involved. Leave to appeal must be obtained from the Commissioner or, failing that from the Court of Appeal: Social Security Act 1980, s.14. There is a three-month time limit, which can only be extended for good reasons.

From the Employment Appeal Tribunal

Again the appeal to the Court of Appeal is only available where a point of law is involved. Application is made initially to the EAT, but if that fails, it may be renewed before the Court of Appeal: Employment Protection (Consolidation) Act 1978, s.146.

The Grounds of Appeal

The notice of appeal must set out clearly and completely, shortly and simply, the grounds of appeal. The Court of Appeal has very wide powers to remedy deficiencies in the decision under appeal and the grounds of appeal are not restricted in any way. They must show the error in the court below or the tribunal and the relief being sought. It is important that the grounds of appeal are full because any omission can only be cured with the leave of the Court of Appeal. The detailed rules governing appeals to the Court of Appeal in civil cases can be found in O.59 of the Rules of the Supreme Court.

The Powers of the Court of Appeal

In general terms the Court of Appeal has all the authority and jurisdiction of the court or appellate authority from which the appeal is brought (Supreme Court Act 1981, s.15). Indeed it is now clear that the Court of Appeal may on appeal even exercise a power conferred on the court below after the date of the judgment against which the appeal is lodged (*Attorney-General* v. *Vernazza*, [1960] AC 965). Though the appeal is said to be 'by way of rehearing', it is not a re-creation of the trial with witnesses giving evidence again before the appeal court. The appeal will be limited to the matters raised in the notice of appeal, and normally only legal argument will be presented. In theory it is possible to raise new points not dealt with in the pleadings or argument in the trial, but the Court of Appeal is reluctant to exercise the power to admit them, since it smacks of allowing the running of alternative arguments where those run at trial have failed. Where evidence is relevant, the court almost always relies on the chairman's notes of evidence in tribunal proceedings, on the county court judge's note, or on the transcript. It is difficult to persuade the Court of Appeal to alter a finding of direct fact by the trial judge. The court takes the view that it has not had the benefit of seeing the witnesses, hearing their evidence and forming opinions as to the weight to be attached to it. Accordingly, they will not lightly interfere. There is more chance of persuading the court to substitute its own finding of inferential fact from the direct facts, because this goes to the conclusions drawn by the trial judge from direct facts. The best example is a conclusion that direct facts do or do not amount to contributory negligence, which will always be an inference drawn in the light of the facts found.

It is possible to appeal against the amount of damages awarded by the trial judge and here the Court of Appeal will amend the amount if the trial judge has applied an incorrect principle of law or has awarded a sum which is clearly inconsistent with awards in comparable cases. The appeal court will only interfere if there is a significant divergence from the norm; here again they allow the trial judge a margin of appreciation because that judge has seen the parties and heard the evidence. Different principles apply to awards by juries, which are used only rarely in civil cases, usually in defamation cases. There is here the traditional reluctance to interfere with decisions of jurors (*Cassell* v. *Broome*, [1972] AC 1027). In certain cases the ordering of a retrial will be the appropriate solution where the damages appear excessive because the jury has taken into account irrelevant matters, or has not considered relevant matters (*Rubber Improvement Ltd* v. *Daily Telegraph Ltd*, [1964] AC 234). Recent high awards of damages in libel cases have led the Court of Appeal to a greater willingness to interfere.

The Court of Appeal has power to receive fresh evidence only on special grounds. The test for the admission of fresh evidence is laid down in *Ladd* v. *Marshall* ([1954] 1 WLR 1489) and was approved by the House of Lords in *Skone* v. *Skone* ([1971] 1 WLR 812). Three conditions must be satisfied:

the evidence could not have been obtained with reasonable diligence at the trial; and
if given at the trial, the evidence would probably have had an important influence on the result of the case; and
the evidence is apparently credible, though it need not be incontrovertible.

These rigorous tests mean that the Court of Appeal hears fresh evidence only rarely; it will certainly need to be satisfied that the appeal is not being used merely as an attempt to argue the case in a different way. If the matter cannot be resolved by the Court of Appeal, it has power to order a retrial.

The civil division of the Court of Appeal enjoys much wider powers to order a retrial than the criminal division. Some have already been mentioned; others relate to jury trial. In addition to these the Court of Appeal has powers to order the retrial of a case tried before a judge alone in the following cases:

where there has been improper admission or exclusion of evidence;
where there has been surprise, as where the trial judge allows the case to proceed on a basis other than that pleaded without giving the other side an opportunity to consider the new material;
where there have been irregularities in the course of the trial, as where the judge intervened so much that proper cross-examination was precluded (*Jones* v. *NCB*, [1957] 2 QB 55).

The final power to mention is not a power exclusive to the Court of Appeal, nor is it a power whose exercise disposes of the appeal. This is the power to make a reference to the Court of Justice of the European Communities seeking an authoritative interpretation of a point of European Community law relevant to the determination of the dispute before the court (RSC O.114). Any court or tribunal may make such a reference, and final appeal courts must make a reference where the point of European Community law is relevant to its decision (EEC Treaty, Article 177). The effect of a reference is to suspend the proceedings before the referring court until the Court of Justice has handed down its opinion which is then applied by the referring court to the dispute before it.

Managing the Business of the Court of Appeal

Significant changes were made by the Supreme Court Act 1981 in the arrangements for the management of the business of the civil division of the Court of Appeal. Prior to the implementation of the Act the civil division had no staff of its own except the clerks to the Master of the Rolls and the Lords Justices of Appeal. As a result much judicial time was taken up with administrative matters and with interlocutory matters which did not justify the use of the time and expertise of the judges. In December 1978 the unpublished report of a Working Party headed by Lord Scarman recommended the establishment of a Registrar of Civil Appeals having both judicial and administrative functions. The Act made provision for such an office, which has now been established and has already contributed to increased efficiency in the division. The Act also made provision for some appeals to be disposed of by courts composed of two judges rather than three. There is now a clear hierarchy of powers exercisable by the Registrar, and by one, two or three judges of the division. The most important points to note are as follows. The Registrar has power to deal with most interlocutory matters arising on appeal, though there is provision for review of his decisions by a single judge with the possibility of appeal with leave to a full court. The single judge may review decisions of the Registrar and make interim orders outside the Law Terms. Most importantly, of course, the single judge may decide applications for leave to appeal. Refusals of leave by a single judge are final.

Two judge courts will normally deal with appeals concerning interlocutory matters and may hear any final appeals with the consent of the parties. In addition two judge courts are competent to hear appeals from county court decisions and most appeals from the High Court where the amount of the claim or counterclaim does not exceed the county court limits (Court of Appeal (Civil Division) Order 1982, SI 1982: 543). Where the court consists of an even number of judges who are equally divided, the case must be re-argued before an uneven number of judges before appeal to the House of Lords is possible. The principal work of three judge courts will now be the determination of appeals from the High Court where the amount of the claim or counterclaim exceeds the county court limits. Of course, it will remain open to the court to list any appeal which involves important points before a court of three or more judges.

The importance of the role of the Master of the Rolls as head of the civil division of the Court of Appeal should not be overlooked. The Master of the Rolls sets the tone of the court and can control the distribution of business among his colleagues. The matching of judges to cases can, of course, have an effect on the outcome of appeals. It will be the Master of the Rolls who decides whether an appeal is so important that it should be referred to a court composed of more than three judges, even though decisions of such courts formally have no greater weight than those of three judge courts. A good modern example is the decision of the former Master of the Rolls, Lord Denning, to convene a special court of five judges to hear the appeal in *Davis v. Johnson* ([1979] AC 264) concerning the scope of the county court's jurisdiction under the provisions of the Domestic Violence and Matrimonial Proceedings Act 1976 to exclude a person from premises in which that person has a proprietary interest. The problem was that there were two previous decisions of the Court of Appeal, by which the court would normally be bound, which would, contrary to the justice of the case, have denied a remedy in the case before the court. The device of a court of five judges was adopted to add weight to the reconsideration of the earlier cases. The case was taken on appeal to the House of Lords, who upheld the decision of the Court of Appeal on the merits, but rebuked the Court of Appeal for not following its own previous decisions. We shall return later in this chapter to the doctrine of precedent.

As part of the campaign to increase the efficiency of the civil division of the Court of Appeal, the Master of the Rolls, Sir John Donaldson (as he then was), has introduced a number of innovations following the recommendations of Lord Scarman's Working Party (*Practice Note*, [1982] 1 WLR 1312, as amended by *Practice Note*, [1983] 1 WLR 598). The first is the early listing of cases in which it appears that the only purpose of the appeal is to secure some advantage by preserving the *status quo* pending the outcome of the appeal. The example given was of a tenant against whom an order for eviction had been made securing further time in residence by appealing. Early listing is seen as likely to remove the incentive for such appeals (Donaldson, 1983). The average delay in the hearing of appeals in 1983 by two judge courts was six to seven months, but before three judge courts was between 12 and 14 months.

The second innovation is more interesting and raises wider issues. In a *Practice Note* in April 1983 ([1983] 1 WLR 1055) Sir John recommended the submission shortly before the hearing of the appeal of 'skeleton arguments' by counsel for the parties. These would also be exchanged between counsel. The contents of the skeleton arguments should be a list of numbered propositions expressed in no more than one or two sentences which counsel proposed to argue. References to authorities and to documents, to which counsel intends to refer in his or her submissions to the court, should be annexed to the skeleton arguments. Counsel should also ensure that there is annexed any material which counsel would expect the court to note in detail. The judges hearing the appeal will read the skeleton arguments prior to the hearing along with the notice of appeal and the judgment appealed. The benefits of skeleton arguments are seen to be:

the saving of time because the need for longhand notes is obviated;
the elaboration of the substance of the appeal which is not usually apparent from the notice of appeal;
the provision of an aide-memoire for convenience of reference for counsel.

The *Practice Note* emphasized the informal nature of the arrangements and stated that counsel should not be inhibited from departing from the skeleton arguments. Their use was not envisaged in every case; express reference is made to the submission in simple appeals only of material counsel would expect the court to note in detail.

The use of skeleton arguments has been popular with the Court of Appeal, but met with some resistance from some members of the Bar (Blom-Cooper, 1984). Their use has now been refined and extended (Donaldson, 1990a). The current guidance is contained in a 1989 *Practice Direction (Court of Appeal: Presentation of Argument)* ([1989] 1 WLR 281 as amended by [1990] 1 WLR 794). Skeleton arguments are now compulsory in all appeals before the Court of Appeal except in cases of urgency or where the court otherwise directs. Paragraph 3 of the Direction specifies the requirements as to content:

> The purpose of a skeleton argument is to identify not to argue the points. A skeleton argument should therefore be as succinct as possible. In the case of points of law, it should state the point and cite the principal authority or authorities in support with references to the particular page(s) where the principle concerned is enunciated. In the case of questions of fact, the skeleton argument should state briefly the basis on which the Court of Appeal can interfere with the finding of fact concerned, with cross-references to the passages in the transcript or notes of evidence which bear on the point.
>
> In the case of respondents whose arguments will be simply that the judgment of the court below is correct for the reasons given, counsel for the respondent can send in a letter to that effect in lieu of a skeleton argument. Where, however, the respondent is going to rely on any authority or refer to any evidence which is not dealt with in the judgment of the court below, a respondent's skeleton argument must always be lodged.
>
> Skeleton arguments are *not* pleadings and, save in exceptional cases . . . need not answer the skeleton arguments of the other side.

The skeleton arguments must be accompanied by a chronology of events, which must be contained in a separate document for ease of consultation. Skeleton arguments are to be exchanged between the parties and four copies delivered to the court 14 days in advance of the hearing.

The issue raised by these developments is whether the principle of orality upon which English trials and appeals proceed is the best way of dealing with appeals. The English requirement of oral presentation of the whole of the case stands in marked contrast to the rules obtaining in other jurisdictions. The judges have repeatedly rejected the introduction of written briefs into English civil procedure, but Sir John Donaldson's proposals and their development over the past five years are a step in the direction of a written stage in appellate procedure, despite the somewhat ambivalent caveat added at the end of the *Practice Note*:

> It cannot be over-emphasised that skeleton arguments are not formal documents to the terms of which anyone will be held. They are simply a tool

to be used in the interests of greater efficiency. Experience shows that they can be a valuable tool. The judges of the court all hope that it will be possible to refine and extend their use.

This caveat is echoed in the statement in the explanatory introduction to the 1989 Practice Direction that the Court of Appeal remains 'firmly wedded to its long established tradition of oral argument in open court'.

In *Mardas* v. *Official Receiver* (*New Law Journal*, 24 November 1989, p. 1597) Lord Donaldson said:

One of the points of skeleton arguments is this. Judges ought, when they are pre-reading a case, to be able to pick up the skeleton argument, and they ought actually to be able to start with the skeleton argument, which would tell them in very succinct form the background facts and what the points are.

Appellate procedures in the United States rely on the submission of written briefs by each side followed by limited oral argument, upon which a strict time limit is placed. The Evershed Committee in 1953 considered the introduction of such procedures in the Court of Appeal but rejected them. The principle of orality was considered to contribute to unanimity in decision making because of the thorough sifting and testing of argument in unrestricted oral argument. This teamwork aspect of the work of the Court of Appeal would be lost if written briefs were read individually by judges prior to limited oral argument. The strongest objection raised by the Evershed Committee was that the system would not fit easily into the division of labour between solicitors and barristers. It was stated that solicitors would not find it possible to prepare the written briefs, and that it would be unfair to expect them to do so. If barristers were to be instructed to prepare written briefs, they would need to be remunerated fairly for the work and there would be a resulting rise in costs (Evershed, 1953). The conclusions of the Evershed Committee, particularly with regard to the division of work between solicitors and barristers, are open to challenge. The real problem is that if solicitors prepare the written brief, there is much less of a case for denying them the right of audience to argue that brief before the court. Indeed to suggest that solicitors might not be equipped to prepare written briefs is rather odd, since much of the paperwork in litigation is done by solicitors, though traditionally counsel settle documents to be used in court.

The rejection of written briefs was repeated by Lord Evershed in 1962 in a *Practice Note* ([1962] 1 WLR 395). An interesting attempt was made in 1966 by Michael Zander, acting as solicitor for the appellant, to introduce a written brief into the Court of Appeal. Though received in the case before it, Danckwerts LJ said that the submission of such a document was 'wholly irregular and contrary to the practice of the court and. . . should not be allowed as a precedent for future proceedings' (*Rondel* v. *Worsley*, [1967] 1 QB 443, p. 509). Lord Scarman's Working Party also rejected the introduction of written briefs. If the introduction of skeleton arguments works well, and the indications are that it does, then the case against fuller written briefs becomes less easy to answer. The principle of orality clearly belongs to an age in which the speedy production of multiple copies of documents was a slow labour-intensive exercise. In the age of photocopiers and word processors, the case against written procedures is more difficult to sustain.

To save time when judgment is given, the practice has been adopted of stating the disposition of the case in open court, but of providing printed copies of the full judgments to the parties' lawyers and to the representatives of the press in court. This is a further, but eminently sensible, erosion of the principle of orality.

The current volume of appeals to the Court of Appeal from all sources is about 1630 cases a year, of which 930 will be final appeals and 700 will be interlocutory appeals. The major sources of appeals are the county courts which generate about 300 final appeals and the QBD of the High Court which generates about 400 final appeals. About one in five appeals succeeds in whole or in part (Judicial Statistics, 1988).

Appeal to the House of Lords

From the Court of Appeal

In civil cases a precondition to any appeal from the Court of Appeal to the House of Lords is the obtaining of leave from either the Court of Appeal or the Appeal Committee of the House of Lords, which consists of three Law Lords. Leave will only be granted if the appeal involves a point of law of general public importance. In those cases where no time for appealing is fixed by statute or by order of the House, the time for appealing is three months from the date the judgment of the Court of Appeal was handed down. The proper procedure is to apply first to the Court of Appeal, but if leave is refused, the application may be renewed before the Appeal Committee within one month of the refusal of leave by the Court of Appeal. The Appeal Committee will hear oral argument before deciding whether leave should be given.

The criteria which seem to be applied by both the Court of Appeal and the House of Lords in deciding whether leave should be granted are (Blom-Cooper and Drewry, 1972):

Does the case raise a point of law of general public importance?
Does the appeal appear likely to succeed?
Has the case resulted in significant differences of opinion in the courts below?

It is common for conditions to be attached to the grant of leave. The most common condition is that the appellant must bear the costs of the appeal whatever the outcome. This is almost standard in appeals by the Inland Revenue. The justification is that a respondent should not be put at further risk of costs by virtue of the Revenue's wish to have final authority on some aspect of taxation law, which will inevitably be of general application.

The use of a written procedure was pioneered in the House of Lords where each party has for some years been required to lodge a 'Case' with the court which is very similar to the skeleton arguments more recently introduced in the Court of Appeal. The Case did not appear to play an important part in the process of decision making in the House of Lords during the period under review (1957 to 1973) in Alan Paterson's book *The Law Lords*, which indicates that both counsel and the Law Lords in practice diminished the effect of the written Case in the arguing of the appeal (Paterson, 1982). A similar conclusion had been reached in an earlier study covering the period 1952 to 1968 (Blom-Cooper and Drewry, 1972). If this remains true today, it is probably because the House does not have the same pressures placed on its time as the Court of Appeal and is able to devote as much time as it wishes to oral argument.

Appeals to the House of Lords are heard by the Appellate Committee of the House, which consists of those members of the House qualified to deal with its judicial business. This should be distinguished from the Appeal Committee which considers applications for leave to appeal. Following oral argument the Law Lords inevitably take time to consider their opinions. The opinions are printed and handed down to the parties rather than being read aloud. The House has no power to implement its own decisions, which are transmitted to the trial judge to be converted into enforceable judgments or orders.

From the High Court

In some cases appeals may proceed directly from the High Court (not from county courts or tribunals of first instance) to the House of Lords. Part II of the Administration of Justice Act 1969 introduced the procedure universally known as the 'leap-frog' procedure to deal with those cases where determination by the Court of Appeal might not be the most effective way of disposing of the case. The conditions to be met before a leap-frog appeal can take place indicate the type of case the legislature had in mind. Two conditions must be met before there can be such an appeal:

1 the trial judge must grant a certificate which is only available where:
  (a) the parties consent, and
  (b) a point of law of general public importance is involved
     (i) which relates to the construction of legislation, or
     (ii) in respect of which the trial judge was bound by a decision of the Court of Appeal or House of Lords
  and which in either case was fully considered by the trial judge or in the previous decisions by which the trial judge was bound; and
2 the House of Lords must give leave on the basis that the case is one which ought to be heard by the House.

It should be noted that both the trial judge and the House of Lords have discretions. Trial judges are not required to grant certificates where the conditions are met; they simply have power to grant certificates. The restrictive conditions governing the leap-frog appeal reflect the usual caution over the introduction of innovations and the real misgivings some members of the judiciary had over the introduction of the procedure. These were that the House would be inundated with appeals relating to the interpretation of statutes and that the House would not have the benefit of the careful consideration of the case before it went up to the House (Drewry, 1973). The conclusions drawn by Drewry in 1973 remain apposite today. The use of the leap-frog appeal has been surrounded by considerable caution and the very stringent conditions to be met before such an appeal can be taken has meant that there have been very few such appeals. In 1988 there were four. A further reason for the small number of appeals is that there is only a small pool of cases involving principally the interpretation of legislation or the resolution of conflicting cases. There is also the problem of breaking with tradition; the House of Lords is accustomed to having the assistance of judgments from the Court of Appeal following full and careful consideration of detailed argument on the points of principle involved in an atmosphere which, though busy, is not quite so frenetic as that of the High Court.

It is not clear why the consent of the parties should be a precondition to leap-frog appeals, and the issue was contentious when the Bill was debated in Parliament. If it is appropriate for a case to go direct to the House of Lords it seems wrong that a litigant should be able to frustrate what appears to be a proper course. No doubt if such a condition were not written into the Act, the trial judge and the House of Lords would have regard to the significance of the adoption of the procedure for litigants and to their wishes in exercising their respective discretions to grant a certificate or leave to appeal. It seems that the absence of transcripts of evidence, argument and judgment in the county court explains why the leap-frog procedure does not apply to decisions of county courts. This is surely right, even though in cases like *Davis* v. *Johnson*, which began in the county court, situations can arise in which there is not only an important point of interpretation to be decided, but also binding decisions of the Court of Appeal to be considered. Such cases could be met by adopting for civil cases a procedure similar to the Attorney-General's reference in criminal proceedings. Such a procedure would allow the Attorney-General to refer a point of law of general public importance arising in any litigation to the Court of Appeal or House of Lords. References to the House of Lords would be available following a decision of the Court of Appeal, but could also be allowed from either the county courts or the High Court where the Attorney-General was satisfied that the criteria for the grant of a certificate under Part II of the Administration of Justice Act 1969 were met. To grant a power to make references on points arising other than in connection with litigation would present difficulties in the selection of points for reference. Furthermore the judges have never relished answering hypothetical points.

The Case Load

The House of Lords is not overworked. The number of civil appeals is small. In 1988 there were 144 petitions for leave to appeal in civil cases. Six were withdrawn, 100 were refused and 30 were allowed. In the same year 78 appeals were determined including four leap-frog appeals. In 34 cases the House affirmed the decision of the Court of Appeal, while in 19 cases the decision of the court below was reversed (Judicial Statistics, 1988). It is fair to say that 1988 was a typical year for the House of Lords.

The Functions of Civil Appeal Courts

The Impact of the Doctrine of Precedent

The doctrine of precedent ensures that decisions of the Court of Appeal and House of Lords are of the greatest importance for lawyers and litigants alike. The doctrine of precedent requires that trial judges follow decisions of the Court of Appeal and House of Lords. The Court of Appeal itself is, subject to limited exceptions, bound by its own previous decisions and is always bound by decisions of the House of Lords. The House of Lords is, as we shall see, no longer bound by its own previous decisions and enjoys a unique power to reshape legal principles established by an accumulation of case law. With his tongue firmly in his cheek, Mr Justice Murphy, the colourful judge of the High Court of Australia (roughly the equivalent of our Court of Appeal), has described the doctrine of precedent as follows:

> Then there is the doctrine of precedent, one of my favourite doctrines. I have managed to apply it at least once a year since I've been on the Bench. The doctrine is that whenever you are faced with a decision, you always follow what the last person who was faced with the same decision did. It is a doctrine eminently suitable for a nation overwhelmingly populated by sheep. As the distinguished chemist, Cornford, said: 'The doctrine is based on the theory that nothing should ever be done for the first time.'

To state that trial judges are bound by decisions of the Court of Appeal and House of Lords seems remarkably straightforward, but the multiple judgments of the Court of Appeal and of the House of Lords immediately make the issue more complex. The solution has been to separate the propositions made in judgments into two categories: those of binding authority and those of persuasive authority. Indeed some propositions falling into the second category are of such little weight as to amount to virtually no authority at all, while others are so significant as to be more important than those apparently of binding authority. Only that part of the judgment classified as binding authority is required to be followed in a similar later case. The key to unlocking the secret of the system of precedent is the ability to unravel lengthy individual judgments in order to identify the key propositions of law relevant to the essential facts of the litigation. This will reveal the reason for the decision, known among lawyers as the 'ratio decidendi' (reason for deciding) of the case. This is the binding authority of the decision. Unravelling cases is not, as some commentators have suggested, a formalistic process. It is rather one which results from the process of 'legal reading', that is, the reading of the text against the background of 'the legal reader's access to a store of specifically legal relevant contexts' (Davies, 1987).

Attempts have been made to offer formulae for determining the ratio decidendi of cases, but few have proved to be really satisfactory. Too much emphasis on the search for the ratio decidendi of cases can be misleading. Though it is the ratio that will be binding, the significance of other statements (*obiter dicta*) which have only persuasive authority may be considerable. For example, faced with the ratio of a two to one majority decision in the Court of Appeal as against dicta of three judges in the House of Lords agreeing with the dissent in the Court of Appeal and casting doubt on the correctness of the majority opinion, but not expressly overruling it, it is clear that the Court of Appeal must follow the dicta of the House of Lords rather than the ratio of their earlier decision, so paradoxically preferring the persuasive to the binding authority. Courts also avoid the slavish copying of earlier decisions by the technique of distinguishing cases. The judge in the later case finds some relevant fact in that case of sufficient importance to justify a different approach from that adopted in the first decision.

The use of cases as precedents therefore involves an evaluation of the weight of propositions, both of binding and of persuasive authority, and of their application to the facts of the instant dispute. In evaluating the weight of propositions, the following factors will be relevant:

1 Greater weight is given to propositions by judges of courts higher in the hierarchy of courts.
2 Greater weight is given to propositions contained in judgments where the judges took time to consider their judgments. This is indicated in the law reports by the abbreviation *cur. adv. vult* (*curia advisari vult* which translates 'the court wishes to be advised') at the end of the judgments. Judgments in the House of Lords are always reserved, but in the much busier Court of Appeal many judgments are delivered extemporaneously after very brief deliberations.
3 Greater weight is given to propositions which have been repeated by judges in a number of cases.
4 Greater weight is given to propositions in cases where the decision was unanimous.
5 Greater weight is generally given to propositions which have stood the test of time.
6 Greater weight is given to propositions which appear to be broadly consistent with the general law governing the area in which the proposition arises.
7 Greater weight will usually be given to propositions which have met with general approval among lawyers and commentators. But if, for example, the Law Commission in a law reform proposal has suggested that a proposition is ripe for alteration by statute, that would seriously erode the importance of the proposition.

The doctrine of precedent depends upon courts lower in the hierarchy respecting the authority of previous cases. As an intermediate appellate court the Court of Appeal is bound by its own previous decisions and by decisions of the House of Lords. It now seems clearly established that the Court of Appeal may only depart from one of its own previous decisions in four circumstances. The first three exceptions were spelled out by a six judge Court of Appeal in *Young* v. *Bristol Aeroplane Co. Ltd* ([1944] KB 718):

1 When faced with two conflicting decisions of its own, the Court of Appeal is entitled and bound to decide which it will follow.
2 The Court of Appeal is bound to refuse to follow a previous decision of its own which, even though not expressly overruled, cannot in its opinion stand with a subsequent decision of the House of Lords.
3 The Court of Appeal is not bound to follow a decision of its own if it is satisfied that the decision was given *per incuriam*. A decision is given *per incuriam* if it appears to have been made in ignorance of relevant statutory provisions or binding case law (*Morelle* v. *Wakeling*, [1955] 2 QB 379).
4 The Court of Appeal is not bound to follow an interlocutory decision made by two judges of the Court of Appeal which it considers to be wrong (*Boys* v. *Chaplin*, [1968] 2 QB 1).

Once cases disposed of by two judges under the new rules for the determination of final appeals become common, there will, no doubt, be an attempt to extend the decision in *Boys* v. *Chaplin* to such cases, though that will require reconsideration of the current view that the weight of authority in the Court of Appeal does not depend on the number of judges hearing the appeal.

Lord Denning as Master of the Rolls fought long and hard to persuade his colleagues that the Court of Appeal should free itself from the fetter of being bound by its own previous decisions just as the House of Lords had done in the 1966 *Practice Statement* (see below), and also suggested that the Court of Appeal was free to refuse to follow decisions of the House of Lords which were considered to be clearly wrong (Carty, 1983). Lord Denning and the few colleagues agreeing with him met with little success in either case. In *Cassell* v. *Broome* ([1972] AC 1027) and *Miliangos* v. *George Frank (Textiles) Ltd* ([1976] AC 443) the House of Lords made it clear that the Court of Appeal is bound by decisions of the House of Lords whatever its views as to the correctness of those decisions. Lord Denning's views on the liberation of the Court of Appeal from the obligation to follow its own previous decisions were crushingly rebuffed in *Davis* v *Johnson* ([1979] AC 264) in which the authority of *Young* v. *Bristol Aeroplane Co Ltd* was re-affirmed. With the retirement of Lord Denning, it seems that the issue has been laid to rest for some time, since his successor, Lord Donaldson, and most of the current Lords Justices of Appeal do not appear to share the views of the former Master of the Rolls.

Until 1966 the House of Lords was also bound by its own previous decisions having so decided in *London Street Tramways* v. *London County Council* ([1898] AC 375). But in 1966 the Lord Chancellor, Lord Gardiner, with the concurrence of the Law Lords, announced that in future the House would regard itself as free to 'depart from a previous decision when it appears right to do so'.

A principal justification for the change was said to be that it unduly restricted the proper development of the law (*Practice Statement*, (*Judicial Precedent*), [1966] 1 WLR 1234). The decision to change the rules of precedent in the House of Lords was not a sudden one. By 1960 the judicial approach in the House of Lords, which has been summed up by Alan Paterson as 'be fair, be consistent, don't legislate', was beginning to be seen as too restrictive and the potential conflicts between the requirements of fairness, consistency and creativity were being recognized. By a process described by Paterson as 'Dissimulation', the Law Lords began to violate one of the three expectations of judicial activity necessary to do justice in individual cases while, nevertheless, appearing to uphold all three expectations. The years 1962 to 1966 immediately prior to the issuing of the Practice Statement were marked by considerable judicial creativity (Paterson, 1982).

It was always envisaged that the House of Lords would use the freedom to depart from its own previous decisions sparingly, but in the years following the Practice Statement the potential impact of the new freedom was narrowed by the addition of a series of riders. The effect of these riders was to stress the need for certainty in decision making. Thus it was considered inappropriate to overrule a previous decision if:

> this would defeat the legitimate expectations of those who had acted in some way in reliance on the old authority; or
>
> this would change the interpretation to be given to particular statutory provisions; or
>
> the House could not foresee all the consequences of the change proposed; or
>
> the whole area of law in which the question arose is in need of comprehensive reform.

The main types of case appropriate for the application of the Practice Statement appear to be those which will rectify some uncertainty which has arisen in the case law or which are outmoded or unjust in relation to some broad issue of principle. The sparing use of the Practice Statement is confirmed by the statistics: the use of the Statement was made 39 times between 1966 and the end of 1989, but in only 12 cases has it been applied to overrule a previous decision. The main importance of the change of practice in 1966 is that it allowed the Law Lords to accept an innovatory role and to avoid the practice of 'Dissimulation'. The removal of the shackles of the doctrine of precedent also confirms the special role of the House of Lords as a court of supervision.

Do we Need Two Levels of Appeal Court?

The distinction between supervision and review and the discussion of the differing roles of the Court of Appeal and House of Lords provide part of the answer to this question. But the small case load of the House of Lords and the expense of bringing a second appeal have produced suggestions that there is no need for the second appeal if the Court of Appeal were to be free to reconsider its own previous decisions. In considering the merits of such suggestions, it is important to realize that the House of Lords is also the final appeal court for cases originating in Scotland and Northern Ireland which have their own legal systems. Without the House of Lords there would be no institutional link between these legal systems in which there is considerable overlap of legal rules. Blom-Cooper and Drewry concluded that there was a role for the House of Lords and argued that the House of Lords was neither unfitted to retain its present judicial role nor prohibitively expensive to use. Such conclusions are surely right. Once the distinction between review and supervision is grasped, there is surely sense in having a special type of final appeal for cases involving issues of supervision, which allows more leisurely consideration of the issues than is possible in the Court of Appeal. Though the Court of Appeal is also a court of supervision, it appears to be too busy to be able to devote as much time and thought as is needed to such cases. But what is also clear is that it is unfair to litigants that they should meet the cost of a second appeal, one of the principal purposes of which is to resolve issues of law of general public importance. Such issues should, as currently occurs in most tax cases, always be litigated at the public expense. The discretionary nature of the grant of leave to appeal to the House of Lords avoids any suggestion that there might be abuse of such an approach.

Are the Judges Fitted for the Task of Making Law?

It will be clear from the description of the functions of the Court of Appeal and House of Lords that they make law to meet the needs of cases arising before them and lay down guidelines for judges in courts below. Even in cases involving the interpretation of legislation the judges' choices between competing or differential readings of the words of the statutory material involve judicial creativity or innovation. The doctrine of precedent restrains tribunals and the trial judges in the county courts and in the High Court from digressing into frolics of legal innovation, but even the trial judge will be presented from time to time with issues upon which there are no binding precedents. After all every great House of Lords decision, which does not involve a departure from precedent, began with the presentation of issues at first instance. So to a limited extent all judges are involved in the process of supervision and the gradual accretion of legal rules by layer upon layer of precedent. All judges face choices in the process of adjudication. Nevertheless the overwhelming majority of trials turn on the establishment of facts and the matching of those facts to well settled legal rules. Simon Lee has argued that judges' creativity ought to vary according to four factors:

1 Does the case involve statutes or common law (the latter allowing more freedom)?
2 Where is the judge in the courts' hierarchy (the higher up, the more creativity is suitable)?
3 Is the subject matter such that creativity or justice is more important?

4 What is the likelihood of other institutions of government correcting any injustice? (Lee, 1988, p. 202)

Given the greater creative role of the judges in the appellate courts, it is appropriate to question whether they are fitted for the task of supervision. Today appellate judges, apart from the Lord Chancellor, are in practice recruited exclusively from among the best High Court judges, who after serving the Court of Appeal may be elevated to the House of Lords. This is a quite extraordinarily narrow group within the legal profession. Until the passing of the Courts and Legal Services Act 1990, only barristers could become High Court judges. Not only will the years at the Bar have moulded the barrister, but 'judicial qualities' will have been noted under the Lord Chancellor's system for recording the progress of barristers. Dossiers on barristers, known as 'yellow sheets' (actually pink cards), are kept by the Lord Chancellor's Department which record the progress of the barrister and judges will pass on comments, both favourable and unfavourable, about barristers appearing before them. By the time a barrister is considered for judicial appointment, the dossier will contain considerable information about him or her. In addition there will be discreet enquiries about the barrister's personal life. Finally there will be an interview with the Lord Chancellor. No applications are invited for High Court judgeships, though they are for Circuit judgeships (Shetreet, 1976; Lord Chancellor's Department, 1990). This system of selection for elevation to the High Court bench and for promotion to the Court of Appeal and House of Lords results in the character of the judiciary seeming to be self-perpetuating.

The system secures a marked uniformity among the puisne judges and consequently among the appellate judges. It would also seem to discriminate against women and ethnic minorities (Cohen, 1982a). The time spent on the High Court bench will also impose its further stamp upon the potential appellate judge. The typical appellate judge will be at least 60 years of age, white, male and educated at public school and at Oxford or Cambridge and have lived in the insular world of the Bar for more than 30 years. There is clearly much scope and a very strong case for broadening the representation of the legal profession, both practising and academic, on the appellate bench. Where issues of supervision are involved, the necessity for practice at the Bar as a qualification for office is much harder to sustain than in relation to trials and appeals involving review.

Against this background, it is hardly surprising to find assertions made that judges consistently support 'the conventional established and settled interests' and that this role of preserving stability is in conflict with the role of the judiciary as protectors of the liberties of the individual (Griffith, 1987). Professor Griffith's book *The Politics of the Judiciary* first published in 1977 caused a considerable stir in documenting such assertions with many examples. On judicial creativity Professor Griffith was worried that judges' emotional and personal prejudices became, perhaps unconsciously, a part of their decision-making process, and therefore lacked impartiality. The perceived need to ensure stability in society took precedence over fairness and justice. But no recipe for remedying the perceived deficiency was offered.

In an article responding to the gauntlet hurled down by Professor Griffith, Lord Devlin does not deny the homogeneity of attitudes of the appellate judges, but goes on to argue that this is probably inevitable. Lord Devlin concludes:

> To my mind none of the evidence, general or specific adds much to the inherent probability that men and women of a certain age will be inclined by nature to favour the status quo. Is it displeasing to the public at large that the guardians of the law should share this common tendency? (Devlin, 1978, p. 509)

But in the context of a consideration of judicial creativity, or perhaps lack of it, the selection of the judiciary and their 'politics' in the sense used by Professor Griffith seem to be marginal considerations. Even in the United States' Supreme Court with its overtly political processes of appointment, it seems that, in deciding landmark cases embodying sweeping reforms of the law, the justices do not always fully appreciate the significance and social consequences of their decisions (Horowitz, 1977). This is despite, in addition to the special process of appointment, the presentation of elaborate written briefs and in appropriate cases 'Brandeis briefs' containing detailed economic and social data pertinent to the issue being litigated.

In the English appellate courts it may be true to say that change that can be based on reasoning by analogy and the evolutionary development of legal rules is the most that can be expected, and that major changes of direction require legislation which, to overcome the bias of judges in favour of the *status quo*, must be unequivocally expressed. While permitting a degree of creativity, the doctrine of precedent, even in the House of Lords, operates to limit the changes in the law which the judges are willing to make. The judges can develop the law, but major exercises in 'judicial legislation' are not perceived as appropriate. Indeed if there is any validity in the argument that the narrow background and insularity of judges renders them unfitted to make decisions with significant broad social consequences, there is some merit in a system which limits their ability to change the law and reserves such questions for full consideration by a democratically elected legislature. But there is scope for innovation and change both in the composition and procedures of appellate courts (Bell, 1983). The greater use of written procedures has been mentioned. Other possibilities are the use of a broader range of *amicus curiae* briefs in cases involving issues of supervision. For too long the modernization of the appellate courts has been geared towards the management of case loads rather than with equipping the appellate judges better for the task of the development of legal rules.

Part IV

The Delivery of Legal Services

15

The Legal Profession

Introduction

Growth and Problems

After a period of modest growth in the 1950s, both branches of the legal profession in England and Wales experienced major growth in the 1960s and 1970s. In 1963 there were approximately 20,000 solicitors and 2000 barristers. By 1989, this had grown to about 55,000 solicitors and 5000 barristers.

Growth in the size of the legal profession occurred during the time when consumer movements were coming of age. It became fashionable and acceptable to criticize the delivery of professional services. The legal profession was not immune from this trend, particularly in relation to the perceived poor performance and high cost of conveyancing work (Joseph, 1980). It was argued that across a range of services, costs were too high, the service to the client was poor and that the legal profession was failing to meet the needs of all sections of the community. The ground swell of concern continued at a sufficient level that the issue could not be ignored. The Labour Government of the day responded by establishing in 1976 the Royal Commission on Legal Services (Benson Commission, 1979) with wide terms of reference. It was to examine the structure, organization, training and regulation of the legal profession and to recommend those changes that would be desirable in the interests of justice.

Over the years Royal Commissions have been noted for the lack of impact made by their recommendations, but there can be no doubt that the profession was frightened by the Benson Commission. They feared structural change and the loss of monopolies on property transfer work, in probate and in the conduct of litigation. In particular, the threat to conveyancing work was viewed as undermining the main fee earning activity of many practices. It was a source of great satisfaction to both branches of the profession when the Benson Commission's Report in 1979 did not propose any radical change, though the Report was generally unpopular with other commentators. One editorial described it as 'characterised by an over-anxiety not to offend the professional establishment'.

The Benson Commission's Concept of a Profession

What is clear to anyone reading the report is that the Benson Commission accepted that the practice of law was a professional activity and that professions display a number of common characteristics:

> the existence of a central organization or governing body representing the profession and having powers of control and discipline over its members;
> the function of giving specialist advice and services in a specialized field of knowledge;
> entry and training are controlled by the profession itself and are dependent on a formalized system of education and training;
> the activity is self-regulated, enabling the requirement of high standards in relations with clients, usually higher than that imposed by the general law;
> the first and paramount responsibility of the members of the profession is to act in the best interests of their clients.

The existence of these characteristics required the independence of the profession from interference by government. Without independence, the interests of the client cannot be a first and paramount consideration. The self-regulation of the profession and the high standards demanded of its members are said to be the justification for the monopolies enjoyed by those engaging in the activity and by the restrictive practices permitted.

The Calm Before the Storm

The period of calm and stability which followed the publication of the Report of the Benson Commission was short lived. Perhaps the profession became too complacent about their privileged position, but three events can be identified as catalysts for the current period of dramatic change.

The first event was the scandal which has come to be known as the Glanville Davies affair. The failure of the Law Society to act effectively in dealing with complaints against a solicitor and respected member of the Council of The Law Society, Mr Glanville Davies, attracted enormous publicity and led to a complete breakdown of public confidence in the Law Society's ability to regulate professional conduct. Mr Davies did not contest an application by the aggrieved client, Mr Parsons, that he should be struck off the roll of solicitors following the reduction on taxation of a grossly inflated and inaccurate litigation bill from £197,000 to £67,000. The litigation and the subsequent enquiries by the Lay Observer and by the Law Society (known as 'the Ely Report') revealed an appalling catalogue of errors, insensitivity and lack of sound judgment (Lay Observer, 1984; Law Society, 1984). Despite radical revision of the complaints procedures, there remains dissatisfaction about the handling of complaints similar to those concerning police complaints procedures considered earlier in this book (Newbold and Zellick, 1987).

The second event was the ending of the conveyancing monopoly. In 1983

Austin Mitchell introduced a Private Member's Bill proposing the establishment of licensed conveyancers able to undertake residential conveyancing in competition with solicitors. This Bill failed but the Government undertook to introduce its own legislation on conveyancing in the Parliamentary session 1984–5 with the same objective. The Government honoured its undertaking and included the extension of the conveyancing monopoly to licensed conveyancers in the Administration of Justice Act 1985. The effect of this change has not been as dramatic as had been feared. Conveyancing work has become more competitive, but solicitors have not lost substantial amounts of work to the modest number of licensed conveyancers who have set up in practice. Much more fear has been engendered by the proposal that banks and building societies be allowed to offer conveyancing services. Such bodies have a very large, almost captive, clientele since many of those buying houses will go first to the bank or building society to arrange to borrow the money to buy the house.

The third event was the liberalization of the restrictions on advertising, which had previously permitted only institutional advertising such as the 'See a Solicitor' series of leaflets. The removal of restrictions was, in part, a reaction to the threat of competition from licensed conveyancers. From a position where individual advertising was considered inconsistent with the professional image of solicitors and where there were rules determining the size and style even of the name of the practice on its premises, The Law Society moved speedily to a virtually deregulated advertising regime. The sole remaining restraint is the requirement that the advertising must not impair the solicitor's independence and integrity and must not bring the profession into disrepute. Sending brochures and leaflets to clients, and advertising in local newspapers and some specialist journals are now common, though larger well-established firms seem to do less advertising than smaller and newer practices. Many solicitors still obtain business through 'networking', that is, establishing a network of friends and business contacts likely to refer business to the solicitor. It is common for solicitors to build cordial relationships with estate agents, building societies and even with the custody officer at the police station, in order to secure referrals. Solicitors also participate in social activities likely to get them and their firms known to potential clients. In 1967 Abel-Smith and Stevens asserted that 'solicitors tend to be active members of rotary clubs, golf clubs, rugby football clubs and to become freemasons and leading churchmen' (Abel-Smith and Stevens, 1967, pp. 142–3). More recent empirical research tends to confirm this assertion (Podmore, 1980).

These three events also coincided with a period when the character of legal work was changing. The 1980s saw an explosion in corporate, commercial and financial services work on such a scale that there is currently a shortage of lawyers, despite the admission of record numbers of new entrants to the profession in recent years (The Law Society 1990).

There is no doubt that the professions are today under attack. Privileges and self-regulation are no longer accepted as necessary corollaries of professional status. For some, the chill wind of competition is again blowing through their offices. The abolition of many remaining monopolies and restrictive practices is again on the political agenda.

The Great Reform of the Legal Profession

The great reform of the legal profession is the result of three major enquiries into the legal profession within a decade. The first is the Royal Commission on Legal Services (Benson Commission, 1979), which has already been mentioned. The second is the joint committee set up by the General Council of the Bar and The Law Society, chaired by Lady Marre, which reported in July 1988 (Marre Committee, 1988). The third and by far the most important is the trio of Green Papers (Cm 570, 571 and 572) issued by The Lord Chancellor in January 1989 followed by a White Paper (Cm 740) in June 1990 and culminating in the Courts and Legal Services Act 1990.

The Benson Commission

The Royal Commission on Legal Services, which was chaired by a lay person and had a majority of lay members, devoted three years to its study of legal services. It took voluminous evidence, undertook its own research studies, and engaged in lengthy consultation and deliberation. The Report published in 1979 runs to four volumes. There is much of value in the Report and implementation of many of its recommendations would undoubtedly have resulted in improvements in the system for delivering legal services.

The Benson Commission's unpopularity with commentators (though not with lawyers) is based on its recommendations that the *status quo* be retained in three areas seen by the profession as crucial: the retention by barristers of a monopoly on rights of audience in the higher courts, the retention by solicitors of the monopoly on conveyancing work and the division of the profession into solicitors and barristers. In 1983 the Government accepted the Report, though it has never been debated in Parliament. The Government indicated that implementation of a number of recommendations was subject to resources becoming available or would need to await an appropriate legislative opportunity.

The Marre Committee

When solicitors lost the conveyancing monopoly with the enactment of the Administration of Justice Act 1985, they turned their attention to the advocacy monopoly enjoyed by barristers in the higher courts. The absurdity of the monopoly was brought to public attention when Cyril Smith MP's solicitor sought the leave of the High Court to read out an agreed statement in settlement of a libel action, because he considered the fee proposed by counsel for doing this to be 'unnecessarily expensive'. Leave was refused at first instance and in the Court of Appeal, though a few months later a *Practice Direction* ([1986] 2 All ER 226) was issued indicating the collective view of the judges that solicitors should be permitted to appear in the High Court or Court of Appeal in formal or unopposed proceedings.

There followed a public and acrimonious debate between representatives of solicitors and barristers on the issue of rights of audience. The General Council of the Bar responded by proposing a joint committee with The Law Society to consider the future of the legal profession. The Marre Committee was born, but its report was a great disappointment. Its deliberations had been hurried, its request for evidence stressed the need for a brevity viewed by many as excessive and it lacked sufficient resources to produce a credible alternative to any Government proposals. The credibility of the final report was further damaged by the Note of Dissent attached by the barrister members and some independent members on the proposed extension of rights of audience.

The Marre Committee concluded that unless the professions themselves initiated change, it would be forced upon them. Commercial considerations should not alone determine the future supply of legal services and the profession should retain only those rules which are 'essential for the maintenance of professional standards in the public interest'. The biggest area of unmet need was identified as the provision of social welfare law, particularly in rural districts, in parts of London and in the urban conurbations of the Midlands and the north of England. Realism was needed in providing new services because of resource constraints. Informational and education initiatives were encouraged.

On legal aid, the Committee essentially recommends the *status quo*, but does recommend the extension of legal aid to tribunal proceedings. Law centres and other advice agencies should receive funding from the Legal Aid Board, but the idea of a national legal service and of a public defender system were disapproved. The controversial part of the report related to rights of audience, where the majority recommended the creation of a Rights of Audience Advisory Board which would recommend to The Law Society the licensing of suitably qualified solicitors to act as advocates in the Crown Court. Employed lawyers should also be entitled to rights of audience in the courts.

Lord Mackay's Proposals

In January 1989 Lord Mackay issued three Green Papers: *The Work and Organisation of the Legal Profession (Cm 570)*; *Conveyancing by Authorised Practitioners (Cm 572)* and *Contingency Fees (Cm 571)*. The Green Papers are short, sharp and to the point. They seem to depend more on policy preferences than research and to reflect the Government's preference for action not words, for speedy response rather than lengthy debate, and perhaps also a deep disregard for the theoretical overview. Notions of 'value for money', 'efficiency' and 'market forces' are firmly embedded in these reports. They state that the Government believes that free competition between the providers of legal services will, through the discipline of the market, ensure that the public is provided with the most efficient and effective network of legal services at the most economical price. The mood of deregulation is tempered only by reference to the need to assure the public of the competence of providers of legal services.

The debate which the Green Papers generated has been fully chronicled elsewhere (Cownie, 1990; Donaldson, 1990b), but the response to the proposal that rights of audience should in future depend on certificates of competence in advocacy rather than membership of a particular branch of the profession met a predictably hostile response from the Bar and a response verging on the intemperate from the judges. The subsequent White Paper, *Legal Services: A Framework for the Future (Cm 740)*, adopted a different tone, referring rather more to the requirement for legal services to be responsive to clients' needs than to notions of competition and the discipline of the market; but in content the proposals actually gave little ground on key points.

Extended rights of audience are to be permitted, both for present advocates in more courts and for new classes of advocates. For certain classes of work (small claims, debt cases and housing cases in the county courts) there will be no restrictions at all on rights of audience; the only control will be the court's discretion to restrict the involvement of unruly or corrupt representatives. The Government believes that it is for the professional bodies and other organizations whose members provide legal services to satisfy the courts and the public that their members are competent to undertake representation. Professional bodies will produce rules of conduct for such activity having regard to advice from an Advisory Committee to be set up by the Lord Chancellor.

The concession to the Bar is that any person called to the Bar will have rights of audience in all courts on completion of pupillage, dependent only on their compliance with rules of conduct made by the Bar. Once the new Act is in force, any change to the rules relating to education training and conduct will be subject to the concurrence of the Lord Chancellor, Lord Chief Justice, Master of the Rolls, President of the Family Division and Vice-Chancellor, who will act having regard to advice received from a new Advisory Committee on Legal Education and Conduct.

The Law Society becomes a recognizing authority under the new scheme and so will be able to recognize a solicitor as qualified as an advocate in a particular court or courts, again subject to rules on education, training and conduct which will parallel the arrangements for the Bar. Again there will be no loss of existing rights of audience; solicitors will be recognized as having competence to be advocates in the lower courts. The gain for The Law Society is that they will be able to certificate solicitors who have undertaken further training entitling them to rights of audience in the higher courts. This in turn opens the way to appointment to the High Court bench for solicitors.

The new Act removes the monopoly on starting and conducting litigation. The Government considers that this unnecessarily hinders the ways in which the provision of legal services might develop. Anyone suitably qualified will be permitted to undertake this work. The Government will licence authorizing bodies which may include bodies other than The Law Society and the General Council of the Bar.

The Advisory Committee on Legal Education and Conduct will play a central role in the revised arrangements for supervising legal education and ensuring satisfactory standards of conduct by those entitled to undertake legal services. The functions of the Advisory Committee will be to advise on questions that arise as to what qualifications are necessary for providing legal services connected with litigation and what requirements are necessary to ensure proper standards of conduct. An annual report will be presented to the Lord Chancellor and will be laid before Parliament. Professional bodies are to be placed under a statutory duty to have regard to advice from the Advisory Committee in preparing rules of competence and conduct for their own members.

The Courts and Legal Services Act 1990

The proposals which require legislative change for their implementation have been included in Part II of the Courts and Legal Services Act 1990 (White, Robin, 1991). This lays down a general statutory objective of making provision for new or better ways of providing legal services and a wider choice of person providing them, while maintaining the proper and efficient administration of justice. The Advisory Committee on Legal Education and Conduct is established. Chaired by a judge of the High Court or a higher court, it has 16 members, a majority of whom must be persons other than practising or academic lawyers. The system of advocacy licensing is also detailed in the Act. There are a multitude of other very significant changes on specific matters relating to monopolies and styles of practice. But these do not impact dramatically on the overall work of the profession.

The Organization of the Profession

A Divided Profession

The legal profession in England and Wales is divided into solicitors and barristers, with the latter being considered the senior branch of the profession. The solicitor gives advice and has the conduct of the business of the client from day to day and will retain a barrister to carry out a specific task in handling the client's business. Solicitors (subject to very limited exceptions) alone have the right to brief counsel, who will be called in as the occasion demands to give specialist advice, to draft documents or to act as advocate in the higher courts. The barrister is currently alone entitled to act as advocate in the higher courts. Each branch of the profession has its own system of entry and training, its own governing body and its own rules of conduct and discipline.

The distinction between the two branches of the profession is an artificial one. There are, in fact, no tasks exclusive to one branch. Solicitors regularly appear as advocates in the lower courts and, by special fiat of the Lord Chancellor, in some Crown Courts which are geographically remote from barristers' chambers. Equally, there are many barristers who very seldom appear in court, spending virtually all their time on written opinions on the law. Over the years there has been much debate on the fusion of the two branches of the profession.

The issue of fusion was considered by the Royal Commission which unanimously concluded that the legal profession should continue to be divided. Advocates of fusion, who represented a minority among those who submitted evidence to the Royal Commission, criticized the divided profession on a number of grounds: duplication, inefficiency, delay, and inaccessibility. Duplication of effort arises because convention demands the involvement of both solicitor and barrister where only one need be involved. Barristers do not appear in court alone; the solicitor, or a representative of the practice, must also be present. Clients must consult solicitors even if their only need is for an opinion from counsel. No convincing answer has been given to this criticism; all that is offered is the general argument in favour of a specialized division of the profession which is free from hour to hour to engage in advocacy and other specialist work.

Inefficiency obviously arises because of the necessity to reduce everything to written instructions. Conferences at an early stage are only common in major litigation. Very frequently counsel will only begin to prepare on the night before the case is to be heard and will only meet with the client on the morning of the hearing. If the brief has been badly prepared, there cannot be effective representation. Nor does the system guarantee that the barrister of the solicitor's choice will be able to take the case and in minor cases, last minute changes of barrister are fairly common. The Royal Commission's response to this criticism was to note that fusion might not improve matters and to suggest that a more detailed set of standards should be prepared for both solicitors and barristers on the preparation and handling of briefs. The argument in favour of a divided profession which found favour with the Royal Commission was that the existence of a separate branch of the profession ensured that there was a body of specialist advocates available to all solicitors, which would be dispersed if the two branches were fused.

There is some merit in the Royal Commission's reasoning, but it does not seem to warrant so total a separation of the two branches of the profession as exists currently. Ultimately the issue may not be that important, because the impact of fusion for clients may well be minimal. In order to allow time for attendance in court to represent the client, office administration probably demands that there be separation of preparation and advocacy. Furthermore even in a fused profession, the barristers in chambers in the Inns of Court and elsewhere would undoubtedly enter into partnership as specialist trial advocates and do agency work for other solicitors, whose own staff were unable to act as advocates in every case or where the complexity of the case justified bringing in a specialist advocate. On the other hand, there would be much greater flexibility for clients and lawyers, and much more control by the instructing client who would have direct access to the advocate in the case. No party would be able to shelter behind the barriers inevitably created by the divided profession.

Often ill-informed and repetitive, the debate has tended to ignore the interests of the client and has frequently been conducted by those whose minds are already made up on the issue. Increasingly, the distinction is being blurred and fusion will eventually arrive in some form. The provisions on advocacy rights in the Courts and Legal Services Act 1990 provide a further blurring of the distinction.

Solicitors

Solicitors are increasingly becoming the dominant branch of the profession despite the historical recognition that they are the junior part of the legal profession. Solicitors are governed by The Law Society, established by Royal Charter in 1831, which also acts as the main professional association of solicitors. The Law Society acts through its Council which is composed of 70 solicitors, 56 of whom are elected by members of the Society with the remaining 14 being elected by the Council itself. There are also 121 autonomous local law societies, which have an important role to play in the formulation of policy by The Law Society.

Admission to practice requires the completion of three stages of training: the academic stage, the vocational stage and the apprenticeship. The academic stage of training is satisfied by completion of a qualifying law degree containing the six core subjects or by passing the Common Professional Examination. The six core subjects are Constitutional and Administrative Law, Contract, Tort, Criminal Law, Land Law, and Equity and Trusts. The second stage of training is the Solicitors Final Examination taken after a further year of study at one of the professional schools. This is known as the vocational stage of training, which is designed to provide a bridge between the academic stage of training and what might be labelled the clinical stage of training in articles.

Though the subjects available as part of law degree courses have increased enormously in range in recent years, the balance of courses offered is still weighted considerably in favour of 'practical' subjects reflecting traditional private law concepts of property rather than the 'new property' in the many entitlements deriving from the public law that regulates the welfare state (Abel, 1982; Zander, 1978).

The final stage is two years' apprenticeship to an established solicitor, known as articles of clerkship, which can be regarded as the clinical stage of training during which the skills of managing an office, interviewing clients, writing letters, instructing counsel and handling client money are learned. Articled clerks, recently renamed trainee solicitors, are paid salaries, which have in recent years become increasingly attractive. The salary will naturally depend on the size and range of work of the practice in which the trainee solicitor is articled, but The Law Society sets down recommended minimum salaries and can refuse to register articles where the salary is less than this figure. On satisfactory completion of the period of apprenticeship, trainee solicitors are entitled to be formally admitted as solicitors and to describe themselves as such. They may not set up in practice on their own account for a further three years.

Once admitted, the solicitor is required to maintain a practising certificate, for which a substantial annual fee is charged. The solicitor must also contribute to the compensation fund, which makes good any losses suffered by clients when a dishonest solicitor makes off with their money. All solicitors other than employed solicitors are also required to take out compulsory professional indemnity insurance as a condition of the grant of the annual practising certificate.

Barristers

The barristers' governing bodies are more complex than those of solicitors. They are the barrister's own Inn of Court, the Senate of the Inns of Court and the General Council of the Bar, often known simply as the Bar Council. In order to become a barrister it is necessary to become a member of one of the Inns of

Court: the Inner Temple, the Middle Temple, Lincoln's Inn or Gray's Inn. Each Inn is governed by benchers appointed by existing benchers. The Inns are very powerful and wealthy institutions which rent chambers (offices) for the large majority of London barristers. There is also a collegiality within each Inn which maintains for the members dining and library facilities and, some would argue, a retreat from the real world.

The Senate of the Inns of Court consists of 101 barristers (some of whom will be judges) representing the profession of barrister; some are appointed by the benchers of each Inn, some are *ex officio* members like the leaders from each of the six circuits, and some are elected by members of the Bar. The Senate's powers are essentially supervisory and policy making, enabling the four Inns to speak with one voice on matters of common interest.

Though admission to the Bar is still largely the domain of the individual Inns, the formal education of the trainee barrister is centralized through the Inns of Court School of Law run by the Council of Legal Education, which is a committee of Senate. The other governing body for barristers is the Bar Council whose membership derives much less from the Inns; it is the barristers' elected representative body. The Bar Council is responsible for the maintenance of professional standards and represents the general interests of the Bar in its relations with outsiders. There is considerable overlap in membership of the Senate and Bar Council. The establishment of the Senate does not yet appear to have resulted in any discernible shift of power away from the individual Inns (Hazell, 1978; Benson Commission, 1979).

The training of barristers can, like that of solicitors, be divided into the same three stages: academic, vocational and apprenticeship. The requirements of the academic stage are common to both branches of the profession. The vocational stage for the barrister consists of a year at the Inns of Court Law School followed by Bar Finals. Success in Bar Finals entitles the candidate to admission to the Bar, known as call to the Bar provided that they have completed the quaint requirement of eating the necessary number of dinners in their Inn. Following call, candidates can call themselves barristers but may not yet practise as such. A one year period of apprenticeship to an established barrister must be undertaken. In marked distinction to the solicitors' branch of the profession, the pupil barrister may not earn any money during the first six months of pupillage and there are only limited opportunities for earning in the second six months of pupillage. This places financial constraints on qualification as a barrister which do not exist for intending solicitors. The award of bursaries and scholarships can mitigate the difficulties the system causes and very recently the Bar has taken on board the need to change the system so that the equivalent of salaries can be offered during pupillage.

Barristers are all sole practitioners, though they work in sets of offices (called sets of chambers) in groups of between 12 and 20 sharing central services notably of a clerk but also secretarial and other services. Each set of chambers is required to have at least one clerk, who performs the functions of office administrator and accountant, business manager and agent. Work coming in from solicitors is allocated among members of the chambers by the clerk, who also negotiates the fee for the brief. The clerk therefore has some control over the flow of work for each barrister in the chambers. A senior clerk takes a commission of between five and ten per cent of the brief fees rather than a salary, which can exceed the earnings of many of the barristers in the chambers. (Flood, 1983).

After around ten to fifteen years in practice, successful barristers can consider applying for promotion to Queen's Counsel, known as 'silk' from the material of which the QC's formal gown is made. Queen's Counsel are appointed by the Queen on the advice of the Lord Chancellor, who will normally consult senior members of the judiciary. Being a Queen's Counsel brings status, high income, and relief from some of the more tedious paperwork done by barristers. It may also often be a step on the way to judicial appointment in the High Court.

Socialization

Socialization refers to the mechanisms by which the profession reproduces the motivations and attitudes regarded as appropriate for the practice of law. The lengthy period of training required for admission to either branch of the profession has a socializing effect on entrants to the profession. The character of the profession is thus maintained. Since the standard route of entry is graduate entry, the social profile of graduates is the starting point for consideration of the social profile of the profession. The social composition of undergraduate law students is predominantly middle-class in origin and outlook (Benson Commission, 1979; McDonald, 1982). The social composition of admitted solicitors is remarkably similar to the profile of law students, but the socialization process involved in qualifying to practise at the Bar dramatically increases the preponderance of persons from professional and managerial backgrounds. The process in both branches of the profession impacts adversely on women and ethnic minorities, who, even when they do enter the profession, tend to be relegated to lower status work (Hazell, 1978; Podmore and Spencer, 1982; Cohen, 1982b and 1982c; Abel, 1988).

The traditions and customs of each branch of the profession tend to determine the form of education and training rather than any objectively determined educational needs. The eating of dinners as a precondition to call to the Bar and the serving of pupillage as a precondition to practice at the Bar are the most obvious examples of socialization processes. For potential solicitors the apprenticeship to an experienced solicitor in the form of articles of clerkship performs the same function. The apprenticeship is the period when the motivations and attitudes important for the practice of the law are inculcated and reinforced.

It seems inevitable that the social profile of lawyers is going to be markedly different from that of society at large because the social profile of persons attaining the level of educational achievement required for admission to higher education does not itself correspond with that of the whole community. The differences, however, go beyond this, most notably at the Bar. This has important consequences for the delivery of legal services, which are only now being slowly realized. The social class composition of lawyers compared with particular client groups appears to make it easy for some to consult lawyers while presenting barriers to other sections of the community. Poorer working-class groups do not seem to perceive lawyers as providing a service for them. Law centres have tried to address this problem, but it is difficult to isolate the factors which make law centres more accessible to working-class clients. The offering of a free service and the ability to advertise have obviously been key factors having little to do with questions of social class composition, though they have much to do with socialization since law centres perceive their role very differently from those in private practice.

Monopolies

One common feature of professions is the claim that their services are more than business transactions and that this aspect of the delivery of professional services justifies in the public interest monopolies that would not be acceptable in the ordinary industrial and commercial arena. Many of the traditional monopolies applicable in the legal profession are under attack and some are on the point of disappearing. There have always been surprisingly few monopolies though they have become principal protectors of the exclusivity of the legal profession. These are the conveyancing and probate monopolies, restrictions on instituting litigation and on rights of audience. There is no general monopoly on the giving of legal advice, but the monopolies that do exist have been very effective in reserving most legal work for solicitors and barristers. There has been some encroachment in specific areas such as employment law advice and welfare benefits advice where tribunals with their generous rights of audience are major institutions.

Barristers and solicitors together with certificated notaries (who are normally also solicitors) and licensed conveyancers enjoy a statutory monopoly which makes it an offence for any other persons to draw up or prepare documents connected with the transfer of title to property for payment. This is commonly known as the conveyancing monopoly.

Solicitors, barristers and certificated notaries enjoy a statutory monopoly over the drawing up or preparation of the executor's affidavit and account; these are formal documents which must be obtained before probate can be granted. Like the conveyancing monopoly, the probate monopoly affects only a small part of the work involved in the administration of the estate of a deceased person. In both cases the practical effect of the monopolies is in most cases to reserve all the work for solicitors (and in the case of property transfer, licensed conveyancers). By practice rule barristers do not undertake conveyancing and probate work falling within these monopolies. Despite popular opinion to the contrary there is no monopoly over the preparation of wills. Both the conveyancing and probate monopolies are extended under Part II of the Courts and Legal Services Act 1990 to authorised practitioners.

Restrictions connected with litigation cover two situations. First, only solicitors may begin and conduct litigation on behalf of others. Secondly, there are rules restricting rights of audience. Both will be affected by the implementation of the Courts and Legal Services Act 1990. Obviously individuals may begin litigation on their own account and represent themselves in those proceedings, but otherwise only solicitors and barristers have the right to act as advocates in courts and only barristers in the higher courts, other than on formal or unopposed business. Legal executives and lay advisers have rights of audience before judges in chambers and in certain proceedings before Masters and Registrars. It is important to note in this context that courts have an inherent power to permit anyone to act as advocate, though this is seldom exercised except for the massive exception which at one time allowed police officers to act as prosecutors in the magistrates' courts. Rights of audience before tribunals are much wider as noted in chapters 12 and 13.

Restrictions on rights of audience ensure that persons appearing as representatives before courts have a minimum level of competence as advocates. Most of the argument has related to the divided profession's respective rights of audience discussed above, with much of the argument centring on solicitors being granted full rights of audience before the higher courts, especially the Crown Court.

The monopoly over the initiation of proceedings has proved to be most contentious in relation to claims assessors who deal with accident claims on a contingency basis taking part of the compensation as remuneration. Because few such cases proceed to trial it was argued that claims assessors should be able to issue proceedings on behalf of their clients. These claims were rejected and the rule that a solicitor be involved was seen as protecting the client who might otherwise be advised to settle too early or for too little to maximize the claims assessors' cash flow (Winn, 1968). The Courts and Legal Services Act 1990 opens the monopoly to authorized litigators who are members of bodies approved by the machinery set up in Part II of the Act.

The Work of the Profession

This section focuses on solicitors since they remain the initial point of contact for those seeking legal services from the profession. With some 15,500 outlets for their business, solicitors are likely to remain for some time the principal providers of legal services even if there is considerable expansion of alternatives to the use of solicitors for some legal work (The Law Society, 1990). What follows is a description of a typical general practice, but this description should be set against the increasing stratification of legal practice in England and Wales. For example, 60 per cent of all solicitors now practice in London, many doing commercial and financial services work for corporate clients in very large firms, some with over 400 lawyers in post. Outside London, there has also been a trend towards larger practices seeking to soak up the commercial work which remains in the provincial cities of England and Wales. Yet there are still large numbers of small, modestly supported and equipped practices. These are where the ordinary citizen goes for the help of a lawyer.

The type of practice which the ordinary citizen is most likely to encounter is the partnership of between two and four solicitors, who will employ one assistant solicitor, one articled clerk (trainee solicitor), two legal executives and seven clerical staff. About half of all firms of solicitors fell within this profile, while about one in six firms have five or more partners (Benson Commission, 1979, vol. 2, Section 16). The annual statistical surveys produced by The Law Society continue to show the predominance of the two to four solicitor partnership. Only one in 25 practices has more than ten partners.

For many years solicitors' practices have employed non-lawyers to do professional work. Formerly known as managing clerks, this body of employees has been known as legal executives since 1963 when the Institute of Legal Executives was established. The Institute has worked hard to ensure recognition of the professional work done by such staff and operates its own qualification procedures. Associates of the Institute must have served in a solicitor's office for three years and have passed four examination papers in law and Fellows must be over 25, have served eight years in a solicitor's office and have passed a further three examinations from a list of subjects offered by the Institute. These three papers are said to be of the same standard as the six Law Society's finals papers. There is no requirement that a person holds a qualification from the Institute in order to be employed as a legal executive. It is estimated that over half the legal executives working in solicitors' practices hold no formal qualification in law at all.

The Royal Commission on Legal Services commissioned a survey into the use of lawyers' services and the matters upon which they consulted lawyers. The survey did not include use of lawyers by business clients. In so far as the typical client can be identified from the survey information, he is likely to be a male owner-occupier aged between 25 and 34 and be himself a member of the professional or employers and managers socio-economic group. Incidence of lawyer use drops off dramatically for those over 45, for those renting their homes, and is markedly less for those from the skilled manual and own-account and semi-skilled or unskilled manual socio-economic groups. There was no significant regional variation in the incidence of lawyer use, despite earlier evidence of considerable regional variations in the concentration of solicitors (Foster, 1973b).

Table 1   *Royal Commission on Legal Services survey on work of solicitors*

	%
Conveyancing and related matters	35%
Wills and probate	21%
Matrimonial work	12%
Crime (including motoring)	7%
Personal injury claims	7%
Consumer problems (including insurance)	4%
Employment rights	1%
Welfare rights	less than 0.5%

Table 2   Podmore Survey on work of solicitors

	Mean Score
Conveyancing	6.65
Wills and probate	5.41
Matrimonial work	5.18
Personal injury claims	4.60
Crime	4.52
Company and commercial	4.03
Tax advice	3.60

The enquiry into matters about which the public had consulted lawyers in 1977 confirmed the generally accepted division of work by lawyers. The results are set out in table 1.

The survey did not include work for the business client. A different kind of survey conducted among 103 West Midlands practices showed that company and commercial advice and taxation advice often associated with the drafting of wills were regarded as important categories of work (Podmore, 1977). The results are reproduced in table 2. Firms were asked to rank categories of work on a seven point scale; from 0 representing 'not important at all' to 7 representing 'extremely important'.

The Podmore survey indicated that on average 15 per cent of a practices' time would be taken up with company and commercial work. The survey is perhaps also significant for the total absence of any importance being placed on welfare law work. More recent surveys confirm these general findings (Chambers and Harwood, 1990).

Paying for Legal Services

The Basis of Charging and the Control of Fees

The income of solicitors and barristers in private practice comes from the fees paid by clients. Solicitors and barristers in private practice are in business and must make a profit to survive. This section will focus on solicitors' charges but will only consider them in outline. There are two important distinctions to make: that between contentious and non-contentious business, and that between private payment of fees and legal aid.

Contentious business is work involving litigation, while non-contentious business is the rest of the solicitor's work of which the most important component will be conveyancing and probate work. The broad basis of all private charges of fees is what is fair and reasonable having regard to the complexity of the matter and its importance to the client. This translates in reality into the use of time charging plus a mark-up for the profit element and for the care and conduct of the matter. For the latter, half of one per cent of the value of the matter to the client is common. Clients are often aggrieved by the size of the bill delivered at the conclusion of the business brought to the solicitor and, save perhaps recently for conveyancing work, advance estimates of total costs are not common.

There are three ways clients can challenge the fees charged. First, they can always return to the solicitor to seek more details of the basis of charging; many bills are uninformative about this. Secondly, they can require the solicitor to obtain a remuneration certificate from The Law Society to show whether the fees are fair and reasonable. This involves the solicitor submitting full details of the transaction for consideration by The Law Society. If the fees certified by The Law Society are lower than those in the bill, only the lower sum is recoverable by the solicitor. No solicitor can sue for fees unless the client has been told about the remuneration certificate procedure. The use of the procedure is free and the bill can only be lowered; it can never be increased.

At any time, even after requiring a remuneration certificate, the client may apply to a High Court taxing master for taxation of the bill. Taxation is a formal process of verification of the fairness and reasonableness of the charges. The applicant pays the costs of taxation if the bill is reduced by one-sixth or less. Neither procedure is commonly used, but taxation is hardly used at all, which is not surprising in view of the costs risk. The main recommendations of the Royal Commission, which found that three-quarters of all clients had no complaints about their bills, was that more information in writing should be given to clients about the basis of charges at the time the solicitor is first instructed.

Costs in contentious cases are more complicated because a successful party may normally recover some of the costs from the losing party. In this context formal taxation of costs on the standard basis has a major role to play, though in minor cases costs may be agreed between the parties without the need for taxation.

Finally, in cases involving legal aid, legal aid rates are established by regulations and it will be these which determine the amount payable to the solicitor out of the Legal Aid Fund for work done whether contentious or non-contentious. It is a breach of the legal aid regulations for a solicitor to receive money for fees from a client who is legally aided other than the contribution payable under the Green Form scheme.

Legal Aid

Fear of costs is one of the major inhibitions which prevents clients from consulting lawyers. It is a fear which often arises out of ignorance, because for those on low to middle incomes, some assistance may be available under the various components of the legal aid scheme. A number of choices were made on the introduction of legal aid after the Second World War, which have affected its development. These might now be labelled 'fundamental principles' and it is important to bear them in mind when looking at the limitations of the legal aid scheme (Pollock, 1975):

1 There should be free access to all courts within the jurisdiction and to legal services to make such access effective, including access to assistance which avoids the need to resort to litigation.
2 Persons receiving legal aid should make such contribution to the cost of legal services as they are deemed able to afford having regard to their resources.
3 Persons eligible for legal aid should have a free choice of lawyers and the services provided should be of the same quality as those available for fee-paying clients.
4 Lawyers offering legal services under the legal aid scheme must remain professionally independent.
5 Lawyers should be fairly and reasonably remunerated for work done under the legal aid scheme.

The obvious impact of these principles has been to graft the legal aid scheme onto the existing structure of private practice. Persons within the scheme are provided with an indemnity against the cost of legal services subject only to the payment of the contribution. The legal aid scheme developed over the decades as a means of paying for a lawyer in connection with litigation work. Its impact has been greatest in personal injuries litigation and matrimonial proceedings and in the defence of those charged with serious criminal offences. These aspects of the legal aid schemes were fully discussed in the parts of the book on the civil and criminal justice systems.

An attempt was made in the Legal Advice and Assistance Act 1972 (now consolidated in the Legal Aid Act 1988) to extend the scope of legal aid beyond the confines of civil and criminal litigation. Since April 1973 the Green Form scheme has been available. This is the simplest component of legal aid, but alterations and adjustments to it make it best to think of it as encompassing a number of different types of help.

Standard Green Form work is the basic part of the scheme. Any person is entitled to ask for advice on any question of English law except one concerning conveyancing services, wills or a step in proceedings. Those over 70 and certain other vulnerable groups are entitled to receive advice and assistance connected with wills. The solicitor or some other member of the practice will conduct a simplified means test using a green form and a key card to determine financial eligibility. If the client is happy to pay any contribution required, the solicitor is authorized to provide up to two hours of work. The work which can be done is any work a solicitor normally does other than representation in a court or tribunal. It is even possible for the solicitor to draft a submission for the client to present personally in a court or tribunal. Obviously the time limit may not be enough to enable the solicitor to complete the client's business. If this is so, the solicitor may seek an extension from the Legal Aid Board, who, if satisfied that there is a need to spend further money, will authorize further expenditure. There is no limit to the number of different problems which can be taken to a solicitor under the scheme. In undefended divorce cases a higher initial time limit of three hours' work applies.

Assistance by way of representation (ABWOR) is best thought of as a simple and easily administered type of civil legal aid for particular types of litigation. ABWOR covers certain civil litigation, but is administered on arrangements more like Green Form than civil legal aid. Potentially ABWOR can be used for any proceedings. Currently the main cases for which it is used are:

> applications to the domestic panel of the magistrates' court for various kinds of matrimonial relief;
> representation of parents in care proceedings;
> applications to Mental Health Review Tribunals;
> applications concerning certain prisoners before Prison Visitors.

If legal aid becomes available in other tribunals, ABWOR is almost certain to be the legal aid component used.

The intention behind the introduction of the Green Form scheme was to extend the range of services offered by solicitors which would be covered by legal aid. Unfortunately this expectation has not been fulfilled. Three-quarters of Green Form work is made up of advice on divorce and family matters and on criminal cases. It is also often used to pay for the preliminary work involved in making applications for civil and criminal legal aid. New ways of delivering legal advice and assistance are being explored by the Legal Aid Board including schemes which will franchise certain work to specific firms or agencies rather than making such advice available from any solicitor (Smith, 1989).

Looking at the legal aid scheme overall, it is clear that it offers nothing new in the system for the delivery of legal services. The scheme is neatly dovetailed into the established system of private practice. No attempt has been made to see the needs of legally aided clients as different from those of fee-paying clients. Yet as we shall see in the next chapter, with poorer clients the problem is not simply one of providing lawyers for people who cannot afford them from their own resources.

For the areas of work traditionally offered by lawyers, the legal aid scheme provides very good coverage for the poor. For the rich the cost of legal services is not a barrier to the use of lawyers. But the legal aid financial limits all have cut-off points. Income above the prescribed figures operates as a bar. This has left a section of the community without effective access to legal services for expensive litigation. A number of alternatives have been suggested. The use of contingent fees, whereby lawyers recoup their fees from damages recovered but agree to accept no fee if the case is lost, have been rejected despite the ability to operate such schemes alongside legal aid and the English system of costs (White, Robin, 1978). A limited version of the Scottish speculative fee is included in the Courts and Legal Services Act 1990.

Another alternative which is attracting increasing attention is the development of legal expenses insurances against such risks which has been welcomed and sponsored by The Law Society (White, Robin, 1984).

Complaining about Lawyers' Services

Key Distinctions

Following the Glanville Davies debacle, The Law Society completely revamped its complaints machinery in an effort to regain some credibility with the public. But there remains a key distinction between complaints of negligence and of other deficiencies which determines whether The Law Society will investigate complaints. The Law Society takes the view that the remedy for negligent work is to sue the negligent solicitor for compensation. Because of difficulties experienced in the past over finding one solicitor prepared to take negligence actions against other solicitors, The Law Society has established Negligence Panels. These are essentially lists of solicitors experienced in negligence claims, who will offer an initial one hour consultation free of charge. There is also an arbitration scheme under which many negligence claims are settled.

The Solicitors Complaints Bureau

The creation of the Solicitors Complaints Bureau (SCB) in September 1986 was The Law Society's answer to critics of the complaints machinery. The SCB has its own budget, appoints its own staff and operates from its own premises. It runs as a quasi-autonomous organization. The SCB is a convenient name to describe three elements involved in the consideration of complaints about solicitors: the staff of the Bureau, the Investigation Committee and the Adjudication Committee. Most complaints are dealt with by staff of the Bureau. Complaints can cover any aspect of the solicitor's work, excluding negligence. It can include inadequate professional services or 'shoddy work' and the definition of this concept has proved to be a difficult one for the SCB. Inadequate professional services are services which fall below an acceptable standard, but are short of negligent work. The dividing line is a thin one. The single largest cause of complaint is delay by solicitors in the handling of client matters.

Persons wishing to complain but who have difficulty in explaining their case will be put in touch with a solicitor on the Interview Panel, who will see the complainant and will help to put together the information needed for presentation to the SCB. This service is free. Once the complaint is received by the SCB, it is logged onto the computer and allocated to a section. There an Investigation Officer will consider the documentation and decide whether the solicitor about whom the complaint has been filed has a case to answer within the powers of the SCB. Those sending in inadequate documentation may be referred to a solicitor on the Interview Panel before the matter proceeds further. If there appears to be a case to answer, the observations of the solicitor will be sought on the complaint. In serious cases, the request for observations is accompanied by a warning that if disciplinary proceedings result from the investigation, the reply may be used in those proceedings. A copy of the solicitor's reply is then sent to the complainant together with a comment from the Investigation Officer. Sometimes complaints end at this point.

Where the complaint is of shoddy work, the solicitor's file is called for and is passed to an experienced report writer for detailed comment. It is then vetted by a second report writer and if there is any divergence of view, the opinion of a third report writer will be sought. The solicitor's observations are sought in any case where shoddy work is found and the solicitor can request further consideration by a review panel of practising solicitors. A conclusion that the complaint reveals no evidence of shoddy work will be communicated to the complainant and solicitor, if necessary through a solicitor on the Interview Panel.

If the complainant remains unhappy about the conclusion, the file must be referred to the Investigation Committee, since in these circumstances only they can conclude the investigation. Where the complaint of shoddy work is found to be substantiated, the Investigation Officer prepares a report on the case for the Adjudication Committee, who have the final power of decision. Such cases will, however, first be considered by the Investigation Committee.

The Investigation Committee consists of eleven members of whom only four are solicitors. The functions of the Investigation Committee are to review cases which the Investigation Officer wishes to terminate as not substantiated but the complainant does not and cases where the Investigation Officer is referring the file to the Adjudication Committee. It has power to recommend further investigations. The Investigation Committee also has a general monitoring function over the handling of complaints by the SCB.

The Adjudication Committee consists of 18 members: nine members drawn from The Law Society Council, three other solicitors and six lay members. All the disciplinary powers of The Law Society have been delegated to the Adjudication Committee. The Adjudication Committee can take a broad range of actions in relation to complaints: it can:

call for a file to investigate a complaint of misconduct or shoddy work;
order an inspection of a solicitor's accounts;
in serious cases, intervene in a solicitor's practice to protect the interests of clients;
intervene to recover a particular item;
refuse, or impose conditions on, practising certificates;
prohibit a solicitor from taking an articles clerk;
control the employment of a solicitor who has been suspended from practice or struck off the roll of solicitors;
control the employment of solicitor's clerks;
order payment of interest on client's money;
order payments out of the Compensation Fund where a person has lost money as a result of a solicitor's dishonesty;
issue rebukes relating to solicitor's conduct;
require a solicitor to take specific action, such as compliance with an undertaking;
order a solicitor found guilty of shoddy work to remit fees, waive the right to fees, or to rectify a mistake at his or her own expense;

take disciplinary proceedings against a solicitor before the Solicitors Disciplinary Tribunal;
dismiss a complaint.

The Adjudication Committee is therefore the body with teeth. In 1989 the SCB
received 21,000 complaints. Most were disposed of at the Investigation Officer
stage, though an interesting innovation in 1989, which is to be extended
nationally, is local conciliation by experienced solicitors designated as Local
Conciliation Officers. In 1989 the Adjudication Committee dealt with 2729
cases. Complaints of shoddy work accounted for 345 cases; in 271 a financial
penalty was imposed and in 49 no further action was taken (SCB, 1989). Power
is given in the Courts and Legal Services Act 1990 to award compensation of up
to £1000 to a client who has been the victim of shoddy work.

In December 1990 The Law Society announced a major reorganization of the
SCB including the introduction of an appeals procedure. Three divisions are to
be established to deal with:

conduct matters;
compensation and inadequate professional services; and
conciliation.

The current Adjudication and Investigation Committees will combine to
become the Adjudication and Appeals Committee, split into sub-committees of
two solicitors and one lay member each. A policy advisory committee is established which will report annually to the Council of The Law Society. The appeals
procedure will be available to both complainants and solicitors.

The Solicitors Disciplinary Tribunal

The Solicitors Disciplinary Tribunal is wholly independent of The Law Society
and its members are appointed by the Master of the Rolls. The Tribunal sits in
groups of three: two lawyer members and one lay member. The principal function of the Tribunal is to determine applications in respect of solicitors relating
to allegations of unbefitting conduct or breaches of the rules relating to professional practice, conduct and discipline. Most applications are made by The
Law Society through its Adjudication Committee, but it is open to anyone to
make application to the Tribunal without recourse to The Law Society. The Lay
Observer also has power to make applications. The penalties available to the
Tribunal include striking a solicitor off the roll of solicitors, suspension from
practice, the imposition of a money penalty not exceeding £5000, and payment
of all or part of the costs of the application.

The Lay Observer

The Lay Observer, who must be neither a solicitor nor a barrister, is appointed by the Lord Chancellor to consider the investigation of complaints about solicitors. The Lay Observer makes an annual report to Parliament. There are no more than about 300 complaints to the Lay Observer each year and it is rare for the Lay Observer to criticize The Law Society's handling of a complaint.

The Lay Observer has been replaced with a Legal Services Ombudsman with rather wider powers than the Law Observer under provisions contained in Part II of the Courts and Legal Services Act 1990.

Complaints about Barristers

The Bar also has a complaints machinery, but it is less complex than that relating to solicitors. Many of the complaints emanate from judges rather than members of the public and relate to conduct in court. Complaints are investigated by the Professional Conduct Committee of the Bar, which considers a written report from a barrister who has been given the task of investigating the complaint. Substantiated complaints may result in applications to the Bar Disciplinary Tribunal, which can disbar the barrister, suspend from practice, order to repay or forgo fees, or order various types of rebuke to be administered.

Professions: an Outmoded Concept?

There has been much criticism of the theoretical framework within which the enquiries of the Royal Commission proceeded, which has been characterized as 'functionalist' and criticized as being 'discredited in contemporary sociology of law' (Thomas, P. 1982).

Professor Abel has offered an alternative analysis of legal services (Abel, 1982). Building on the work of other sociologists, he notes that professions as producers of services can only really control supply of those services by controlling the supply of members of the profession. By the turn of the century law and most of today's major professions had acquired this control by the system required for entry to the profession and by securing monopolies over certain types of work. But since around 1945 the gateway to the legal profession has changed. It has ceased to be effectively wholly within the control of solicitors and barristers through the system of articles of clerkship and pupillage, for which premiums and pupillage fees were paid and which were generally obtained by the exercise of patronage, and through professional examinations conducted by the profession.

The growth of universities and polytechnics teaching for law degrees has led to expectations, which have been largely fulfilled, that a law degree provides a gateway to professional qualification. Though non-graduate entry to the profession is still possible, it is very much the exception to the more normal graduate entry. This loss of control over supply resulted in dramatic increases in the numbers of lawyers noted at the start of this chapter. The increase in numbers led the profession to turn its attention to the stimulation of demand for legal services, called by Abel 'demand creation'. It seems that private demand is almost fully met, and so the focus of attention has been in public demand creation. Major initiatives have been the growth of the legal aid schemes and duty solicitor schemes, support for generalist advice services like the Citizens Advice Bureaux and legal advice centres, which generate work for lawyers, and the serious attempt made by the profession to recover control over law centres, which is described in the next chapter.

The dilemma presented by all these initiatives is that they affect the homogeneity of the profession. A heterogeneous profession is not nearly as powerful. The market initiatives can also backfire, particularly in the private sector, where alternatives to the use of professional advisers or self-help are seen as viable. The claim to exclusive competence also becomes harder to sustain in an environment of market competition, as is evidenced in the area of conveyancing. Abel even suggests that, whereas the latter half of the nineteenth century saw the rise of the professions, the latter half of the twentieth century will see their demise. He concludes with a new image for the lawyer:

> The lawyer today, and even more tomorrow, is an entrepreneur selling his services in an increasingly competitive market, an employee whose labour is exploited, an employer exploiting subordinates – all increasingly dependent upon state or capital for their business and therefore increasingly subject to their control. Although the ideal of professionalism will undoubtedly linger on as an ever more anachronistic warrant of legitimacy the profession as an economic, social and political institution is moribund. (Abel, 1982, p. 48)

Another eminent commentator on the legal profession takes a less gloomy view than Professor Abel. Cyril Glasser draws attention to the move away from complete self-regulation, the increasingly heterogeneous rather than homogeneous character of the legal profession and changing ideologies about the delivery of legal services, and suggests that a new type of professionalism is emerging. He says:

> In a recent major study of professional society since 1800, Professor Harold Perkin has produced an altogether different analysis. He sees much of the structure of modern British politics as a battle between 'the public sector ideal of an egalitarian, compassionate and caring state run by well paid professionals and the private sector ideal of equal opportunity for those who are able to climb the corporate ladder of success and compete in the struggle for survival of the fittest corporation.' He argues for a new professional society for late twentieth century Britain which does not fall into the rival pits of corporate neo-feudalism and the authoritarian state. (Glasser, 1990 p. 9)

Concluding Comment

There can be little doubt that the typical practice is still populated by middle-class lawyers catering for the needs of middle-class clients. It will be located in or near the centre of commercial activity in a town or in a prosperous suburb with a high incidence of owner-occupation (Foster, 1973b). The bulk of the work and income will come from conveyancing and related matters, but there is likely to be some degree of specialization within the firm in three areas: litigation; business and commercial work; and wills and probate. It is likely that much routine conveyancing will be conducted by unadmitted staff, that is, legal executives, with minimum supervision, leaving the solicitors free for more complex conveyancing and for the specialist work. This typical profile is not intended as a criticism, nor should it come as a great surprise. A concentration on profitable work is perfectly natural if the provision of legal services is seen as a business activity. Practice seems at variance here with the pious noises sometimes emanating from The Law Society that solicitors' practices provide a service equally attractive to all sections of the community. We can also conclude that, though legal aid provides valuable support for traditional legal work, it does not break new ground in ensuring that poorer sections of the community receive adequate delivery of legal services.

16

Legal Services: New Methods of Delivery

Introduction

The great challenge to the legal system, to an independent legal profession and to the judiciary is to ensure that legal services are available to all who need them at a cost they can afford. The erosion of the legal aid scheme is leading lawyers to abandon work under it and the private practice of law in the competitive era of the 1990s is tending to concentrate on the more profitable areas of work to the exclusion of work for poorer sections of the community. The two areas targeted for expansion in a survey of public use and perception of legal services in 1989 were legal and financial advice connected with pensions and with setting up businesses (Jenkins et al., 1989).

There are gaps in the provision of legal services. Divorce and crime are the only two areas of private practice where the poorer sections of the community have any significant contacts with lawyers. These types of work are, of course, not exclusive to the poor. This chapter will consider other needs and the difficult concept of the unmet need for legal services. The attempts made by law centres and other agencies to fill the gap will be discussed, together with the issue of who should manage delivery of legal services to ensure that an adequate service is available to all who need it.

Unmet Need for Legal Services

The phrase 'unmet need for legal services' has been surrounded by controversy and confusion. There is disagreement about the precise meaning of virtually every word, and even disagreement about whether the phrase is capable of meaningful definition. Though most commentators accept that there is unmet need, there is little agreement on its extent or about appropriate responses to it.

First it is necessary to consider what is meant by 'legal services'. The Royal Commission on Legal Services construed the expression as referring to those services:

which should be available to any person or organisation requiring advice or assistance of a legal character whether payment for the service is made from public or private funds.

Unfortunately the Report immediately goes on to qualify this broad definition by making it clear that it had in mind only services provided by qualified lawyers and excluded from the definition advice by 'lay persons' (Benson Commission, 1979, paras.2.1–2.4). A preferable definition of legal services is to be found in the Report of the Royal Commission on Legal Services in Scotland where the wide role of non-lawyers in providing legal services is recognized and such a service is characterized as 'no less a legal service than when it is done by a solicitor'. This Report adopts a much more consumer-oriented approach and defines legal services as:

> . . . advice information or assistance involving a knowledge of rights and obligations conferred by law, and of legal procedures, whether provided by a lawyer or otherwise. These services may include action taken on behalf of a client, or facilities used by a client (whether the client is an individual, a group or an organisation). (Hughes Commission, 1980, para.2.2)

Lord Mackay's Green Paper *The Work and Organization of the Legal Profession* rather blandly states that:

> legal services are concerned with the advice, assistance and representation required by a person in connection with his rights, duties and liabilities. (para.2.1)

But it is clear that Lord Mackay was not limiting himself only to the work done by solicitors and barristers.

Armed with these definitions, few would argue with the following examples of situations in which there is a need for legal services (White, Richard, 1973):

1 where a person fails to recognize a problem as having a legal aspect to it and so takes no further action to seek out legal services;
2 where a person recognizes a problem as having a legal aspect but is ignorant either about the existence of a relevant legal service or about his or her own eligibility to make use of it;
3 where a person recognizes a problem as having a legal aspect and identifies a legal service as relevant and available but, because of some barrier, such as fear of costs or ignorance of legal aid, chooses not to make use of the service;
4 where a person recognizes a problem as having a legal aspect and as requiring legal services, but finds no developed legal services available; no legal action is taken because no service is available.

The obvious solutions to these various needs will differ. In the second and third cases, strategies which increase public awareness of the legal aid schemes would resolve some of the difficulties. The last case requires changes in the services and skills offered by lawyers and legal advisers while the first case is particularly problematic because it begs the questions of what constitutes a legal problem and what constitutes need.

These are the two areas where confusion has been injected into the debate. The definition of a 'legal problem' is highly dependent upon the perceptions of the definer. If legal services are seen as contributing to the amelioration of the situation, it will be defined as a legal problem, but if the problem appears rather to be shortage of money or some lack of competence in the individual, the problem will be defined as a social problem. Many lawyers in private practice have categorized problems concerning the range of rights deriving from the public law that regulates the welfare state, most notably in the area of welfare benefits, as social problems simply because they have typically had no involvement in these areas. Others who see law and legal strategies as a means of giving power to a section of the community lacking in power and influence would adopt a very wide definition which almost subsumes both legal and social problems under one heading.

As though this was not confusing enough, we then find very obvious difficulties with the definition of 'need'. The term is often used without any regard to the fact that need is a relative concept. Need tends to be related to resources available and to be constantly redefined and adjusted with the ebb and flow of resources. The acuteness of need is also relative to the circumstances of the individual. The poor person in low quality rented housing where the landlord allows the roof to fall into disrepair and let in water can only hope to secure a weatherproof roof by reliance on the landlord's obligation to repair. The rich man whose luxury rented house develops a leaking roof has the wealth to choose to pay for the repair and argue about the matter afterwards. He may even choose not to pursue the matter further. The poor person's need may be said to be more acute. There is then the question of how the need is satisfied. Is it always necessary to have the advice of a qualified lawyer? In many welfare law areas alternatives to lawyers are being used increasingly to pass on basic advice on legal rights and to negotiate claims for clients. Because of the monopolies given to lawyers, they often need to be brought in for the difficult case where litigation is involved and representation is needed.

The increasing use of lay advisers has also raised questions as to whether the appropriate solution is always the legal solution. This can be encapsulated in the question of whether the poor tenant with the leaky roof needs a lawyer or a ladder (Lewis, 1973). If the relative costs of public provision of a lawyer and of a roofing contractor were the same, it may be better to pay the roofer rather than the lawyer. This would leave unresolved the problem of what, if any, action should be taken against the defaulting landlord. Perhaps the state could have a right to recover the roofer's costs from the landlord.

Attempts to quantify unmet need for legal services are problematic, but a number of attempts have nevertheless been made. An early study which matched individuals own recognition of their need for advice in a number of areas with the action they actually took produced evidence of considerable perceived unmet need. There was also a clear correlation between high incidence of taking advice and those matters which we saw in the last chapter to be important areas of solicitors' work (Abel-Smith et al., 1973). Virtually every respondent who identified the need for advice in buying a house consulted a solicitor, but in relation to employment problems only four per cent took advice from a solicitor. Thirty-four per cent took advice from some other source while 62 per cent took no advice at all. For social security problems the figures were even worse: three per cent consulted solicitors, 16 per cent took advice elsewhere and 81 per cent took no advice despite their own perceived need for some advice. The study of need in personal injury cases discussed in chapter 10 provided similar evidence of alarming cases where no action had been taken by victims of accidents who felt someone else was to blame for their injuries (Genn, 1982).

The Benson Commission's own Users' Survey sought information about matters not taken to solicitors even though respondents felt that advice from a solicitor might be useful. One in eleven respondents identified such matters. The most common matter was neighbour disputes, and the other commonly mentioned matters were consumer complaints and problems with employment and social security. In a number of cases the respondents resorted to advice from friends, the local council or from a Citizens Advice Bureau. One third of respondents identified cost as the major reason they had not taken advice from a solicitor.

These findings led the Benson Commission to conclude that there were two main reasons why legal services 'are, in some areas and for certain classes of society, not available'. The first was the inadequacy of legal aid for certain types of work, notably those involving tribunal representation. The second was a combination of ignorance, powerlessness and a shortage of resources. Five factors were identified as principal contributors to this unmet need:

  a lack of knowledge of the rights offered by the law and of the remedy offered by the use of legal strategies;
  a lack of lawyers working in the areas of law where the problems arise;
  a lack of information about lawyers working in the areas of law where the problems arise;
  a reluctance to consult a lawyer about the problem for fear of what might be involved, particularly cost;
  the public image of lawyers inhibits approaches to lawyers by poorer sections of the community.

In a report which is devoid of any express theoretical framework, it is difficult to identify the reasons underlying particular conclusions. The Benson Commission seems to accept as the causes of unmet need a combination of the 'poverty' theory and the 'legal incompetence' theory. The first simply asserts that poverty is the major cause of unmet need, but empirical studies do not seem to bear this out. For the poor do use solicitors on marriage breakdown and for criminal defence work, both substantial parts of lawyers' practices. Equally the middle classes do not use lawyers very much for advice with employment or consumer problems.

The legal competence theory suggests that unmet need arises predominantly among the poor because they do not recognize their problems as legal nor do they perceive lawyers as a resource available for them save in very specific areas. Because they are almost always 'one-shotters' arguing cases against 'repeat-players' they also lack power. For repeat-players the matter is routine and they are used to using the law and lawyers, while for the one-shotter the matter is traumatic and unfamiliar at every stage (Carlin et al., 1966; Galanter, 1974).

Zander rejects both these explanations (Zander, 1978). He prefers, but does not totally accept, the 'social organization' theory of Mayhew and Reiss (Mayhew and Reiss, 1969) because this provides a better explanation of the incidence of lawyer use by rich and poor alike. This theory links particular types of work with networks of social contacts. Thus acquisition of real property, or divorce, or writing a will or administering an estate become areas where lawyer use is taken for granted by all sections of the community and where lawyers have responded by providing the service expected. In other areas the social links and networks are not as well developed and the incidence of lawyer use will not be as high. Examples would be personal injuries litigation and minor crime. For Zander the key to variations in the incidence of lawyer use is contact with a knowledgeable and trusted lay person who identifies, or confirms the identification of, the problem as requiring the services of a lawyer. But this alone is not enough, because the referral needs to be backed by sympathetic, relevant and fruitful help from a lawyer.

Whatever the disagreements about the definition of unmet need, there is general agreement that there is a gap between certain new rights that are legally recognized and their observation and enforcement. These rights have arisen principally in the areas of welfare law, a generic label referring to the law relating to housing, social security benefits, mental health, discrimination, employment, immigration and nationality, and the welfare of children. One solution to the problem is commitment to making these rights effective by ensuring genuinely accessible legal services in all these areas (Cappelletti, 1978). Many of these rights have a special significance for the poor because they are rights relating to basic human needs: housing, a source of income and respect for the dignity of the person. It is precisely in these areas that law centres have made a major contribution. They have also developed a system of trusted referral and effective response which has been the source of their success in getting clients to use their services. This process is sometimes called 'mobilizing' a clientele. Law centres and those working for the poor are often labelled public sector legal services to distinguish them from solicitors in private practice.

The Notion of Public Sector Legal Services

Using Salaried Lawyers

The fundamental principles of the legal aid scheme were considered in the last chapter and it was noted that the effect of these principles was to dovetail legal aid into the system of private practice. Sociologists point to this as an example of successful demand creation by the legal profession (Abel, 1982). However, in its evidence to the Rushcliffe Committee whose report formed the basis of the Legal Aid and Advice Act 1949, which introduced the modern legal aid scheme, The Law Society had argued strongly for a salaried component as part of the scheme. It was proposed that there should be a network of advice centres employing solicitors which would provide advice and assistance in those parts of the country with only sparse provision of legal services. Provision was made in the 1949 Act for this scheme, though it was never implemented.

By 1958 The Law Society had changed its mind and proposed that advice and assistance could be more economically provided by solicitors in their own offices rather than by salaried lawyers. The new proposals were accepted and eventually came to fruition with the introduction in April 1973 of the Green Form scheme. When proposals for the new scheme were first introduced in 1968, The Law Society also proposed the appointment of salaried Advisory Liaison Officers to ensure that all sections of the community would get to know about the facilities offered by the legal aid scheme and where these facilities were available. In essence Advisory Liaison Officers were to be a salaried task force within the legal aid scheme drumming up legal aid business for lawyers in private practice. It was envisaged that the Liaison Officer would, for example, hold referral sessions at Citizens Advice Bureaux to discover the nature of clients' problems and to provide introductions to solicitors in private practice. Seton Pollock puts it very frankly in his history of the first 25 years of legal aid:

> For solicitors in private practice to be diverted by undertaking 'missionary' activities to attract work to themselves would be wasteful, would be a recipe for professional problems and would reduce their availability to do the very work so attracted. What is needed is a link between them and those who need, but would otherwise not obtain, those services and this would be the basic function that the Advisory Liaison Officer would perform. (Pollock, 1975, p. 125)

Following the publication of the Society of Labour Lawyers pamphlet *Justice for All* (see below), The Law Society amended its proposal to include the use of Advisory Liaison Officers to set up permanent salaried offices and to offer a broader range of work including litigation in the magistrates' and county courts. Provision was made in the Legal Advice and Assistance Act 1972, and later included in the consolidating Legal Aid Act 1974, for the establishment of the scheme but it was never brought into force. The idea was probably sound in 1949, but by 1972 it was an idea whose time was past. To understand why, it is necessary to consider what was happening elsewhere in the development of salaried legal services for the public.

Three Phases in the Response to Unmet Need

It is possible to identify three phases in the response to the problem of unmet need. The first was the development of the legal aid scheme, the second was the perception of legal services as a social service using recognized legal strategies in order to make rights effective, and the third is the questioning of whether traditionally accepted legal strategies are the most appropriate response to particular problems (Paterson and Nelken, 1984). By 1972 developments within the second phase were well under way. In the 1960s in the United States President Lyndon Johnson had announced his 'War on Poverty' and the Economic Opportunity Act 1964 had established the Office of Economic Opportunity (OEO) which in turn established a 'Legal Services Program' which set up several hundred neighbourhood law offices at public expense. The policy of these law offices was not simply to provide legal services on an individual basis but also, and principally, to secure law reform. The Director of the OEO Legal Services Program put it thus:

> We cannot at the same time provide every indigent with a lawyer, treat all his problems legal and personal, work devotedly to change the statutes and court holdings that have placed our clients in a disadvantageous position, and develop the theories to win the battles of tomorrow as well as today . . . . [T]he primary goal of the Legal Services Program should be law reform, to bring about changes in the structures of the world in which the poor people live in order to provide on the largest scale possible consistent with our limited resources, a legal system in which the poor enjoy the same treatment as the rich. (Johnson, 1974, p. 133)

In 1966 and 1967 the Lord Chancellor's Advisory Committee on Legal Aid considered, and rejected, proposals for a similar system of neighbourhood law firms of salaried lawyers (Zander, 1978). The idea was, however, enthusiastically embraced by the Society for Labour Lawyers, whose 1968 pamphlet *Justice for All* recommended a pilot project on the feasibility of neighbourhood law firms in England, and the Conservative Political Centre's 1968 pamphlet *Rough Justice* also expressed cautious approval of experiments in the area.

The recommendations were again rejected by The Law Society and the Government (Zander, 1978). Undaunted, independent groups of young lawyers and community workers, inspired by the American experience, began planning new means of delivering legal services. Some began by setting up legal advice centres where lawyers from private practice offered their services as volunteers to provide surgery style consultations in the evenings without charge. Some later matured into fully fledged law centres (Cooper, 1983).

The Legal Aid Efficiency Scrutiny

The latest look at the problems of delivering legal services to all is the Legal Aid Efficiency Scrutiny conducted by a team of four respectively from the Lord Chancellor's Department, the Treasury, the Church Commissioners and the Prime Minister's Efficiency Unit. The Scrutiny Report, which led to the White Paper *Legal Aid in England and Wales: A New Framework* (Cm 118), found a lack of coordination in existing arrangements with overlap between the work done by solicitors under the Green Form scheme and the Citizens Advice Bureaux. The Scrutiny proposed a restriction in Green Form availability relating to legal advice which simply enabled a person to arrange their own affairs. This referred to the drafting of wills, conveyancing and probate work. But the Scrutiny felt that Green Form should be abolished altogether and a radical new approach adopted to the delivery of generalist legal advice.

The Scrutiny proposed that in future the first point of contact on basic legal problems should be the Citizens Advice Bureaux, which would be upgraded to meet the demand. It would become the responsibility of Legal Aid Area Directors to get the best service possible within nationally agreed criteria on access, competence and emergency advice provision within the budget allocation provided by the Legal Aid Board, who would take over the administration of legal aid from The Law Society. Naturally The Law Society opposed the proposals, not because it wished to retain the administration of legal aid, but because it amounted to a rationing of legal advice rather than an increase, both in terms of access and quality. The Law Society's arguments received a boost when research into the scheme conducted on behalf of the Lord Chancellor's Department (Baldwin and Hill, 1988) reported that it was a crucial element in publicly funded legal services. The notion that much of the advice given under the scheme represented consultations by members of the public over trivial matters was dispelled. Furthermore more people are helped under the Green Form scheme, which accounts for 20 per cent of the legal aid budget than are helped under all other forms of legal aid put together. Client satisfaction with the help they received was also high.

Nor were the proposals acceptable to the Citizens Advice Bureaux, who seemed to stand to gain much from acceptance of them. The proposals were viewed as part of a cost-cutting exercise and the Citizens Advice Bureaux had no confidence that the resources would be provided to meet the need for legal services its own records showed existed. The National Association of Citizens Advice Bureaux (NACAB) also frankly admitted that Citizens Advice Bureaux were insufficiently well established to assume the responsibility for first-line general legal advice for all.

The White Paper modified the Scrutiny's recommendations, though the administration of legal aid was to be transferred from The Law Society to the Legal Aid Board, which would have a more managerial approach to the administration of legal aid. The proposed abolition of the Green Form scheme was rejected. Instead the Government proposed that the Green Form scheme could be improved 'to provide better service at lower cost' and that some use could be made of advice agencies. Powers would be taken to enable the Legal Aid Board 'to make alternative arrangements for the provision of advice and assistance for particular categories of work where this would be a more efficient way of providing the service'. These proposals were given substance in provisions contained in the Legal Aid Act 1988. The Legal Aid Board is in the process of 'franchising' certain aspects of legal advice and assistance under pilot schemes. Michael Zander sums up the Scrutiny and White Paper as follows:

In short, the White Paper was a bleak document with the hand of the Treasury written plainly all over it. It was certainly the most depressing official document on legal aid and legal services since the scheme was established in the late 1940s and became the model for developments in legal aid all over the world. There is not a word in it which could be said to indicate recognition of the fact that many citizens continue to suffer from inadequate access to justice. (Zander, 1988, p. 71)

Public Interest Law

The label 'public interest law' was devised in the United States and imported into the United Kingdom (Dhavan, 1986) where it was 'a compendium phrase to gather together a cluster of movements seeking to mobilize law and legal services on behalf of the disadvantaged'. It encompasses the espousal of the public interest by any person or group. The concept has had an important effect on the debate on the provision of legal services, especially concerning the practice of law in law centres. Dhavan concludes:

Public interest law is not just concerned with giving the disadvantaged access to lawyers but with creating a greater consciousness about entitlements and devising ways and means in which these entitlements can be won. Accepting that the life of law is larger than litigation, it seeks to use a combination of skills and community involvement to develop the law and restructure legal processes to benefit the disadvantaged. Despite considerable opposition and a low-key public law system, public interest law has been established as an important emerging part of the English legal system. (Dhavan, 1986, p. 38)

One conclusion to emerge from consideration of the notion of public interest law is that the legal aid scheme only has a limited role to play in bringing legal services to all sections of the community. This system of funding legal services, whereby solicitors in private practice provide the same service for legal aid clients as for private clients but with payment of their fees coming from the public purse, fails to see the problems of the poor and disadvantaged as collective problems. The problem is an individual problem brought by an individual client to an individual solicitor. That solicitor then deals with the case on an individual basis. In truth, the problem may reflect a group problem which will not be solved by providing an individual remedy for the client. An example will give life to this notion. Suppose that a client comes to an individual solicitor complaining that the house let to the client's family by the local council is damp and in poor repair. The client wishes to secure a transfer to a house in better condition. The solicitor, under the Green Form scheme, collects evidence of the state of the house and writes to the local council, who ultimately agree to transfer the family to another house. The client is naturally pleased, but only the symptoms and not the cause of the problem have been tackled. The local council subsequently relets the damp house to another family, who may take no action. Though the case may be put forward as a success for legal aid, the public interest in improving the quality of housing stock has not been tackled. Public interest law involves more than servicing individual cases. It can also involve community legal education, law reform, negotiation on behalf of interest groups, lobbying, involvement in alternative methods of dispute resolution, legal research, monitoring the efficacy of enforcement procedures, and publicity.

Law centres have sought to tackle both the individual needs of clients and the collective needs of the community in the work that they do. They have also brought into the arena other providers of legal services which have not previously been recognised as part of the network of legal service delivery. Principal among these institutions are the Citizens Advice Bureaux, but there are a host of other agencies providing both general and specialist advice both to individuals and groups.

The Central Issue of Funding

Major achievements have resulted from experiments in the delivery of legal services, but all have struggled over the issue of funding. This type of legal service delivery cannot generate in fees from clients the sums necessary to run the service. Such developments have been dependent on public funding from central or local government. This funding has proved to be volatile and to be subject to political whim. Securing a sound financial base for the new systems for delivering legal services remains one of the priorities for these valuable initiatives.

The Law Centre Movement

Early Days

The first law centre to open was the North Kensington Neighbourhood Law Centre in 1969 (Byles and Morris, 1977; Cooper, 1983). Since 1969 there has been a steady growth of law centres. No official figures are kept because law centres have been set up on local initiative and on a number of different models. Today there are about 60 law centres: about half are to be found in London and the remainder in large provincial cities. Most are funded by a mixture of charitable funding, and local and central government funding. The development of law centres occurred outside the control of The Law Society and initially without its official encouragement. Though solicitors in private practice have been and continue to be involved in the management of law centres, The Law Society has no policy control over the operation of law centres. Its only involvement arises because it is the regulator of professional conduct and is the body responsible for granting the waivers of the Solicitors Practice Rules needed to accommodate law centres' working methods.

The Law Society's rejection of the idea of neighbourhood law firms was based upon considerations of expense and its commitment to ensuring that expansion of legal services took place in the context of the legal aid scheme, which, of course, channels work to solicitors in private practice. The language of the rejection of the idea was surprisingly strong at times. For example The Law Society said that the new scheme:

> contemplates a radical departure from the concept of legal aid as so far developed in this country and, by introducing a separate and distinct legal service, it would exercise a divisive social influence. (Law Society, 1968, para.20)

To test the hypothesis that a legal aid practice could be set up and work effectively, The Law Society in co-operation with the Greater Manchester Legal Services Committee set up the experimental firm of Cooper & Pearson in Manchester in May 1977. The firm was set up on traditional lines and was not allowed to advertise. The object of the project was to assess the demand for welfare law practices in inner city areas and the commercial viability of meeting the need by the establishment of new practices in such areas. The firm experienced problems from the outset in mobilizing a clientele in areas of work other than the traditional legal work of solicitors. Very little welfare law work was received. The partners felt that the prohibition on advertising was a major inhibition in this respect. It also seems that remuneration for legal aid work makes it unattractive and forces practices to take on traditional work to secure an acceptable cash flow. This is confirmed by other figures produced by legal aid practices elsewhere (Zander, 1978; Cooper, 1986). Cooper & Pearson lost money and in May 1980 the firm was taken over (Cooper, 1983).

The initial hostility of The Law Society to law centres has evaporated. Law centres are now accepted as making an important contribution to the provision of legal services and The Law Society made a concerted effort in its evidence to the Benson Commission to persuade it to recommend that The Law Society should have control over law centres. They did not succeed, nor do they seem likely to do so in the foreseeable future. The Law Society's early opposition to law centres was based on two grounds. First, that the creation of salaried lawyers in law centres was expensive and unnecessary: a cheaper way of meeting the same objective was to raise the profile of legal aid work in private practice and to use Advisory Liaison Officers. The second was undoubtedly the fear of competition. Experience has shown that, far from taking work from solicitors in private practice, law centres generate work from clients who have not previously used lawyers. Evidence given to the Benson Commission confirms this and The Law Society in its own evidence concedes the point. Indeed in some areas private practices have become established in the shadow of law centres and receive considerable work on referral from the nearby law centres. The Law Society is also involved with law centres in its capacity as regulator of the profession. The Law Society now lays down special rules relating to the practice of law in law centres, which restricts the work which may normally be done there. The solicitor may not generally act in conveyancing or commercial matters, divorce proceedings, probate matters, except for personal applications relating to small estates, personal injuries litigation where the expected damages are unlikely to exceed

£3000, and criminal cases involving those aged 21 or more (Law Society, 1990, p. 221).

Individual law centres have been set up on local initiative. There is no standard structure or style of work. It will be for the local group to identify the style of practice for its law centre. This represents one of the major differences between law centres and the private profession. Whereas partners in private practice decide the work that the firm will do and the resources that will be devoted to each department within the firm, in law centres it is the management committee, which is usually representative of the community from which the clients are drawn who determine the allocation of resources and priorities. In effect the clients control the practice rather than the lawyers. The Law Centres Federation (LCF), formerly the Law Centres Working Group, does attempt to monitor the development of law centres and enables law centres belonging to the LCF to speak with one voice on matters of common concern. Though it offers advice and information to groups trying to set up law centres, the LCF is careful to avoid plugging one particular ideology of law centres. Many, it seems, have not really thought about such matters prior to starting work and only develop a particular style of practice in the light of experience.

John Hendy of the Newham Rights Centre, a London law centre, made a major contribution to the debate on styles of practice by identifying five different approaches to legal services for the economically underprivileged. These are not necessarily mutually exclusive, though each has its own unique attributes and considerable implications for the allocation of resources within the law centre (Newham Rights Centre, 1975).

The first approach, which is also the most conservative, argues that poverty is no longer really a problem and so there are few, if any, problems peculiar to the poor. Therefore no change is required in systems for the delivery of legal services. This approach has few supporters. Not even The Law Society adheres to this view.

The second approach accepts that there is a gap between the promise and reality of rights for the underprivileged and the need to make those rights effective. It goes on to argue for genuine access to legal services for the poor by an expansion of legal services. The traditional solicitor–client relationship is retained, though some flexibility of approach is possible to include the use of community workers and the permissibility of educational outreach activities. Nevertheless the emphasis remains on the provision of legal services to individual clients.

The third approach follows from the recognition that the legal problems of the poor do not exist in isolation from their social problems. The poor not only suffer from legal deprivation but also from social grievances. To respond to individual cases is to ignore the underlying disease by merely providing relief for a symptom. Once this is accepted it becomes more important to focus on the social grievance as a whole and to direct attention to the class of clients suffering the grievance rather than to respond to the individual complainant. Securing a remedy for the individual may do little for the class. This approach is still rooted in the use of traditional legal remedies but on a group basis rather than on an individual basis. Equally where the law does not recognize a social grievance, a legitimate strategy will be to lobby for changes in the law.

The fourth approach seems rather more radical because it appears to move away from the traditional practice of law. It certainly does so in regarding the legal remedy or strategy as only one of a number of possible solutions to a grievance. In doing so, it accepts the limited capacity of the law to secure significant change. It recognizes that the poor lack power and seeks to assist in giving them power to secure change by programmes of community development, community organization and self-help. Law centres adopting this approach will frequently be found advising on the legal form an organization should take, writing constitutions for groups and advising them on how best to achieve the objectives and goals they have chosen for themselves. Though often challenged as overtly political, in terms of function law centres adopting this approach have much in common with lawyers advising large corporations. Provided that the law centre lawyers avoid domination of the groups they are involved with and simply serve their needs as perceived by them, their action is clearly not political.

The fifth approach is based on a Marxist analysis of society and rejects the capacity of law and legal services to effect any redistribution of wealth. Since law is seen as a tool of the capitalist classes designed to secure power and wealth for the ruling class, it would be futile to expect the law to contribute to the alleviation of poverty. Most subscribers to this view join the revolution rather than law centres!

Most law centres adopt the third or fourth approaches, or a combination of the two. It is sometimes suggested that law centres become involved in group work as a forced alternative to work with individuals because they are inundated with individual cases. An appreciation of the above approaches shows that this is a fallacy. Unfortunately this fallacy is not always recognized. As we shall see shortly, the Benson Commission does not appear to have understood the importance of the group work approach.

Profile of a Law Centre

At this point it will be helpful to describe a law centre. Rather than attempt the impossible of producing a synthesis of the various models currently operating, it is better to describe just one law centre. That chosen is the comparatively large law centre in Leeds, the Harehills and Chapeltown Law Centre. The centre was established in 1978 as the only law centre in Leeds and though it does not have a rigidly defined catchment area, it is principally concerned with meeting the needs of the Harehills and Chapeltown communities, where there is a high concentration of ethnic minorities both Asian and Afro-Caribbean. The law centre is located in shop-front premises on the Roundhay Road on a main bus route in the area where Harehills runs into Chapeltown. It is funded primarily by grants from the Lord Chancellor's Office and from Leeds City Council.

There are four admitted lawyers, seven general workers, an administrator/book-keeper and a part-time general worker. Over half the staff are from the ethnic minorities. In the 1980 Annual Report the centre described itself as follows:

> We are an agency in which there is a strong element of user control. This is not seen by all as a virtue, but we see it as an incontrovertible fact that in areas like Harehills and Chapeltown it is only through bodies identifiable by the community as by them, of them, and for them, that any real advancement can take place. This is perhaps just our way of stating the widely accepted doctrine of community self help.

The staff is organized into issue based units. There are five units: housing, immigration and nationality, crime and policing, welfare rights and employment. Each member of staff belongs to two units, but is expected to retain a broad knowledge of all areas of social welfare law. The centre is open to the public between 10.00 am and 4.00 pm each day except Wednesday. Two members of staff (on a rota basis) run the front desk and the switchboard, thus providing direct access to an adviser from the centre. If the matter is complex, the client will be seen by a member of the appropriate unit. Immigration and nationality, housing and welfare rights cases are the most frequently met categories of cases. The centre also offers a 24 hour emergency service with members of staff taking it in turns to be 'on call'. There is involvement by solicitors from private practice who offer free advice sessions at the centre on Tuesday evenings and Saturday mornings. The centre does individual case work, group work and educational work and is anxious to keep them in balance. There is what seems to be a perennial worry among law centres: that of keeping the individual case work within bounds so that time is available for the group work activities.

The Harehills and Chapeltown Law Centre has a management committee composed of 28 members. Seventeen represent the communities of Harehills and Chapeltown, five, the 'professionals' (Council, The Law Society, the Bar and local advice agencies) and there are four co-opted members chosen for their special expertise in areas not otherwise covered on the committee. The emphasis on user control is important, and the strong community base is seen as vital in developing confidence in the centre among the community. The 1980 Annual Report put it this way:

> In practice a lot of money seems to us to have been wasted in the past on providing agencies and services which the community experiences as imposed on them, and to which, accordingly, they do not actively respond, or learn from. . . . The law centre represents a different kind of approach to tackling these problems – one which seeks to harness the initiative locked up in the communities and develop resources within the community itself to enable people to play a much greater part in solving the problems.

The Benson Commission's Proposals

Law centres were well established when the Benson Commission called for evidence and there was a massive volume of evidence submitted about their work and potential. The response of the Benson Commission is disappointing because the Commissioners failed to understand the importance of the new initiatives which seek to release enterprise within communities to enable them to solve their own problems. A distinction which separates the practice of law in law centres from that in private practice is that between reactivity and proactivity (Stephens, 1982; Stephens, 1990). This is an abbreviated way of referring to the five approaches discussed above. The reactive approach is that of private practice: the lawyer remains passive and only responds to the legal problems of clients who seek out the lawyer's services. The proactive approach goes beyond the traditional lawyer–client relationship and reaches into communities 'to encourage collective and concerted action by neighbourhood groups' (Stephens, 1982, p. 109). The notions of reactivity and proactivity can be seen as opposite ends of a spectrum of operational philosophy.

The Benson Commission was unhappy with a proactive approach to the provision of legal services. While acknowledging the beneficial work of law centres generally, the Commission regarded the decade from 1969 to 1979 as one of experimentation. For the Commission the time for experimentation was over; it had a model for law centres which it proposed should become the official model. The security of central funding would only be available to those law centres complying with all the criteria laid down for the official model. These new law centres were called Citizens Law Centres. Most notably an embargo would be placed on 'general community work'. Law centres doing this type of work are described in the Report as follows:

> [These centres] like to work for the community at large or sections of it, rather than for individuals. They often seek to attack the roots of problems by organising groups to bring pressure to bear on landlords, local authorities and central government either to improve working, housing or living conditions or to urge changes in priorities of public expenditure so as to meet urgent needs or to promote changes of a similar character. (Benson Commission, 1979, para.8.19)

Such work is said to be inappropriate for a legal service for three reasons, which clearly indicate that the Commission failed to understand the function of group work. The reasons put forward are:

that the purpose of a legal service is to bring legal advice to all those in its area who would not otherwise receive it;

that general community work involves only sections of the community served whereas a legal service should be seen as willing to act for anyone who needs its services;

that general community work cannot be done while maintaining a position of providing an independent service.

Citizens Law Centres would offer legal services of the same type and on the same terms as private practice, being obliged to use the legal aid scheme and to require the payment of any assessed contributions from clients. Though many law centres use legal aid where they feel it is appropriate, many waive the payment of contributions. Nor did the Commission seem to like the pluralism which exists in law centres both in their structure and organization. They proposed considerable national standardization and to this end recommended the creation of a new national agency which would hold the purse strings and be able to direct certain aspects of centres' work and organization. There would still be local committees, but the role of 'local advisory committees', by contrast with existing management committees, is considerably reduced. The carrot of financial security is dangled before existing law centres to entice them into the new structure.

The proposals have been described as 'corporatist' by which is meant disguised state regulation (Elliott, 1980), as leading to 'the emasculation of the current law centre movement' (Stephens, 1982) and as 'seeking to nurture and support these important innovatory schemes by bludgeoning them into a rigidly centralised bureaucracy' (LCF, 1980). There is no doubt that implementation of the Benson Commission's proposals would mean that the poor would only be offered individual case work subject to all the restrictions of the legal aid scheme, even though the Commission elsewhere proposes significant extensions to the legal aid scheme. Given the evidence by law centres of their being inundated by individual cases, this would be both expensive and ineffective for the reasons given above. The Government appears to have quietly shelved the proposals. Existing law centres have certainly made it clear that they would have nothing to do with the new system.

Law Centres Today

Today Law centres have shown a remarkable ability to survive confirming the Benson Commission's statement that they have an influence out of all proportion to their numbers. Their survival is the more remarkable given their general lack of national organization:

> Law centres, whilst working a system that has many exciting possibilities for radical public interest development, are dogged by underfunding, a failure to keep experienced lawyers, inequitable distribution, very bad public relations and publicity output, and an almost total lack of co-ordinated back-up systems. (Cooper, 1986, p. 189)

Law centres appear to be searching for a new strategy and focus in the enterprise culture of modern Britain (Stephens, 1990). There is a paradox in their role. On the one hand they wish to retain their strong local links and responsiveness to local communities. On the other hand they wish to be seen as the focus of a new national salaried element with a network of law centres in all major urban areas. The new strategy that seems to be emerging is to recognize the central role that will be played by the private sector and to argue for a strong legal aid scheme, but also to bring within that scheme wide availability of general advice and accessibility to specialist public interest work which would belong with law centres. Viewed in this way, the ground between the law centre movement and the Legal Aid Board does not seem so wide. Nor are the figures required to implement such a scheme completely unimaginable, though there would need to be a dramatic increase in the Legal Aid Board's budget before implementation could become a reality.

Alternatives to Lawyers

The Notion of Para-Legal Advisers

New initiatives in legal services have not only involved qualified lawyers. The rise of lay advisory agencies has been phenomenal, so much so that it has been described as 'a new social service' (National Consumer Council, 1977). Much of the advice available from this new service is related to social welfare law and to consumer law. The agencies giving this advice are likely to be trades unions, Citizens Advice Bureaux, welfare rights teams, consumer advice centres, money advice centres, housing aid centres, neighbourhood centres run by social services departments and a whole host of specialist agencies. What they have in common and what distinguishes them from law centres is that generally advice is given by lay advisers who are not under the direct or indirect supervision of a qualified lawyer. Many such services devote the whole of their time to the provision of legal advice; they frequently appear as advocates before tribunals and are increasingly being granted discretionary rights of audience before registrars in county courts. The term para-legal adviser has grown up in the literature to describe those giving legal advice and doing legal work who are not qualified as solicitors or barristers.

The principal feature of many lay advisory agencies is that they give routine free legal advice on a massive scale to members of the public at very low cost (Kempson, 1987; Kempson, 1989). They act as an important filter for both private practice and for law centres to whom cases of difficulty are frequently referred. It would, however, be wrong to assume that such agencies only deal with the routine. For example, it is becoming standard practice for welfare rights advisers to argue cases with great competence before the Social Security Commissioners, and specialist agencies like MIND (National Association for Mental Health) employ lay advisers whose knowledge of mental health law is a match for any lawyer.

There is little wrong with this pluralism in the delivery of legal services. However, two problems can be identified. The first is the issue of quality control. Because the legal profession enjoys no monopoly on the giving of legal advice, there is no restriction on the establishment of a legal advice service and no formal check on the competence of advisers. Many agencies are scrupulous in their internal requirements for proper training before advisers are let loose on clients, but other are more casual. It is difficult for the consumer of legal services to discern the competence of the adviser. The client group most likely to use the free services of a lay adviser may not realize that the general principles of tort law on professional negligence apply to all such advisers and may not take action in the face of negligent advice which causes loss. The second problem is the price paid for pluralism. Faced with the multiplicity of agencies, how does the client choose where to go and which agency is most appropriate for his or her problem? There is something of a lottery about whether the right client gets to the right agency at the right time to be best dealt with. Attempts at the coordination of services seem doomed to failure. There is such a wide range of funding bodies and philosophies that it would be impossible to bring them all together. It may be that such coordination would result in the loss of the varied skills and traditions which make such agencies popular.

The diversity of agencies and advisers indicates how multi-faceted the provision of legal services is. Consumers of such services may be in the best position to judge their worth; consumers of legal services have proved remarkably astute in sifting the good from the bad and the fruitful from the useless.

The Citizens Advice Bureaux

The Citizens Advice Bureaux (CABx) are seen as having an important role to play in the future delivery of general legal advice. There is a national network of independent bureaux in all major towns and in some rural areas with some 900 outlets. Local bureaux are members of the National Association of Citizens Advice Bureaux (NACAB). The CABx provide frontline advice on a range of matters, but increasingly they are delivering legal advice and conducting representation before tribunals. Some employ a community lawyer who will handle more complex matters in-house. They typically operate from well-located, open-fronted offices near a central shopping district. There is no means test and no matters excluded from their range of services. They are extremely cheap to run because most of their work is done by trained volunteers. Salaried staff often includes only a manager, deputy manager and some secretarial support. Funding of individual bureaux is commonly a combination of NACAB funding and funding from local authorities in its catchment area (Citron, 1989; Richards, 1989).

NACAB provides some finance, which it receives from Government, and a wide range of support for local CABx, including a superb information system upon which advisers can rely in giving advice and which is designed to be easy to use for the trained lay adviser. NACAB also lays down national standards for the service, which includes guidance on opening hours, staffing, training and suitability of premises. It is also the national voice for the CABx.

The development of legal advice through the CABx is, however, patchy. The best approach law centres in their expertise and innovation. The worst remain rather amateurish in their work. Until recently, NACAB has not viewed itself as a central player in the legal services debate, but it does have the largest national coverage of advice provision. It is certain to be an influential actor in the development of a total strategy for the delivery of legal services. It may, indeed, become the logical first point of contact for anyone with a legal problem as the

Legal Aid Efficiency Scrutiny had suggested. The proposal failed on two grounds: the paucity of funding on offer and the lack of maturity of the CABx network for the task.

Managing the Delivery of Legal Services

The Need for an Overview

The Benson Commission had recognized the need for some body having overall responsibility for the management of legal services. The Commission proposed the establishment of a Council on Legal Services, whose functions would be:

to review and to carry out research on the provision of legal services;
to prepare proposals for the more effective provision of legal services of any description;
to review implemented proposals and, if so directed, to accept responsibility for the implementation of proposals;
to carry out any other functions in connection with the provision of legal services assigned to it.

The upward reporting, and receipt of direction, would be to and from the Lord Chancellor. It is unfortunate that the Government has rejected this proposal.

Looking at the experience in other countries there does seem to be a broad consensus that the management of legal services requires the participation of both consumers and providers of legal services. There is evidence of this process of democratization in this country with increasing participation by lay people in the work of regulation of the profession. No one is suggesting that a central body should take over the control of the powerful private profession. To do so would erode the sacred notion of the independence of the profession. However, legal services are increasingly a matter of public provision and even the private profession draws considerable fee income from the public funds of legal aid. There is clearly room for some body to oversee and comment on all public sector spending on legal services. The creation of a Council on Legal Services would have been the first step towards the creation of such a body in this country. Some of the functions of the Council on Legal Services are performed by the Lord Chancellor's Advisory Committee on Legal Aid whose remit is limited and which can only hope to persuade by the irrefutability of its arguments. There is also the Legal Aid Board, but its independence of thought is constrained by the budgets available to it.

In this connection the recommendation of the Benson Commission that regional legal services committees be created is to be welcomed. These committees, with full-time liaison officers, would be based on legal aid areas and have responsibility for assessing the needs for legal and para-legal services in their regions and how they should be met, as well as for coordinating regional services. The proposal builds on the successful work of the experimental North West Regional Legal Services Committee (see below).

To suggest the need for some central policy-making body is not to suggest the bureaucratization of legal services. It is possible to develop a national policy which accommodates local or regional policy variations. But without some national coordination it is possible for some regions to be inadvertently starved of the resources and ideas needed for appropriate provision of legal services while other regions are favoured.

A Ministry of Justice?

There is an arguable case that the time has come to create a Department of Justice. The idea was first floated in 1918 by the Haldane Committee, because of the problems caused by issues of law being covered by a number of ministries. That position has got much worse as regulation has penetrated more and more activities. There are now at least eight Government Departments charged with various aspects of the administration of justice, with the nearest to an overall remit being the Lord Chancellor's Department. This is unsatisfactory. The creation of a single Department of Justice in which responsibility for justice matters would be concentrated would also serve to make the Government more readily accountable to Parliament because there would be a Minister of Justice in the House of Commons. Government legal business could be coordinated through the Department of Justice, who would take over responsibility for the drafting of legislation and break the Parliamentary draughtsmen's stranglehold on outdated legislative drafting techniques which result in legislation barely comprehensible to lawyers let alone members of the public.

There are two areas of the administration of justice where there is concern to secure a degree of independence from the government of the day. The first is judicial appointments and the second is the administration of legal aid. These functions could be handed over to a Judicial Commission and a Legal Services Commission respectively. These would be independent Commissions voted funds by Parliament to enable them to carry out their functions. The idea of a Legal Services Commission has been part of the policy of the Legal Action Group since at least 1974. The Legal Action Group, an influential group which campaigns for greater access to justice, identified as shortcomings of the existing system:

> the legal rights of many citizens were going by default because of ignorance of those rights and an inadequate legal aid system;
> the uneven geographic distribution of existing legal services, both in the form of solicitors' practices and advice agencies;
> the concentration of solicitors' practices in the commercial centres of towns and in wealthier suburbs;
> the absence of subsidies to encourage practices to set up in 'unpopular' areas;
> the absence of a national policy on law centres;

a reluctance by some sections of the community to use solicitors in private practice because of fear of cost, inconvenience of location and office hours, and cultural and psychological barriers.

The Group's response was to call for a fresh approach to the provision of legal services based on:

a definition of need for legal services from the consumer's point of view, rather than leaving it to the lawyers to choose the services they are prepared to provide and to lobby for funds to pay for them;

legal services being seen as a branch of the social services, with a category of essential legal services identified for which non-means tested legal services would be available to all;

a move away from viewing legal services as the parochial concern of solicitors and barristers.

The Legal Action Group called for a complex mix of more lawyers, greater use of para-legals, active encouragement of self-help, new specialist courts and tribunals, and simplified procedures, and a new administrative structure (Legal Action Group, 1977). Essential legal services would include matters relating to occupation of residential accommodation, custody and care of children, personal injuries, protection against arbitrary action by employers, defence of persons accused of crime, income maintenance, immigration and discrimination.

The proposed Legal Services Commission would be an independent body funded by Government grant and responsible for all publicly financed legal services. Its remit would be wide, including:

the monitoring of legal services;

the efficient allocation of public funds to ensure adequate provision of legal services to all sections of the community;

the allocation of funds to a salaried sector;

the running of the legal aid scheme;

the investigation of the scope for savings by changes in, and simplification of, legal procedures;

to provide information for the public on the availability of legal services;

to promote an active policy for improving the quality of legal services by remaining continually responsive to consumer needs.

In the exercise of its functions the Legal Services Commission would be advised by a network of regional advisory councils composed of both providers and consumers of legal services from both the private and public sector. The broad idea was attractive to the Benson Commission, whose report in November 1979 proposed the establishment of a Council on Legal Services. The proposed model for the structure of a Department of Justice can be seen in chart form in figure 7.

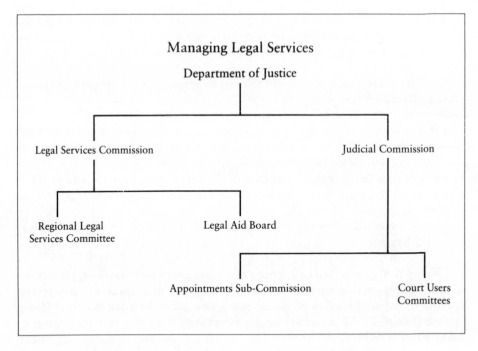

Figure 7   Managing Legal Services

While there is no hint that a Ministry of Justice will be created, the proposed
Legal Services Commission and Judicial Commission could easily be established
under the Lord Chancellor's Department which would be a big step in the right
direction. There are, however, two existing bodies which might claim to be
serving the purposes of the Legal Services Commission. The first is the new Legal
Aid Board, established under the Legal Aid Act 1988, and the second is the Lord
Chancellor's Advisory Committee on Legal Aid. This latter body was established
to provide some element of independent oversight of The Law Society's management of the legal aid scheme on behalf of the Government. The problem with
the first is that, although it has some executive capacity, it is thought by some
to lack the independence necessary to be an effective provider of legal services.
The Lord Chancellor's Advisory Committee has, by contrast, a splendid track
record of thoughtful, well-researched advice, which has unfortunately largely
been ignored. There is a cloud over its future now that the Legal Aid Board has
been established.

Finally, there is also the new body proposed by the Lord Chancellor in the
Green Papers and established by the Courts and Legal Services Act 1990: the
Advisory Committee on Legal Education and Conduct. There is a suggestion
that this raises constitutional issues because it could allow a Lord Chancellor
to interfere with the independence of the profession, by, for example, directing
how the defence of certain politically sensitive matters should be handled,
which might remove the prime obligation to act in the best interests of the client

without misleading the court. But significant revamping of this body and its merger with the Legal Aid Board would effectively be the creation of a Legal Services Commission especially if it was given a decent budget.

The 1989 Report of the Lord Chancellor's Legal Aid Advisory Committee recommend the establishment of a network of regional legal services committees. The model is the existing North Western Legal Services Committee referred to earlier in this chapter, the only such Committee which is fully operational. This Committee covers legal services in Greater Manchester, Lancashire and Cumbria; and each of these three areas has a regional sub-committee. Membership is drawn from advice agencies, including the CABx, the probation service, practising lawyers, local government officers, magistrates, the police, libraries, law centres, churches and tertiary education. The Committee exercises a coordinating function in the provision of legal services in the region and produces publicity material. The Advisory Committee calculates that a national network of six such Legal Services Committees on the North Western model would cost a mere £350,000.

Other recommendations by the Advisory Committee include the national funding of law centres and the funding of 125 resource lawyers in advice agencies up and down the country. The Committee has also been a champion of the extension of legal aid for some tribunal cases, and has been joined recently by another Government advisory body, the Council on Tribunals, in this call for an extension of legal aid to such cases.

One consequence of this sort of recognition of the significance of public sector legal services is that the role of The Law Society, and to a limited extent, the General Council of the Bar, would be restricted to that of professional associations of solicitors and barristers. They would provide just one input, representing the private sector, rather than the sole input, into issues involving the delivery of legal services. That is, of course, an important input because the nature of legal services, especially corporate legal services, is such that they will always be a privately funded sector. The professions can hardly complain if others step in to fill the gap in provision left by the profession itself.

Conclusion

In terms of the numbers of lawyers working in law centres and other advisory agencies, their significance is minimal. There are around 50,000 solicitors in private practice compared with no more than about 200 solicitors in law centres. Yet the importance of the public sector cannot be ignored. Why should this be so? The main reason is that the law centre movement has marked a shift away from reliance upon the legal profession to identify the legal needs of the public and to respond to them. The impetus for law centres and public provision of legal services outside the legal profession and liberated from the constraints of legal aid came from consumers rather than providers of legal services.

The mood of the late 1960s and early 1970s undoubtedly acted as a catalyst. The question of the provision of legal services has ceased to be an issue just for lawyers. The public sector will undoubtedly grow, but the private sector will not wither and die. Michael Zander points out that the ratio of private sector to public sector lawyers in 1978 was 340:1 in England and Wales but only 80:1 in the United States. The private sector will continue to be the main source of legal services for most people. The permanence of law centres, however, also seems certain. Despite perennial worries about funding and severe cuts in public expenditure, law centres have continued to be established and to grow. One likely development must be national funding of law centres, though this will have to be on some other model than that of Citizens Law Centres as proposed by the Benson Commission.

One heartening development in recent years has been the forging of under-standings between the private profession and law centres. Initial scepticism and hostility, coupled with fears of losing legal aid clients to law centres, have tended to evaporate as law centres have become established and as the private profession sees them meeting different needs and actually generating work for the private profession. There is surely nothing wrong with a system which offers different styles of practice to different types of clients. The need being met by the private sector is that of the wealthy and middle-class clients and of businesses, together with civil and criminal litigation for all sections of the community supported by legal aid. The public sector is tackling the needs of the poorer communities and is contributing to the movement to make rights effective.

These developments have coincided with a more critical mood on the part of consumers and providers, so that deficiencies in the operation of the legal system are highlighted and the role of law in achieving social policy goals becomes more overt. These issues tend to be unsettling; yet in the long term they are a sign of a healthy system. The result will be evolutionary change in the systems for the delivery of legal services in this country. In criticizing the Report of the Benson Commission it is sometimes forgotten that it proposed a considerable increase in public spending on the provision of legal services. Few would deny that legal ser-vices are comparatively under-funded. The argument is about the best allocation of funds and the most cost-effective system of delivery. What is missing from the debate is a sound foundation of principles upon which the provision can be based and perhaps also a tone which is less critical of the traditional provision of legal services than the mood of the times demands.

Many analyses of the role of lawyers stress the role of looking after the interests of clients. This involves fighting for clients, counselling them, con-structing powerful and persuasive arguments for their cases whether in litigation or otherwise, influencing decision makers and presenting clients with choices and information about the consequences of those choices. To these must be added the skills of managing and organizing transactions (Podmore, 1980). These are skills which will always be needed in both the public and private sectors, and so both are likely to flourish.

Part V
Recurring Themes

17

Recurring Themes

Introduction

We have now examined the claims most frequently met within both the criminal and civil justice systems. We have considered the contribution of tribunals to the development of the civil process, and we have examined the system for the delivery of legal services to individuals caught up in the criminal or civil process. Questions have been raised and conclusions drawn about the adequacy of our legal system for providing a just solution to the issues raised before it. In this chapter a number of recurring themes will be identified and discussed.

Adversarial *versus* Inquisitorial Procedures

The English legal system adopts the adversarial system of dispute resolution even where it seeks to provide assistance for those who come before the courts and tribunals of the system without an advocate to speak for them. This often leads to suggestions that all the deficiencies of the English system could be removed by the adoption of inquisitorial procedures. The principal difference is that whereas the adversary system places the onus of collecting and presenting evidence on the parties, the inquisitorial system places a duty upon the judge to investigate and inquire into the facts and the law upon which the claim is based. In terms of civil procedure this results in the absence of a concentration on the ultimate trial of the issue that pervades the English system, even though trial is a rare occurrence. The process in countries with civil law traditions is more diffuse. Typically there are three stages. First, there is the preliminary stage at which pleadings less formal than in the English system are filed and a hearing judge is appointed. Secondly, there will be the evidence-taking stage at which the hearing judge takes evidence and prepares a written report on the case. Thirdly, there is the decision-taking stage at which a bench of judges, of whom one will be the hearing judge, consider the report on the case together with the lawyers' written submissions on the law. They will hear oral argument only on selected issues and make a decision as to the outcome of the claim before them (Merryman, 1969). Written procedures play a large part.

In France the procedures in civil cases are as follows. The lawyers (*avocats*) file their pleadings (*conclusions*), following which a hearing judge (*juge des mises*) is appointed. At the evidence-taking stage, the *juge des mises* supervises the collection of evidence which is placed in a *dossier* which includes a summary of the evidence and report on the case prepared by the *juge des mises*. *Conclusions* continue to be exchanged throughout the case, particularly on legal issues raised. The *juge des mises* may pursue avenues of enquiry not suggested by the parties' *avocats*. He may not make any conclusions as to facts or law, but he does have a continuing supervisory role and does prepare the *dossier*, which is the written record on the basis of which the bench of three judges (the *juge des mises* will be one of the three) will decide the case following the final hearing (*audience*). The *audience* rarely lasts more than an hour or two. It will be seen that there is no culminating event equivalent to the English trial; there is rather a continuing trial with evidence presented early in the process.

As Sir Jack Jacob has noted (Jacob, 1987), both systems assume the contradictory character of the dispute they are called upon to determine, but employ different ways to reach that determination. It is possible to envisage the adversary system operating with a high degree of intervention from the judge. The essence of the adversary system is that it is for one of the parties to prove certain facts crucial to the claim. Often, especially where one of the parties is unrepresented, there will be a startling inequality between them. An interventionist approach from the judge can reduce that inequality. The unanswered question is whether it can remove the inequality. Only if such strategies can remove the inequality is it right to say that litigation without representation is possible. What few would dispute is the need for courts and tribunals to be friendlier places for litigants to use whether with or without lawyers.

The Concept of Due Process of Law

In English law there is no formal legal rule requiring the resolution of disputes to be by due process of law. Though there are similarities, care should be taken not to confuse the concept with that contained in the Fourteenth Amendment to the United States Constitution, which ordains that no State in the Union 'shall deprive any person of life, liberty or property, without due process of law'. Professor Atiyah concludes that the concept of due process of law in this country is a combination of three ideals:

 that adjudication is open;
 that each party has a right to be heard (that is, to adduce evidence and to present argument); and
 that the decision maker is impartial.

He notes that due process of law involves more than merely a trial by 'process authorised by a law validly made by Parliament', because in a formal sense Parliament is free to pass any law it wishes and this would include a law abolishing the ideals of due process in the judicial settlement of disputes. But Professor Atiyah considers it 'unthinkable that the concept. . . could be swept away like this' (Atiyah, 1983).

However we have seen that a formal trial is a rarity in the English legal process in both criminal and civil matters. The bulk of criminal cases is disposed of by guilty plea in both magistrates' courts and the Crown Court. Such proceedings cannot be said to display in any meaningful sense the ideals of due process. Openness is lacking in that important processes are hidden, masked behind the single word 'guilty' which is almost the limit of the defendant's right to be heard. In these cases impartiality of the judge is an irrelevance. In civil cases dealing with major personal injuries claims, the impact of insurance and the settlement of so many claims by negotiation dramatically reduces the significance of adjudication. In contract claims there is seldom any consideration of, or challenge to, the merits of the claim. In small claims in the county court the requirements of due process are ineffective. The adjudication of the dispute may claim to be open, fair and impartial, but if the procedures are too complex and legal aid provides no assistance, the right to be heard becomes illusory.

Does all this mean that yet again there is a gap between the rhetoric of due process and the actuality of the experience of those caught up in the legal process? Not necessarily. But it is necessary to extend the focus of due process to include not just the final adjudication of the dispute but also every preliminary stage leading up to adjudication. This requires a broadening of the ideals of due process. The key must be the requirement at every stage that those involved in the process make choices freely and on an informed basis. The notion of informed choice requires the availability of an independent adviser whenever someone is faced with a choice but lacks the knowledge upon which to base an informed and genuine choice. The requirement is of special importance in a legal system rooted in the adversarial tradition where party initiative is required throughout the whole process. It is in the nature of the adversarial process constantly to confront participants with the need to make choices concerning the preparation and conduct of their cases. For this reason mere simplification of procedures without any fundamental change in the responsibilities of litigants for the presentation of their cases is unlikely to secure lasting benefits.

The adoption of inquisitorial procedures does not mean the redundancy of the lawyer or legal adviser, though any process of dispute settlement designed to be used without a lawyer or legal adviser must be genuinely inquisitorial in function if it is to be fair to the parties. It may be more fruitful to consider due process more in terms of information and informed choices throughout the process than in terms of the qualities of the rare final determination of a dispute by contested adjudication before a court or tribunal. Instead of asking 'has there been due process?' we should ask the broader question 'has there been access to justice?'

Access to Justice

The concept of access to justice is far wider than that of due process, which is subsumed within this concept. The concept is argued and developed in the major Florence Access to Justice project whose results are published in six volumes (Cappelletti, 1978). Access to justice involves focus on two basic purposes of the legal system. First, the legal system must be equally accessible to everyone, and that access must be effective. Secondly, access to the system must lead to results that are individually and socially just. The emphasis on individual and social justice does not allow the problems of, for example, the litigant seeking redress following the purchase of a defective radio for £5 to be ignored.

The access to justice approach has developed as a consequence of the modern notion of the equality of all citizens and has grown out of developments in the provision of legal aid for the poor and of the growth of identifiable group interests for the protection of, for example, the rights of employees, of consumers, of ethnic minorities and of women. The access to justice approach moves beyond merely providing representation to consideration of 'the need to relate and adapt the process to the type of dispute'. Though the access to justice project was concerned with the civil process, its underlying philosophy can easily be transferred to the criminal process. It requires an examination of processes to determine whether there are structural imbalances or inequities in the system and to effect change to redress any imbalances, inequities or insufficiencies. It accepts a pluralism in methods of dispute resolution, but above all focuses on the needs of participants in the process. The report does not demand the abolition of the full adversarial trial, but would reserve it for disputes where so slow, expensive and formal a process is warranted.

As a model for small claims adjudication it is, not surprisingly, rejected as inappropriate. The access to justice approach demands a particularity of comment that is inappropriate in a short concluding chapter. Readers will have noted particular comments on particular systems of dispute resolution elsewhere in this book. The remainder of this chapter will therefore be devoted to comment on two recurring themes: the role of lay persons as decision makers and the provision of assistance and representation as a solution to problems of access.

The Role of Lay Persons as Decision Makers

The use of lay men and women as adjudicators in the legal system is widespread and is not unique to the English system. The use of lay persons has consequences for the operation of the system. There must be a clear understanding of the role of the lay members who cannot be expected to have a complete command of the law relevant to the issue before them. Professor Stein concludes that 'the association of laymen in the legal process tends to limit the issue to a clear-cut question which they can readily answer without having to give reasons.' He adds that a similar limitation applies to the remedies open to a lay court (Stein, 1984). The English legal system uses lay members as adjudicators in both criminal and civil cases. Justices of the peace deal with the bulk of criminal cases. Juries determine issues of fact in trials on indictment and are used on rare occasions in civil cases. Expert lay members can be called upon to sit with High Court judges in Admiralty and commercial cases. Finally, lay members sit alongside lawyer chairmen and women in tribunals.

The consequences of their involvement are considerable. Professor Stein considers that lay adjudicators are superior to professional judges in the application of general standards of conduct and gives as examples the notions of reasonableness, fairness and good faith. He also considers an important contribution by them to be the provision of 'an antidote against excessive technicality' and 'some guarantee that law does not diverge too far from reality'. Because they are not experts lay decision makers present a very real danger that the dispute may not be resolved in accordance with the prescribed rules of law, but rather by some general notion of fairness between the parties. In some circumstances the decisions made by lay adjudicators may not be appealable. The making of decisions in accordance with the prescribed rules of law is an inherent aspect of due process of law. Many criticisms of the old supplementary benefit appeal tribunals, often at that time composed wholly of lay members, was that adjudication of claims was based on whether the claimant was seen as deserving rather than on the legal rules of entitlement.

The modern tribunal composed of lawyer and two lay members presents an opportunity to develop a model of adjudication that combines the merits of lay decision making with legal competence. The participation of lay members does seem to lead to general public confidence in the fairness of the process. It can also dramatically widen the social experience represented by the decision makers. What is important here is the broadest representation consistent with the demands of the task. Appointments of lay members of tribunals seems currently too locked into the system for the appointment of justices of the peace, which hardly seems likely to result in the representation of a wide cross-section of the community. The key role of lay members, apart from their breadth of experience, will be in ensuring that procedures do not become too full of mystery, and to ensure that litigants before them are not reduced to passive spectators in a process designed to resolve their disputes. Perhaps more than any other change, moves to ensure that parties understand what is going on will increase effective access to justice. Lay members sitting regularly will obviously, and rightly, become familiar with the legal framework within which they are operating. Perhaps to ensure that the lay input is always well represented, it would be worth considering limiting the appointment of lay members (and possibly also lawyers as chairmen and women) to terms of five years with a compulsory period before reappointment. Such a move may also encourage broader representation since more lay members would be needed.

If the pattern of joint decision making can be made to work effectively in tribunals, then it might be extended to adjudication in the magistrates' courts where the role of clerk would be taken over by a lawyer in the chair sitting with two lay justices. Reasons for decisions could then be required, as they are currently required of tribunals. Again to reduce the incidence of the 'professional' lay adjudicator, there might be an embargo on holding more than one lay 'judicial' appointment at any given time. Of course, if the tribunal model becomes widely accepted, then adjudication of small claims would seem to be an obvious candidate for disposal in this manner, though a change to an inquisitorial procedure genuinely accessible to litigants in person would be the most beneficial change. But changes in structures even as dramatic as those suggested will not alone be enough if abandonment of claims continues to be of major significance because the process and law are too difficult to understand alone.

The Role of Advice and Advocacy

The Benson Commission considered the role of advice and advocacy principally in the context of representation before tribunals. As explained in chapter 13 the Commission made three recommendations to tackle the problem of representation: the simplification of tribunal procedures, the development of lay advice and representation, and the extension of legal aid.

The Government accepted these recommendations in principle 'subject to further consideration being given to timing and the availability of resources' (Government Response to Benson, 1983). Unanswered questions relate to how the complementarity of roles of lay and legal advisers will operate, and when, in the current climate of Lord Chancellor's concern about legal aid expenditure, resources for an extension of legal aid to tribunals is likely to be available. Nor has any attempt been made to establish criteria for distinguishing those cases where applicants might reasonably be expected to represent themselves from those where representation either by specialist lay adviser or by lawyer is appropriate. The 1990 Genn study (Genn and Genn, 1990) may inform the Lord Chancellor's thinking in this area.

The current restrictions on the availability of legal aid mean that solicitors are not viewed as a major source of advice in tribunal work either by themselves or by potential clients. The main sources of help are public sector and voluntary agencies like law centres, legal advice centres, representation units, welfare rights units and CABx. As noted above representation may not be available in all cases where initial advice and assistance has been offered.

Following a study of advice and advocacy services, principally in connection with welfare benefits, Roger Lawrence proposed a two-tier system for lay agencies with the first tier of generalist advisers available in CABx and similar agencies filtering the difficult cases for reference to a second-tier specialist representation service (Lawrence, 1980b). The proposal ignores the role of the legal profession and would be very expensive to implement if adequate numbers of staff were to be funded to enable representation to be widely available. Any proposal should acknowledge the issue of complementarity; even if the Benson Commission's recommendations are rejected, it is a fact of life that the legal profession has a role to play in this area, and would become far more involved if legal aid were extended. Certainly the role of the legal profession becomes significant once industrial tribunal work is taken into account.

The final issue which makes representation such a difficult question is that of the style of representation. It is axiomatic to say that the style of representation should be appropriate to the forum, but the pluralist approach to representation means that a tribunal is likely to see all types and styles of representation from the confrontational aggressive approach adopted by some Claimants Union representatives to the highly formalized performance of a lawyer used to appearing before the courts. Both would seem to be inappropriate. Studies have shown that claimants prefer proceedings in which they are involved and participate (Bell et al., 1974; Bell, 1975). The lower levels of formality before tribunals do mean that claimants are less stage-managed and can become far more involved in the presentation and argument of their cases. This has led experienced tribunal advocates to argue in favour of a style of 'joint representation' or 'co-operation' (Lawrence, 1980b). This means working with the claimant, advising on the legal framework within which the decisions are made, and avoiding reducing the claimant to the status of a passive participant in the process, whose only role is to give evidence. It is difficult to achieve joint representation, requiring time and patience in the preparatory stages. This style is contrasted with that of 'co-option', which occurs when the adviser takes over the claim and does not involve the claimant save to take instructions and to give evidence at the hearing. Claimants represented effectively using the co-operative style of representation are likely to have a far higher opinion of the process regardless of the outcome when compared with the litigant who has understood little of what is going on and has hardly participated in the decision-making process. But too much is sometimes made of this issue of style. The co-operative style is obviously preferable whatever the forum. A common division of responsibilities is to reserve factual issues for the claimant and legal issues for the representative.

Effective advice and representation in tribunals will undoubtedly result in more sittings of tribunals, but under the present system seems to be the only way of ensuring that claimants' cases are put fully to, and more importantly considered fully by, tribunals. In the long term it may well prove to be quicker and cheaper than changing to a fully inquisitorial system designed to be used by claimants without advice and representation.

It seems unlikely that there will be major changes in the predominantly adversarial style of dispute resolution in the foreseeable future. If this is so, advice, assistance and representation are of considerable importance in helping litigants to cope with the system. Yet we have seen that there are enormous gaps in the provision of legal services both in the criminal and civil process. In proceedings before magistrates' courts large numbers of defendants are unrepresented and alarmingly few defendants receive any legal help prior to charge or summons. For major civil claims matters are not quite as bad, though in debt cases debtors seem all too readily to submit to the claims of creditors. In the areas of small claims and of tribunal adjudication which were designed for use without representation, there is inadequate assistance available and the dramatic differences in the success rates of represented and unrepresented litigants indicates a failure in the design of the system. The solution for these difficulties is the ready availability of advice and assistance, and, in many cases, also of representation. Such representation must be of a quality and price to match the dispute. For less complex matters the use of para-legal workers is a real possibility. The legal aid scheme providing, albeit at lowish rates of remuneration, expensive lawyers for litigants may not be the best solution to the problems of lack of assistance and representation.

There is a need for a broader consideration of the means of delivering legal services which encompasses both the public and the private sectors and which does not ignore the important contribution of para-legals. At present The Law Society and the Bar seem to regard the non-professionally qualified as irrelevant in considering policies for the delivery of legal services. The need for a more representative body to oversee such policies is urgent. More public money needs to be spent on legal services. There is much merit in the argument for increased spending on law centres, but there is also a need for a salaried public litigation service. Such a service could be split into criminal and tribunals divisions. A salaried body of solicitors, barristers and para-legal workers could then be available to represent individuals with claims before criminal courts and a wide range of tribunals. Small claims are excluded because, with increased funding, lawyers and others working with consumer groups and in consumer advice centres could take on this work. A major contribution of increased use of para-legals is that the background and social composition of the providers of legal services is likely to be dramatically widened. The issue of the competence of para-legals would need to be addressed, but, just as the profession of legal executive has developed within the private sector, and will probably come of age with the solicitors' loss of the conveyancing monopoly, there is no reason why para-legals should not develop an organization similar to the Institute of Legal Executives with the ability to certificate its members.

The law has become too complex, even when unnecessary mystification is removed, for all members of society to act for themselves in claims which reach the stage of formal adjudication. Where help is available, for many people it unfortunately tends to be too little and too late, except for serious criminal offences and major civil claims. For this reason more resources should be devoted to legal education in schools and to the provision of effective advice and assistance at the earliest stages of claims. The concept of access to justice for all demands greater recognition of the need to inform individuals of their rights and of the choices available to them in securing enjoyment of those rights.

Concluding Comment

It would be easy to end on too pessimistic a note and to leave the reader with a picture of a legal system which is rotten to the core. This is clearly not so. It is, however, wrong to be complacent and to accept that the current system offers individual and social justice to all who invoke its processes. There is a place for bold and innovative reform based on a clear understanding of the strengths and weaknesses of the present system. The seeds of ideas for innovation and experimentation can be found in the present system. If we build on its strengths and seek to remove its weaknesses, the legal system of tomorrow can be more effective, more equitable, more open and more understandable than the system of today.

Bibliography

Abel, R. 1982: 'The Politics of the Market for Legal Services'. In P. Thomas (ed.), *Law in the Balance: Legal Services for the 1980s*, Oxford: Martin Robertson, p. 6.

Abel, R. 1988: *The Legal Profession in England and Wales*, Oxford: Basil Blackwell.

Abel-Smith, B. and Stevens, R. 1967: *Lawyers and the Courts*, London: Heinemann.

Abel-Smith, B. and Stevens, R. 1968: *In Search of Justice*, Harmondsworth: Penguin.

Abel-Smith, R., Zander, M. and Brooke, R. 1973: *Legal Problems and the Citizen*, London: Heinemann.

Adamsdown Community Trust 1978: *Community Need and Law Centre Practice*, Cardiff: Adamsdown Community Trust.

Adler, M. and Bradley, A. 1975: *Justice Discretion and Poverty – Supplementary Benefit Appeal Tribunals in Britain*, London: Professional Books.

Anderson Committee 1965: *Report of the Joint Working Party on the Enforcement of Judgments, Orders and Decrees of the Courts of Northern Ireland*, Belfast: HMSO.

Anon. 1957: 'Appeals to the House of Lords' [1957] Crim LR 566.

Applebey, G. 1978: *Small Claims in England and Wales*, Birmingham: Institute of Judicial Administration.

Applebey, G. 1979: 'Small Claims in England and Wales'. In M. Cappelletti (ed.), *Access to Justice*, 1979, vol. II p. 683, Alphen aan den Rijn: Sitjhoff and Noordhoff.

Applebey, G. 1987: 'Justice within Reach? – A Review of Progress in Reforming Small Claims' 6 Civil JQ 214.

Ashworth, A. 1984: *Sentencing in the Crown Court*, Occasional Paper No. 10, Centre for Criminological Research, University of Oxford.

Ashworth, A. 1987: 'The "Public Interest" Element in Prosecutions' [1987] Crim LR 595.

Ashworth, A. 1989: 'Criminal Justice and Deserved Sentences' [1989] Crim LR 340.

Atiyah, P. 1987: *Accidents, Compensation and the Law*, (4th edn), London: Weidenfeld and Nicolson.

Atiyah, P. 1983: *Law and Modern Society*, Oxford: Oxford University Press.

Baldwin, J. 1974: 'The Compulsory Training of Magistrates' [1975] Crim LR 634.

Baldwin, J. 1976: 'The Social Composition of the Magistracy' 16 Brit J of Crim 171.

Baldwin, J. and Hill, S. 1988: *The Operation of the Green Form Scheme in England and Wales*, London: Lord Chancellor's Department.

Baldwin, J. and McConville, M. 1974: 'The Acquittal Rate of Professional Criminals: A Critical Note' [1974] 37 MLR 439.

Baldwin, J. and McConville, M. 1977: *Negotiated Justice*, Oxford: Martin Robertson.

Baldwin, J. and McConville, M. 1978: 'Allegations against Lawyers' [1978] Crim LR 744.

Baldwin, J. and McConville, M. 1979a: 'Plea Bargaining and the Court of Appeal' 6 Brit J of Law and Soc 200.

Baldwin, J. and McConville, M. 1979b: *Jury Trials*, Oxford: Clarendon Press.

Baldwin, J. and Mulvaney, A. 1987a: 'Advance Disclosure in the Magistrates' Courts: Two Cheers for Section 48' [1987] Crim LR 315.

Baldwin, J. and Mulvaney, A. 1987b: 'Advance Disclosure in the Magistrates' Courts: How useful are Prosecution Summaries?' [1987] Crim LR 805.

Bankowski, Z. and Mungham, G. 1976: *Images of Law*, London: Routledge and Kegan Paul.

Barnard, D. 1985: *The Civil Court in Action*, (2nd edn) London: Butterworths.

Barnes, J. and Webster, N. 1980: *Police Interrogation: Tape Recording*, RCCP Research Study No. 8, London: HMSO.

Bartle, R. 1990: 'A Deviation from Crime' *New Law Journal*, 26 October 1990, p. 1494.

Bases, N. and Smith, M. 1976: 'A Study of Bail Applications through the Official Solicitor by Brixton Prisoners in 1974' [1976] Crim LR 541.

Beale, H. and Dugdale, A. 1975: 'Contracts between Businessmen: Planning and the Use of Contractual Remedies' 2 Brit J of Law and Soc 45.

Beeching Commission 1969: *Report of the Royal Commission on Assizes and Quarter Sessions*, Cmnd 4153, London: HMSO.

Bell, J. 1983: *Policy Arguments in Judicial Decisions*, Oxford: Clarendon Press.

Bell, K. 1975: *Research Study on Supplementary Benefit Appeal Tribunals. Review of Main Findings: Conclusions: Recommendations*, London: HMSO.

Bell, K., Collison, P., Turner, S. and Webber, S. 'National Insurance Local Tribunals – A Research Study' [1974] 3 J Soc Pol 289 and [1975] 4 J Soc Pol 1.

Benson Commission 1979: *Final Report of the Royal Commission on Legal Services*, (Benson Commission), Cmnd 7648, London: HMSO.

Benyon, J. 1986: 'In the Limelight: the Changing Context of Policing'. In C. Bourn and J. Benyon (eds) *The Police: Powers, Procedures and Proprieties*, Oxford: Pergamon Press, pp. 3–42.

Benyon, J. and Bourn, C. 1986: (eds) *The Police: Powers, Procedures and Proprieties*, Oxford: Pergamon Press.

Beveridge Report 1942: *Report on Social Insurance and Allied Services*, Cmd 6404, London: HMSO.

Birch, D. 1989: 'The PACE Hots Up: Confessions and Confusions under the 1984 Act' [1989] Crim LR 95.

Birks, M. 1980: *Enforcing Money Judgments in the County Court – How to Obtain Payment without a Solicitor*, April 1980, Form EX 50C, London: Lord Chancellor's Department.

Birks, M. 1984: *Small Claims in the County Court – How to Sue and Defend Actions without a Solicitor*, (revised November 1984), Form EX 50, London: Lord Chancellor's Department.

Blake, A., Bridges, L. and Cape, E. 1988: *The Duty Solicitor's Handbook*, London: Legal Action Group.

Blom-Cooper, L. and Drewry, G. 1972: *Final Appeal – A Study of the House of Lords in its Judicial Capacity*, Oxford: Clarendon Press.

Blom-Cooper, L. 1984: 'The Changing Nature of the Appellate process' 3 Civil JQ 295.

Bottoms, A. and McClean, J. 1976: *Defendants in the Criminal Process*, London: Routledge and Kegan Paul.

Bourn, C. 1979: 'The Pearson Proposals in Outline'. In D. Allen, C. Bourn and J. Holyoak, *Accident Compensation after Pearson*, London: Sweet and Maxwell.

Bridges, L., Carter, J. and Gorbing, S. 1982: 'The Impact of Duty Solicitor Schemes in Six Magistrates' Courts' LAG Bulletin, July 1982, p. 12.

Brink, B. and Stone, C. 1988: 'Defendants who do not ask for bail' [1988] Crim LR 152.

Brown, D. 1987: *The Police Complaints Procedure: A Survey of Complainants' Views*, Home Office Research Study No. 93, London: HMSO.

Brown, D. 1989: *Detention and the Police Station under the Police and Criminal Evidence Act 1984*, Home Office Research Study No. 93, London: HMSO.

Burney, E. 1979: *J.P.: Magistrate, Court and Community*, London: Hutchinson.

Buxton, R. 1990: 'Challenging and Discharging Jurors' [1990] Crim LR 225 and 284.

Byles, A. and Morris, P. 1977: *Unmet Need – The Case of the Neighbourhood Law Centre*, London: Routledge and Kegan Paul.

Cain, M. 1986: 'Who loses out in Paradise Island?' In I. Ramsay (ed.) *Debtors and creditors*, London: Professional Books.

Cantley Working Party 1979: *Report of the Personal Injuries Litigation Procedure Working Party* (Cantley Report), Cmnd 7476, London: HMSO.

Cappelletti, M. (ed.) 1978: *Access to Justice*, (6 vols), Alphen aan den Rijn: Sitjhoff and Noordhoff.

Carlen, P. 1976: *Magistrates Justice*, Oxford: Martin Robertson.

Carlin, J., Messinger, J. and Howard, S. 1966: 'Civil Justice and the Poor – Issues for Sociological Research' 1 Law & Soc Rev 9.

Carty, H. 1983: 'Precedent and the Court of Appeal: Lord Denning's Views Explored' 1 Legal Studies 68.

Chambers, G. and Harwood, S. 1990: *Solicitors in England and Wales: Practice, Organisation and Perceptions*, London: The Law Society.

Citron, J. 1989: *Citizens Advice Bureaux: For the Community by the Community*, London: Pluto Press.

Civil Justice Review 1988: *Civil Justice Review. Report of the Review Body on Civil Justice*, Cm 394, London: HMSO.

Clayton, R. and Tomlinson, H. 1987: *Civil Actions against the Police*, London: Sweet and Maxwell.

Cocks, R. 1983: *Foundations of the Modern Bar*, London: Sweet and Maxwell.

Cohen, P. 1982a: 'Born to Judge' LAG Bulletin, August 1982, p. 8.

Cohen, P. 1982b: 'Bar Racism on Trial' LAG Bulletin, April 1982, p. 6.

Cohen, P. 1982c: 'Racial Discrimination among Solicitors' LAG Bulletin, May 1982, p. 11.

Conroy, D. 1971: 'Do Applicants Need Advice or Representation?' *The Future of Administrative Tribunals*. Edited transcript of proceedings of a conference held at the Institute of Judicial Administration, University of Birmingham, April 1971, Birmingham: Institute of Judicial Administration.

Conservative Political Centre 1968: *Rough Justice*, London: Conservative Political Centre.

Consumer Council 1970: *Justice out of Reach*, London: Consumer Council.

Conway, A. 1980: 'The London Small Claims Court' [1980] LAG Bulletin 231.

Cooper, J. 1983: *Public Legal Services: A Comparative Study of Policy, Politics and Practice*, London: Sweet and Maxwell.

Cooper, J. 1986: 'Public Interest Lawyers in England and Wales'. In J. Cooper and R. Dhavan (eds) *Public Interest Law*, Oxford: Basil Blackwell, pp. 161–92.

Cork Committee 1982: *Report of the Review Committee on Insolvency Law and Practice (Cork Committee)*, Cmnd 8558, London: HMSO.

Cownie, F. 1990: 'The Reform of the Legal Profession or the End of Civilization as we Know it'. In F. Patfield and R. White, *The Changing Law*, Leicester: Leicester University Press, p. 213.

Cross, R. 1962: 'The Criminal Evidence Act 1898 and the House of Lords as a Court of Criminal Appeal' 78 LQR 407.

Cutts, A. 1982: 'Has the Bail Act Made Any Difference?' *New Law Journal*, 25 November 1982, p. 1089.

Dashwood, A. 1972: 'Juries in a Multi-Racial Society' [1972] Crim LR 85.

Dashwood, A. 1974: 'The Jury and the Angry Brigade' 11 Western Australia L Rev 245.

Davies, C. 1970: 'The Innocent who Plead Guilty' *Law Guardian*, March 1970, p. 9.

Davies, J. E. 1986: 'Delegalisation of Debt Recovery Proceedings: a Socio-Legal Study of Money Advice Centres and Administration Orders'. In I. Ramsay (ed.) *Debtors and creditors*, London: Professional Books.

Davies, M. 1987: 'Reading Cases' 50 MLR 409.

Dell, S. 1971: *Silent in Court*, London: Social Administration Research Trust.

Devlin, P. 1978: 'Judges, Government and Politics' 41 MLR 501.

Devlin, P. 1979: *The Judge*, Oxford: Oxford University Press.

Devlin Committee 1976: *Report of the Committee on Evidence of Identification in Criminal Cases*, (Devlin Committee), HCP 338 [1975–6], London: HMSO.

Dhavan, R. 1986: 'Whose Law? Whose Interest?' In J. Cooper and R. Dhavan (eds) *Public Interest Law*, Oxford: Basil Blackwell, pp. 17–48.

DHSS 1978: *Social Assistance: A Review of the Supplementary Benefit Scheme in Great Britain*, London: HMSO.

DHSS, 1983: *Social Security Statistics 1983*, London: HMSO.

Dickens, L. et al., 1985: *Dismissed. A Study of Unfair Dismissal and the Industrial Tribunal System*, Oxford: Basil Blackwell.

DoE 1981: W. Hawes and G. Smith, *Patterns of Representation of the Parties in Unfair Dismissal Cases: A Review of the Evidence*, DoE Research Paper No. 22, London: HMSO.

DoE, 1984: *Employment Gazette*, March 1984, p. 127, London: HMSO.

DoE 1988: *Consultation Paper on Industrial Tribunals*, London: Department of Employment.

Donaldson, Sir J. 1983: *The Times*, 5 October 1983, p. 10.

Donaldson, Lord, 1990a: 'Review of the Legal Year 1989–90' *New Law Journal*, 9 November 1990, p. 1569.

Donaldson, Lord, 1990b: 'Reform of the Legal Profession' 40 CLP 1.

Donoughmore Committee 1932: *Report of the Committee on Minister's Powers* (Donoughmore Committee) Cmd 4060, London: HMSO.

Donovan Committee 1965: *Report of the Interdepartmental Committee on the Court of Criminal Appeal*, (Donovan Committee), Cmnd 2755, London: HMSO.

Donovan Commission 1968: *Report of the Royal Commission on Trades Unions and Employers' Associations*, (Donovan Commission), Cmnd 3623, London: HMSO.

Downey, B. 1961: 'Administration of Justice Act 1960' 24 MLR 261.

Drewry, G. 1973: 'Leapfrogging – and a Lords Justices' Eye View of the Final Appeal' 89 LQR 260.

Duff, P. and Findlay, M. 1983: 'Jury Vetting – The Jury under Attack' 3 Legal Studies 159.

East, R. 1985: 'Jury Packing: A Thing of the Past?' 48 MLR 518.

East, R. and Doherty, M. 1984: 'The Practical Operation of Bail' Legal Action, March 1984, p. 12.

Economides, K. 1980: 'Small Claims and Procedural Justice' 7 Brit J of Law & Soc 111.

Elliott, M. 1980: 'The Royal Commission on Legal Services: The Theoretical Background' [1980] JSWL 1.

Evershed Committee 1953: *Final Report of the Committee on Supreme Court Practice and Procedure*, (Evershed Committee) Cmd 8878, London: HMSO.

Farmer, J. 1974: *Tribunals and Government*, London: Weidenfeld and Nicolson.

Farquharson, D. 1986: 'The Role of Prosecution Counsel: Report by a Committee under the Chairmanship of the Hon. Mr Justice Farquharson' *Law Society's Gazette*, 26 November 1986, p. 3599.

Feeney, F. 1984: 'Advance Disclosure of the Prosecution Case' Home Office Research Bulletin 17 p. 15.

Feeney, F. 1985: 'Advance Disclosure of the Prosecution Case'. In Moxon, D. (ed.) *Managing Criminal Justice*, p. 94, Home Office Research and Planning Unit, London: HMSO.

Findlay, M. and Duff, P. 1988: *The Jury under Attack*, London: Butterworths.

Fisher Inquiry 1977: *Report of an Inquiry into the Circumstances leading to the Trial of Three Persons on Charges arising out of the Death of Maxwell Confait and the Fire at 27 Doggett Road, London SE6,* (Fisher Report) HCP 90, London: HMSO.

Fiss, O. 1984: 'Against Settlement' 93 Yale LJ 1073.

Flood, J. 1983: *Barristers' Clerks*, Manchester: Manchester University Press.

Foster, K. 1973a: 'The Manchester Arbitration Scheme – An Interim Report' [1973] LAG Bulletin 190.

Foster, K. 1973b: 'The Location of Solicitors' 36 MLR 153.

Foster, K. 1975: 'Problems with Small Claims' 2 Brit J of Law & Soc 75.

Franks Committee 1957: *Report of the Committee on Administrative Tribunals and Enquiries* (Franks Committee) Cmnd 218, London: HMSO.

Freeman, M. 1981: 'The Jury on Trial' [1981] CLP 65.

Frost, A. and Howard, C. 1977: *Representation and Administrative Tribunals*, London: Routledge and Kegan Paul.

Galanter, M. 1974: 'Why the "Haves" come out ahead: Speculation on the Limits of Legal Change' 9 Law & Soc Rev 95.

Galligan, D. 1981: 'Guidelines and Just Deserts: A Critique of Recent Trends in Sentencing Reform' [1981] Crim LR 297.

Genn, H. 1982: *Meeting Legal Needs?* Oxford: Centre for Socio-Legal Studies.

Genn, H. 1987: *Hard Bargaining: Out of Court Settlement in Personal Injury Actions*, Oxford: Clarendon Press.

Genn, H. and Genn, Y. 1989: *The Effectiveness of Representation at Tribunals*, Lord Chancellor's Department.

Glasser, C. 1990: 'The Legal Professor in the 1990s – Images of Change' 10 Legal Studies 1.

Government Reply to Miscarriages of Justice 1983: *The Government Reply to the Sixth Report of the Home Affairs Committee Session 1981–2 HC 421 Miscarriages of Justice*, Cmnd 8856, London: HMSO.

Government Response to Benson 1983: *The Government Response to the Report of the Royal Commission on Legal Services*, Cmnd 9077, London: HMSO.

Greer, D. 1971: 'Anything but the Truth: The Reliability of Testimony in Criminal Trials' 11 *Brit J of Crim* 131.

Gregory, J. 1976: *Crown Court or Magistrates' Court*, London: HMSO.

Gregory, J. 1987: *Sex, Race and the Law*, London: Sage.

Griffith, J. 1955: 'The Crichel Down Affair' 18 MLR 557.

Griffith, J. 1987: *The Politics of the Judiciary*, (3rd edn) London: Fontana.

Guide to Conduct, 1990: *The Guide to the Professional Conduct of Solicitors*, London: The Law Society.

Hall, A. 1984: 'Bail: Appeals' [1984] LAG Bulletin 145.

Hall Williams, J. E. 1988: *The Role of the Prosecutor*, Aldershot: Avebury.

Hansen, O. 1983a: 'Little Changes to Police Bill' LAG Bulletin, March 1983, p. 3.

Hansen, O. 1983b: 'Outside Parliament Opposition Mounts' LAG Bulletin, April 1983, p. 3.

Harman, H. and Griffith, J. 1979: *Justice Deserted: The Subversion of the Jury*, London: NCCL.

Harris, D., Maclean, M., Genn, H., Lloyd-Bostock, S., Fenn, P., Corfield, P. and Brittan, Y. 1984: *Compensation and Support for Injury and Illness*, Oxford: Clarendon Press.

Harris, N. 1983: 'The Reform of the Supplementary Benefit Appeal System' [1983] JSWL 212.

Harrison, J. 1987: *Police Misconduct: Legal Remedies*, London: Legal Action Group.

Hayes, M. 1981: 'Where Now the Right to Bail?' [1981] Crim LR 20.

Hazell, R. (ed.) 1978: *The Bar on Trial*, London: Quartet Books.

Holdsworth, W. 1956: *A History of English Law*, (7th edn, A. Goodhart and H. Hanbury) vol. I, London: Methuen.

Home Affairs Committee 1982: *Miscarriages of Justice*, 6th Report of Home Affairs Committee of the House of Commons, HCP 421, London: HMSO.

Home Affairs Committee, 1990: *Crown Prosecution Service: Fourth report of Home Affairs Committee*, April 1990, HCP 118, London: HMSO.

Home Office 1989: *Committal Proceedings: A Consultation Paper*, London: Home Office and Lord Chancellor's Department.

Hood, R. 1972: *Sentencing the Motoring Offender*, London: Heinemann.

Horowitz, D. 1977: *The Courts and Social Policy*, Washington DC: The Brookings Institution.

Hughes Commission 1980: *Report of the Royal Commission on Legal Services in Scotland*, (Hughes Commission), Cmnd 7846, London: HMSO.

Hunter Committee 1988: *Report of the Enforcement of Judgments Review Committee (Northern Ireland)*, Belfast: HMSO.

Irving, B. 1980: *Police Interrogation: A Case Study of Current Practice*, RCCP Research Study no. 2, London: HMSO.

Irving, B. 1986: 'The Interrogation Process'. In J. Benyon and C. Bourn (eds) *The Police: Powers, Procedures and Proprieties*, Oxford: Pergamon Press, pp. 136–49.

Irving, B. and Hilgendorf, L. 1980: *Police Interrogation: The Psychological Approach*, RCCP Research Study no. 1, London: HMSO.

Ison, T. 1972: 'Small Claims' 53 MLR 18.

Jacob, J. 1987: *The Fabric of English Civil Justice*, London: Stevens.

James Committee 1975: *Report of the Interdepartmental Committee on The Distribution of Criminal Business between the Crown Court and Magistrates' Courts*, (James Committee), Cmnd 6323, London: HMSO.

Jenkins, J., Skordaki, E., and Willis, C., 1989: *Public Use and Perception of Solicitors' Services*, London: The Law Society.

Johnson, E. 1974: *Justice and Reform: The Formative Years of the OEO Legal Services Program*, New Brunswick: Transaction Books.

Joseph, M. 1980: *The Conveyancing Fraud*, London: Michael Joseph.

Joseph, M. 1984: *Lawyers Can Seriously Damage Your Health*, London: Michael Joseph.

Judicial Statistics 1988: *Judicial Statistics for the Year 1988*, Cm 745, London: HMSO.

Jukes, M. 1978: 'Reply: Tribunals – Justice for All?' *Industrial Society*, September/ October, pp. 5–6.

JUSTICE 1964: *Criminal Appeals*, London: Stevens.

JUSTICE 1968: *Home Office Review of Criminal Convictions*, London: Stevens.

JUSTICE 1970: *The Prosecution Process in England and Wales*, London: Justice Educational and Research Trust.

JUSTICE 1974: *Going to Law: A Critique of English Civil Procedure*, London: Stevens.

JUSTICE 1982: *Compensation for Wrongful Imprisonment*, London: Stevens.

JUSTICE 1987: *Industrial Tribunals*, London: JUSTICE.

JUSTICE 1989: *Miscarriages of Justice*, London: Justice Educational and Research Trust.

Kempson, E. 1987: *Advice Services in Oldham. A Review of Current Provision and Patterns of Use*, Oldham: Oldham Metropolitan Borough.

Kempson, E. 1989: *Legal Advice and Assistance*, London: Policy Studies Institute.

King, M. 1973: *Bail or Custody*, (2nd edn), London: Cobden Trust.

King, M. 1976: 'Roles and Relationships in Magistrates' Courts' [1976] LAG Bulletin 7.

King, M. 1977: *The Effects of a Duty Solicitor Scheme: An Assessment of the Impact upon a Magistrates' Court*, London: Cobden Trust.

King, M. 1981: *The Framework of Criminal Justice*, London: Croom Helm.

King, M. and May, C. 1985: *Black Magistrates*, London: Cobden Trust.

Knight, M. 1970: *Criminal Appeals. A Study of the Powers of the Court of Appeal, Criminal Division on Appeals against Conviction*, London: Stevens.

Knittel, E. and Seiler, D. 1972: 'The Merits of Trial by Jury' [1972] CLJ 316.

LAG Bulletin 1983a: 'Dangerous Intransigence' LAG Bulletin, March 1983, p. 1.

LAG Bulletin 1983b: 'A Bill Beyond Repair' LAG Bulletin, April 1983, p. 1.

Law Centres Federation (LCF) 1980: *A Response to the Royal Commission on Legal Services*, London: Law Centres Federation.

Law Society 1968: *Legal Advice and Assistance*, London: The Law Society.

Law Society 1984: *Report of The Law Society Council's Committee of Enquiry into The Law Society's Treatment of the Complaints of Mr L.A. Parsons against Mr G. Davies and Mr C. Malim*, (The Ely Report), February 1984, London: The Law Society.

Law Society, 1990: *Annual Statistic Report 1990*, London: The Law Society.

Lawrence, R. 1980a: 'Solicitors and Tribunals' [1980] JSWL 13.

Lawrence, R. 1980b: *Tribunal Representation*, London: Bedford Square Press.

Lay Observer 1984: 'The Lay Observer's Letter to Mr Leslie Parsons Regarding Mr Glanville Davies', *Law Society's Gazette*, 14 December 1983, p. 3203.

Lee, S. 1988: *Judging Judges*, London: Faber and Faber.

Legal Action Group 1977: *Legal Services: A Blueprint for the Future*, London: Legal Action Group.

Legal Aid Handbook 1990: *Legal Aid Handbook 1990*, London: Sweet and Maxwell.

Leicestershire Constabulary 1989: *Annual Report 1988*.

Levenson, H. 1981: 'Uneven Justice – Refusal of Criminal Legal Aid' LAG Bulletin, March 1981, p. 106.

Levin, J. 1982: 'Legal Insurance?' LAG Bulletin, August 1982, p. 13.

Lewis, C. 1981: 'The Voluntary Bill of Indictment' *Law Society's Gazette*, 16 December 1981, p. 1442.

Lewis, P. 1973: 'Unmet Legal Needs'. In P. Morris, R. White and P. Lewis, (eds) *Social Needs and Legal Action*, p. 73, Oxford: Martin Robertson.

Lister, R. 1975: 'SBATs – an urgent case for Reform'. In M. Adler and A. Bradley, *Justice Discretion and Poverty – Supplementary Benefit Appeal Tribunals in Britain*, p. 171, London: Professional Books.

Lord Chancellor's Department 1990: *Judicial Appointments: The Lord Chancellor's Policies and Procedures* (2nd edn), London: Lord Chancellor's Department.

Lord Chancellor's Department 1987: *The Claims Registry: Computerisation of County Court Procedures in Debt Cases*, London: Lord Chancellor's Department.

Lord Chancellor's Department 1988: *Today's Magistrate*, London: HMSO.

Lord Chancellor's Department 1989: *Judicial Statistics 1988*, London: HMSO.

Lustgarten, L. 1986: *The Governance of Police*, London: Sweet and Maxwell.

Lynes, A. 1976: 'Unemployment Assistance Tribunals in the 1930s'. in M. Adler and A. Bradley, *Justice Discretion and Poverty – Supplementary Benefit Appeal Tribunals in Britain*, p. 5, London: Professional Books.

Macaulay, S. 1963: 'Non-Contractual Relations in Business: A Preliminary Study' 28 Am Soc Rev 55.

Mack, D. 1976: 'Full-Time Major Criminals and the Courts' 39 MLR 241.

Macmillan, J. 1983: 'Industrial Tribunals – A Defence and Some Proposals for Reform' *Law Society's Gazette*, 30 November 1983, p. 3091.

Mair, G. 1988: *Bail and Probation Work: the ILPS Temporary Bail Action project*, Home Office Research and Planning Unit Paper 46, London: HMSO.

Mark, R. 1973: *Minority Verdict*, The 1973 Dimbleby Lecture, London: BBC.

Marre Committee, 1988: *A Time for Change: Report of the Committee on the Future of the Legal Profession*, (Marre Committee), London: The General Council of the Bar and The Law Society.

Marshall, G. 1978: 'Police Accountability Revisited'. In D. Butler and A. Halsey, *Policy and Politics*, London: Macmillan.

Mayhew, P., Elliott, D. and Dowds, L. 1988: *The British Crime Survey 1988*, Home Office Research Study no. 111, London: HMSO.

Mayhew L. and Reiss, A. 1969: 'The Social Organisation of Legal Contacts' 34 Am Soc Rev 318.

McBarnet, D. 1981: *Conviction, Law, The State and the Construction of Justice*, London: Macmillan.

McCabe, S. and Purves, R. 1972: *The Jury at Work*, Oxford: Basil Blackwell.

McCabe, S. and Purves, R. 1974: *The Shadow Jury at Work*, Oxford: Basil Blackwell.

McCabe, S. and Sutcliffe, F. 1978: *Defining Crime: A Study of Police Definitions*, Oxford: Basil Blackwell.

McConville, M. and Baldwin, J. 1981: *Courts, Prosecution and Conviction*, Oxford: Clarendon Press.

McConville, M. and Morrell, P. 1983: 'Recording the Interrogation: Have the Police got it Taped?' [1983] Crim LR 158.

McCorquodale, S. 1962: 'The Composition of Administrative Tribunals' [1962] PL 298.

McDonald, P. 1982: 'The Class of '81 – A Glance at the Social Class Composition of Recruits to the Legal Profession' 9 J of L & Soc 267.

McMullen, J. 1984: 'An Analysis of the Power of Review by Industrial Tribunals of Their Own Decisions' 3 Civil JQ 12.

Meador, D. 1973: *Criminal Appeals – English Practices and American Reforms*, Charlottesville: University Press of Virginia.

Merryman, J. 1969: *The Civil Law Tradition*, Stanford: Stanford University Press.

Micklethwait, R. 1976: *The National Insurance Commissioners*, London: Stevens.

Mirfield, P. 1984: 'The Future of the Law of Confessions' [1984] Crim LR 63.

Moir, E. 1969: *The Justice of the Peace*, Harmondsworth: Penguin.

Moody, S. and Tombs, J. 1982: *Prosecution in the Public Interest*, Edinburgh: Scottish Academic Press.

Morgan, P. 1985: *Modelling the Criminal Justice System*, Home Office Research and Planning Unit Paper 35, London: HMSO.

Morgan, R. 1989: 'Remands in Custody: Problems and Prospects' [1989] Crim LR 481.

Morris Committee 1965: *Report of the Departmental Committee on Jury Service*, (Morris Committee), Cmnd 2627, London: HMSO.

Moxon, D. 1988: *Sentencing Practice in the Crown Court*, Home Office Research Study No. 103, London: HMSO.

Nardulli, P. 1979: 'The Caseload Controversy and the Study of Criminal Courts' 70 *J of Crim L and Criminology* 89.

National Audit Office 1989: *Review of the Crown Prosecution Service*, HCP 345 1988–9, London: HMSO.

National Consumer Council 1977: *The Fourth Right of Citizenship: A Review of Local Advice Services*, London: National Consumer Council.

National Consumer Council 1979: *Simple Justice*, London: National Consumer Council.

National Consumer Council 1980: *Model Code of Procedure for Small Claims Divisions of County Courts*, London: National Consumer Council.

National Consumer Council, 1991: *Out of Court*, London: National Consumer Council.

National Consumer Council and Welsh Consumer Council 1983: *Consumers and Debt*.

National Consumer Council 1989: *Ordinary Justice*, London: HMSO.

Newbold, A. and Zellick, G. 1987: 'Reform of the Solicitors' Complaints Procedures: Fact or Fiction?' 6 Civil JQ 25.

Newham Rights Centre 1975: *Report and Analysis of a Community Law Centre 1974–5*, London: Newham Rights Centre.

Nottinghamshire Constabulary 1989: *Annual Report 1988*.

Office of Fair Trading 1981: *Redress Procedures under Codes of Practice*, December 1981, London: Office of Fair Trading.

Office of Fair Trading 1986: *Consumer Dissatisfaction: a Report on Surveys undertaken by the Office of Fair Trading, 1986*, London: HMSO.

Ogus, A., Barendt, E., Buck, T. and Lynes, T. 1988: *The Law of Social Security*, (3rd edn), London: Butterworths.

Packer, H. 1968: *The Limits of the Criminal Sanction*, Stanford: Stanford University Press.

Pannick, D. 1988: *Judges*, Oxford: Clarendon Press.

Paterson, A. 1982: *The Law Lords*, London: Macmillan.

Paterson, A. and Nelken, D. 1984: 'Evolution in Legal Services: Practice without Theory' 3 Civil JQ 229.

Payne Committee 1969: *Report of the Committee on the Enforcement of Judgment Debts*, (Payne Committee), Cmnd 3909, London: HMSO.

Pearson Commission 1978: *Report of the Royal Commission on Civil Liability and Compensation for Personal Injury*, (Pearson Commission), Cmnd 7054, London: HMSO.

Philips Commission 1981: *Report of the Royal Commission on Criminal Procedure*, (Philips Commission) Cmnd 8092–I, London: HMSO.

Phipps, J. 1990: 'Warrants of Execution in the Recovery of Consumer Debts in the County Court. A Lost Opportunity for Change?' 9 Civil JQ 234.

Podmore, D. 1977: 'The Work of Solicitors in Private Practice' *Law Society's Gazette*, 20 July 1977, p. 636.

Podmore, D. 1980: *Solicitors and the Wider Community*, London: Heinemann.

Podmore, D. and Spencer, A. 1982: 'The Law as a Sex-Typed Profession' J of Law and Soc 21.

Pollock, S. 1975: *Legal Aid – The First 25 Years*, London: Oyez.

Potter, D. and Stansfield, D. 1950: *The National Insurance (Industrial Injury) Act 1946*, (2nd edn), London: Butterworths.

Powis, D. 1977: *The Signs of Crime: A Field Manual for Police*, Maidenhead: McGraw-Hill.

Prevezer, S. 1962: 'The Criminal Jurisdiction of the House of Lords' [1962] CLP 102.

Pullinger, H. 1986: *The Criminal Justice System: the Flow Model*, Home Office Research and Planning Unit Paper 36, London: HMSO.

Reiner, R. 1985: *The Politics of the Police*, Brighton: Wheatsheaf.

Renton, R. and Brown, H. 1972: *Criminal Procedure According to the Law of Scotland*, 4th edn by Gerald Gordon, Edinburgh: W. Green.

Richards, J. 1989: *Inform, Advise and Support: The Story of Fifty Years of the CAB*, London: Lutterworth Press.

Riley, D. and Vennard, J. 1988: *Triable-Either-Way Cases: Crown Court or Magistrates' Court*, Home Office Research Study No. 98, London: HMSO.

Roskill Committee 1986: *Report of the Fraud Trials Committee*, London: HMSO.

Sanders, A. 1977: 'Does Professional Crime Pay? A Critical Comment on Mack' 40 MLR 553.

Sanders, A. 1985: 'Prosecution Decisions and the Attorney-General's Guidelines' Crim LR 16.

Sanders, A. 1986: 'An Independent Crown Prosecution Service?' [1986] Crim LR 16.

Sanders, A., Bridges, L., Mulvaney, A., and Crozier, G. 1989: *Advice and Assistance at Police Stations and The 24 Hour Duty Solicitor Scheme*, London: Lord Chancellor's Department.

SCB 1989: *Solicitors Complaint Bureau Annual Report 1989*, London: Solicitors Complaints Bureau.

Scott, I. 1977: 'Appeals to the Crown Court following Summary Conviction'. Paper delivered to SPTL Criminal Law Group, September, 1977.

Scottish Consumer Council 1988: *Debt Advice in Scotland*.

Sealy, L. and Cornish, W. 1973: 'Juries and the Rules of Evidence' [1973] Crim LR 208.

Shapland, J., Willmore, J. and Duff, P. 1985: *Victims in the Criminal Justice System*, Aldershot: Gower.

Sherwin, M. 1975: 'The Westminster Small Claims Court' [1975] LAG Bulletin 65.

Shetreet, S. 1976: *Judges on Trial*, Amsterdam: North Holland.

Sieghart, P. 1986: 'Reliable evidence, fairly obtained'. In J. Benyon and C. Bourn (eds) *The Police: Powers, Procedures and Proprieties*, Oxford: Pergamon Press, pp. 267–78.

Silkin, S. 1983. 'The Shape of Prosecutions to Come' *The Lawyer*, October 1983, p. 14.

Skyrme, T. 1983: *The Changing Image of the Magistracy*, (2nd edn), London: Macmillan.

Smith, A. T. H. 1983: 'The Prerogative of Mercy, The Power of Pardon and Criminal Justice' [1983] PL 398.

Smith, A. T. H. 1984: 'Criminal Appeals in the House of Lords' 47 MLR 133.

Smith, D. et al. 1983: *Police and People in London*, 4 vols, London: Policy Studies Institute.

Smith, J. 1986: 'The new rules of evidence'. In J. Benyon and C. Bourn (eds) *The Police: Powers, Procedures and Proprieties*, Oxford: Pergamon Press, pp. 251–67.

Smith, P. 1986: 'Small Claims: Back to an Adversarial Approach?' 5 Civil JQ 292.

Smith, R. 1989: 'The Board, the Future and the Franchise' *New Law Journal*, 19 May 1989, p. 687.

Society of Labour Lawyers 1968: *Justice for All*, London: Society of Labour Lawyers.

Softley, P. 1980a: 'Sentencing Practice in Magistrates' Courts' [1980] Crim LR 161.

Softley, P. 1980b: *Police Interrogation: An Observational Study in Four Police Stations*, RCCP Research Study No. 4, London: HMSO.

Southgate, P. 1986: *Police-Public Encounters*, Home Office Research Study No. 90, London: HMSO.

Sparks, R., Genn, H. and Dodd, D. 1977: *Surveying Victims: A Study of the Measurement of Criminal Victimisation, Perspective of Crime and Attitudes to Criminal Justice*, Chichester: John Wiley and Sons.

Spencer, J. 1982: 'Criminal Law and Criminal Appeals – The Tail that Wags the Dog' [1982] Crim LR 260.

Steer, D. 1980: *Uncovering Crime – The Police Role*, RCCP Research Study No. 7, London: HMSO.

Stein, P. 1984: *Legal Institutions – The Development of Dispute Settlement*, London: Butterworths.

Stephens, M. 1982: 'Law Centres and Citizenship: The Way Forward'. In P. Thomas (ed.) *Law in the Balance: Legal Services in the 1980s*, Oxford: Martin Robertson.

Stephens, M. 1990: *Community Law Centres: A Critical Appraisal*, Aldershot: Avebury.

Stone, C. 1988: *Bail Information for the Crown Prosecution Service*, Wakefield: Association of Chief Police Officers.

Stone, R. 1989: *Entry, Search and Seizure*, (2nd edn) London: Sweet and Maxwell.

Street, H. 1975: *Justice in the Welfare State*, (2nd edn) London: Stevens.

Tarling, R. 1979: *Sentencing Practice in Magistrates' Courts*, Home Office Research Study No. 56, London: HMSO.

Thomas, D. 1978: *Principles of Sentencing*, (2nd edn) London: Sweet and Maxwell.

Thomas, D. (ed.) 1983: *Current Sentencing Practice*, London: Sweet and Maxwell.

Thomas, P. (ed.) 1982: *Law in the Balance: Legal Services in the 1980s*, Oxford: Martin Robertson.

Thomas, R. 1982: 'A Code of Procedure for Small Claims: A response to the demand for do-it-yourself litigation' 1 Civil JQ 52.

Thomas, R. 1988: 'Alternative Dispute Resolution – Consumer Disputes' 7 Civil JQ 206.

Thompson, D. 1983: *A Guide to Proceedings in the Court of Appeal, Criminal Division*, reproduced in [1983] Crim LR 415 and at 77 Cr App R 138.

Titmuss, R. 1971: 'Welfare, "Rights", Law and Discretion' 42 Pol Q 113.

Touche Ross Management Consultants 1986a: *Study of the small claims procedure, produced for the Lord Chancellor's Civil Justice Review*, London: Touche Ross.

Touche Ross Management Consultants 1986b: *Study of debt enforcement procedures, produced for the Lord Chancellor's Civil Justice Review*, London: Touche Ross.

Tucker Committee 1954: *Report of the Departmental Committee on New Trials in Criminal Cases*, (Tucker Committee), Cmd 9150, London: HMSO.

Van Bueren, G. 1983: 'Statutory Class Action' LAG Bulletin, August 1983, p. 7.

Vennard, J. 1980: *Contested Trial in Magistrates' Courts*, RCCP Research Study No. 6, London: HMSO.

Vennard, J. 1982: *Contested Trials in Magistrates' Courts*, Home Office Research Study No. 71, London: HMSO.

Vennard, J. 1984: 'Disputes within Trials over the Admissibility and Accuracy of Incriminating Statements: Some Research Evidence' [1984] Crim LR 15.

Vennard, J. and Riley, D. 1988: 'The Use of Peremptory Challenge and Stand By of Jurors and their Relationship to Trial Outcome' [1988] Crim LR 731.

Walker, R. 1985: *The English Legal System*, (6th edn) London: Butterworths.

Weatheritt, M. 1980: *The Prosecution System: Survey Prosecuting Solicitors' Departments*, Royal Commission on Criminal Procedure Research Study No. 11, London: HMSO.

Weller, S., Martin, J. and Ruhnka, J. 1984: 'In-Court Assistance to Small Claims Litigants' 3 Civil JQ 62.

Whelan, C. 1987: 'The Role of Research in Civil Justice Reform: Small Claims in the County Court' 6 Civil JQ 237.

Whelan, C. 1990: 'Small Claims in England and Wales: Redefining Justice'. In C. Whelan (ed.) *Small Claims Courts: A Comparative Study*, Oxford: Clarendon Press, p. 99.

White, Richard 1973: 'Lawyers and the Enforcement of Rights'. In P. Morris, R. White and P. Lewis, *Social Needs and Legal Action*, p. 15, Oxford: Martin Robertson.

White, Robin 1977: 'The Bail Act – Will It Make Any Difference?' Crim LR 338.

White, Robin 1978: 'Contingent Fees – A Supplement to Legal Aid?' 41 MLR 286.

White, Robin 1982: *Legal Services in Leicester – A Report for Leicester City Council*, Leicester: University of Leicester.

White, Robin 1984: 'Legal Expenses Insurance' 3 Civil JQ 245.

White, Robin 1986: 'A public prosecution service for England and Wales'. In J. Benyon and C. Bourn (eds): *The Police: Powers, Procedures and Proprieties*, Oxford: Pergamon Press, pp. 193–210.

White, Robin, 1991: *A Guide to the Courts and Legal Services Act 1990*, London: Fourmat Publishing.

Whitesides, K. and Hawker, G. 1975: *Industrial Tribunals*, London: Sweet and Maxwell.

Widgery Committee 1966: *Report of the Committee on Legal Aid in Criminal Proceedings*, (Widgery Committee), Cmnd 2934, London: HMSO.

Wilcox, A. 1972: *The Decision to Prosecute*, London: Butterworths.

Wilkins, L. 1980: 'Sentencing Guidelines to Reduce Disparity' [1980] Crim LR 201.

Willink Commission, 1962: *Final Report of the Royal Commission on the Police*, (Willink Commission), Cmnd 1728, London: HMSO.

Willis, C. 1984: *The Tape Recording of Police Interviews with Suspects: an interim report*, Home Office Research Study No. 82, London: HMSO.

Willis, C., Macleod, J. and Naish, P. 1988: *The Tape Recording of Police Interviews with Suspects: a second Interim Report*, Home Office Research Study No. 102, London: HMSO.

Winn Committee 1968: *Report of the Commitee on Personal Injuries Litigation*, (Winn Committee) Cmnd 369, London: HMSO.

Wood, J. 1989: 'The Serious Fraud Office' [1989] Crim LR 175.

Woolf, H. 1988: 'A Hotchpotch of Appeals – The Need for a Blender' 7 Civil JQ 44.

Wraith, R. and Hutchesson, P. 1973: *Administrative Tribunals*, London: George Allen and Unwin.

Zander, M. 1968: *Lawyers and the Public Interest*, London: Weidenfeld and Nicolson.

Zander, M. 1969: 'Unrepresented Defendants in the Criminal Courts' [1969] Crim LR 632.

Zander, M. 1972a: 'Unrepresented Defendants in Magistrates' Courts' [1972] 122 *New Law Journal* 1042.

Zander, M. 1972b: 'Legal Advice and Criminal Appeals: A Survey of Prisoners, Prisons and Lawyers' [1972] Crim LR 132.

Zander, M. 1974a: 'Are Too Many Professional Criminals Avoiding Conviction – A Study of Britain's Two Busiest Courts' 37 MLR 28.

Zander, M. 1974b: 'The Acquittal Rate of Professional Criminals: A Reply' 37 MLR 444.

Zander, M. 1975a: 'Cost of Litigation: A Study of the Queen's Bench Division' *Law Society's Gazette*, 25 June 1975.

Zander, M. 1975b: 'Legal Advice on Appeal: The New Machinery' [1975] Crim LR 364.

Zander, M. 1978: *Legal Services for the Community*, London: Temple Smith.

Zander, M. 1979a: 'Operation of the Bail Act in London Magistrates' Courts' 129 *New Law Journal* 108.

Zander, M. 1979b: 'The Investigation of Crime: A Study of Cases Tried at the Old Bailey' [1979] Crim LR 203.

Zander, M. 1988: *A Matter of Justice. The Legal System in Ferment*, London: I B Tauris.

Author Index

Subject Index